LANDRY: THE LEGEND AND THE LEGACY

LANDRY:
THE LEGEND AND THE LEGACY

By Bob St. John

WORD PUBLISHING

NASHVILLE

A Thomas Nelson Company

JH

LANDRY: THE LEGEND AND THE LEGACY

Published by Word Publishing, a unit of Thomas Nelson, Inc.,
P. O. Box 14100, Nashville, Tennessee 37214.

ISBN 0-8499-1670-4

Parts of the present book have appeared in slightly different versions in *Landry*
(Waco, TX: Word, 1979) © Word, Inc., and *The Landry Legend* (Dallas: Word,
1989) © Bob St. John, both by Bob St. John.

Printed in the United States of America
00 01 02 03 04 05 BVG 9 8 7 6 5 4 3

ACKNOWLEDGMENTS

My special thanks to Frank Luksa, Charlie Waters, Roger Staubach, and so many of the players I came to know during what I consider the best years for the Dallas Cowboys. Alicia and Tom Landry Jr. were great to me during such a tragic time of their lives. The sports staff of the Dallas Morning News *was also helpful. But most of all, I'm grateful to my wife, Sandy, who spent almost as much time as I did getting this project into shape.*

DEDICATION

For Alicia Landry, one of those special, unforgettable people who can light up your life with a smile.

CONTENTS

FOREWORD

~:~

I CONSIDER MYSELF EXTREMELY FORTUNATE not only to have played for Tom Landry but also to have become his friend. There is no one I admire and respect more. He will always be a beacon of hope, someone we can look up to when our country's leaders and sports figures don't measure up to what we would like them to be. Tom Landry used his Christian faith as his guiding light in life, helping him maintain those wonderful characteristics of honor, integrity, loyalty, and not only doing the very best you can but trying to do the "right thing."

I was hardly his ideal of what a professional quarterback should be, because instead of staying in the pocket and looking for receivers, I'd scramble, or take off running, if I couldn't find anybody open. Yet we were able to work together because we had the same competitiveness and will and drive to win. I think he came to see some value in my mobility, but I'm sure he didn't always appreciate my scrambling or, perhaps, my attempts to, well, loosen him up a bit. Once during practice he didn't like the way I ran a play. So with his gimpy knee and all, he lined up at quarterback and showed me exactly how he wanted the play run. He told me to do it just like he did. So I limped right through it. He just looked at me. Some of my teammates believed they saw a trace of a smile on his face, but I was never sure.

We know that he was one of the greatest coaches the game of football has ever known. Considering his twenty straight winning seasons with different casts of players and his innovations and ability to foresee what a player's ability might become, I believe him to be the best ever in his profession.

But I'm even more impressed by him as a Christian, one who lived his religion rather than just talking about it. He was a devoted family man and worked hard for many charities. In his quiet way, he helped and brightened the lives of so many people.

I'm glad Bob St. John emphasizes that part of Landry's life in this book, although as in his two previous biographies on Tom Landry, there's plenty of football too. I can't think of anyone more qualified than Bob to write this book. When Bob covered the team, we respected and trusted him. He's written several books about the Cowboys, including coauthoring my first book, *First Down, Lifetime to Go*, with Sam Blair. He's observed Tom Landry for years and gotten to know the sides of him many people never saw. By reading this book, you will come to know those too.

—ROGER STAUBACH

PROLOGUE

⁓:⁓

IN THE EARLY EVENING of February 12, 2000, time seemed to stop for countless people when that quiet, dignified "Man in the Hat," Tom Landry, passed away at Baylor University Medical Center in Dallas, Texas. He had affected so many lives, perhaps because he represented traits we hoped for in ourselves and wished for in others. And we admired him for the person he was. Now, he was not a noted diplomat, a national leader, a crusader for social reforms, or a religious icon. Yet his image, his presence, his influence, his popularity far transcended those of a great football coach.

Tom's longtime friend and former assistant coach Gene Stallings captured the mystique of Landry's popularity when he remarked, "When I went to Rome on vacation, I took the pope a football signed by Coach Landry. I never got to talk to the pope, but I left it anyway because I figured he'd sure want it."

Landry was a deeply religious man, a family man in both words and actions, and a man who displayed class and grace in the best and worst of times and worked tirelessly for charities and Christian causes. In these times of political scandals, shootings in our schools, and diminishing family values, in these times when some sports idols wear greed and disgrace like medals of honor and appear to choreograph their religion for prime time like victory dances in the end zone, Tom Landry brought honor back into focus. He was as we once would have had our sports heroes be, unpretentious and modest, exhibiting none of the taunting, in-your-face attitude of so many today. And he wasn't just a sports hero, he was a real hero and a Christian hero, whose faith was not reserved for Sundays and religious holidays. Landry certainly found his accomplishments and good deeds gratifying, but he did not flaunt or brag about them. Doing them was reward enough.

The Dallas Cowboys organization was the public stage upon which Landry would gain widespread notoriety. The Cowboys were winners, and the popularity of "America's Team" and the "Man in the Hat" spread far and wide. Obviously, Landry was one of the NFL's all-time great coaches and innovators. Yet the grace with which he conducted himself on and off the field, no matter whether he won or lost, was felt beyond mere sports. After he was so abruptly fired by Jerry Jones following the 1988 season, we seemed to gain a more accurate perspective and Landry's legacy grew.

The most meaningful tribute to Landry's coaching ability was his twenty straight winning seasons with different casts of players. Landry's teams were in the playoffs eighteen of twenty-nine seasons, won thirteen division titles, made five of a dozen NFL title game appearances, and won two of five Super Bowls. Since the NFL and AFL merged in 1966 but still played separate championship games to determine which team went to the Super Bowl, Dallas actually played in two more NFL title games, in 1966 and 1967, narrowly losing to Green Bay each time.

After Landry had completed his twenty-sixth year coaching the Cowboys, a fan gushed over his record, and Landry's reply was typical of him and his often-overlooked sense of humor. Landry thanked the guy, smiled, and replied, "Another way of looking at it is that I haven't had a promotion in twenty-six years."

The Cowboys fell on hard times Landry's final three seasons, finishing 7–9 in 1986, 7–8 in 1987 (the game with Buffalo was canceled), and 3–13 in 1988. Then, as he laid plans he believed would make the team winners again, he was fired. It has always been said that Dallas fans have a short memory and only fall in step behind winners, their motto being "What have you done for me lately?" Yet two months after Landry was fired, there was a "Hats off to Tom Landry" celebration in downtown Dallas. In an outpouring of support, more than fifty thousand people crowded around City Hall Plaza, and an estimated one hundred thousand filled the streets to watch him pass by in a parade. It is difficult to imagine another coach with a losing record for three straight years, one whose final season was the worst since the team's beginning in 1960, attracting such a huge gathering. When Landry heard there was going to be a special day for him, he asked his wife, Alicia, "Do you think anybody will be there?"

Sure, Tom Landry had his shortcomings, as we all do. He was unwavering about his system. His great power of concentration and, especially in the early years, his feeling that humor had no place in football made him seem to some cold and uncaring. But as Lee Roy Jordan, who praised Landry as a great innovator and the "epitome of a good person as a man, a father, and a coach," explained, "Sometimes he didn't communicate with people real well but did things through example and was certainly a leader by example."

Many players had been buddies with their rah-rah high-school and college coaches, but Landry was different. He would always say he couldn't get too close to his players because it might cloud tough decisions he had to make regarding personnel. Yet sometimes his cover slipped. Drew Pearson recalled seeing that usually hidden side of Landry in 1976 when twelve rookies, who would become known as the "Dirty Dozen," made the team, meaning veterans had to be cut. When Landry announced the cuts to the team, Drew said, "he actually stood there and started crying. We were all shocked. We'd never seen that side of him. He had to leave the room. We all felt like we wanted to cry because he did. That showed the compassion and care he had for all his players."

Some players didn't always agree with what Landry did or said, but as Roger Staubach pointed out, "He was our coach, and we did love him. Some more than others, but no one, no one I know of, didn't completely respect him."

"I loved my parents but didn't always appreciate what they had done until I became a parent myself," said Dan Reeves, a very successful NFL coach who was with Landry for sixteen years as a player and an assistant coach. "It was like that for me with Coach Landry. I gained more respect for him and the great job he did when I became a head coach. Coach Landry had so much effect on so many lives. He got his faith across in subtle ways. It never was a pushy situation or that he forced it on you. He did it by example."

So Tom Landry's life inspired those who knew him as well as those who had met him only casually or not at all. He inspired celebrities and stars, the rich and poor, and ordinary people for whom the limelight is but a distant flicker. In life he was a wonderful role model, a hero, and in death practically immortal. And it was his death that made us pause and think, and be reminded once again of a special person who touched our lives in such a positive way by only being himself. His death became a realization, a confirmation, of what his life had meant to us.

CHAPTER 1
Death and Remembrance

~:~

While the world at large saw him as a coach who led his team to twenty consecutive winning seasons, we who knew him saw him as a friend, as a coach. We discovered that he seemed to care more about us as people, especially as we were going through times of pain, than he did about his own success. Others view him as a good man. We who walked alongside him admired him as a great man, great in integrity, great in generosity, great in faithfulness, great in commitment, and especially great in humility.

—DR. CHARLES R. SWINDOLL
President, Dallas Theological Seminary

THE NEW CENTURY BEGAN, and soothsayers of doom, disaster, and chaos disappeared in the shadows when the Y2K transition brought for the most part not even mild inconvenience. Armageddon did not come, the sky did not fall, and preparation kept computers from going wild. It was, however, a very painful time for the Landrys. Tom Landry's battle with leukemia took a turn for the worse, and in January he was re-admitted to the hospital.

As news of Landry's condition spread, his admirers everywhere prayed and waited in vigil, spoken and silent, for what they feared to be the inevitable. There was such an outpouring of concern that a special hotline was established so callers could get updates on his medical condition. Landry had always been such a rock, a picture of health and vitality, that people felt this just couldn't be happening to him. He was so . . . so indestructible. Even his family felt that way, and his wife, Alicia, would later say, "I just couldn't believe it was happening to him, not Tommy. He was always so strong and healthy. . . . It just couldn't happen to him."

~:~

LANDRY HADN'T BEEN FEELING WELL long before he was diagnosed in May 1999 with acute myelogenous leukemia, a cancer that prevents the normal manufacture of blood cells, results in anemia, and interferes with the function of vital organs. At the April 1999 Tom Landry Fellowship of Christian Athletes Open, friends noticed the coach didn't look well. But he was there as usual, socializing and having his picture taken with participants. The FCA was one of Landry's special causes, and he was a major reason for its success.

Tournament director Jim Myers, Landry's friend and longtime assistant at the Cowboys, later recalled, "He was tired and just didn't look like himself. I thought maybe he'd just been sick, never dreaming of what was happening to him."

Tito Nicholas had known the coach since they were U.S. Army Air Force cadets in World War II. "It was a very hot day, but he never complained about feeling bad," said Tito. "He was just out there as usual. It was important to him to visit with the golfers as they finished. So I was playing gin after my round, and he walked in. I looked up, and he had that slight grin on his face and said, 'I see you're playing as bad as ever, Nicholas.' But, no, he just didn't look like his usual self." Nevertheless, Landry helped the tournament be successful. It netted $578,000 for the FCA.

It was at another of his favorite charities, Happy Hill Farm, that Landry made his final public appearance that same April. Ed Shipman and his wife, Gloria, founded Happy Hill Farm, which is near Fort Worth, Texas, between Granbury and Glen Rose. It provides a haven for boys and girls who are unwanted and have been discarded by society. Landry, in spite of his health, flew there to be with the kids.

"Just before Easter, I played golf with him in a foursome," recalled Landry's son, Tom Landry Jr. "He shot an 83. He seemed tired, yet he was still able to play that well. Nobody knew just how sick he was."

That May the Landrys attended a baseball game of grandson Ryan's, who played for Trinity Christian Academy in Dallas. Landry was late for the game because he'd just learned at a visit to his doctor that he had leukemia. Paul Corley, a friend of Landry since the late 1950s, was also at the game. Paul was a neighbor of Ryan's parents, Kitty and Eddie Phillips, and was there to cheer for Ryan.

"I noticed them [Tom and Alicia] hurrying in about the fourth inning," recalled Paul. "They took a seat by us, and I thought Tom looked very tired. I had no idea that an hour before he'd learned he had leukemia. . . . But as you would expect, he handled it very well."

Dr. Ken Cooper is founder of the Cooper Aerobics Center and Cooper Clinic in Dallas. Dr. Cooper and his wife, Millie, were also old friends of the Landrys. And Coach Landry was a longtime patient of Dr. Cooper.

"I never saw him depressed, and I never saw him weep," said Dr. Cooper. "He just accepted the diagnosis. He was going to live with it. The Lord had dealt him those cards, and in his typical stoic manner he went on with his life. Tom had great strength during that time. No, I never saw him break down at all. He was an amazing man."

Later that May, Landry and Roger Staubach were honored with Lifetime Achievement awards by the Bobby Bragan Youth Foundation, another charity that helps needy youngsters. Tom was unable to attend, but Alicia accepted the award for him. "Treatment is on schedule, and he's handling it well, except for being bored," she said. "We're still hoping for remission. The doctors are cautiously optimistic. . . . Tommy has been through every John Wayne film twice. He followed the World Series on television. He reads books and walks thirty minutes in the hall each day. He walks fast too."

There was, of course, optimism and hope that he'd win what turned out to be the final battle of his life.

~:~

THERE WAS A GREAT OUTPOURING OF CONCERN for Landry when he entered the hospital for the first time that May. The *Dallas Morning News* was flooded with letters and e-mails. They came from well-wishers in every state, the tiny island of Guam in the North Pacific, and foreign countries, including the Netherlands, Poland, Mexico, Canada, and Australia. In the first five days alone some seventeen hundred e-mails were received. Cowboy fans, people uninterested in football, and even supporters of the Washington Redskins and Minnesota Vikings wrote to say they were praying for him and to thank him for what he had meant in their lives. They sent poems and notes with sentiments like: "The standard you set as a coach and a man is not equaled in today's sports world. Thank you for the example"; "Get well soon, and we'll keep you in our prayers"; "We need more classy people here on earth than they do in heaven."

Frank Dudley sent a letter from Togo, an independent country in West Africa where he was serving as a Southern Baptist missionary: "My mom is from Mission [Texas], and you have always been a hero for me, both on the football field and in the Kingdom of God. . . . I am praying for you from here. God bless you and heal you and give you peace." Michel Beaupre from Quebec, Canada, wrote, "You are more than a coach; you are the kind of human being this planet will never have enough of."

Having written two biographies on Landry and knowing him since covering the Cowboys from 1967 through Super Bowl IV in January 1978, I believed I knew how he would be coping with the situation. He would be handling it much better than those closest to him. Furthermore, he would be doing all he could to ease their burden. He would be dealing with leukemia as he had other setbacks in his life: calculating his options, praying, then coping with whatever he faced.

Landry's reaction to his chemotherapy treatments seemed so typical. During a late August interview at his North Dallas office with *Dallas Morning News* sports columnist Frank Luksa, Landry was very composed and in control. As far as being diagnosed with leukemia, he remarked, "It didn't bother me over-much. If the Good Lord wanted to take me, it was OK with me. I'd just go ahead with chemotherapy. Amazing how well that went. I didn't have a very difficult time at all."

Charlie Waters and Cliff Harris, All-Pro safeties for Landry during the 1970s, hold an annual golf tournament to benefit CASA (Court Appointed Special Advocates), whose members volunteer their time and resources to help abused and abandoned children. The 1999 tournament was being held in September, and Charlie and Cliff decided to combine the tournament with a birthday party for Coach Landry, who would turn seventy-five on the twelfth of that month. "Our main concern was that he might not feel well enough to attend," said Charlie. "But we were assured by his family that he was looking forward to being there."

The party was held in a large banquet room at the Fairmont Hotel, and players who couldn't attend sent videotapes wishing Coach Landry a happy birthday. Danny Reeves, busy coaching the Falcons, couldn't make it but told Coach Landry on videotape how happy he was that the coach was feeling better, adding, "Whatever success I've had I owe directly to you." Mike Ditka offered, "You're still my biggest hero. God bless you." Bob Hayes, tears in his eyes, said, "You've given me so much." Tony Dorsett, whom Landry once counseled through a divorce, commented how Landry had pushed the players to a higher level individually and as a team. He also spoke about how wonderful it was being with Landry's Cowboys during such a great time as the 1970s and 1980s. Ed "Too Tall" Jones thanked Landry for the fourteen years he was with the team. Indeed, Jones said he thanked Coach Landry for those years every time he saw him.

After the videos had been played and the players in attendance told the coach what he meant to them, Landry stood up. His voice broke as he said, "We had some great years, but none of it would ever have happened without you guys."

"Mrs. Landry later told me how Coach Landry loved every minute of the party," said Charlie. "He'd been through the chemo treatments, but you never would have known it. He stayed there all four hours and was wearing this little bolo tie because the party had a Western theme. He just looked so great. He really did. That kind of gave you hope. . . . Then the next day he went back into the hospital."

Something Landry said in 1981 when the Cowboys were still enjoying great success comes to mind. Reflecting on his legendary career and his life, he said, "I just hope that when it's all over, I've helped some people have a better life because they've known me somewhere along the way. I don't care if I'm in the Hall of Fame or whether I'm remembered for any other reason than that."

~:~

LANDRY WAS RELEASED from the hospital on November 21, 1999, for what would be the last time to be home with his family. He was readmitted in January 2000. For a while the chemotherapy seemed to be working, giving the family hope. Then it didn't. Landry was surrounded by his family when the end came on the evening of February 12. He had said he was ready to go, and they knew his undying faith had prepared him for the great hereafter.

"If Coach Landry isn't in heaven, we're all in trouble," said Roger Staubach.

When Jim Myers heard the news, he felt "lonesome and lost, because something was missing from my life. His death was such a tremendous loss for me, for everybody. I couldn't just pick up the telephone and talk to him. You hurt but don't know what to do about it."

Jim in turn called Tex Schramm. "We all knew it was coming, but when something like that actually happens it still really hits you," said

Tex. "It's tough to think you'll never see or talk to him again. A key reason people felt we were America's Team was because they could see Tom Landry standing on the sidelines wearing that hat and they knew all the good things that he stood for."

Drew Pearson learned of Coach Landry's death when he got a call from Dallas's Channel 11. Later recalling the feelings he had, Drew said, "I just needed to be alone and reflect on what had happened and figure out how to deal with it. In the course of grieving, I experienced a gamut of emotions . . . shock, denial, anger, confusion, frustration, fear, helplessness, numbness. Eventually, I felt a sense of acceptance. There really is no death, no end, there is only transformation. Coach Landry has now made that transformation. He now exists in a new time, a new place. He now exists in a new reality, and because of that, so do we. Our relationship has now transformed from the physical to the spiritual. It certainly has not ended. Instead of talking to him face-to-face, I now communicate with him through prayer."

Landry's friend Dr. Billy Graham said, "The death of Tom Landry has come as a shock to me and to Christians everywhere. Tom was one of the greatest Christian gentlemen I ever knew."

Fan Phil Klan wrote in a letter to the *Dallas Morning News*, "Somehow, I felt a closeness to him that I cannot explain. I feel a loss that is more than a great Cowboy passing, but the void left from the death of a great person. He died as he lived, quietly, with dignity, and his faith firmly intact."

Fans left flowers and messages near a likeness of Tom Landry at Texas Stadium and under a sign that read, "Dallas Cowboys World Champions 1971, 1977, 1992, 1993, 1995" on a wall by the team's offices at Valley Ranch. One placard proclaimed, "Legends Never Die. You'll always be in our hearts." A man and a woman stood silently with their small son. Their heads were bowed, and the woman brushed back a tear. People of all ages stopped to reflect, to pray, and some spoke words to Landry, believing he would hear them. His death was announced over CNN and other national networks and written about in newspapers around the country. It received important media play in New York, where fans remembered his days with the Giants and had followed his career with the Cowboys. Flags flew at half-mast at the state capitol, at schools, at businesses, and in front yards. Beloved "Peanuts" creator Charles Schulz died the same day as Coach Landry. Ironically, Schulz had joined such people as Nancy Reagan, Art Linkletter, and Bob Hope as a recipient of the Landry Medal, awarded by California Lutheran College to people who make great accomplishments and possess great integrity.

Mike Thompson of the *Detroit Free Press* inked a cartoon showing Coach Landry with his arm around Schulz, personified as his character Charlie Brown, as they walked through the Pearly Gates. Landry was telling him, "Now, a few pointers on kicking the football." If you're a fan of "Peanuts," you know Charlie needed all the help he could get booting the football.

The Landry family was flooded with letters from around the country as people expressed their condolences and offered their prayers. Some were addressed only to "Tom Landry, Dallas, Texas." One man wrote, "I'll always remember him as that great man who raised the standard and set an example for all of us." There were letters from New York Giants and Green Bay Packers fans who admired Landry.

And one woman wrote Alicia, "He touched my heart in so many ways [from the time] I was a little girl growing up in the 1960s" until he passed away. She added she still had a letter she'd framed that Landry had written her son. A man who was dying of liver disease wrote how he met Landry once on "Fan Day" at practice. "It was a brief encounter, yet in that moment of a handshake, a smile, the twinkle of his eyes, I received confirmation of all I hoped would be a part of Coach Landry's spirit. He was so genuine."

A man from Mission, Texas, told how he admired Landry for his values, his faith in God, and his honesty and integrity, adding, "My only regret is that my children, five and three, will not get to meet him. They will know about him through me, however." Several letters were from people who had named their sons and daughters "Landry." One woman wrote that when her son asks where he got his name, she will tell him "about Tom Landry and his love of Christ." Another woman told the family how impressed she had been as a child watching Coach Landry at football games. Later she heard him speak at an FCA convention and determined "he truly transcended and touched every generation from young kids to those of my parents' generation. What a gift from God! Thank you for sharing the life of your husband and father with the many fans of the Cowboys and for allowing us to consider him part of our family."

Joe Gibbs had been Landry's rival as coach of the Washington

Redskins. By his own admission, Joe experienced burnout, and he left a very successful career in the NFL to become a NASCAR team owner. He was at the Daytona 500 when he heard about Landry's death. Joe said that when he came to the NFL the "one person I would have loved to have been like was Tom Landry. The reason is not so much what he accomplished in football. It wasn't the wins and losses but the kind of person he was. Tom was a great moral person and led a lot of people to Christ.

"I was amazed at how fresh he always seemed to be on the sidelines. Toward the end of the year, I'd look over there and he'd look like he was taking a stroll in the park with his hat on and everything. I'd look like I'd been kicked and beaten and slammed all over the place."

Later at one of the three memorial services for Landry, Roger Staubach talked about how Coach Landry had so thoroughly prepared the team for Super Bowl VI on January 16, 1972. The Cowboys had fallen short the year before in Super Bowl V and had experienced disappointment after disappointment in other big championship games. They were being called the team that couldn't win the "Big One." Roger recalled that he'd never, ever been on a team that was more prepared, more ready to play, leaving no stone unturned, than in the 26–3 victory over Miami.

"That football game was the most fun I've had in my life," continued Roger. "Coach Landry was carried off the field. He was smiling. I believe he was that prepared when he took his last breath on Saturday night. He didn't want to go, but he was prepared for what he knew would be his future, to meet his Lord, to have eternal happiness."

⌣∴∾

SOME FOUR HUNDRED FORMER PLAYERS, assistant coaches, family members, and closest of friends gathered at the invitation-only private funeral service and burial late on the Wednesday afternoon following Landry's death. It was held at the Sparkman/Hillcrest Funeral Home, Mausoleum, and Memorial Park, a massive, serene refuge of manicured lawns, tree-lined paths, and sculptured red-tipped bushes in the midst of a busy, bustling commercial section of North Dallas.

In addition to the private funeral and burial, a memorial service was held at noon on Thursday at the Highland Park United Methodist Church, where Landry had been a member for forty-three years. A final tribute, which was open to the public, began at 4:00 P.M. at the Morton

H. Meyerson Symphony Center in downtown Dallas. Alicia wanted the players present at all three services. "It was so comforting to have them there," she said. "I appreciated them being there so much. They were such an important part of our lives."

Frank Gifford and Sam Huff, friends from Tom's days with the New York Giants, were at the three services. And so were players who'd played with the Cowboys from the team's beginning until Landry was fired. There were great players there and average ones and some who'd hardly made a mark with the team. Charlie Granger, then a rookie from Southern University, was cut from the team during the 1961 season. But he was there from Louisiana. Former players came from Louisiana, California, Washington, Virginia, all around Texas, and of course, the Dallas area. Fullback Don Perkins, one of the brightest stars of the 1960s, traveled from Albuquerque, New Mexico, because Coach Landry meant so much to him as a coach and as a man. "It was not a consideration that I wouldn't be here," he said. "To me it was a given."

Dick Nolan, who had played and coached with Landry since his days with the Giants, was in San Francisco dealing with a family emergency when he heard about Tom's death. He drove more than nine hundred miles for the funeral and memorial services.

Jeff Rohrer, a backup linebacker in the 1980s, made the trip from California as well. "Coach Landry totally influenced my life and my family's life," he said. "It's important for all the guys on his teams to be here no matter what you're doing or who you are. You should be here."

Baldness or white hair notwithstanding, many former players looked as if they could still play a few downs, while the years had changed so many others. Sure the years had aged them, but not their feelings for the man who had touched their lives.

"Guys were here from our first team in 1960," said Gil Brandt, the third member of the Schramm-Landry-Brandt triumvirate that built the team into a dominant power. "There must have been over one hundred players. That was the greatest testament you can have to what they thought of Coach Landry. It was the first time so many of them had ever gotten back together, and he was the only person who could have caused it to happen. It'll never happen again."

The largest group of players attended the private burial services. Cliff Harris remembered, "As I looked around at everybody, I thought how so many of us didn't fully realize what a strong impact Coach

Landry had on our lives until after he passed away. We learned things from him that affected the rest of our lives. He was such a strong Christian, and just being around him made you want to do the right thing. We moved in that direction without even being aware that it was his influence that caused it.

"It was difficult to realize he was actually gone. There was a void in our lives. I was filled with two strong emotions: very sad and very happy. Sad that he was gone, but happy to have been a part of a great man's life."

Mike and Diana Ditka were in Palm Springs, California, on holiday when they heard of Landry's death. They cut their trip short and hurried to Dallas. By the late 1960s, Mike's career as a Hall of Fame tight end with the Chicago Bears was over and he was struggling with the Philadelphia Eagles. His first marriage was on the rocks, and if there was a light at the end of the tunnel, it was on the blink. Then Landry brought him to Dallas. He was so happy to be out of Philadelphia and get a new start with the Cowboys that his whole outlook was rejuvenated.

Mike played four years for the Cowboys, including in their Super Bowl VI victory over Miami. He certainly showed the old fire. He was in an automobile accident before a game, suffering cuts and bruises and knocking his teeth loose. When a dentist told him he couldn't play the game because he might lose his teeth, Mike replied, "Then pull them." Mike stayed on to become one of Landry's assistants. He never forgot what Landry did for him.

"Coach Landry gave me a second chance as a player and gave me my first chance as a coach," he said. "He taught me the game of football from his perspective and taught me how to teach other people the game. He was the classiest act in coaching. He was the best in my opinion.

"He was a great coach but a greater man. And probably misunderstood by so many people who thought he was a plastic man. He wasn't. He was a caring, emotional person in control of the situation.

"He projected the right image of never letting the game be bigger than life. I always appreciated him, but I don't think I fully appreciated him until later. I loved him for what he meant to my life and what he meant to the game."

Harvey Martin's All-Pro career ended prior to the 1984 season, probably prematurely, because he became involved with the wrong people, those who lie in wait in the dark corners of fame and money. He developed an addiction to drugs, and his life hit rock bottom. After many failures and a newfound faith in God, Harvey had been straight for three and a half years when Tom Landry died. During the services, he remembered, "Coach Landry stood by me and tried to help me during that terrible time of my life. I'm sorry I didn't listen, but I was so messed up then. When I got my life back together, I'd see him at different speaking engagements and tell him how much I appreciated that he tried to help me. If I'd only listened."

Thomas "Hollywood" Henderson's promising career ended when Landry had enough of his behavior and cut him at midseason in 1979. He's now a recovering alcoholic who is very outspoken on the dangers of alcohol and drugs, which ruined his career and might eventually have cost him his life. By his own admission, he didn't particularly like Landry when he was playing for him, but all that changed. Like Harvey, Thomas regrets he didn't ask Landry for help, believing that if he had he might have avoided all his problems.

"Tom Landry was the greatest man I ever knew," said Thomas. "He should have cut me. He was like a father to me, but I didn't realize it when I was playing for him. He made me accountable for my actions and disciplined me when I'd loaf or do something wrong. I just didn't receive it well back then."

The players crowded into the chapel before the funeral services were to begin, and many viewed the body before taking their seats. Landry was dressed as immaculately as he dressed in life. He wore his NFL Hall of Fame tie and a blue blazer. One of his famous fedoras was placed by the casket. As people do in death, he seemed smaller than in life, and it was obvious that the cancer and treatment had taken their toll.

"He didn't look at all like himself, but I'm glad I got to get one last look at the coach who meant so much to me," said Drew Pearson.

Charlie Waters stood in the back of the chapel and became aware that there was total silence. "Usually at funerals people mill around and talk and then meander into the chapel about ten minutes before the service starts," he said. "This time everybody came into the chapel early. The place was completely packed, and it was like everybody knew they had to be there early, a testimonial to Coach Landry's discipline."

The Landry family wanted players to visit with each other, to interact because they hadn't seen each other for so many years, so an announcement was made that the service would be delayed. It seemed to break the ice, and the players began to greet one another and talk.

Dr. Howard Hendricks, a Dallas Theological Seminary professor who had been the Cowboys' chaplain from 1974 to 1982, presided over the funeral service and burial at Sparkman/Hillcrest. He spoke of Coach Landry's character, confidence, conviction, and compassion. "His character was formed in the person of Christ. His confidence was driven by the power of Christ. His conviction was based on the promises of Christ, and his compassion was modeled after the passion of Christ.

"The greatest crisis in America is the crisis of leadership, and the greatest crisis of leadership is the crisis of character. Everybody would like to have character, but few can define it although everybody knows it when they see it. They saw it in him."

Dr. Hendricks mentioned the Landrys' daughter, Lisa, who died of cancer in 1995, and continued, "Unlike many in our generation who have both feet firmly planted in midair, all his decisions were obviously based on his convictions. His convictions were forged in the furnace of real life with the loss of Lisa [and] the graceless firing as a coach."

He also told anecdotes, such as the time he accompanied the Cowboys on a team trip to Philadelphia. After the game, buses waited to take the Cowboys to the airport to board their flight home. Landry was patiently signing autographs when a team official told him they needed to leave for the airport. Landry said, "I've got to sign an autograph for my young friend here."

Tom Landry Jr. asked Charlie Waters, Drew Pearson, Pettis Norman, Tony Dorsett, Bob Lilly, Mel Renfro, Randy White, and Dan Reeves to carry the casket from the hearse to the gravesite. Bob Hayes, somewhat overcome with emotion, joined them. They placed the casket under the tent in front of the Landry family, adjacent to the grave. The afternoon was gray, with low-hanging clouds and threats of rain.

"I think about the people there and how we held him in such high respect and how he really was a humble man," recalled Charlie. "No matter how humble we are, we're all guilty of bringing attention to ourselves in some way. We still want recognition for what we do. I don't think Coach Landry ever felt that way. I believe he did think of himself as being somewhat of a genius in football and believed that his system was flawless. But he never brought attention to himself when the team was so successful. He just went on to the next game plan, the next week. He felt very confident he was right, but I never heard him do anything to bring attention to himself. All of us are guilty of that, but he wasn't."

Players remembered how Landry was patient with them. Charlie thought about how the low point of his career became a turning point because of Coach Landry. Charlie, who would eventually move to strong safety and become an All-Pro, was pressed into playing corner-back early in his career. He didn't have the speed to guard the wide receivers. During a 1973 game with the Rams in Los Angeles Coliseum, Charlie was beaten for three touchdowns, although he was mistakenly given "credit" for four by national television announcers. He recalled it felt more like seven. Perhaps Landry remembered he also had played cornerback for the Giants by using his wits rather than speed.

"After the game Coach Landry came into the team meeting, and I was ready to face the music. That's another thing he taught me, to take the heat, just stand up and take it. Then he announced, 'You know Charlie had a rough game. But if we had forty-five guys who played as hard as he played, we wouldn't lose a game.' I had played terribly, and he was under heavy siege from everybody to bench me. Yet he said that. That gave me great confidence when I could have lost it. When he did that, he got me for life. I would have run through a brick wall for him. He just had such patience and insight into human nature."

Landry would have appreciated the way the services went. Drew Pearson later said, "Mrs. Landry and the family were such a reflection of what Coach Landry was all about. They just handled it with such class, such dignity. Of course they had their private moments to deal with all the emotions you go through when you lose a husband, a father, a grand-father. But publicly they presented a strong, classy, dignified image."

If you've ever been to a full military funeral, then you know how impressive it can be. At Landry's burial, there was a twenty-one-gun salute, and two members of the military color guard folded the flag and presented it to Alicia. A bugler played the haunting postlude taps. Those at the gravesite were then asked to focus their eyes to the south. With explicit timing, the silence was broken by a shattering crescendo as F-16's burst out of the clouds in diamond formation, banked, and then disappeared. Everybody was then asked to look to the north. Once again as if on key, four World War II standard training planes, the type in which Landry likely learned to fly, approached in what seemed slow motion compared to the jets. As they passed overhead, one plane peeled out of the formation, banked upward, and left the others in what is called the "Missing Man Formation" in honor of a lost pilot, Tom Landry.

"Everybody had remained fairly composed, but when the planes flew over I guarantee you there wasn't a dry eye in the crowd," said Drew. "We just all lost it."

Tom Jr. then took Landry's hat and placed it on the coffin before the family was escorted away. Unplanned, Charlie Waters walked over to the coffin and placed his hand on it in a solemn, last good-bye. Others followed. Burton Lawless, whose career and life had almost ended in the early 1980s when a tractor he was driving capsized on him, limped badly. But he, like others, felt drawn to be there.

Then Tom Landry's body was placed in its final resting place in the family plot. His spirit, his legend and legacy, will never die.

ON THURSDAY, FEBRUARY 17, television crews, reporters, and fans began gathering outside the sandstone-colored Highland Park United Methodist Church two hours before the noon celebration and remembrance for Tom Landry began. The Landrys had requested that only family and the extended list of friends attend and that no cameras be brought into the sanctuary. Their wishes appeared to be respected, although members of the media interviewed former Cowboy stars as they entered and left the church and fans asked for autographs. Across the street at the construction site of Southern Methodist University's new Gerald Ford Stadium, workers had placed a sign on a flatbed truck that read, "R.I.P."

The historic church, begun in 1916 and located at the edge of the SMU campus in affluent North Dallas, now has some twelve hundred members. The showplace and centerpiece of the huge church complex is the New Gothic Revival sanctuary, built in 1926 with flagstone walkways surrounded by ageless oaks and magnolias. At times, Tom Landry would speak at the services in that sanctuary. Seldom have members been more moved than on Palm Sunday in 1996 when Landry gave his testimonial and told how his faith had helped him cope with the tragic loss of his younger daughter, Lisa, who was only thirty-seven at her death. And when the church had a membership drive, people were not terribly surprised if Tom Landry knocked on their door.

Dr. Leighton Ferrell was senior pastor of the church for twenty-three years before turning over those duties to Dr. Mark Craig. "Tom would do anything you asked for the church," recalled Dr. Ferrell. "If you asked him to speak to six people or six thousand, he'd say, 'Sure, I'll be glad to do it.' Tom and Alicia were at church every time they were in town. If there was a home game on Sunday, they'd go to the early morning service at 8:30. Other coaches in that position wouldn't have been there. They would have been out there planning, fretting over the game plan, and stalking around. He did a lot of things in the church I don't think anybody knew about."

Landry taught Sunday-school classes for young people whenever he could, and each spring he spoke at the annual confirmation youth banquet where sixth-grade kids are moved up to the next level. In 1991, he was one of the keynote speakers with future governor George W. Bush for the church's "Capital Funds Campaign," in which $7 million was raised for the church.

"Parishioners were just in awe of him," continued Dr. Ferrell. "One gentleman said he sat down in the pew and looked over and this big fellow and his wife were sitting next to him. He said they looked at each other and the big fellow said, 'Hi, I'm Tom Landry and this is my wife, Alicia.' The gentleman said he almost fell out of the pew.

"Another man told me not long ago that one of the greatest experiences his children remember from when they were growing up is going to the communion altar on Sunday and having Tom Landry kneel by them. I'm sure that's true for others too. It's something they'll never forget."

Church member Bob LaPrada said he never really knew Landry but years ago took his grandsons, Spence Graham and Rob and Shaun Ireland, to hear Tom speak to a men's group at the church. "We walked up to him and he said, 'Hello, Bob,' and boy, my grandsons were so impressed that I knew Tom Landry." The boys also had their picture taken with Landry. They're grown now, but Bob said they still talk about the time they met Tom Landry.

Larry Wansley, the former FBI agent in charge of counseling and security for the Cowboys during the Landry years, was out of town in conjunction with his job in security for American Airlines when Landry died but returned to attend the memorial service. Before the service began, he said, "Coach Landry had such a profound influence on me that I had to be here. I remember being in his office talking to him the day he was packing up to leave the team. He talked about his players and his relationships with them. As I sat there, I was aware of being in the presence of greatness."

Tito Nicholas was in the audience, sitting next to former Cowboy Jeff Rohrer. "I just don't think people will ever be aware of some of the nice things Tom did for people," he said, recalling a personal incident many years earlier when Tito's twins, Dana and Nicky, were attending Trinity Christian Academy, a private school, with Lisa Landry. At that time, Tito also had older children in college and couldn't afford to send the twins back to Trinity for their senior year. Apparently Lisa mentioned this to her father, and Tom asked Tito to stop by his office.

"We talked about our bad golf games and how the Cowboys would do that year," said Tito. "Then Tom got to the point and said how important it was for the twins to finish at Trinity. Nicky was on the football team, Dana was on the pep squad, and all their friends were there. I told him I just couldn't afford it. He said it was already taken care of and I shouldn't worry. I told him I couldn't do that, and he said it was too late. Years later when I could afford to pay him back, he wouldn't accept the money. I bet there are a lot of stories out there like that about Tom."

Dr. Kenneth Dickson, another former pastor at Highland Park United Methodist Church, said, "Tom Landry is a great gift. Tom would say that the greatest gift of all gifts is God's love. So on this day, we are here to celebrate two great gifts: the gift of Tom Landry and the gift of God's love. Both are worthy of our praise and worthy of thanksgiving and indeed worthy of our celebration."

Dr. Craig, senior pastor of the church since 1995, didn't know Landry that well but told the audience of some two thousand people how he'd visited Landry in the hospital during the past Christmas season. "The greatest gift I ever received was the opportunity for a brief visit with Mr. Landry at the foot of his hospital bed last Christmas," he began, then paused to wipe away a tear. "Most of what happened is just a blur to me now. I just stood there and cried. I asked myself, Why am I crying? And I realized it was because I was standing in the presence of greatness. And when you do that it's a very emotional thing. Tom Landry was a great gift to his family, to his church, and to this nation."

Dr. Craig then remarked that there were only two people in his life whom he feared calling by their first names, his father and Tom Landry. "Like Moses who meets something transcendent, there's some holy ground there that you just do not walk on. And I felt like that was a boundary that was holy. I think he was a holy man, and I think he was a man . . . nearly a saint to me."

Tom Landry Jr., who was in business with his father in the Landry Investment Group, Inc., reminds me of his father. He has his father's gait, minus the limp, and at the service held himself straight as he walked to the pulpit. In spite of his great grief, he was able to stay in control as he talked about his father. He told about one of the hundreds of letters his father received that last time he was in the hospital. A father wrote reminding Coach Landry about his son Paul, who died in a New York hospital in 1979 at the age of fourteen. Paul was an avid Dallas Cowboys fan, and Coach Landry heard about him. So he called the boy and talked to him. Then he said, "Paul, I want to introduce you to our quarterback, Roger Staubach." The boy was able to visit with Roger and excitedly told his mother, "Wow, Mom! I've just talked to the Dallas Cowboys coach Tom Landry and Roger Staubach. Wow! Coach Landry wants me to keep on fighting."

"Later that year, my son died," wrote Paul's father. "Tom, you might think your phone call was a small thing. But my wife and I hold it in our hearts as a cherished memory of a moment of pure joy for Paul, one that brought him an enduring source of strength. Thank you for giving the blessing of your great love to Paul."

"I'm the luckiest person in the world to have the finest man I ever met happen to be my father," said Tom Jr.

Roger Staubach was having a difficult time over Landry's death. Landry and Staubach certainly had differences of opinion, yet over the years they developed a mutual respect and love for each other. Roger spoke at the church and would do so again at the public gathering at the Meyerson. "This is the most difficult thing I've had to do," he said. "It's more difficult than playing in a Super Bowl." As he spoke from the heart in each service, he paused at times to collect himself.

"A chunk has been taken out of me by the death of Coach Landry. . . . Tom Landry had a decency about him that was unsurpassed. He achieved great fame while not seeking it. Everyone knew he wasn't a phony. He just didn't put on airs, not ever. He did things for the right reasons. That's what his Christian religion taught him to do . . . the right thing, the things that helped others. His dedication to the FCA and to the ministries of Billy Graham, his work for charity, his desire to help child after child, friend after friend . . . so many other things are testaments to his character and to his faith. Tom Landry was there for people when they needed him. He was there for his country in World

War II. He was there for his community, for his team, and most important, for his family.

"Coach Landry was able to keep things in perspective. He knew what was important in life, and he helped us understand that his road was the high road. He didn't dwell on defeat. He looked to the next play, the next game, the next season. He was our rock, our hope, our inspiration. He was our coach."

Alicia, Tom Jr., and the Landrys' daughter Kitty received guests after the church ceremonies. It was obvious that Alicia was in great pain, but she greeted each and every one of us. I was reminded just how much I liked and respected her. While Tom never said a word, except maybe in a kidding way, when I was critical of him, Alicia would tease me about some of my shenanigans when I covered the team and let me know if she didn't like something I'd written about her husband. I liked her even better for that, for speaking up for her husband. She has class, loyalty, honor . . . all the things associated with her husband.

Alicia smiled, hugged, and shook hands with each person as we struggled for the right words to say at such a terrible time. It broke your heart to see her in such pain, the depth of which only she knew. Alicia and Tom had been married for fifty-one years and faced the joys and heartbreaks of life together. They were a part of each other and no doubt would be again someday. But now he wasn't there anymore. It was difficult for her to imagine going on without him, but she had her children and grandchildren and knew they needed her and that she must go on. That's what Tom would have wanted.

Alicia asked all the players to stop by the Landry home after the memorial service, where she visited with each one. Bob Breunig had been there earlier in the week with his wife, Mary. "We'd taken a cake over. I'd never been in his home before, but it was so warm there with Alicia, their children, and their grandchildren. And it made me realize the guy was just as human as can be. He went home and faced the challenges, the frustrations, the disappointments and pain, and all those things we all go through."

Alicia and her family, mentally and emotionally spent, prepared for the final tribute at the Morton H. Meyerson Symphony Center. The public was invited, and there would be complete live-television coverage, offering those not in attendance a chance to hear what Tom Landry meant to so many people while reflecting on what he meant to them.

Death and Remembrance

꒰꒱

THE MORTON H. MEYERSON SYMPHONY CENTER for performing arts is located in downtown Dallas by the Arts District. Because of the earlier service at the church, the "Tribute to the Tom Landry Legacy" at the Meyerson didn't start until 4:00 P.M., a time that coincided with the early rush hour and caused fears of a possible traffic jam. That possibility, plus limited first come, first serve seating, prompted city officials to urge the public to watch the service on television. That advice was heeded.

Cowboys owner-general-manager-and-whatever-else-he-wants-to-be Jerry Jones had offered use of Texas Stadium for the final tribute, but the Landry family preferred the more dignified, appropriate setting of the Meyerson. It was a full house. People came dressed in everything from suits to Cowboy T-shirts and caps. They were young and old, easily recognizable faces and others known only to family and friends. Jones and his wife, Gene, were there, as were new Cowboys coach Dave Campo and Troy Aikman, who had commented earlier how he'd have loved to have played for Tom Landry.

Jones issued a statement calling Landry the single most important figure in the history of the Dallas Cowboys. "His legacy and his influence, however, extend far beyond this organization. In one individual, Tom Landry captured the essence of this sport, the spirit of this state, and all of the virtues that athletic competition provides our society. . . . He will remain an inspiration for as long as young men and boys play this game, and his name—and his presence—will be forever woven throughout the fabric of American football."

Blake Martin left class at Scofield Christian School in Lake Highlands to attend the Meyerson tribute. His parents had told him Tom Landry was a great football coach but an even greater Christian. "I wish I could be like him," said Blake. As did many others, Blake brought flowers. Everybody brought memories.

They listened to players tell amusing and inspirational stories about Coach Landry and how he impacted their lives and to Ann Murchison, widow of Cowboys founder Clint Murchison Jr., praise Alicia and what she had meant to Tom. And they listened to Dr. Charles Swindoll, president of Dallas Theological Seminary, and to former Cowboys chaplain Dr. Tony Evans of the Oak Cliff Bible Fellowship put Tom's life in perspective. There was laughter . . . and quiet tears.

At 4:00 P.M., a color guard marched to the stage, stopped, and presented arms as Tommy Loy, a fixture with his trumpet at Cowboy games for twenty-two years during the Landry years, played the national anthem. Dr. Swindoll, presiding, called the gathering a tribute "to a man who has touched and impacted all our lives. . . . He left the world a better place than he found it. . . . He defied mediocrity. He embraced priority, the right priority of God, family, and then your work, football."

Dr. Evans led the audience in prayer: "This honoring is a time to recognize the great God of this great man who unapologetically gave tribute to the source of his strength. And when such a God produced such a great man, how can you be silent about that."

National Football League commissioner Paul Tagliabue told the audience that if there was a Mount Rushmore for the NFL, the profile of Tom Landry, wearing his trademark hat, would be there. "Tom Landry himself was one of the greatest gifts ever given to the NFL. The spirit and values of Coach Landry will always be with us in the National Football League. . . . He truly was not just the greatest Dallas Cowboy and legendary New York Giant, Tom Landry was the genuine article, a legend across the entire history of pro football." Landry's legacy, Tagliabue continued, went far beyond his football accomplishments and "is one of towering achievements, modest demeanor, discipline, teamwork, straight talk, loyalty, commitment, and faith."

Tex Schramm recalled when he first hired Landry after the 1959 season and said the coach's death "marks today a closure for a great individual, who along with a bunch of young men, made the Dallas Cowboys something special, made the team represent something special to the rest of the country. Tom is up there looking, and I just hope we can fulfill the great things in our personal life that he did."

Then Ann Murchison spoke: "I'm sure the first words Tom heard when he went to heaven were, 'Well done, good and faithful servant,' and I want to say the same thing to you, dearest Alicia. Well done, good and faithful servant." She talked about how Tom and Alicia were a reflection of each other. "If you know her, you know him. If you know him, you know her. I know of no more lovely, supportive wife than Alicia Landry. She was the revelation of his own good, kind heart, and he hers. . . . You were a rare and precious jewel to Tom, Alicia. Side by side, you loved, raised children, enjoyed grandchildren, dreamed, and shared the heartbreak of losing a beautiful daughter. . . .You lit up Tom's life. You two lived a great love story. . . .You were Tom's hero."

When Landry was an assistant coach with the New York Giants in 1956, he picked Sam Huff to be the NFL's first middle linebacker in his new, innovative 4–3 defense. At the Meyerson, Huff fondly remembered those days when many of the players and coaches lived in the same hotel in New York. He recalled seeing Tom Jr. playing in Central Park, how Landry would drill him hours on hours about the intricacies of the new formation. Then he looked over at Alicia and added, "He married the most beautiful lady that I have ever met. She is still the most beautiful person that I have ever met."

Landry's defense was precise. He strongly believed if each player did exactly what he was supposed to do the opposition would be stopped. Sam brought laughs, especially from empathetic Cowboy players, when he told of intercepting a pass and coming off the field in triumph, expecting to be congratulated. "Landry just looked at me and said, 'You must play my defense. Your pass drop was the wrong way. You cannot do that. You must play my defense.' All I said was, 'Yes sir.'" Sam concluded, "My greatest moment in sports was the day Tom Landry inducted me into the Pro Football Hall of Fame."

Don Perkins mentioned how when he played for the Cowboys in the 1960s, the country was racially divided. "One thing I can appreciate as a player is that we, as Cowboys, transcended that. . . . Tom was a big reason for that. In spite of things around the country, it never affected us. You see the old players here today and a handshake isn't enough. We end up in an embrace."

During the time of the Civil Rights movement, Ann Laws, then executive secretary of the national and regional NAACP, wrote to a number of celebrities asking them to be on her advisory committee. In those days, some famous people shied away from becoming involved. But Tom Landry and the late U.S. District Judge Sarah T. Hughes were among the first to respond and offer their support. Their names were printed on the formal invitations to hear Roy Wilkins speak at the Adolphus Hotel in downtown Dallas. The NAACP was able to make twenty thousand dollars from the event.

Don continued, "Football isn't about winning and losing but being the best you can be. I learned that firsthand through practical experiences with Tom Landry. We miss you, Tom. We love you."

Bob Lilly recalled his rookie year when he played defensive end. It was only when Landry later moved him to tackle in 1963 that he became one of the NFL's all-time greats. "I had a broken foot, a torn-up thumb, a torn-up knee," he said. "I wasn't supposed to play in this game. Coach Landry came to me and said, 'We've only got four linemen, Bob. It looks like you're going to have to play.' So I did, and then on Monday he said, 'That's the worst game I've ever seen a defensive end play in my life.'" Bob paused and then continued, "He was my coach, like my second father. He instilled principles, integrity, and character in us that we probably lost when we went to college. When I went to that first meeting and he told me his priorities [God, family, football], I thought he was kidding. When I was thirty-five years old and had quit football, I realized his priorities in life were the ones I wanted in my life. I know many of my peers have done the same thing. . . . I've tried to impart those things to my children."

Rayfield Wright praised Landry's great insight when he moved him from tight end to offensive right tackle, where he became All-Pro. At the time, Rayfield wasn't so sure it was a good idea. He especially wasn't sure it was a good idea when his first assignment was to line up against the great Los Angeles Rams defensive end Deacon Jones. On the first play, Rayfield was listening to Roger call signals when Deacon said, "Does your mother know you're on the football field?" Rayfield said he never heard the rest of the snap count because he was knocked flat on his back. "I rolled over toward our sidelines and focused on Coach Landry's eyes," he said. "He did not have to say a word, but I could feel what he was saying: 'Get up. Get up.' Well, I got up, and Mr. Jones had a tough day after that."

Many feel Drew Pearson should be in the Cowboy Ring of Honor and perhaps even strongly considered for the NFL Hall of Fame. During the 1970s and early 1980s, he made the tough catches, the clutch catches, such as the famous "Hail Mary" pass from Roger Staubach that beat Minnesota, 17–14, in the 1975 divisional playoffs. But Drew put the meaning of his career in perspective for the audience.

"I cannot believe I played the game for eleven years in a league like the NFL for a team like the Dallas Cowboys for Coach Tom Landry. And I don't need to be in the Hall of Fame or Ring of Honor to punctuate my career. What counts and punctuates my career more than anything is that I played eleven years for Coach Tom Landry. You can't get any more respect than that.

"When my children and recent grandchildren ask me about my days in the NFL, about my catches or the Hail Mary, I'll simply say I played eleven years for Coach Tom Landry. They will know about Coach Tom Landry and his great success as a coach. They will know about his great success as a person and about the legacy he has left. I expect their response will be, 'You must have been a good player to play for such a man for eleven years.'"

When adversity struck, Drew realized just how much Coach Landry cared for him. Drew was driving the car in the tragic accident in 1984 in which his brother was killed. Drew was also badly injured and could no longer play football. Coach Landry was there for him and his family during that terrible time. He comforted Drew's family and repeatedly came to the hospital to visit him. He even brought Drew in as an assistant, trying to ease the pain of not being able to play again.

So Drew told the audience how Coach Landry was there for him during the good times, and the bad times, and how he loved him. "We are all going to miss Coach Landry, but we all know if we do the right thing and live our lives the way he did, we'll have the opportunity to meet him again."

Randy White, the guy you now see on commercials, was very shy when he joined the Cowboys. He was so afraid of Coach Landry that he was unable to speak when he talked to him. He would just make noises. "I was so intimidated that for a long time I don't think he thought I could make a whole sentence," said Randy, the NFL Hall of Fame defensive tackle. Then Randy told about a special time he had with Coach Landry. Randy's father died before the final regular-season game of 1977. Randy hadn't mentioned this to anybody but his friend, middle linebacker Bob Breunig. Bob in turn told Coach Landry, who told Randy to take all the time he needed to be with his family. Randy said he wanted to play, and Coach Landry said, "That's fine, but go to your family right after the game."

"I'll never forget my whole life a moment I shared with Coach Landry," said Randy. "When the defense was going to be introduced to go on the field, we were all standing there. I had tears in my eyes. Coach Landry came over and shook my hand, and he had tears in his eyes when he said how sorry he was about my dad. . . . I will never forget him. The thing I respect most about Tom Landry is that he didn't just talk the talk, he walked the walk."

"Two months ago, I spoke to Coach Landry on the telephone," said Danny Reeves. "I didn't know at the time that it would be my last chance to talk to him. I just wish I had thought, along with others here today, to use the three most beautiful words in the English language and told him, 'I love you.'"

Roger Staubach was the man who brought the team back from the brink of defeat so many times, the guy who was best when the pressure was worst. At the Meyerson, Roger paused several times to keep his composure as he related humorous and meaningful stories about Coach Landry.

"We've all experienced lots of relationships in our lives, but we keep going back to the one we had with Coach Landry. Even though we didn't think at the time that he was listening or paying any attention to us, we now know that he was. He was committed to us, and you don't find that commitment in life very often. . . .The essence of Tom Landry's faith was that he did not give up. He never gave up! He set his eyes on what he could not see but knew in his heart to be true. That is the way he lived here on this earth and one of the reasons people loved and respected him. This is why he won for twenty straight seasons. This is why this relatively quiet, shy man, who wasn't much for small talk, didn't seem to smile much, and was very stoic, could walk into a room and the room would light up and he'd become the center of attention. He didn't want to be the center of attention, but he deserved to be. This is why he was so loved by his family and the millions more who never had the privilege of meeting him."

Roger closed by reading one of Coach Landry's favorite poems:

His love is greater than the expanse of the sea.
He died a cruel death to save you and me.

Although we continue to sin day after day,
He forgives us and leads us back to his way.

His path is straight and narrow, you see.
But if we follow his leading, in his will we'll be.

This world gives no lasting pleasure.
But his kingdom is full of riches beyond measure.

Remember to always look above the sun.
Until that final day when his will shall be done.

The Lord, in his glory, will ride on a cloud.
And the trumpets will blast in the heavens so loud,

To call his children home at last,
Never to look back to those things that are past.

Our bodies will become glorious and perfectly made.
For Christ made sure our ransom was paid.

The poem was written by Lisa Landry Childress. "Coach, give our love to Lisa," Roger concluded. "We miss you both."

⌣∙〜

DR. SWINDOLL DIRECTED HIS CLOSING REMARKS first to Alicia. "All of us have tried to say how much you have meant to us, throughout the seasons and all these wonderful years you have spent with your loving partner. Your grief is almost beyond description. You have been a rock of Gibraltar. . . . And we love you, we respect you."

Then he continued, "Tom Landry was not one to sermonize or to cram his faith down anybody's throat. He taught by example as you have heard time and again from those who played for him and coached alongside him and those who have known him up close as well as from a distance. Rather than trying to force anyone to believe what he believed, he lived his faith in a life of uncompromising character wherever he went in whatever circumstances he found himself. . . .

"His marriage to his beloved partner for over fifty years spoke eloquently to a society where married partnership quickly erodes. His example taught us the value of marital fidelity. His deep and rarely mentioned grief over the loss of his beloved daughter Lisa taught us all how to go through fire of affliction without being burned by bitterness."

Dr. Swindoll spoke of Landry's unselfish compassion for the needs of others, whether in giving a boy his autograph or talking to a teenager about saying no to drugs. He told how Landry had lent his "name and untarnished reputation" to help churches, community groups, and charitable organizations reach their goals for donations.

"He made lasting impressions on all of us as we stood back and watched and we admired him all the more. . . . Tom Landry was a man of grace. It was because years earlier he had met on his own the God of all grace, through a personal relationship with His Son, Jesus Christ, in whom Tom believed with all his heart . . . and became the man God intended him to be. . . . He lived his life ready to die, for a man is not ready to live if he is not ready to die."

To conclude the Meyerson tribute, the Dallas Children's Chorus and the Dallas Baptist University were joined by the audience in singing that wonderful testament to redemption, "Amazing Grace." Written in the eighteenth century by Englishman John Newton, a slave trader who found God then became a minister and fought to abolish slavery, it was one of Tom Landry's favorite hymns.

> Amazing grace, how sweet the sound, that saved a wretch like me.
> I once was lost, but now am found, was blind but now I see.
> 'Twas grace that taught my heart to fear, and grace my fears
> relieved.
> How precious did that grace appear, the hour I first believed.

People lingered inside and outside the Meyerson after the tribute as if they didn't want that final memorial, a closure in a way, to end. Those in attendance and people watching at home continued to talk about Landry and his career, the funny and tender things the speakers had said. They remembered Landry's career, this game or that game, and that he was fired and speculated on what might have happened had he continued to coach the Cowboys for a few more years. This is something we'll never know, although there is no doubt that after Landry was fired his life continued to be gratifying and meaningful.

CHAPTER 2
Retirement: Good Deeds and Charities

‿⁚‿

Coach Landry reminded all of us that there are still a lot of good people in sports and in the world in general. He represented the best of the Cowboys, the best of all of us, not only here but also around the country and even abroad because Dallas is an international city.

—ROGER STAUBACH

MANY PEOPLE would have reached the breaking point if the door had been so abruptly slammed on such a big part of their life, something they loved and in which they had been very successful, as it was for Tom Landry when he was fired in 1989 from his position as head coach of the Dallas Cowboys. Now, Tom Landry was certainly disappointed and hurt when he was fired and had initial concerns about how he might fill the empty spots in his life away from football. But he accepted that God had something else in store for him and found that shining light. From that late February day in 1989 when his football career ended until his death eleven years later in another February of a new millennium, he was as busy as ever. He devoted even more time to philanthropy, Christian work, and making a difference in people's lives, one on one. He also went into business with his son, Tom Jr., and was in great demand as a motivational speaker. And he was able to spend much more priceless time with his family.

When Landry was in football, the family was able to make only infrequent trips from Dallas to their getaway home near Austin in the Hills of Lakeway. Once he left the Cowboys, the Landrys became regular commuters to Lakeway in Tom's Cessna Centurion 210. It was a short plane trip, and a landing strip nearby allowed them to be at the house in a matter of minutes. The Landrys built their two-story, white stucco, Italian villa–style house in the mid-1980s. The house backed up to the eighteenth fairway, about thirty yards from the green, in an elite development about forty-five minutes from downtown Austin. Jack Nicklaus designed the private golf course and has a home at Lakeway. The Landrys' daughter Lisa and son-in-law Gary Childress also lived nearby. Tom and Alicia welcomed trips to Lakeway even more when their third grandchild, Christina Childress, was born.

It was so pleasant and peaceful at Lakeway. A creek ran on the south side of the house, and deer could be seen wandering around the area. The Landrys liked to sit on the patio on the second floor of their house and watch the golfers below or simply enjoy the fading traces of daylight. And sometimes they would talk about Austin and the appeal it had for them.

TO MOST PEOPLE WHO HAVE LIVED IN AUSTIN, especially if they lived there when they were young, the city remains the best of places, like a first love. It is certainly a wonderful place to be when you're as young as Tom and Alicia were when they first lived there. They met and fell in love at the University of Texas in Austin, so Austin and its surrounding area was always a memorable part of their life together.

Certainly, Austin has changed a great deal since the Landrys were at UT. The Hills of Lakeway development is just another part of the ever-expanding capital city, which has grown by leaps and bounds in the last two decades. The population is now some five hundred sixty thousand, UT has fifty thousand students, and a modern double-deck freeway goes through the downtown area. Highways that once bordered the city are now engulfed in the city proper. And as is the case with Dallas, Fort Worth, Houston, and San Antonio, small towns that once were outside Austin are now connected in most everything but name.

Although politics and education remain the backbone of the city's economy, Austin has become a high-tech city with numerous research- and science-oriented industries. Many now see it as a smaller version of Dallas and Houston, and yet in spite of the continual rush into future expansion, it still retains a great deal of its unique atmosphere. And atmosphere is something that can't be manufactured or prefabricated, because it simply is there or it isn't.

Scholz Beer Garten was for generations a traditional meeting place for students, writers, would-be writers, politicians (coming up and going down), professors, and athletes. Many go elsewhere now. But Austin still has classic old homes and parks with rock paths winding under giant oaks, and the Colorado River still snakes its way along the edge of downtown and helps form beautiful lakes around the city. And tourists and sweethearts can still go up on Mt. Bonnell and look down at the city and the Colorado.

Austin has Barton Springs, one of the nation's largest and most beautiful spring-fed swimming pools, and it is a city where William "Sydney" Porter, better known as O. Henry, once worked for the local newspaper (his home has become a popular museum) and where J. Frank Dobie taught at UT. Short miles to the southwest is the stunning Hill Country with its soft, rolling hills, spring-fed streams, and oaks and cedars and pecans and wildflowers of blue and red and yellow. Sure, Austin has changed a lot in recent years, but for people like Tom and Alicia, it can still conjure memories of pleasant times.

~:~

WHEN LANDRY WAS FIRED in 1989, Alicia recalled, he looked "worn, tired, and thin," but after a while he became "relaxed, rested, and happy." She said retirement agreed with him, although he was doing so much he hardly seemed to have retired. Landry himself said the transition from football was a lot easier than he'd imagined it would be.

"He just moved on to the next challenge," said Tom Jr. "The Cowboys changed when he left. The people he knew and worked with were also gone. It would have affected him more if the players, coaches, and everybody had still been there and he was the only one gone."

Landry did quickly detach himself from the Dallas Cowboys because the people who'd joined him in making the team so popular and so successful were let go too. He wrote in his 1990 autobiography, *Tom Landry:* "As sad as that realization is, I know no one can take away the memories—memories shared with so many people who played and worked together to create a football team and a proud tradition that made Dallas, Texas, renowned throughout the world as the home of the Cowboys. For a time at least, America's Team."

It saddened him to see the new management deliberately dismantle so many years of tradition. After Landry was dismissed, Tex Schramm, Gil Brandt, Doug Todd, other office personnel and scouts, and all but two of his assistant coaches were fired or forced out. Key players Randy

White and Danny White were encouraged to retire, and Herschel Walker was traded. Even Tommy Loy, who for twenty-two years had played "The Star-Spangled Banner" on his trumpet before games, was replaced. It was Jerry Jones's team, and he wanted his own people to establish the new Dallas Cowboys. His team would be very successful and, at this writing, has won three Super Bowls. But his Cowboys are unlike the team Landry coached. There certainly have been some good guys on the team, but overall, the aura, the class personified by Tom Landry, has been missing.

⌣∶∾

WHILE AT LAKEWAY, Landry could play golf with his son, Tom Jr., his sons-in-law Gary Childress and Eddie Phillips, and his old friends Wade Spillman and Bill Sansing. Sansing observed that Landry seemed to get better and better over the years and once fired a 32 in a 9-hole club tournament. Landry was a powerful golfer, capable of driving the ball 270 yards. He carried a 14-handicap because he didn't play often but was capable of shooting in the high 70s. And he was known to have made spectacular shots. During a tournament in Houston, Landry's team was getting ready for what appeared a playoff with another group. Their opponents pitched onto the green, but the playoff never materialized. Landry immediately hit a hole in one. "Under pressure," said Tom Jr., "he would just take it to another level."

Spillman grew up with Landry in Mission, Texas. "Tom was my dearest and oldest friend," he said. "There won't be another person like Tom Landry. He's an extraordinary person, a paragon. I can remember so many things about him, so many kindnesses." One was so typical of Landry. "Years ago my sister had lost her husband to cancer and was working with the Cancer Society. She called me and said she was wondering if Tommy might be willing to serve as its chairman. So I asked him, and he said he would do it but was very apologetic because he felt he just didn't have time to give it the proper attention. 'But I'll tell you what,' he said. 'I'll do it next year and make sure I have enough time to do it right.' And he did."

People who have this preconceived image of the stone-faced, unsmiling Landry might not imagine this scene: He loved to romp on the floor and play around with his grandchildren. As Alicia once remarked, "You don't see that grim face you see on the sidelines when

30

he's playing with the grandkids. You see laughs and smiles." The grand-kids called Alicia "Honey" and Tom "Coach" (but once when granddaughter Jennifer was young she became confused and called Alicia "Coach").

There were great times at the Hills of Lakeway, and sure, commuting was quick and simple, with one frightening exception.

ON AN OVERCAST FRIDAY AFTERNOON in March 1995 with low visibility, Landry was flying Alicia and other members of the family to Austin for the weekend in his Cessna. He'd left Dallas's Love Field and was flying on instruments above the clouds just south of Dallas near Ennis. All at once the oil temperature gauge went over the top, signaling engine failure. Landry knew the Ennis airfield was nearby and hoped he could make an emergency landing there. Just as he brought the plane below the clouds, visibility returned. But the engine blew out. He realized there was no way he could make the airfield without power, as the plane began a powerless glide to the ground.

Clifford Norman, an Ennis schoolteacher, seemed to speak for all the bystanders watching the aircraft's eerie descent when he said, "That plane's going to crash!"

Typically, Landry remained cool, more calculating than frightened. "It wasn't that much of a problem bringing her in, but you never know what the field is like where you're landing," he later said, knowing that any small obstruction could flip his light plane. Landry set the Cessna down on a vacant lot behind the high-school football field and walked away with his family members. Nobody was hurt, and there wasn't a scratch on the plane.

"It was frightening, but I knew Tommy was in control," said Alicia.

Fifty-one years earlier, Landry, who had just turned twenty, was copilot on a B-17, one of the legendary Flying Fortresses, returning from a bombing run over Germany during World War II. Engines on the plane sputtered then died, and the plane dropped to about a thousand feet while under fire from antiaircraft. Just before the crew bailed out, Landry thought to adjust the fuel mixture. The engines came back alive, and the crew made it back to England. Another time his plane ran out of gas and crash-landed in France. Trees sheared both wings, and the nose of the plane went into a tree. All walked away. Recalling those episodes and his latest adventure, Landry said, "Well, I hope I haven't run out my string."

~:~

IN 1989, Tom Landry and Tom Jr. opened the Landry Investment Group, Inc., a holding company with investments in oil and other businesses. In addition, Landry was listed with a number of bureaus that furnish speakers for meetings and events, and could practically name his five-figure price. He was also getting offers to do commercials and could have made appearances three or four days a week. He had become a one-man conglomerate.

Tom Jr., who handled Landry's endorsements and appearances, explained, "One of Dad's speeches was entitled 'Commitment to Excellence,' and the theme of that speech was an ideal that was central to my father's beliefs. 'The quality of a man's life is in direct proportion to his commitment to excellence.' It was this commitment to excellence in all aspects of my father's life that made him great. It could be his job, it could be his family, it could be his Christian faith, and it could be compassion and feelings for other people. It was simply an effort to strive to do the very, very best in whatever a person was doing."

Landry and his son were in business for ten years, and yet Tom Jr. never ceased to be surprised at how much his father accomplished. "He got so much done without you even realizing what he was doing," he said. "He'd send all the thank-you notes, all the letters and things like that. . . . He did so many things none of us knew about. He'd write a letter of encouragement to someone who was having problems or take time to call them. He'd answer letters from fans. The only way we'd find out about those things was usually by accident. He just never mentioned them."

Shortly after Landry's death, Tom Jr. made a call to discuss the possibility of a high-school event being named after his father. An older man answered the phone and immediately began telling him about a special time when he was in the seventh grade. In conjunction with the FCA, Coach Landry had come by his school to talk to the kids at 7:30 A.M. Landry spoke to them about how important it was to do the right thing even though it might not be popular with their peers.

"The guy said that years later he was at a party with friends, drinking beer and all, when he remembered what Dad had told them," continued Tom Jr. "So he left the party because of that speech Dad had made so many years earlier. Another impressive thing is that it happened during football season. Here's a guy who is head coach of a world-championship team, taking time to go over there at seven-thirty in the morning to talk to a group of unknown kids. If I hadn't made that call, I'd never have known about that."

Jim Reeves had a car dealership that was one of the ticket outlets in the early days of the Cowboys franchise. He's now in the Veterans Administration Hospital in Bonham, Texas. At the VA, he befriended a guy named Don Bingham, but by the summer of 1998, his friend was dying of cancer. Don didn't talk much about his past to the guys at the VA. But he did open up to Jim. He told him how he'd played for the Chicago Bears when they lost the NFL championship game to the New York Giants. That was when the Giants had a cornerback named Tom Landry.

"Don was deathly ill, bedridden, and fading fast, so I called Coach Landry," said Jim. "He was on vacation, but his secretary said he'd return my call when he got back. The day he got back, he called me. I was wondering if he might come to Bonham and see Don, but his schedule was heavy after vacation and he couldn't make it. He remembered Don, though. I don't think Coach Landry ever forgot anybody. So he suggested we hook up a conference call, and we did. Coach Landry called Don, and they must have talked for thirty to forty minutes. I listened part of the time as they talked about the old days when they played, what they'd been doing since, and all sorts of things. Ol' Don was lit up like a Christmas tree after that. When he hung up, you could just see the change in him. I think that conversation added another ninety days to his life.

"Very few people knew Don had played pro football, much less that he knew Tom Landry. After that call, everybody was talking about Don. Yes, he died about three months after that."

Landry once called me to ask if I would write a column about Buddy Dial, who played for Landry in the mid-1960s but was having a terrible time. If I decided to do something on Buddy, Landry said, he'd rather I not mention him. The *Dallas Morning News*, with its vast circulation and exposure, had always been a great format to help people by writing about them, although I was often accused of overplaying my hand as a columnist. Buddy was an all-American at Rice University and a star in the NFL at Pittsburgh. But he fell on hard times with the Cowboys. He suffered injury after injury, underwent five back surgeries, and lost a kidney. He became hooked on painkillers and spent years trying to overcome the problem. In the process, he lost his house, his wife, and most of his worldly possessions and could no longer work. In addition, he fought the NFL for years before he was awarded full disability benefits.

During his playing days, Buddy weighed 190 pounds, but when I talked to him, his weight had dwindled to 132 pounds. He was living with his mother and had difficulty getting around, but he was going to a pain clinic and had never stopped fighting to put his life back together. He had once been a hero, a star, but had become a forgotten man. He also had some bitter feelings about the Cowboys. After my column appeared, he heard from numerous friends and former teammates. I honored Landry's wishes, and Buddy never knew the column was his idea.

"I read the column and showed it to Dad," said Tom Jr. "He never mentioned it was his idea. See what I mean.

"Working closely with Dad, I was better able to understand him. We were working on this complicated deal. I had it all figured out and went into Dad's office to discuss it with him. He was very patient and let me finish talking about it before commenting. He wanted me to describe it to him completely. Finally I said, 'Dad, what do you want to do?' He said, 'I want to do what's fair.' That's the way he did business and lived his life."

Landry was far from forgotten after football. Bill Clements, governor of Texas when Landry was fired, and other politicians and civic leaders urged him to run for office. Within a short time after he was fired, President George Bush appointed Landry to the President's Drug Strategy Council. The $16 million sports medicine and research center at Baylor University Medical Center was named after him. Dallas mayor Annette Strauss, an avid Landry fan, appointed him chairman of the International Sports Commission, created to lure top sports events to the city. He served the commission until it disbanded in 1996. He was even inducted into the Washington, D.C., Touchdown Club. The honors continued over the years. In 1996, an elementary school in the Dallas suburbs of Carrollton–Farmers Branch was named after him.

In January 1990, Landry received his greatest sports honor when he was elected into the NFL Hall of Fame in his first year of eligibility, less than a year after he'd been fired. He was both surprised and thrilled. "It was a great honor for me," said Landry. "I never expected it to happen.

I'd always looked at it as a player's honor, although a few of us coaches have sneaked in there."

On August 4, Roger Staubach, who'd become a close friend of Landry after retiring, made the induction speech, something Landry had done for him at his Hall of Fame induction in 1985. Landry's famous fedora was placed in the Pro Football Hall of Fame in Canton, Ohio. Curator Don Smith said, "We thought about a playbook, but that's kind of technical. When you think of Tom Landry, you think about his hat."

Of course, the hat was Landry's trademark. He'd started wearing it as an assistant coach with the New York Giants when hats were a popular item. Even then, he dressed well on the sidelines, feeling a person should dress as if he were going to work in the business world. Besides, the hat warmed his head in the New York winters. Later, Resistol Hats of Dallas began sending him a selection of hats each year and even came out with the "Tom Landry Signature Line."

In his Hall of Fame acceptance speech, Landry credited the players for putting him in the position to be honored. Tex Schramm and players Bob Lilly, Mel Renfro, Tony Dorsett, and Randy White would also make the Hall of Fame. When he was inducted into the Dallas Cowboys Ring of Honor in 1993, Landry again credited his players for any success he had. The Ring of Honor is reserved for players and coaches who make great contributions to the team. Landry's name was inscribed above the Cowboy bench at Texas Stadium. With that honor, he joined his former players, including Don Perkins, Don Meredith, Bob Lilly, Mel Renfro, Roger Staubach, Randy White, Lee Roy Jordan, Chuck Howley, and Tony Dorsett. Cowboy owner Jerry Jones had been trying for three years to get Landry to come to the stadium to accept the honor. Tom had said he was busy with other things, but he'd finally relented.

Fans and former Cowboy employees are still bitter about Landry being let go by Jones, but no one can remember Landry being outwardly critical of Jones. Landry didn't linger; he went on with his life.

"I never heard Tommy say a bad word about anybody," said Alicia.

"I never saw him bitter," said Jim Myers, Landry's longtime assistant. "I saw no public display of bitterness. He was able to put the past where it was supposed to be and go on."

"When he was fired, it turned out to have the opposite effect than some people thought it might," said Landry's friend Paul Corley.

"Instead of having lingering bad feelings, he gained strength from it. Fans, friends, the media, and everybody rallied around him because of the way he was treated. He became an even bigger legend."

Sportscaster Pat Summerall, an old friend Landry had coached when he was with the Giants, moved to the Dallas area in the mid-1990s. "I didn't realize how strong his impact was in Dallas until I moved here. And as I go around the country, I realize it became even stronger after he left football."

"Dad just didn't dwell on the past," said Tom Jr. "He would just close the door to the past and open up another one and move on to the next challenge. It saved a lot of time.

"He was amazing. He had great success in business just like in everything else he did, whether it was football, charities, or whatever. He was supremely confident but didn't need validation other than knowing he'd done his best. He recognized the job at hand, got it done, and didn't blow his own horn."

Well, there *was* one thing Tom Landry could not do. He couldn't sing a lick. In the small town of Mission, where Landry grew up, there weren't a lot of people in high school. So young people often participated in a number of activities. Landry, a popular superathlete, was pressed into duty with the boys glee club. Aware of his musical limitations, Landry decided he would just move his lips instead of actually singing. Had he not done this on his own, the glee club director probably would have suggested he do so. So there was some concern when Tom agreed to do a commercial for Quality Inn in which he would pop out of a suitcase strumming a guitar and singing.

"When we were negotiating the deal, we thought about getting Willie Nelson or somebody to dub in the singing," said Tom Jr. "But they worked with him and decided to let him sing, and it turned out great."

So here comes Landry, dressed in fedora, coat, and tie, popping out of a suitcase, picking and singing, "Mamas, don't let your babies grow up to be Redskins," then adding, "You didn't think I was going to say *Cowboys*, did you?" He played off his serious, stern demeanor, which made the commercial funnier than ever and very popular. A commercial he did for American Express during the NFL strike in 1982 worked well for the same reason.

That one was shot on the movie set of a western town. Landry is dressed in western hat, trail coat, and boots and comes riding into town.

He ties his horse to the hitching post and walks into the saloon, never changing his expression. As he's surrounded by Washington Redskins, he calmly says, "Do you know me? I'm one of the best-known cowboys in Texas. A lot of people don't recognize me in this cowboy hat. That's why I carry my American Express card." As he walks out with this stern look on his face, the swinging doors of the saloon knock over the Redskins following him. The commercial became one of the best business-related commercials in history. People in the business said Landry could get one hundred to four hundred thousand dollars per commercial for, say, an automobile company. That's the same amount paid some movie stars. But he only did one other national commercial.

He was hired for a Frito Lay commercial that was first aired during the 1993 Super Bowl. The cast also included Mike Ditka, Lawrence Taylor, Boomer Esiason, Phil Simms, Eric Dickerson, and John Elway. In the commercial, Landry bets the others they can tell the difference between Frito-Lay and another chip. They lose the bet, and when it comes time to think of the way they can pay up, Landry tells them, "Well, I'm sure I can think of something off the top of my head." So the others are required to shave their heads, and through the magic of makeup, it looks very much as if they had.

These commercials changed the misconception many people had that Landry seldom smiled and lacked a sense of humor. Those closer to him knew better.

Mike Ditka was one of the toughest guys to ever play in the NFL and was known for his hot temper. Yet Landry intimidated Mike and the most feared players on the team. Tom didn't kick or scream and seldom yelled. But he just gave them "That Look," a feared, cold stare that went right through you. It was worth hundreds of words.

Landry was very competitive on the golf course but much looser than he was on the football field. Once in 1970, when Mike Ditka was still a tight end for the Cowboys, he was playing golf with his pal Tito Nicholas. After Mike chipped onto the green with an 8-iron, he left the club on the fairway. When he had use for the 8-iron again, Tito yelled through the trees separating them from the previous fairway, "Did anybody pick up Ditka's 8-iron!"

Somebody yelled back that he'd picked up the club, so what. Ditka yelled he'd like to have the club back. Then the voice said, "Well, I might throw it right in the lake." Ditka became angry and replied, "If you throw it in the lake, I'll throw you in after it!" The voice on the other side of the trees replied, "Tito, how do you think Mike will like playing in Buffalo next year?" They recognized the voice as Landry's, and Mike turned white and subdued. Later they all laughed.

Landry's secretary, Barbara Goodman, often brought him hot tea in the morning in his office. Once her timing was off and she walked in the door as Landry was walking out. They bumped, and she spilled hot tea all over him. She apologized profusely, but he told her she shouldn't worry about it. When she asked him if she could bring him another cup of tea, he said, "Yes, thank you. But could you toot your horn next time?"

Once, Tony Dorsett fell off a horse during a team outing. The following day before practice, Landry walked by Tony's locker and said, "There's ol' Hopalong Cassidy."

On another occasion, Don Meredith was having a bad day throwing during training camp. One of his passes was especially wild and Don said, "Well, I'll be an SOB!" Landry, standing nearby, remarked, "That wouldn't help your passing."

Landry was much more uptight during the early years of the team, and Meredith, and the other quarterbacks for that matter, were a little reluctant to try to loosen up the coach. The exception was Staubach. During a game in Texas Stadium, Roger noticed the coach in a familiar posture, deep in thought, arms folded and staring up toward the hole in the roof. Roger approached Landry and said, "Now I know where you get your plays." Landry, momentarily distracted, resumed thinking about his next move on the field.

One practice session Landry didn't like the way Roger executed a certain play. In spite of his gimpy knee, Tom got under center and ran the play himself. "Roger, do it just like I did," he said. So Roger limped when he ran the play. Everybody laughed. Some said Landry had slight traces of a grin on his face while others said he never changed his expression.

He certainly was capable of making fun of himself and his image, so perhaps he laughed later.

After Walt Garrison retired, he was asked if he'd ever seen Coach Landry smile. "No, but I was only around him for nine years," replied Walt.

Landry was absolutely meticulous in preparation for a game, leaving nothing to chance. Once, free safety Cliff Harris became confused during a strategy session before a particular game. Landry was diagraming a blitz in which it appeared that if each back flared out as receivers Cliff would have to cover both of them.

Very nervously, Cliff raised his hand and told Landry that he had him covering two guys at once. Landry said, "They both won't go out." When Cliff asked him what if they did, Landry, straight-faced, replied, "Then cover the one they throw to."

Strong safety Charlie Waters also became very puzzled during a long conversation with Landry. Preceding a particular game, Staubach was ailing and his status was unsure. Jack Concannon, brought in as a backup, was having all sorts of problems. Landry appointed player-coach Danny Reeves, who had been a college quarterback, the number one backup quarterback. He knew that Charlie had played a little quarterback at Clemson, so poof, he became the number two backup. "But in college they quickly moved me from quarterback to wide receiver," volunteered Charlie. "There was some reason for that."

All week during practice, Charlie never took a snap, never practiced a down at quarterback. He was getting very worried. "Friday before the Sunday game it was raining, so we were riding on a bus to a practice field in Garland. I usually avoided sitting by Coach Landry but made sure I was near him that day because I was getting very nervous about playing quarterback without any practice."

"Uh, hey Coach Landry, today is Friday, the game is Sunday. If Danny gets hurt and I have to play, don't you think I should take a snap or two? I'd hate to go in there cold."

Landry then went off on this long tangent about when he played defensive back for the Giants and was forced to fill in cold when the top two quarterbacks were injured. Landry explained that he had to go in without any preparation at all but that he did pretty well. Then the following week he practiced a little at quarterback, and sure enough, injuries forced him to play the position again. That time he was awful.

Then Landry became silent. Finally, Charlie asked, "Coach, excuse me, but what does that have to do with my situation? What's the moral?" Landry responded, "I want you to go in there cold."

Even sportswriters following the team didn't escape Landry's dry wit. In 1970, the football Giants were still playing games in Yankee Stadium. One Sunday as we went into the press box, officers were there. They searched our typewriter cases and briefcases and even looked under the tables and chairs. When we found out somebody had called and threatened to blow up the press box, we were a little uneasy. (Blackie Sherrod did ease the tension somewhat about the bomb threat. Blackie had eaten one of those infamous press box hot dogs with hard buns, and he quipped, "Don't worry, men! I just ate it!")

After the game, we asked Landry what would have happened if we'd all been blown up. With that expressionless look, he replied, "Hmm. I suppose we would have observed thirty seconds of silence and then continued to play with all enthusiasm and vigor."

During the years I covered the Cowboys (1967 through the Super Bowl of 1978), we were always having pickup kamikaze basketball games during training camp with visiting coaches, Landry's assistants, and innocent bystanders. When I badly injured my foot and suffered cracked ribs in a friendly game, trainers Don Cochren and Larry Gardner put me on the players injury report they gave to Landry each day. They said he grinned bigger than usual and continued reading the report. Thereafter, Landry would sometimes look at me, shake his head slowly, and remark, "St. John, I'm glad you're not my responsibility." Many times when I saw him over the years, I suspected he was still thinking the same thing.

Once at training camp, reporters Frank Luksa, Carlton Stowers, and Deanne Freeman all grew beards, styled in a shabby way. They approached Landry one day after practice, and Landry deadpanned, "Every time I see you guys coming, I want to call security."

⌣∴⌣

THE FAMILY ALWAYS ENJOYED GOING TO LAKEWAY. After Lisa died, they sold the Lakeway house and built another one farther west at the Lakeside development, closer to where their granddaughter Christina lived. Neighbors always talked about seeing Tom and Christina riding in a golf cart and how she was always laughing and having a wonderful time with her grandfather "Coach."

Lisa Landry Childress loved kids and always wanted a child of her own. She even got a degree in child development and became a teacher so she could be close to young people and perhaps make a difference in their lives. Lisa had tried to become pregnant for five years. She hoped and prayed she could have a baby. Her dreams were answered in the spring of 1991 when her doctor told Lisa and her husband, Gary, that

Lisa was pregnant. They immediately began making plans for the baby. But a month later, they received a shocking setback. During a routine sonogram, doctors discovered Lisa had a rare form of liver cancer with three large tumors.

Landry would later recall how devastated the rest of the family was but that Lisa had such a wonderful outlook on life that it helped brighten their outlook. She was placed on the transplant list, and doctors decided the best chance to save Lisa's life was to abort the baby. But Lisa told them there was no way she was going to abort the baby that God had given her. She refused to take treatments for cancer from February until the baby's birth, further endangering her own life. Family videos show her proudly standing sideways and proudly patting her stomach. She was so happy in spite of everything and had this big smile on her face.

During a Cesarean procedure in which Christina was born on August 20, doctors discovered the three tumors on her liver were growing fast. If Lisa didn't have a transplant in two months, she'd be dead. A donor was found, and ten days after the birth of her daughter, Lisa underwent a successful transplant, although there had been another scare. While doctors were performing surgery, they found a swollen lymph node. They had to check to see if it was malignant before continuing the surgery. If cancer had shown up outside the liver, they wouldn't have performed the transplant. It turned out to be benign.

There was still another crisis when drugs did not stop rejection of the liver. Landry knew a doctor in Pittsburgh who had had success with another antirejection drug. It was tried and was successful for Lisa. Pictures show her holding Christina and, again, looking happy. You'd never have known what she'd gone through.

"She wanted a baby more than anything in her life and believed God had blessed her so she could have Christina," recalled family friend Milla Jones, vice president of Baylor Health Care Systems Foundation. "She was a very shy person but really came out of her shell and became a spokesperson for donor awareness. She was an incredible model for donor awareness. She was wonderful, just wonderful."

Lisa took every opportunity to speak at schools and churches and tell people about her experience in order to call attention to donor and transplantation programs. Sadly, a checkup a year after the transplant showed lesions on her lung. Doctors removed those, but new lesions came back in greater numbers. Seven of the dozen lesions were malignant. These too were removed, but Lisa had finally succumbed to a losing battle with cancer. She was only thirty-seven when she died in May of 1995. Christina was nearly four.

⌣∴∽

EVEN AFTER DEATH, Lisa continues to share her message because family and friends formed the Lisa Landry Childress Foundation. Her sister, Kitty Landry Phillips, is executive director, and Milla Jones oversees the foundation, which is located in the Baylor Health Center Foundation offices.

The Lisa Landry Childress Foundation has as a primary goal to further public awareness of the need for donating organs and tissue. Additionally, the foundation has formed partnerships with institutions and organizations across the state and developed programs for implementation in school curricula, youth programs, and church groups.

Tom Landry and Gary Childress took part in the foundation's "Pass It On" video, which is included in an ever-growing fourth- to eighth-grade youth education program. The video helps youngsters understand the donor process so they can, hopefully, pass the information along to their parents. On the video, Landry and Gary talk about how an unknown donor's gift of life was so important to Lisa.

"When Christina was born, it was just an answer to a prayer for Lisa," said Gary. "She loved every second she had with Christina. After Lisa had her transplant . . . she took every opportunity to tell how fortunate she was to have gotten the transplant and how much she owed to the donor family. . . . The four years we had with Christina were the best years of our lives. Lisa's greatest wish was that she would live long enough for Christina to remember her, and she did. Christina has wonderful memories of her mommy."

Landry said the four years of life a donor gave Lisa "were the happiest times she had with Christina because she was teaching her the things she needed to know to be a young lady someday. The important thing was that she had that chance to raise Christina for those years. She had that opportunity because of a transplant."

Milla Jones would later say, "Lisa lived every day as a blessing from God through a total stranger's unselfish gift. Up until the last six months of her life, she continued to work for donor awareness. Her inner strength came from her incredible faith. That was something she learned from her parents.

"It has been such a blessing in my life to have gotten to know the Landrys. You see so much bad in this world, and then when you get to know people like the Landrys you realize that there is good in the world and, through faith, you can find it. They were a blessing, an incredible blessing, for those of us here at Baylor."

"Lisa almost made it" to Christina's fourth birthday, Landry told the congregation of the Highland Park United Methodist Church on Palm Sunday, 1996. "She passed away one month before Christina was four years old. But even though Lisa was short a month, Christina knows her mother is waiting for her in heaven."

Landry also spoke about how people ask themselves whether they will be able to handle adversity when it comes. He told how his faith in God, "who is with me in every storm," helped him deal with Lisa's death. And he said of his daughter, "She taught us how to live in grace and with courage and faith."

Landry participated each year in the "Golf with the Legends" annual tournament to raise money for Lisa's foundation. In October 1999, with many former Cowboy and NFL stars participating with celebrities such as Neil Armstrong and Charley Pride, the tournament raised two hundred thousand dollars for the foundation. Oh yes, the logo for the Lisa Landry Childress Foundation is angel's wings. Lisa believed in angels. Lisa Landry Childress believed in angels.

❦

TOM LANDRY HAD HEARD about the Fellowship of Christian Athletes and was intrigued by the possibilities it had of influencing young people. So in 1962 when he was invited to an FCA summer camp in Estes Park, Colorado, he gladly accepted. He was very moved by what he saw that week as some twelve hundred young people and coaches gathered to teach, learn, and explore Christian ideals and lifestyles. The hope was that these young athletes would return to their schools and have a positive effect on their classmates and help them resist the temptations young people face. Athletes always have the opportunity to be great role models.

"I saw that week of inspiration and perspiration and what took place in a short period of time in the life of coaches and athletes," Landry later said. "And I thought this was an ideal platform for me, and so I became involved in the FCA."

Later he would determine, "The FCA is the greatest organization for youngsters I know of. There's no question it will have an effect on them. When a youngster has Christian principles to live by, he's less likely to end up on drugs or in other types of trouble."

"As you know, when Tom gets interested in something, he really goes all out," said Paul Corley, a minority owner of the Cowboys in the Murchison years and a mover on the local business scene. "When he made his decision, the FCA was really struggling."

Paul remembered Landry telling him that if he'd open the doors to the influential businessmen Landry would make the speeches. "I picked out a dozen men and asked them to donate one thousand dollars each. That got it started, and the funds were raised to bring in Bill Krisher to run the local chapter."

"I remember Bill and another guy coming to see Dad when he was still coaching," said Tom Landry Jr. "They laid out some plans they had. Then Dad said, 'You get that done and I'll get the money.' Then everybody just sat there, waiting for him to say something else. Like, Well, anything else? But that was the way Dad was. I certainly became aware of it after he got out of football and we went into business together. He wasn't a small-talk guy. He didn't waste any time. He'd listen and pay attention even if you thought he wasn't, but when it's done, it's done."

"There was no FCA staff anywhere in Texas when I got involved," said Krisher, a former Oklahoma all-American who is now west regional director for the FCA, before Landry's death. "It really took off when he got involved. He was very instrumental in the development of the FCA in the whole Southwest and for the success the organization had around the country.

"Tom Landry is a man who walks with the Lord. He worked so hard with the FCA that he humbled you into wanting to do more than you thought you were capable of doing. It's always exciting to hear him give his witness, and he backs up what he says in his testimony with the way he lives his life."

Landry certainly lightened up during his speeches to the FCA and enjoyed telling the following story, changing the names involved to fit the audience. Once at a roast for Kyle Rote Jr., another devout Christian, Landry told the audience:

"I have this dream where I die and go to heaven. Sure enough, it's a beautiful place. When I arrive, Saint Peter gives me a grand tour. He takes me to a giant room jammed with clocks. I ask him to explain why such a huge and magnificent place has nothing but clocks in it. 'Well, Tom,' Saint Peter says, 'this is the room where we keep check on the daily sins of those people still on earth. We judge each person by the number of revolutions that a person's clock makes. When there's only a small amount of sinning, the clock's hands move only slightly. The more one sins, the greater the revolutions of his clock.'

"'Take that one over there,' Saint Peter said, pointing to the clock of Danny Reeves. 'You'll notice the hands stand at three o'clock, which means Danny has been pretty good lately. Now, look over there at Gene Stallings's clock. Not bad, either, at five o'clock.'

"Then I noticed an empty space where a clock had been and asked Saint Peter why it was missing. Saint Peter smiled at me and said, 'Tom, that one belongs to Kyle Rote Jr. It's been broken down for some time now, and the last time I checked with the people in the shop they were using it for a fan.'"

Landry raised money for the FCA with an annual golf tournament and in other ways, including through a special group of donors called "Tom Landry Associates." Each member of the group agrees to donate ten thousand dollars. "He raised one hundred million dollars for the FCA," said Krisher. One hundred million! "One hundred million," repeated Bill.

When Landry was coaching and his time was limited, he still spent an amazing number of hours on his commitment to the FCA. This was particularly true of the off-season months of April and May, when it wasn't unusual for him to travel across the country, speaking three or four nights a week to high-school and college groups. He flew around the country to talk to large throngs or to a handful of students. He paid his own expenses and donated back to the FCA the money he made speaking. He also joined Lisa and Gary in starting an FCA chapter in Austin and staging an annual charity golf tournament to support the organization there. His work for the FCA greatly increased when his coaching career ended.

"After he retired he really devoted his life to the FCA," said Dan Goddard, assistant Texas director of the FCA. "He was not only flying around the country to make speeches but also flying businessmen from

Dallas to FCA camps so they could see the impact of what we were doing."

"I know one year in the 1990s he went to forty-three states in conjunction with the FCA," said Jim Myers, who runs the Tom Landry Fellowship of Christian Athletes Golf Tournament. In 1999 the FCA also started an annual Tom Landry Excellence of Character Award. Myers was the first recipient.

"It was incredible the ground he covered and the number of schools and young people he reached," said former Cowboy linebacker Bob Breunig, who joined Landry on the FCA board of directors in 1984. "You couldn't count the number of people he recruited and got involved in the FCA. He made hundreds, maybe thousands, of trips to talk to big crowds or a handful of kids in some little town. It didn't matter if they were in Nebraska or Ohio, he'd get into his plane and go. We'll never know the amount of time he spent for the FCA or how many youngsters he influenced."

Don Bentsen Sr., who played high-school football with Landry in Mission, took his grandson and another youngster to hear his old friend speak at an FCA rally. "Tom, my grandson, and I were deep in conversation and it was obvious that my grandson's friend was feeling shy and left out," said Don. "Suddenly, Tom interrupted the conversation and told my grandson, 'I want to meet your friend.' My grandson's friend was beaming, grinning from ear to ear. That's just the kind of man Tom Landry was. He was very thoughtful. The fact of the matter is, you don't have the room to write all the good things about Tom Landry."

FCA president Richard Abel went on some speaking trips with Landry. On a two-day swing in North and South Dakota, said Abel, "Tom gave his usual hard-hitting speech and inspiring message." When Landry completed his speech, a middle-aged man came forward and presented him a check for the FCA. "Tom looked at it, then presented it to me," said Abel. "It was for fifty thousand dollars! As he gave it to me he smiled and said, 'I must be getting to be a better speaker.'"

Abel had once commented that "Tom Landry has probably had the greatest impact and the greatest furthering of the ministry of the FCA than anybody. His commitment to Christ, his example, and his availability and involvement have had dramatic effects on the lives of so many coaches and athletes and the people they, in turn, influenced."

Tom Landry served on the FCA national board and also acted as its chairman. He was also on the board of the Dallas chapter, but it was his work as an ambassador that meant the most to him. After Landry died, current FCA president Dal Shealy commented, "Coach Landry has done more for this ministry than anyone. He gave tirelessly every time he was asked. . . . Jesus Christ is the center of the FCA, the cornerstone, and Coach Landry was a great foundation block on which the FCA has been blessed to build."

~:~

IN THE TERRAIN SOUTHWEST of Fort Worth, Ed Shipman's Happy Hill Farm serves as another chance for youngsters who seem to have had none at all. They are boys and girls, ages twelve to seventeen, who have been abused or whose parents are on drugs, are incarcerated, or can't or won't take care of them. It is a five-hundred-acre working farm with cattle and accredited schools. Living there at one time was a girl whose father and mother were in prison, another girl who had been sexually abused by her father and brother, and a boy who had lived with his mother in an abandoned car in a garbage dump. And there was Tip, who had been in juvenile jail.

Tip had lived his life in poverty and did not know how to use a knife or fork. He had once slugged a teacher at school. The reason he was at Happy Hill Farm was that his only alternative was going back to jail. At Happy Hill, he had problems sleeping indoors on a bed because he'd slept outside most of his life.

Tom Landry was touched by such stories and wrote about the youngsters in *Chicken Soup for the Golden Soul*, which featured heart-warming stories for people sixty and over. He told about his work at Happy Hill and the touching turnabout the youngsters experienced when they found hope again.

"I watched Tip slowly change," wrote Landry. "Over the years as coach of the Dallas Cowboys, I saw a lot of impressive changes as players became more disciplined, more skilled, and more motivated. But the changes I saw in Tip and other bruised and suffering kids like him were far more dramatic than anything I had seen on the football field."

Tip's outlook on life changed drastically at Happy Hill. After leaving the farm, he got a job, had plumbing installed in his mother's house, helped his sisters go to school, and then returned to his old hometown, where he married and now has four kids.

"The dehumanizing cycle of poverty, brutality, and imprisonment has been broken for Tip," wrote Landry. "I love football. Always have, always will. But mending the lives and the hearts of boys and girls like Tip gives me a sense of satisfaction like no other thrill. Giving them a chance at living their dreams is a victory far greater than a Super Bowl."

Tom Landry first learned about Happy Hill Farm from Bob Breunig, who had heard about the place in 1978 and immediately started helping with fund-raising efforts. Bob's wife, Mary, and her mother started a *Cowboy Wives Family Cookbook*, the proceeds of which went to Happy Hill. When Landry became interested in the mid-1980s, he began flying down to the farm, visiting with the kids and helping out in any way he could. Naturally, after he left football his commitment increased.

Landry was on the board of directors of Happy Hill, and as Shipman said, "He was very faithful to us. He was so gracious with his presence, financially and through his own business interests. More importantly, he served as a national spokesperson for us and did several television public service announcements. When Tom Landry lends his name to something, there's going to be a huge impact.

"He always had time for the kids. When he'd come down to the farm they always wanted to be around him. One little boy asked him what they should call him, and he said, 'Just call me Tom.' Of course they couldn't. He was always 'Coach Landry.'

"Tom was genuine. There are guys in professional sports who have two faces. One is a public face and then there's the one that shows who they *really* are. Tom was always the same. There was no facade, no pretense, and he was solid in terms of his Christian commitment. We loved him. We miss him."

There's a full-size bronze bust of Landry in the gymnasium at Happy Hill Farm. He's wearing his hat. The sculpture will always serve as a reminder that Coach Landry was there.

~·:~

IN ADDITION TO HIS INVOLVEMENT in these three significant causes, Tom Landry often spoke at the Billy Graham Crusades around the nation. He began a longstanding partnership with Dr. Graham in 1966 when the noted evangelist asked him and one of his players, wide receiver Frank Clarke, to speak at his crusade in San Antonio. Over the years he answered Dr. Graham's call many times, including at Texas Stadium in 1971.

"When we opened Texas Stadium, Clint Murchison said our organization helped him determine how the traffic should flow, and as a result, he donated one hundred thousand dollars to our crusade," Dr. Graham once recalled, adding, "I consider Tom Landry one of the finest gentlemen I have ever known. I believe him to be the greatest football coach in American history. As long as they play football, Tom Landry will be remembered."

After Landry's death, Jeff Anderson, coordinator of the men's ministry for Dr. Graham, commented, "The Lord has used Tom in a very significant way as a man of integrity."

Landry was also on the board of the Dallas Theological Society and supported the seminary financially for many years. Recalled Dr. Dwight Pentecost, professor emeritus at the seminary, "He said it was very important to him because the seminary stood for many things that were important to him, like his personal relationship with Jesus Christ."

Along with athletes such as Roger Staubach, Joe Green, and Michael Jordan, Landry also worked with the Bill Glass Evangelistic Association, which celebrated its thirtieth anniversary as a prison ministry in 1999.

"Tom Landry is one of the most unselfish people I've ever known," Glass once commented. "When he's worked with us in our prison ministry he's always shown a lot of emotion in what he did and has been very expressive and enthusiastic. Tom has always been a person in the center of attention, and yet there is a great humility about him. It is not a false humility in which a person might degrade himself, but a genuine one. He is confident, purposeful but not self-centered. There is a selflessness about him that is what genuine humility is all about."

Maj. Charles Ellingburg, an officer at a prison in Amarillo, said Landry was very inspirational to the inmates. He would be wearing a suit, the hat, and cowboy boots and stand on a makeshift wooden platform inside the prison to address hundreds of inmates.

"Once I saw him draw a bunch of men aside after the meeting to encourage them, and I'm sure he had quite an impact," said Major Ellingburg.

Of course there are many more charitable works to which Landry contributed and good deeds that only he and the people involved knew about. After he left football, a life opened up to him that was as reward-ing in its way as anything he accomplished in the game. That heartbreaking moment when Jerry Jones fired him was not forgotten but paled in the bigger picture of his life. But although Landry knew that the Lord would lead him to whatever he was meant to do with the rest of his life, he still had to go through the pain and disappointment of being sev-ered from the past twenty-nine years of his life.

CHAPTER 3
Saturday Night Massacre and Sunday Good-Byes

෴

Maybe it [the firing] was the best thing that could have happened to Tom and myself. It might have happened a little too quickly, but as it turned out, Tom had an opportunity to show a lot of class when he went out and people really came forward to let him know how they felt about him. He became a hero again to everybody, even to those who had been critical of him. He always will be a hero. And with both of us gone, an era came to a close.

—TEX SCHRAMM

IT WAS LATE AFTERNOON on Saturday, February 25, 1989, when Tex Schramm and Jerry Jones boarded the new owner's Learjet, with the silver-and-blue Cowboys helmet already painted on the tail, and began the flight from Dallas to Austin. They would be there in less than an hour, but the flight would seem much longer. Jones knew he must confront Tom Landry, face-to-face, to tell him he was fired, and he wasn't particularly looking forward to the prospect. There would be no surprises because the news was out that he had purchased controlling interest in the team from Bum Bright. It also was public knowledge that he was bringing Jimmy Johnson, his longtime friend and roommate and teammate at the University of Arkansas, from Miami as head coach. They would, of course, become former friends when their egos clashed too many times during Johnson's five years with the Cowboys. But the day Jones flew to Austin, Tom Landry was out. Just like that.

Officially, Jones hadn't been approved by the NFL as the Cowboys' owner. But in his enthusiasm, Jones gave no thought to the fact that he had jumped the gun in firing Landry and hiring Johnson and new assistant coaches. Of course, approval was only a formality and would take place in a couple of months. However, NFL owners would later adopt a measure that was referred to by some league officials as the "Jerry Jones Rule" to keep this kind of premature personnel change from happening again. The rule, in effect, prevents prospective owners from making substantial changes in a franchise until the league has actually approved their purchase of a team. But Jones was like someone who had just purchased a new toy, albeit a very expensive one. Owning the Cowboys bordered on fantasy for him, and the Jones juggernaut had begun.

Tex Schramm felt as if a stake had been driven through his heart. He would have trouble controlling his emotions throughout the day he accompanied Jones to Austin and so many days to follow. The organization he had put together, "America's Team," the team with class that others envied and some tried to emulate, was crumbling around him. And the man who'd had so much to do with the team's success and its image was being fired in a classic study of insensitivity.

It wasn't as if Landry and Schramm had seen eye-to-eye in their final years together. The team had had three straight losing seasons and bottomed out in 1988. Even after the 1985 season when, ironically, Landry probably did one of his best coaching jobs by taking what was frankly a mediocre team to the NFL Eastern title, they'd had discussions about what might be done to improve the team. Dallas had beaten division rivals Washington and New York twice each but had also lost by scores of 44–0 to Chicago and 50–24 to Cincinnati during the regular season and 20–0 to Los Angeles in the first round of the playoffs.

Schramm had told Landry he felt some changes were in order, that the coaching staff had aged too much and a youthful infusion was needed. Landry had said he'd rather go with the same assistants one more year, but after a while he had gone along with Schramm, who had initiated the hiring of Paul Hackett to become offensive coordinator and the demotion of Jim Shofner, who later resigned.

During another discussion, Landry had told Schramm, "You probably should start preparing for an orderly transition." The indication was that he would coach one more year, 1986, or perhaps two at the most.

"But later after that season [1985] I seemed to denote a change in his attitude," Schramm recalled. "He wanted a new three-year contract and resisted further changes in the staff, with the exception of replacing the retiring Jim Myers with Jim Erkenbeck."

Landry knew that the team was on a downward trend and that more difficult times were coming, but he felt he could turn the situation around, that he just must turn it around and get the Cowboys back on the winning track. Even after the 3–13 season in 1988, Landry reasoned that the Cowboys easily could have won four or five pivotal games, and the team had continually bounced back from disappointments each week to play well for him. He saw the promise, the light at the end of the tunnel, and announced, two weeks before he was fired, "I'm going to coach into the nineteen nineties."

Schramm didn't particularly want to hear this, feeling that Landry should think of retirement. He felt Tom had thrown down the gauntlet: He was going to continue to coach or Schramm was going to have to fire him.

"At the end of the season [1989], I'll make a judgment in the best interests of the Cowboys," Schramm had said.

Meanwhile, Landry proceeded with his plans for the coming season. One of the first orders of business was to replace Hackett, with whom he'd had philosophical differences and about whom he'd heard reports regarding lack of loyalty.

More than anything, bad luck and some poor draft picks had caused the fall of the Cowboys, but with the 1999 number one pick, which Landry planned to use to get Troy Aikman, other high choices in each round, and a weak schedule, Landry believed the club would be on an upward swing. He felt he knew what needed to be done and made plans to do it. Landry never got the chance. Schramm never had to make a decision about Tom after the 1989 season. It was all taken out of his hands.

Tex was head of the NFL's all-powerful Competition Committee and a key league spokesman in all league matters, especially in dealings with the National Football League Players Association. He was the most prominent NFL official outside of Commissioner Pete Rozelle. Yet he was rendered powerless by the new ownership. An outsider was calling the shots. Schramm dwelled on what had happened and was torn apart. Landry certainly experienced disappointment and anger, but because of his Christian belief that his life was in God's hands, he was able, in the end, to be more philosophical.

It had been Schramm's idea, not Jones's, to fly to Austin to tell Landry in person something he already knew. When they had talked in Dallas that Saturday morning, Schramm had asked Jones if he had contacted Landry. Jones said he had not. "Before you have any press conferences or make any announcements, you need to talk to Tom, and I strongly suggest you do it in person," Schramm had said.

"All right," Jones had answered, "I'll go wherever he is. Austin? Then we'll fly to Austin."

⌣∴∾

NOBODY HAD QUESTIONED Bum Bright's right to sell the Dallas Cowboys or Jerry Jones's right to buy the club. Bright had been actively trying to sell the team he purchased from a dying Clint Murchison five years earlier. He had bought the team and control of the Texas Stadium Corporation for $83 million. Murchison had been well aware of the situation with his health and knew that once the news got out his creditors would call in their loans. So he asked Schramm to find a proper buyer, one who would allow the team to continue to be operated as it had been, without owner interference. Murchison wanted Schramm to continue to be in control, to represent the team and cast votes for the club at league meetings, and to make decisions on behalf of the team. He wanted Landry to remain in charge of all things relating to the team that was put on the field and Gil Brandt to continue to head the scouting.

People such as Landry and Schramm had had much to do with making Murchison's initial investment of $550,000 ($50,000 for the franchise and $500,000 for the players existing NFL teams put in a pool to stock the Cowboys) worth the $83 million Bright paid. They also had a great deal to do with the fact that after five years Bright could sell the Cowboys to Jones for $140 million, including $60 million for the team, $65 million for the stadium, $10 million for the headquarters at Valley Ranch, and $5 million in deferred payments to players. Oddly enough, in the end it would be Bright who totally ignored Schramm in his dealings regarding the sale of the team. He would be the one to place it with a man who would fire Landry and embarrassingly strip Schramm of all his powers and cause his resignation.

Bright was a cold, hard businessman, devoid of sentiment for tradition when there was money to be made. He was a tough, self-made man who made few friends as he butted his way into the high-finance circles. The bottom line for Bright was profit, and the people involved were secondary. Before he sold the Cowboys, he'd lost a great deal of money in oil, real estate, and banking as his financial situation paralleled the weakening Texas economy. He likewise failed to realize expected financial gains on his investment in the Cowboys, who went through lean times on the field, and thus off the field, during Bright's tenure as owner. *Forbes* magazine estimated that Bright's worth had decreased from $600 million to $300 million by 1988, and some with whom he had dealt in the past felt little sympathy for him.

Prior to purchasing the Cowboys, Bright had gained some notoriety on the sports pages by bringing Jackie Sherrill to the coaching position at his alma mater, Texas A&M. There were those in authority at A&M who wanted to keep Tom Wilson as coach, but Bright showed his power as chairman of the school's board of regents. He was almost personally responsible for firing Wilson and luring Sherrill from Pittsburgh as the man of his choice. Sherrill, a wheeler-dealer, brought the Aggies the Southwest Conference championships they sought, but in the end he also brought them bad publicity and problems nobody in the school wanted. The Aggies drew NCAA probation for methods used during Sherrill's regime, and Sherrill resigned after Doug Bedell broke a story in the *Dallas Morning News* that Sherrill had allegedly paid hush money to a former player to keep quiet about some situations that had been going on at A&M.

By 1987 Bright, upset by the plight of the Cowboys on the field, did something Murchison never would have even considered. He criticized Landry to the press. The team had just lost to Atlanta, a team with the worst record in the NFC at the time, by the score of 21–10 in a lackluster performance before a poor crowd in Texas Stadium.

"I get horrified sometimes at our play calling," said Bright. "I've heard we're not using certain players because they haven't been brought along yet. Maybe the problem is we can't utilize the talent of certain guys [he was speaking of number one draft choice Danny Noonan and Herschel Walker] because we don't have anybody in charge that knows what they're doing, other than Tex Schramm. He is the best general manager in the league. I don't want to do the coaching and I don't want to try to run the club, but I'm not satisfied with the results we get. We can't go along like we are."

"He's the owner of the team," said Landry. "He has the right to say whatever he wants."

When asked about Bright's comments, Schramm said, "I'm not even going to recognize the question. There's one thing you don't do in sports, and that's to give a vote of confidence. That has become a kiss of death. When you start trying to break down and isolate what the problems are, you have to remember that during our successful years, everybody shared in that success: The administration received credit for creating the proper atmosphere, the coaches certainly got credit for the job they did, and so did the players for what they accomplished on the field. When you're not having success, you've got to start up the same ladder."

That same year on his weekly radio show, Tex himself had been critical of Landry for the first time, although he later apologized. After the team lost to lowly Detroit, 27–17, Tex told his audience, "Some of the things we're doing are frankly mystifying. It's seldom I'm put in a position of giving the players a reason for losing, but I'm not sure it's all on the players. When things aren't working and you continue to do the same things, it shakes your confidence. There's an old saying: 'If the teacher does not teach, the students cannot learn.'"

Shortly thereafter, Tex issued the following statement: "This is an emotional game, and those things were said under stressful circumstances. I wish I had not said them because they created a misimpression, obviously. I do not have any criticism of Tom's coaching any more than I've had in the past years."

In spite of being critical of Landry, when Bright decided to put the club on the market Schramm recalled Bright told him that he did not want any change in the Landry situation until there was a new owner, who could do whatever he wanted. However, Bright later indicated he'd fire Landry to save Jones the negative reaction he'd get for dismissing a legend.

"Jerry did say Bum Bright begged him to let him fire Landry because the feelings were so strong and the fans and press would really come down on him," said Randy Galloway, *Fort Worth Star-Telegram* columnist and popular sports talk show host. "But Jerry's ego is such that maybe he wanted to be known as the man who fired Tom Landry."

Bright, sixty-eight at the time, would later say he had whittled down seventy-five prospective buyers to five, and only two, Los Angeles Lakers owner Jerry Bush and a Japanese firm, had indicated they would not get rid of Landry immediately if they bought the team. Jones seemed to be the dark horse. But Bright liked him. Jones had come to Dallas from his home in Little Rock in mid-September of 1988 and watched the Giants beat the Cowboys, 12–10, in Texas Stadium. Afterward, he told anybody who would listen that if he bought the team, he would like Jimmy Johnson to coach it. Among those he told was Schramm, who said, "He always seemed to be one of the people on the periphery who was working on the financing. I didn't think any more about it."

"Well, there were a lot of tire kickers out there," recalled Jones. "I cared about the Cowboys and, for instance, didn't want them to be owned by somebody in a foreign country, such as Japan. And, let me say this, I was very up-front from the first about what I was going to do."

Mid-February negotiations between Bright and Jones became serious, unbeknownst to Schramm, and by Tuesday the twenty-first, the deal appeared set. Again, Bright kept Schramm, president and general manager, and Landry, the only coach the team had ever had, completely in the dark.

Landry was going about his business of meeting with his coaches and preparing for the draft and Schramm was becoming excited over the prospect of drafting Troy Aikman. They got an early inkling of what might be going on when KXAS-TV, Channel 5 in Fort Worth, broke the story on its 10:00 P.M. telecast on Thursday, February 23. Sportscaster Scott Murray had pieced together the story, apparently both from sources in Miami and from some of the people helping Bright with the deal.

Schramm received a call prior to the newscast letting him know that the story would be aired. The reporter asked him if the story was true, and he said he knew nothing about it. The following morning, Friday, February 24, Schramm telephoned Bright and asked him what was going on. Bright told him what was happening and to be at his office at 8:30 the following morning.

"The story is out," Schramm told Bright. "What statements can we make?"

Bright told him he could make a statement over the weekend to clarify the ownership. That same Friday morning, Schramm received a call from his good friend Don Shula, coach of the Miami Dolphins. Shula told him that Jimmy Johnson was talking to David Shula, his son and top assistant, about coming with him to Dallas and had also approached his newly hired defensive coach, Dave Wannstedt. Then a reporter from Atlanta called Schramm and informed him that Johnson had been checking around to find out the NFL policy on hiring assistants from other NFL teams after March 1, which was the NFL's deadline. Schramm then knew for sure what was happening and went to Landry's office to tell him.

Landry was being hounded relentlessly by the media but was still doing his job, such as talking to newly hired quarterback coach Jerry Rhome, Hackett's replacement, and defensive coach George Hill. Members of the media kept after him, asking, "Tom, are you being fired?" . . . "Tom, what are your plans for the future?" . . . "Tom, what are you going to do?"

"Well," said Landry, "I'm going to work and then go home when I'm finished."

Randy White, one of the Cowboys' all-time greats who was coming to the end of his career, had been taking all this in. He thought about what Bright had said about Landry after the Atlanta game, about an assistant coach or two not being very loyal, about Schramm not being sure of Tom's future, and about the way the media were hounding his coach.

"It made me sick, watching the whole thing," White later said. "The press was all over him, crowding him and asking him if he was going to lose his job. People were saying negative things about him, and some of it was coming from his own organization. If you ask me, well, Coach Landry knew what he was doing, but some other people in the organization were in a panic and choking. We were aware about all that stuff concerning a member or two of his staff not supporting him. All those things made it tougher on the players too.

"Then here you had Coach Landry just going on and trying to do his job. I tell you, if it had been me, I think I might have punched somebody in the nose."

White grinned and added, "Hey, maybe Coach Landry felt like that too, but he never showed it."

When Schramm went to see Landry that Friday, he told him what he'd found out and added, "Tom, I think it's over." Landry shrugged, took a quick breath as he sometimes would do, and seemed resolved that whatever would be, would be because he couldn't do anything to change it. They chatted for a while about the organization, and Schramm left.

The same day Jones had flown Johnson into town in his private plane because he wanted to get things going. The draft was coming up soon, and they had only a few days if they wanted to hire anybody else off another NFL staff. They quickly proved they would not make, for instance, good secret agents. They went with their wives to eat dinner at Mia's, a popular restaurant that was a favorite of Tom and Alicia.

Dallas Morning News sportswriter Ivan Maisel was there with his fiancée. He saw Jones and Johnson, attempted to talk to them, and telephoned the newspaper to send out a photographer. In the Saturday morning issue of the paper was a large color picture of Jones and Johnson, smiling and apparently celebrating. They were in a restaurant not far from Landry's home, one that he frequented, and were sitting at a table under a wall of pictures of the Cowboys. The final sick irony would have been if the Landrys had also been dining there at the time.

That Saturday morning, Landry saw the picture in the newspaper and read about his apparent impending dismissal but, as was his nature, went on with plans for a customary off-season weekend at his Lakeway retreat near Austin. He flew there that morning with Alicia and Tom Jr. In Austin they met his daughter and son-in-law Lisa and Gary Childress. After lunch they all went to nearby Hidden Hills golf course to play golf.

Schramm met with Jones, Johnson, and Bright that morning. He defended some of the team's policies. Then he began trying desperately to locate Landry, finally tracing him through relatives to the golf course shortly after he'd teed off. Schramm got in touch with the pro there, Jack Bertram, and told him he had an emergency call for Landry. Bertram went to get Tom.

"Tom, this is Tex."

"What's happening?" asked Landry. "Am I okay?"

"It isn't good."

"All right."

"We'll be flying to Austin to see you right away."

Landry left the telephone, caught up with his family on the course, and played golf as if nothing were wrong. Tom was waiting on the street by the club when Jones and Schramm arrived. With Tom Jr., they went into a nearby sales office to talk.

"Tex and I had talked on the flight to Austin about what a great coach Tom Landry was," said Jones. "The whole thing had been a question of timing, and it [the timing] was all off. The story broke and the deal wasn't finalized until too late [for him to have handled the situation with Landry better]. . . . I'd love to have done it the proper way. I'd love to have sat down with Coach Landry and found out if he wanted to be a part of the club in another capacity and let him make the announcement to the press about whatever he wanted to do. The meeting in Austin was . . . solemn, very solemn."

The first thing Landry said to Jones was, "If you're just coming down here for a publicity stunt, you need not have bothered."

"Oh, Tex insisted I talk to you," said Jones, who was very apologetic. "He felt we should meet face-to-face. I'm here now, and so is Jimmy [on board]."

"Frankly," recalled Schramm, "I had trouble keeping my composure. Tom and I had been together twenty-nine years, and the whole thing was beyond my control."

If you did not know Tom Landry, you would have thought he showed no emotion at all. But it was there. "And I've been around him long enough to know it," said Schramm. "At first there was this certain look in his eyes, on his face, that he gets when he's mad. And then, if you knew him, you could tell, he was feeling emotional too."

Landry would later admit that he was emotional because of what happened and angry for the way it was handled. Schramm recalled that Landry let Jones know that the situation could have been handled better. Jones then told Landry that if there was any way he could make it easier on him he would. By that time Landry didn't seem to care, one way or another.

The forty-minute meeting officially ended Landry's twenty-nine-year run as coach of the Cowboys. Witnesses said that when Jones left, his face was ghost white and he was very nervous. Jones remarked, "It was the most inadequate I've ever felt. I want to assure everybody who is interested in the Cowboys and certainly in Coach Landry that he saw my baby blue eyes as quickly as humanly possible under the circumstances. . . . I was so sensitive to his feelings. . . . I was basically trying to say something that couldn't be said. He was magnificent to me for what he had been through. He's special." Later, when he said he wished he had handled the Landry situation differently, he added, "I guess I'll always be thought of as the Darth Vader of the situation."

Landry left the meeting and joined his family for dinner in the clubhouse. Outwardly he didn't seem shaken. In retrospect, he said of the meeting, "I really didn't think about it a lot after that. I really don't keep worrying about things I can't control."

Schramm called from the airport before they flew back to Dallas and told his publicity people to arrange a press conference at the team's headquarters at Valley Ranch for about 8:00 P.M. Schramm and Jones boarded the plane and returned for a press conference that should be shown to public relations students as an example of how not to do one. The media would refer to the press conference as the "Saturday Night Massacre."

⌣∴⌣

THE PRESS CONFERENCE took place in the conference room in the massive, sprawling, single-story sandstone building at Cowboy Center, a two-hundred-acre complex that is the focal point of the twenty-five-hundred-acre Valley Ranch development just north of LBJ Freeway in far North Dallas. Commissioner Pete Rozelle and various sports columnists around the country have called the complex the finest in the country, if not the world. It was Tex Schramm's dream, the house he built with his ideas and innovations and the house Landry built with the great successes his team had on the field.

The press conference served only as a poorly staged coup de grace, and soon Schramm would be gone from the team too. It was a televised bad theater in the real. Members of the media gathered just before 8:00 P.M. to wait for the official version of what they already knew, feeling as though they were at a wake, a funeral. Many of them had been critical of Landry in recent years, especially during the 1988 disaster, and some had called for his resignation. Yet that night, as a group, they were both incensed and sad. Like quarrels or disagreements within a family, it was all right for them to say or do or think this or that critical thing, but they would not tolerate an outsider coming in and treating Landry that way.

Schramm, ashen-faced, led a group into the room. He was sullen, very beaten down, and his eyes were red. It was his lot, if not duty, to introduce forty-six-year-old Jerry Jones, the self-made oil and gas exploration magnate.

Prior to the press conference, Schramm had cautioned Jones that the media would be hostile and that he should get Jimmy Johnson out of town. With ill-conceived reasoning, Jones had planned to introduce his new coach at the press conference. Schramm pointed out that there had been a negative reaction to the fact that Johnson had been in town before Landry heard the official news that he had been fired. There would be strong feelings for Landry and little sympathy for the man who had fired him, much less for the one who had taken his job and begun interviewing coaches while Landry was still going about his work. Jones eventually complied, later telling the press that he felt it inappropriate to have Johnson there. Schramm had also informed Jones of the questions the press probably would ask him and warned that he would not be very popular with the press. Caught up in the excitement of buying the team, Jones apparently still believed that the press and everybody else would be excited too, that they would see him as a young, enthusiastic, aggressive owner who would bring in a man he considered the best, most exciting coach in the country. To Jones's utter dismay, the news of his purchase of the Cowboys and of his hiring Johnson took a backseat to the news of his firing Landry.

Schramm went to the microphone at the podium and said, "I want to introduce you to Jerry Jones, the new owner of the Dallas Cowboys."

Unbeknownst to Schramm or members of the media, Jones had invited to the press conference his family and about twenty-five friends, including three Dallas investors in the club, Charles, Sam, and Evan Wyly. In a totally inappropriate outburst, his supporters stood up and cheered as he entered the room, while others sat silently, staring at them as they would a group caught laughing or cheering at a funeral. Jones acknowledged the cheers and smiled broadly, his eyes dancing like a child who had just seen a new bicycle under the Christmas tree.

And he said, "This is like Christmas to me. The Cowboys are America. They are more than a football team."

Schramm, his head lowered, started back to his seat as Jones walked to the microphone. But perennial jack-in-the-box Ed Smith, a minority owner from Houston, once again throwing himself under the wheels of the moment, had snatched Schramm's chair. Tex glared at him, then stood up the remainder of the press conference.

Smith, who had retained his interest under Jones, had been a staunch Landry detractor, except to Tom's face. Apparently he believed he had learned all there was necessary to know about pro football and the Cowboys by attending games and going on team charter flights after becoming a minor investor when Bright bought the team. Smith was just another burden Landry was carrying in 1988. Once, feeling that old college spirit, Smith approached Landry and asked if he could come into the dressing room and give the players a pep talk prior to a game. Landry had politely refused, showing great restraint by not bursting into laughter.

Now he had come along for another ride, so to speak, with Jones. Smith had tried repeatedly to voice his opinions on the team's plight in 1988, but nobody would listen. Finally, Ted Dawson interviewed him on Channel 4. On the one hand, Smith and his wife had sat near the Schramms and the Landrys on the Cowboys charter flights and always seemed friendly toward them. And yet Smith had been calling Bright for two years trying to get Landry fired, and Smith stated bluntly in the Channel 4 interview that Landry was too old to coach and that Schramm too probably should be fired. Landry was sixty-four; Smith was seventy-two.

During the press conference, Smith said, "He [Landry] should have retired three years ago before he forced *us* to do this." Meanwhile, Jones was bubbling over with excitement in front of a battery of television cameras, reporters, and friends. Then and there, before a media strongly sympathetic to Landry, he immediately began telling everybody what a wonderful man Coach Jimmy Johnson was. He said Jimmy was the best coach in America.

"What Jimmy Johnson will bring us is worth more than if we had five first-round draft choices and five Heisman Trophy winners," he crowed. "History will show that one of the finest things that ever happened to the Dallas Cowboys is Jimmy Johnson."

When he finally got around to Landry, he related how much he had always admired Tom and Tex and how inadequate he felt when he had decided to fly to Austin and talk to Tom eye-to-eye.

Jones would later add, "There were key elements in the business aspects before we talked to Coach Landry. As insensitive as it may seem, and it really is, the real world is that there are owners, and there are people who have built their lives with these teams. And, unfortunately, before those people who have spent their lives building the team can get a message, sometimes the owners have to get together on a deal, and it really isn't fair."

When a question was directed to Schramm regarding the meeting with Landry in Austin, his voice cracked as he began to speak and tears came into his eyes. "It was a very difficult meeting. It was . . . very, very sad. It's . . . tough when you break a relationship . . . a relationship that you've had for twenty-nine years. That's an awful long time. For Tom . . . he was emotional."

Jones admitted it would be tough to live with the tag of "The Man Who Fired Tom Landry." But he continued, "I gave no consideration to retaining Landry, even for one season. I would not have been interested in buying the club if I didn't have Jimmy Johnson with me."

"This is a new generation of coaches and ownership," said Bright. "This is something that must evolve. It happens in every business." He continued that he would like to be remembered as the man who weeded out the prospective owners and settled on the best one, Jerry Jones. "Jerry Jones is going to be the most enthusiastic owner the Cowboys have ever had," Bright added.

Jones then let it be known that he and he alone was the man who would run the club. "My office and my entire business will be at this complex," he said. "I intend to know and have an understanding of the complete situation, an understanding of the player situation, the jocks and socks and TV [contract].

"There is no way in the world that with my enthusiasm and love for what I'm getting ready to do, and the kind of price I'm paying, I could look in the mirror if I don't plan to be a part of everything. I want to understand that everyone associated with it is giving everything he can do." With that, his friends burst into applause, and when Jones was asked the role of Schramm, he said, glancing over his shoulder at Tex, "He's standing a little behind me tonight."

Jones continued, "I will attend every meeting. It's my vote. I'm the owner. This is my life. I intend to invest a lot of time in this. I will be a part of every decision. I won't leave anything to the football people." As we know, he certainly lived up to his words, becoming the most hands-on owner in the NFL and, perhaps, in all professional sports.

Jones indicated that Schramm was still with the team and that he would learn from him, sitting at his knee. He added that he'd like to see Landry, to whom he owed a million dollars for the year left on his contract, stay around in some capacity. There was never a chance he would rehire Landry, much less listen to Schramm. Jones ignored Schramm and, if you will, charged ahead on his fire-breathing horse, carrying his head under his arm . . . the Headless Horseman of Sleepy Hollow.

"There is no substitute for winning," he said, the crescendo of his voice rising, "and we must win. We will win! Winning is the name of the game! We're going to win this year!" His team didn't win that year, or the next, finishing 1–11 in 1989 and 7–9 in 1990, but it certainly did thereafter, racking up three Super Bowl wins.

JEFF ROHRER, a linebacker from Yale who believes in things like a player's freedom of speech, noted, "Two people with an IQ of three could have gotten together and brainstormed for ten minutes and come up with a better way to handle Landry's departure. . . . Bum Bright was the most uninterested and uninteresting owner an NFL team has ever had."

Soon Jones would call a staff meeting and explain that he told the Cowboy employees "point-blank that we had no plans to make changes in the organization, absolutely not. That's a big misunderstanding. We have a new owner, but they shouldn't be afraid. I have no other people than Jimmy Johnson who know one thing about running a football team. Besides, I need them where they are."

"I was at the meeting," said Gil Brandt. "He said, 'It's not my intention to replace any of you. As long as you do your job and not retire, you'll be here.'"

Not long after that the purge began. Jones fired treasurer Don Wilson, who had been with the Cowboys eighteen years, sending him a one-paragraph memo. Then came Doug Todd, the club's popular publicity director, who had also been with the team eighteen years and earlier had been told by Jones, "Everything I see and hear about your department is A-plus." Assistant ticket manager Ann Lloyd, who had joined the team as a teenager and had been with the club more than twenty-one years, was next. Indications later would be that ticket manager Steve Orsini fired her, although some confusion remains over whether it was at Jones's suggestion. Longtime photographic director Bob Friedman and, finally, Gil Brandt, followed. They eventually all received severance pay.

In a speech made later in Arkansas, Jones said that the Cowboy organization had too much fat and had to be trimmed so he could concentrate all his finances on the team he put on the field. He said too that the typical workday of a Cowboy employee consisted of arriving at the office at 9:30 A.M., reading the newspapers, working out, and then leaving at 4:30 P.M. "I don't think it's fair to pick on my people with untruths," responded Schramm, showing amazing restraint. "I'm very proud of the organization we established and the people who contributed. I'd like to know who he was talking about with those references to our working habits. I was around every night until six-thirty or seven, and I saw a lot of familiar faces."

Jones also claimed that during an argument with Schramm, Tex had jumped up and Jones had had to warn him, "Tex, I'm forty-six. You're sixty-seven. Don't come over that desk." Schramm has said that absolutely nothing of this nature ever happened. Jones would later say he had been quoted out of context.

Jones had also commented in Little Rock that Tom Landry was too old to relate to the players. Asked about this, Jones said, "I don't leave things unsaid because they don't look good in print or sound good on television. I'm honest. All my life I've said things that I've made myself accountable for.

"In that particular case, before mentioning Coach Landry to the group, I said men his age make the best leaders in the country, make the best leaders in a giant corporation, make the businessmen. But when it comes to coaching, I told the group, I believed the generation gap that existed between Coach Landry and his players was too much."

"You poll every coach in the National Football League and ask him to name the top four coaches in the league right now," said Gene Stallings, who was then coaching the Phoenix Cardinals, "and every one of them would have Tom Landry on that list. My goodness, the man is sharper and in better shape than most all the rest of us."

"People who haven't been out there in the arena sometimes have no idea what's going on," said Danny Reeves, head coach of Denver at the time. "I keep remembering all the diversified personalities he's had to deal with, and he's always been able to adjust. He's still a fine coach, and I think one of the most amazing jobs I've ever seen was when he won the division with that 1985 team. At best, he had the third-best team behind the Giants and Redskins."

Jimmy Johnson was more prone to try to play the media, unlike Jones, who was inexperienced in the area of public relations and in his early days as owner tended to just say whatever came into his mind. Johnson was very careful in his comments and had only praise for Landry. "I think Tom Landry is one of the finest individuals and finest coaches I would ever hope to know. It hurts me when somebody says I did something out of disrespect to Tom Landry. If I did, I'm sorry. . . . The only thing I can say is that I wanted to be head coach of the Dallas Cowboys. Let me do my thing. Let me work. Let me give effort. Let me show enthusiasm. Judge me for what happens later. It's a great, great honor to come after Tom Landry."

DURING THE "SATURDAY NIGHT MASSACRE," Landry remained in Austin and made plans to return to Dallas on Sunday to begin cleaning out his office. With his actions and comments he handled the situation best.

"It was just one of those things that was predetermined," he said. "Once the owner came in and expressed his sentiments, I was through. There was no place for me. It was just a matter of whether the deal came to a conclusion. Once it did, I was out of a job. There wasn't any question about that. They flew to Austin to see me for nothing. It was obvious I wasn't going to be the coach.

"I'm not bitter at all. I knew what I was doing when I tried to bring this club back. This is the worst scenario, I guess, that could have happened. But I took that chance. I could have very easily quit three years ago, but I felt pretty strong about the team and the direction it was going. I don't regret what I did, staying on.

"I'm going to miss the players. That's going to be the most difficult thing, dealing with that and my coaches.

"It will be hard to slow down. I really feel no different from a coaching perspective than I felt twenty, thirty years ago. I feel the same, and I was really looking forward to this coming season. I thought it was going to be a tremendous challenge and an interesting one. But . . . that's over with. I'm not concerned about that anymore. It's a chapter closed in my life, and I must go on.

"Things could have been handled better, but you have somebody coming in who is awful new to this environment we live in. I'm sure he was very excited about the possibility of owning the Cowboys, and I doubt his thoughts went much further than that."

Landry commented that he didn't know Jimmy Johnson that well. "I can't really judge him. I think he was kind of swept up in the new owner's enthusiasm."

Then he looked back, briefly, on his years with the Cowboys and added, "I don't know if any team in professional football will ever duplicate what happened. The success of that era is something of which all of us who were a part are very proud. It was a great accomplishment."

"Class," said Schramm, noting a word that once was associated with the team, "is created and perpetuated by the individuals who established it. You can go out to the Cowboy Complex and say, 'Boy, this is a great place.' But the feeling for the organization comes from the people inside that complex.

"It's one thing to be a winner. A lot of teams become winners, and they come and go, and it's great to have that as your goal. But it's something special to be a winner and accomplish this with a special sense of style and class. That's what makes one team unique and not just another winner. That style and class were personified by Tom Landry."

"There are relatively few coaches whose careers compare with Tom's," said Pete Rozelle. "He's not only been an outstanding coach but a tremendous role model for kids and our fans. He has contributed a tremendous amount to our league."

Not just in the Dallas Metroplex but throughout the country, Landry had upstaged the new owner and new coach without saying a bad word about either. *Sports Illustrated* praised him, and *People* magazine ran a picture spread on Landry, deciding this was the best way to show the changing of the guard. It seemed at least 90 percent of the columnists and reporters around the country were in Landry's corner.

Tom Landry, the person most affected, seemed the calmest, the person most in control of his emotions. That would change when he came back to Valley Ranch to clean out his office and talk a final time to his team, his last team . . .

⌁⌁

WHEN TOM LANDRY WENT BACK TO HIS OFFICE at the Dallas Cowboy Complex that Sunday, it would be like no other Sabbath. He went there early to pack his personal memorabilia and belongings, his files and the pictures on the wall. It would take him about six hours to clean out twenty-nine years, to put his things, his memories, into simple cartons. It would be a physical and symbolic step toward severing ties with the organization he helped build, the team he loved.

Barbara Goodman, his secretary since 1981, came in during the afternoon when he was about three-fourths finished and began to help him. She recalled he seemed in a good mood. "Coach was such a good person to work for," recalled Barbara. "You could always depend on him. It didn't matter if the team was going good or bad. He never got upset. He was always on schedule and stayed so busy . . . even at the end.

"The mail and calls he got were just astronomical. But he'd return almost every call, answer every letter. The ones he just couldn't, he'd have me call back with a message from him or scribble a note on a letter for me to type and send back. And with all this happening and coaching the team, meeting with media and everything, if something extra came up he'd just take it in stride. I can remember how he'd always handle it."

"I feel bad about this, Coach. I forgot to tell you about this," she'd tell him. Landry'd smile and reply, "Oh, don't worry about it, Barbara. We'll take care of it."

That last Sunday afternoon, the ever-present media came by. A reporter and cameraman from Channel 8 stopped by and, with tears in their eyes, even filmed Landry as he packed. Asked again if he was bitter about the circumstances under which he was let go, Landry again said he wasn't. He did, however, bristle a little at the suggestion that he just didn't know when to retire.

"People say you have to know when to retire, which is a dumb thing to say," remarked Landry. "If people want to go out on top, yeah, it becomes important when you quit if you're afraid of getting into a situation like we've been in the last two or three years.

"But I wasn't afraid of the situation. I wasn't afraid of being fired. That never bothered me. I was never looking for a loophole to get out. I always measured the team. As long as it played hard for me, as it has the last three years, I wanted to stick with it as long as I could help the players. This wasn't an ego thing for me to keep coaching. It's just that I enjoy coaching and I enjoy helping people achieve."

Tex Schramm came by Landry's office. Once again they talked about the era, their era, and reflected on how it was over. It had been obvious to anybody who knew Schramm or looked past the headlines that he wasn't going to stay around and play second fiddle to Jerry Jones. It was just a matter of things settling down a little so he could see what options he had. Landry knew Schramm would be leaving too.

Maybe the season would have turned out all right. Maybe it wouldn't have. Schramm would never have to face the decision of asking Landry to step down. Schramm would later reflect, "Maybe it was the best thing that could have happened to Tom and myself. It might have happened a little too quickly, but as it turned out, Tom had an opportunity to show a lot of class when he went out and people really came forward to let him know how they felt about him. He became a hero again to everybody, even to those who had been critical of him. He always will be a hero. And with both of us gone, an era came to a close."

For months after Landry was fired, mail for him still came in bundles at the Cowboys offices, and Barbara Goodman got help handling it from Marge Kelly, who had been Landry's secretary from 1965 until she retired in 1981.

"Coach had an influence on the way we handled things," said Barbara. "It was so emotionally draining when everything was up in the air about him. Then after it happened we just went on, just rolled up our sleeves and got back to work again. That's what Coach would have wanted us to do."

"He was so patient," said Marge. "I was working with my sister [longtime ticket manager Kay Lang] in the ticket office, but when the opportunity came along to be his secretary, I jumped at it. I'd had a lot of secretarial experience but knew absolutely nothing about football. I thought a coach was somebody who went out and worked with kids in the park on Saturday mornings.

"Ermal Allen dictated the scouting reports to me in those days, and I would take shorthand and type them up for Coach Landry. I knew absolutely nothing about football terminology. I was continually making mistakes, using crazy spellings for terms they used. But Coach Landry never once jumped me about it or bawled me out. Now, I can't say the same thing for Coach [Jim] Myers [offensive line coach]. He was the type who'd let you know exactly how he felt.

"Coach Landry did work hard. There wasn't a lot of idle chitchat, and everybody worked so hard. I can't believe what Mr. Jones said about how everybody came in late and left early. My sister [Kay Lang] used to come in at 4:00 A.M. because she said she could get a lot of work done before anybody else got there."

Both secretaries said they received calls from all types of people, including people from President Bush's office, generals in the Pentagon, religious leaders such as Billy Graham, congressmen, senators, and always, fans.

Trying to throw the ball out of the end zone because all receivers were covered, Joe Montana actually completed the pass to a leaping Dwight Clark for a touchdown to beat Dallas in the final minute of the 1981 NFL championship game, 28–27.

"Dwight Clark's mother was a big fan of Coach, and she used to call him," said Barbara. "People from the Eighth Air Force [Landry served in the group in World War II] were always calling him, and you'd get so many, so very many calls from mothers who'd say they wanted their sons to grow up and be like Coach. They'd write that they wanted their sons to play for him or that they were glad somebody like Coach was around for young people to look up to."

"Coach Landry was such a wonderful family man," continued Marge Kelly. "I always admired him for that, as busy as he was. When his children were growing up and he was working in the office, he'd talk to them all the time and want to know exactly where they were going and with whom. He let them know exactly what time they were supposed to be home. Those kids just loved him.

"When Kitty was working in Austin in Bob Bullock's office, Coach Landry would tell me he wanted to talk to her and ask me to place the call. You know how some young people are when they get out on their own like that . . . they aren't always overly thrilled to hear from their parents.

"But I'd locate Kitty and tell her that her dad was calling. She would always get so excited and say, 'Oh, good!'"

Marge paused, thought for a while, and continued, "Alicia was always so nice too. She was so polite to all of us and had that sweet voice. Once we were working especially hard because Coach Landry and Alicia were leaving on vacation the next day."

Marge answered the telephone that day and it was Alicia, her voice calm and sounding as she always did. "Could I speak with Tommy, please?"

Landry picked up the phone, said a few words, then told Marge he was leaving the office. Alicia had fallen and shattered her elbow.

At one time Landry drank coffee, not tea, in the office. "Then, you remember when the coffee prices skyrocketed?" asked Marge. "They were just outrageous. So one morning Coach Landry walked into the office and said, matter-of-factly, that he thought he'd just start drinking tea." Marge laughed and added, "I could just imagine him hearing Alicia saying, 'Isn't it outrageous what they're charging for coffee now?' And so he just decided then and there he wouldn't drink coffee anymore."

~:~

ON THAT FINAL SUNDAY, Landry started putting down notes about what he would say to his players in his last meeting with them. "It won't be an easy thing to do," he said. And, of course, he was right.

Before he left that day he looked at the door leading to his office. It was hand carved, made of the finest mahogany. Divided into three sections, it had carvings of a Cowboy helmet, the Super Bowl trophy, and a view of Texas Stadium. After Dallas beat Miami in Super Bowl VI, Sam Wing, whose company specializes in wooden window shutters, wanted to do something for Landry to show his appreciation. He talked to woodcarver Ray Kelley, and they constructed the door for Landry's old office in Expressway Towers on Dallas's Central Expressway. When the team moved to Valley Ranch, Landry wanted to take the hand-carved door to his new office. He called the maintenance men at Expressway Towers and asked them to take it down. He was taking the door with him.

⌣:∾

TEMPERATURES WERE IN THE MIDFORTIES, and it was, at times, misty under the oyster sky that Monday morning in February when Tom Landry parked his car and walked into the Cowboy headquarters to visit with his assistants, talk to other administrative staffers, and speak with his players for the last time. He got there very early and was dressed in slacks, white shirt, and tie. He had on a Cowboy warmup jacket to keep out the chill, which had been prevalent, both figuratively and literally, for days.

He went to his office and handed Barbara Goodman some notes for the speech he would make to his players, and she typed them on seven or eight note cards. The media were there early too, hoping to catch him before and after his meeting with the players, which was to begin at 9:00 A.M. Some were there to record everything that might happen and others to interpret what had taken place and to speculate on what they had or perhaps had not heard. Landry smiled at the members of the press and walked over to the weight area, where some of the players had gathered. He shook hands with each player there and cautioned them, "It's really important to stay in shape."

Landry picked up the cards for his speech and went to the huge meeting room, which was in a corner of the locker room between the players' mailboxes and the media workroom. The large meeting room was like the other features in the Cowboys' state-of-the-art complex. It had a futuristic air about it and included such helpful but generally uncommon things as built-in video projectors, wooden paneling for acoustics, and a lighting system found only in the best television production facilities. There were long, thin tabletops mounted in the front of plastic chairs for the players to use.

This was the same place where Landry had held his Monday-morning film sessions in which he went over the previous game with the players, pointing out the good and bad, what was and what might have been. And it was the same room where the "Saturday Night Massacre" debacle was held and where number one draft choice Troy Aikman would later be introduced to the press by Jerry Jones.

There was a hush over the crowd of players as Landry made his way into the room and walked, as always, briskly and straight to the front, his head held high. He carried the cards Barbara had typed and tried to keep his mind on what he was going to say as he stood at the lectern.

The doors closed on the press as Landry entered the room, leaving the media to speculate on and later question what might have taken place. Some of the players weren't sure what was going to happen. Randy White and Ed "Too Tall" Jones weren't even there because they weren't aware Tom would be present. The players were supposed to have reported that morning for a fitness checkup that would help the coaches monitor their progress in the off-season conditioning program. There had been some confusion among them as to just who would administer the test and whether or not their attendance was required.

The players watched and waited. "He stood up there tall and proud," said Everson Walls. "Tom Landry is a statue. Nothing would bring him down."

Landry began, businesslike and in control. "Good morning. This will be the final time I'll be here. This will be our last meeting together."

"The mood in the room changed abruptly when he mentioned it would be the final time we'd meet," said Dave Widell, a rookie offensive tackle in 1988. "Everybody began to realize the power of the moment, the seriousness of the situation."

"I was wishing I'd brought a video camera," said Walls. "It was going to be a special moment, something none of us would ever forget, and I wanted to preserve it."

Landry told the players there was no reason at all to worry about him or the situation. "I plan to face this as I have faced everything else. It's not going to stop me from going on with my life."

He paused, trying to control his voice, which had begun to crack, and the words came more slowly. "Today is the first day of the rest of our lives, and we all will go on. You . . . You'll . . . forget me . . . in a couple of weeks."

"No way," Walls later said. "No way. Any time anybody walks into Texas Stadium, they'll be looking for Tom Landry. In a way, he'll always be there. It's the end of an era, but we'll all remember him for the rest of our lives."

Landry tried to clear his throat. Tears came into his eyes. When a man like that, a man with such control, shows emotion, it means a lot more. It comes from deep within the heart.

"We put our heads down because it was hard to look at him," said Eugene Lockhart, the middle linebacker who is known as the "Mean Machine," the tough guy. "You just hurt so much for him. You knew how much he hated to lose his team. It was a devastating day for the Dallas Cowboys."

Landry reminded the players of something he had said many times: "The way you react to adversity is the key to success. People who succeed react the right way in . . . in adverse circumstances. Right . . . now . . . the situation around here is in turmoil, and how . . . we react will be important . . . important in how the season goes next . . . year. I . . . don't want anyone to concern themselves with what has happened to me but to . . . to look . . . forward to playing football in September."

By this time the tears were falling down his cheeks, but he was going on. Of course he was going on.

"He never asked for sympathy," recalled Herschel Walker. "What he asked for was for us to give one hundred and ten percent next season."

And Randy White would later say, "If I'd known about it, I'd have been at the meeting. Coach Landry used to have those little talks with us before the meetings in that room. He'd have a little message out of the Bible for us. It might relate to life or to our situation, but I got a lot out of his talks. He's been such a great influence on me. It drives me crazy when I hear somebody refer to him as being cold."

And Ed "Too Tall" Jones would later say, "When I got out of football that year [1979] and went to pursue a boxing career, Coach Landry told me, 'Ed, if you ever need anything, if you ever need us, don't hesitate to call.'"

Landry continued to try to talk to the players. "I want you to do everything you can to bring the Cowboys back into the NFL's elite. I . . . I . . ."

Landry had a special feeling for his final team. It had gone 3–13, sure, and hit the bottom in the standings. Yet it had hung in there and fought, and it had a chance to win in the final period in all but the Minnesota game. It suffered so many heartbreaking defeats, incredible bad luck, but each week it would come back and play well again, even when there was nothing to play for other than the game at hand, when any playoff hopes had long since been extinguished.

"I looked up there at Coach Landry," said Ray Alexander, the leading receiver in 1988, "and saw him and listened to him and thought, 'I've helped this great man, this future Hall of Fame coach to a 3–13 record in his last season. What kind of situation is this?' Individually, sure, I had a good year, but that all went out the window when I saw him standing there. I should have done more. I was hurting so much for him in my heart."

David Widell, a fourth-round draft pick from Boston College, had been among the Cowboys who had not played well in the blowout against Minnesota. He'd had an awful day trying to block Viking defensive end Chris Doleman. He too felt bad. Everybody did.

"Some players were surprised by the emotion he showed, but I wasn't because of something that had happened earlier in the year," Widell said. "When I first came here I'd heard he was so detached from his players, that he didn't talk much to them personally or get involved. But I saw that changing.

"Anyway, I was on the life cycle [exercise bike] after practice a couple of days after the Minnesota game and that awful day I'd had. Coach Landry just came up and started riding the bike next to me. You know, he always stays in shape. I was waiting to get reamed out, but he just sat there, riding, and I kept on pedaling."

Finally, Landry turned to him and said, "Dave, you had a rough one, huh?"

"Yeah, Coach, I sure did."

"Well, that's the way you learn in this league, David. Don't worry about it. Just learn from the experience and keep on working. You're going to do just fine."

Widell said what happened really surprised him. "The guys had told me he didn't do things like that," said Widell. "And here he had gone out of his way to say something nice to me, to try to bring me out of it. I'm not an Everson Walls or a Danny White or anybody who's been a star or been here for ten years." During that Monday meeting, Widell watched Landry and wished he could replay the Viking game.

Landry continued his talk, telling the players how much it had meant to him that they had never quit during their last season and how proud he was of that. "That's . . . important for . . . you know, to know that you didn't quit, that . . . we didn't quit. . . ."

Landry broke down completely and could not go on for a while. The room was so quiet around him that it seemed as if nobody was even breathing.

"This is a tough business," said Tom Rafferty, the fourteen-year veteran center who had been around during Super Bowls, an NFL championship, and the 1988 season, "and sometimes we forget to show someone how much we appreciate him."

Safety Bill Bates listened to Landry that last morning and remarked, "Playing at the end of his coaching career I got to see a man who threw himself into his job with the Cowboys. His whole life—besides God and his family—was engrained in the Cowboys. So I got to see an older man look like a thirty-five-year-old on days that we were winning and he felt good and everything was positive. Then I also got to see a sixty-year-old look like a sixty-year-old during the times when we weren't doing that well and maybe he wasn't feeling too good. I got to see both sides of the coin, whereas most people who have seen the Cowboys only see that man in the hat on the sidelines, folding his arms and then making a few gestures of excitement. I saw a lot more than that.

"I was fortunate playing for a man like that, a legend like him. He's influenced so many people that he'll go down in history as one of the greatest of all time. Off the field, his life and the way he handled himself was so inspiring for everybody who was around him.

"There have been a lot of great coaches, but you never heard much about them off the field. You never knew what they were really like. But Coach Landry's whole esteem has been developed because of his attitude both on and off the field. And to know that his relationship with the Lord is number one, that his family is second, and then comes football . . . well, that makes him very special.

"I'll always remember him saying good-bye to us, seeing all the emotion come out that people never got to see. I was honored to be a part of it."

Landry continued but was still having trouble. "The things . . . I'm going to miss the most . . . are the coaches and you . . . you the players . . . ." Landry began to sob.

"Hey," said Jeff Rohrer, "he wasn't the only person in that room who broke down. There were a lot of other people who did. Just to show you what kind of a man he is, he had everybody who wanted to come at that last meeting. There were the veterans but also a lot of free agents and people who hadn't been around him. He had all those feelings, all that weight on his shoulders. . . . I didn't want to sit there and cry, but I couldn't help it.

"The feeling in the air was just so thick I couldn't begin to describe it. I really believe that in his own way he loved everybody in that room. I don't know how many people really understood what transpired in those minutes. That was history in the making. What an honor and privilege to have been in that room for Tom Landry's good-bye."

"There are a lot of things I don't remember," said Danny White. "I guess I've been hit in the head too many times. But that's one day I'll always remember, because it was really bottom line, his gut feelings about the players.

"Forget all those wins and losses and what the record was and what records were set and what great plays were made. All that took a backseat. It was the one time in my experience with him that I saw him coming right from his heart. You could see right through him. You knew exactly what he was saying. He was as pure and raw as I've ever seen.

"I just wish some of the other guys, the Cliff Harrises, Drew Pearsons, Lee Roy Jordans, and guys who had played for him before, had been there. It seems like they should have been."

Landry regained his composure, looked around the room, and said, "I'll be with you in spirit, always. I love you guys. God bless you and your families."

The players gave him a standing ovation. The entire meeting had taken about eight minutes, but it would last them forever.

Members of the media crowded around Landry again when he emerged from the meeting room, listening, leaning closer to hear every word. He talked briefly and went back to his office. As always, he showed great patience and restraint, but then again, Landry always realized the media had a job to do.

Landry went back to his office and chatted with his coaches, such as longtime friends Dick Nolan and Jerry Tubbs. He did separate television interviews for all Metroplex television stations, returned phone calls, and answered letters, such as one from a young woman who was doing a paper on the Green Bay Packers.

Mike Ditka called and Landry talked to him. Then he telephoned Gene Stallings and said, "Well, Gene, here's another guy who had to get out of Dodge."

"How did you do?" asked Barbara Goodman, regarding the last speech he gave the players, the meeting that had worried him so much.

"Okay," he said, then paused and added, "But I didn't make it."

Barbara had brought a camera, and she took pictures of various staff members with Landry, who smilingly obliged. He told everybody good-bye, hugged his secretary, and walked to his car, parked at the front entrance. Cameramen surrounded his car. Tom Jr., who had come to the office to see if his dad needed him, remarked as he looked at the photographers, "This is kind of morbid."

Landry got into the car, and as he started to drive away, players and Cowboy employees stood on the steps outside the main building or looked through their office windows to watch him leave the Cowboys, such a special part of his life. It was as if time had stopped, a final freeze frame embedded in their minds forever. By that afternoon the temperatures had dropped a few more degrees and there was even more of a chill in the air.

CHAPTER 4
Tom Landry Day, 1989

~:~

Tom, the love and respect the people around the country have for you is clearly evident today. You're an inspiration to all who have ever watched or played the game of football, and it is with much pride that we share in the celebration of your special day. I want to thank you for your friendship and support all these years. I can't tell you how much it meant to me. Barbara joins me in sending our best wishes to you and Alicia for every future happiness. God bless you.

—GEORGE BUSH
Former President of the United States

ON A BRIGHT SPRING DAY near the end of April 1989, something very unusual occurred when a vast group of highly diversified people responded almost in unison with an overpowering display of emotion, love, and respect for Tom Landry. There was a fine madness of purpose as upward of one hundred thousand people lined six or seven deep along the streets of downtown Dallas to watch a milelong parade to honor Coach Landry. When the parade ended, some fifty thousand crowded into City Hall Plaza to listen to an array of dignitaries offer grateful recognition to that familiar "Man in the Hat," the man who coached their beloved Dallas Cowboys for twenty-nine years.

After Landry was unceremoniously fired, he seemed to have slipped away. Roger Staubach, Cliff Harris, and a group of volunteers wouldn't allow this to happen. They raised ninety thousand dollars to pay for the ceremony so Coach Landry could get a proper send-off, one befitting someone who had meant so much to so many.

Texas governor Bill Clements and Dallas mayor Annette Strauss gave speeches, and Staubach read telegrams from, among others, then president George Bush and Billy Graham. There was a phone call from Bob Hope. And, finally, the crowd heard Tom Landry for perhaps a final time. The twenty-second day of April 1989 officially became Tom

Landry Day in the city of Dallas, and it was also the day of Tom Landry's parade.

The Dallas Metroplex is too large to be wholly affected by a single event, a single happening, because there are just too many other things going on. Yet the entire area came as close as it could to literally vibrating the day Tom Landry was honored. People forgot what they started to do, what they had meant to do, their problems, their golf games, and what was happening in the world. There was the beginning of the fall of House Speaker Jim Wright, the trial and tribulations of Oliver North, disagreement over abortion issues, and the start of what would become a massive uprising by students seeking a broader democracy in China, a movement that would shake the communist world.

But everything was put on hold because of the man whose image was imbedded forever in the minds and hearts not only of those who followed the Dallas Cowboys but also of the many whose lives he had touched. Once again Landry was the hero he had been before the Cowboys fell on hard times. On that day, the bad years paled or were forgotten in the minds of those who chose to remember instead, as they should have, the great accomplishments of the good ones, the Super Bowls, the unprecedented twenty winning seasons in the NFL.

The tremendous reaction surprised everybody—the fans, the old guard that ran the Cowboys, and the new ownership. "I wasn't surprised that there was so much emotion," said Jerry Jones. "But I think the breadth and depth of feelings for Coach Landry were more than anybody imagined. I would have been more concerned if there had been apathy. I'm deeply glad for the way the fans responded to Coach Landry."

The seeds of the great display of emotion for Tom Landry Day began shortly after the official announcement that the Cowboys had a new ownership, that the new coach would be Jimmy Johnson, and that Landry had been fired. Fans went to Cowboy headquarters at Valley Ranch and left placards and signs on the lawn, protesting what had happened. Soon billboards supporting Landry started going up around town, bumper stickers adorned cars, and blue ribbons appeared on car antennas. Job offers and suggestions for future pursuits were offered almost immediately, a movement to rename Texas Stadium after Landry began, and a trading card from the Bowman Company showing Landry as a defensive back for the New York Giants in 1952 doubled in value. The cards had already surpassed all other post–World War II cards in value, but when he was fired, the prices soared to five or six hundred dollars.

Asked how he felt about Landry being dismissed, NFL commissioner Pete Rozelle said, "I feel like I did when Vince Lombardi died." And Governor Clements suggested at a convention of state leaders from around the country that Landry seek the 1990 GOP nomination for his office.

Kim Jindra, the thirty-two-year-old owner of a computer software publishing company in Denton, Texas, decided immediately after he was fired that Landry should be governor. Kim, who had previously worked in campaigns for Clements and Ronald Reagan, said she'd waited a long time for Landry to leave football so she could become involved in his campaign. "We need somebody like a Tom Landry in public office. We know he's an honest person, and he certainly isn't one of those professional politicians." At her own expense, she issued press releases, placed classified ads in newspapers, and made available "Landry for Governor" bumper stickers. She set up a stand in the semicircle of booths at the edge of City Hall Plaza during the Landry Day festivities. She might have been right about Landry making a good governor. We'll never know. Landry just wasn't interested in running for a political office.

"Tom is a person who stays in control under great stress or fire," said Gil Brandt. "He could handle any kind of job. He's just one of those unique people. If he were running the country or the state as governor, a lot of problems would be solved. But he also would make a fine president of Delta Air Lines. He has a tremendous understanding of so many things."

Major Dallas newspapers, Metroplex television stations, and radio stations took polls and suggested Texas Stadium become Landry Stadium. The polls agreed, but the Irving City Council did not. The late Cowboys owner Clint Murchison Jr. chose Irving as the site for Texas Stadium, bringing that city instant recognition when the team began to play there in mid-1971. When a group of high-school students once suggested to Landry that the stadium be named after him, he said it should bear Murchison's name. But those who knew Clint said he would have wanted it renamed after Landry, a man he loved and for whom he had the greatest respect.

In those days the Irving City Council felt its city was too strongly identified with Texas Stadium to change the name, although members said perhaps a room in the stadium could be named after Landry. Even actor David Keith personally went before the council to try to change its mind. Keith first achieved stardom in the film *An Officer and a Gentleman* and shortly after the Landry Day celebration played Oliver North in a made-for-television movie. He has been an avid Cowboy fan since he was a boy in Knoxville, Tennessee. He went to almost all the games in 1988 and held the earphones for Landry on the sidelines. He even attended a council meeting with then Irving mayor Bob Pierce, who was armed with a poster that, apparently jokingly, said, "What part of NO don't you understand?" At first, Jones seemed receptive to renaming the stadium after Landry, but later he said he didn't believe in naming stadiums after people or retiring jerseys of players, because somebody else might come along who was better, more deserving.

It was not popular that they did not name Texas Stadium after Landry. One fan wrote the local newspapers to suggest that the city rename the Cotton Bowl after Landry and another said Dallas should be henceforth called "Landryville"!

A billboard on Interstate 30, just west of downtown Dallas, read, "Tom Landry. Thanks for 29 Great Years." The employees of a national advertising company talked their superiors into putting up the sign. Another billboard read, "We Love You, Tom," and along the much-traveled North Tollway, one said, "Mother Wurlitzer Says, Exchange the Fat Cat for the Hat. Landry for Governor." The mother in question was Renee Wurlitzer, who said she was very distraught when Landry was fired and that, after praying, it came to her that Landry was destined to become governor.

And it was Landry who threw out the first ball when the Texas Rangers opened the 1989 season against Detroit in Arlington Stadium. There were poems and a dozen songs written about Landry.

Landry Day was covered by all the area media and the wire services and was televised live by the three Metroplex television stations, which fed their respective networks, the American Television Network, and GalaVision, a Spanish-language cable company that made satellite transmissions available worldwide. Mexican publications, the British news service Reuters, *USA Today*, and many others were also represented.

Carlos Puig, reporting for *Proceso*, a news weekly in Mexico City, recalled seeing his editor burst out of his office, hurry over to him, and say, "They're going to fire Tom Landry." Puig responded, "Are you crazy?"

"You can't underestimate Tom's popularity around the world," said Gil Brandt. "I remember when we went to Europe how we'd be walking through an airport and people would start coming up to him, asking for his autograph. He'd ask each person their name so he could personalize the autographs."

So the crowd that lined the streets for what was called the "Hats off to Tom Landry Parade" was everyone. "I hope Bright's oil wells turn to pond water," said Stan Williams, looking down the street for the parade. "He's certainly living down to his true name, Bum."

"The parade is a good way to honor him," said Paul Wright of Dallas. "I hate to see him go, but it is time."

"He should have retired instead of being fired," said Cedric Johnson of Dallas. "He just kept on using the same old plays. How do I feel about him? Well, I'm here."

People held up Landry banners and signs, carried Landry posters and pennants, wore Landry buttons, and waved hand-held fans bearing the likeness of Landry. And there were so many T-shirts being worn and sold, with words such as "Here's to the Hunk in the Hat"; "We Love You, Coach"; "The World's Greatest Tragedies: Chicago Fire, The Titanic, The Alamo, and Losing Landry"; "I (exed-out heart) Jerry Jones."

A woman with four small kids tried to find a place where she could get a better view. The kids seemed to be trying to pull her in all directions, but she moved on, determinedly. People sat on hoods and roofs of cars, roosted on tops of buildings, and looked down from windows of office buildings. They climbed on top of newspaper boxes and stands and scaled posts, hoping to get a glimpse of Landry. A very heavyset woman danced while holding a small child, and other adults placed babies and young children on their shoulders and even their heads so they could get a better view of something most of them were too young to understand.

A man carrying a shoeshine kit stopped in the shade of the entrance to a building. He put down the kit and suddenly began dancing with the music from one of the many bands in the parade. He kept saying, over and over, "What can I say? What can I say?" One of the street people, dressed in a dirty T-shirt, baggy frayed pants, and tennis shoes, took off a blue gimme cap and waved it wildly. "My man!" he shouted. "My man!"

Irene Carnazola stood near a man hanging on to a post. Irene had been an all-time avid Cowboy fan since 1975. She lived in Southern California and had attended almost all the Cowboy games, at home and away, for many years. Sometimes she flew across the country, watched a game, and then flew back home. She was vacationing in Stockholm, Sweden, when she heard the news of the plans to honor Landry.

"I just dropped everything and came to Dallas," she said. "I couldn't miss this."

A lady in a wheelchair, who could not move her arms or legs, was ushered to the edge of the sidewalk, where she could get a better view. The woman pushing her turned the wheelchair to the left so she could look down the street toward the approaching parade and see Landry. Tears came into her eyes as she sat staring, looking, and waiting.

The marchers and floats slowly passed . . . the color guards, the bands, the flatbed trucks and convertibles carrying Cowboy players from the past and present, the Tyler Apache Belles, the Dallas Cowboy Cheerleaders, Louie Thurman riding a twelve-hundred-pound buffalo, Crazy Ray (that grown man who dresses up in a cowboy suit and rides a stickhorse at Dallas Cowboy games), Canadian Mounted Policeman Darryl Karnes ("We've followed Coach Landry for years"), the Patty O-Furniture Precision Lawn Chair Drill Team, stopping and snapping through routines as if to mimic a military precision rifle group, and the Shriners, grown men riding go-carts . . . and the atmosphere was carnival-like as the young and old alike reacted to what almost seemed to be a circus parade.

There were cheers for various parts of the parade, including for former past stars such as Tony Dorsett, Drew Pearson, Ralph Neely, and Walt Garrison, and some people ran out of the crowd, past the guards, to reach up on floats to shake hands with Herschel Walker and Roger Staubach.

"I wouldn't have missed this for the world," said Dorsett, who had had a strained relationship at times with Landry. "It's history, honoring one of the greatest coaches of all time, and I wanted to be a part of it."

"I wouldn't be here if it wasn't a great tribute to a great man," said Neely.

"Nobody's ever been honored in this way in Dallas," said Pearson. "I can't think of anybody who has given the type of service and shown the class that he has in this city. But it's not just for the Cowboys or Dallas, but all around the world. He deserves this. It happened because of the way he lived his life."

"I've never seen this many players [seventy-five] come back for one of our reunions," said Garrison. "It's Tom who brings them back."

There were eighty-six floats in the parade, and then there was one, and then the circus atmosphere ended as the vintage blue 1954 Buick Skylark convertible, carrying Tom Landry, came along. He sat on top of the backseat beside his wife, Alicia. Long before we saw Landry, there were outbursts of cheers as watchers knew he was approaching. Then the man in the straw fedora and light blue sports coat appeared, smiling and waving to the crowd, and people began to shout: "We care for you!" . . . "We love you!" . . . "Love ya, Tom!" . . . "Here, Coach, over here!"

Officials did a good job of holding back the crowd, but they could not stop some fans from rushing out onto the street and extending a hand to Landry, who would offer his hand back . . . a moment's touch . . . and still cameras were snapped and minicams rolled to record him on film that would be looked at again and again. Tom Landry could not believe what was happening.

Some people just stood there and watched the last of the parade pass and saw it slowly disappear down the street and listened to the music fade and the sounds become quieter and quieter. But most people hurried over to the plaza to try to get as close as possible to the speakers platform, situated near City Hall, where the program would be held.

~:~

THE PROGRAM was supposed to begin at noon but would not start until a little later. The day had become warmer, almost summerlike at midday. A soft breeze stirred Old Glory, the state flag of Texas, and the Dallas city flag, flying side by side near the entrance to City Hall Plaza.

Those who were lucky enough to have a place in one of the plastic seats in the sections of chairs below the podium took their seats as quickly as possible. Others crowded as near as they could in lines behind the people who were seated. Some even sat around the nearby concrete pond, close enough to hear the loudspeakers. Four small children took off their shoes and dangled their feet in the water. And people stood or walked slowly past the booths, selling wares and Landry paraphernalia. Alongside them were three makeshift stands upon which the Metroplex television stations had set up temporary headquarters.

Retired USAF Gen. Richard F. Abel, president of the Fellowship of Christian Athletes, to which Tom Landry had given so much of his time, gave the invocation:

"We thank You for the close walk with Your Son Jesus Christ and the work Alicia and Tom Landry have done and the impact they've had, not only on this city and this state, but on the nation and the world. And as a new chapter in this book, the Landry life, opens, we pray, Oh God, that You will uplift them and hold them and use them mightily as You have in the past."

Willa Dorsey was a recording star who had appeared around the world, been nominated for a Grammy Award, and been a guest soloist with the crusades of Landry's friend Billy Graham. She sang the national anthem, backed by orchestra and chorus, as Landry stood at attention, holding his hat in hand over his heart. Tom Landry was the kind of person who still got chill bumps when he heard the national anthem.

Tex Schramm was not there. He had been invited but decided not to attend. "The previous Tuesday it had become public that I was leaving the Cowboys and joining the new football league," he said. "There had been a lot said and written about that, and I was afraid my departure might have caused another wave of criticism and controversy and I didn't want in any way to detract from the total focus on Tom." Schramm had left town, gone to fish on his boat in Key West.

Roger Staubach, the master of ceremonies, received a tremendous ovation as he walked to the microphone on the speakers platform, which faced the crowd below and from which you could clearly see the skyline of downtown Dallas. Staubach said he could think of no one more deserving of such a tribute. "For twenty-nine remarkable years he guided the Dallas Cowboys to win after win, while maintaining the highest integrity of coaching, teamwork, and sportsmanship." He paused, looked into the audience, and added, "That shouldn't surprise anybody because Tom Landry was always such a perfectionist. Like Dandy Don Meredith once said, 'If Tom were married to Raquel Welch, he'd expect her to cook.'" Alicia and Tom laughed along with the crowd.

Staubach read some of the telegrams:

Tom, the love and respect the people around the country have for you is clearly evident today. You're an inspiration to all who have ever watched or played the game of football, and it is with much pride that we share in the celebration of your special day. I want to thank you for your friendship and support all these years. I can't tell you how much it meant to me. Barbara joins me in sending our best wishes to you and Alicia for every future happiness. God bless you.

THE PRESIDENT OF THE UNITED STATES, GEORGE BUSH

As you know, there is no one I have more respect for than you, as a Christian, a professional, and a leader. We were already committed to be in Syracuse for a crusade or we would have been there with you. Congratulations for your great honor today. Nobody deserves it more.

BILLY GRAHAM

Later, a special telephone on the podium rang and Staubach asked Tom to come forward because "somebody wants to talk to you." The audience could hear the conversation over the loudspeaker:

"Hello, this is Tom Landry talkin'."

"Tom, this is Bob Hope."

Hope was in Port Arthur, Texas, doing a benefit for physically handicapped kids and told Landry he'd heard he was being honored and just wanted to say hello and extend his congratulations.

"Tom," continued Hope, "I think everybody feels the same about you. You've done so much for the whole country, not just for Texas but everywhere. You've brought such wonderful entertainment to us over the years . . . and you've been just wonderful."

The crowd began to cheer. "Bob," said Landry, "can you hear that applause? We just appreciate being able to talk to you."

"You've had winning teams for so long that a lot of people thought Tom Landry was the capital of Texas. I mean it. You've done as much for football as you've done for hats. . . . Seeing Tom Landry without a hat is like seeing Tammy Bakker without makeup."

Amid the laughter, Landry said, "I'm sorry. I'm afraid I'm not a very good straight man for you today."

"Tom, I don't know where you're going to coach next or where you're going, but wherever it is, you'll enhance the neighborhood. Believe me."

The cheers grew louder as speakers continued to laud Tom Landry. As we sat there listening to them talk about Landry's career in the past tense, it was difficult to imagine going to Texas Stadium and not seeing that familiar figure in the light blue sports coat, tie, and funny little hat. It was difficult to imagine he no longer would be leading his team out of the tunnel before a game in a limping trot, the result of an old injury, with his head held high and eyes looking forward to the challenge at hand.

And it would also seem odd not to see him on the sidelines during a game, showing almost perfect decorum while others in his profession would jump and scream and jerk as if gripped by some madness. Sometimes Landry would lose control for a moment when he felt a bad call had been made against his team or something very good or very bad had happened, but, mostly, he would remain calm, outwardly anyway.

Roger Staubach read another telegram:

> *After twenty-nine years we'll finally have some peace and quiet on the football field. After all that ranting and raving and throwing your hat into the air over our bad calls, peace will finally come to that great patch with the white lines. Best of health, happiness, and a long life. You will not be like General MacArthur and fade away like the old soldier. You will always be remembered as a coach, a fine person, and a gentleman. We will all miss you.*

THE OFFICIALS OF THE NFL

A contingent from Landry's hometown of Mission listened to the speakers in City Hall Plaza praise Tom Landry, a man who had been born and raised in their town. They had enjoyed riding near the front of the parade in the red convertible that had a sign on its sides identifying them as being from Mission.

Benny Benevides, executive vice president of the Mission Chamber of Commerce, Chamber president Arturo Guerra, and Rubin Femat and Harlan Woods of the Mission Independent School District rode in the car. Others were there from Mission, but they mingled in the crowd and weren't singled out.

"There were a lot of very moving moments," said Benevides. "People in the crowd along the parade would yell and say nice things as we passed. And I heard one woman clearly say, 'Thanks very much for Tom Landry.' That made us all feel tremendous. It was such a splendid way for Dallas to acknowledge his contributions and accomplishments."

Woods had presented Landry with a replica of a chair he had used when he attended elementary school in Mission. That seemed so long ago and far away and, yet, in a way it didn't.

The orchestra and chorus played a medley of armed forces songs, in honor both of our servicemen and, of course, the guest of honor, Tom Landry. Lt. Gen. Ellie Shuler, Eighth Air Force commander of the Strategic Air Command, made his way to the speakers platform.

Lieutenant General Shuler called Landry a great American and a great patriot and said, "Most of us know about his successes on the football field but do not know that long before that he was a warrior and aviator in World War II. . . . Tom Landry answered our nation's call during the critical days of World War II."

He went on to say Landry had been a member of the famous 493rd bombardment group, known as Helton's Hellcats, and had flown thirty combat missions "over the war-torn skies of Europe as a pilot in the legendary B-17 Flying Fortresses."

Landry was awarded the European African Middle Eastern Campaign medal with three combat stars, the American Campaign medal, and the U.S. Air Force medal with four oak leaf clusters. Lieutenant General Shuler explained how "mission after mission gallant airmen like Lieutenant Landry flew hundreds of miles into enemy territory to attack their targets, and inevitably they encountered enemy fighter attacks and murderous fields of flak. Yet, they pressed onward to drop thousands of pounds of high explosives on the targets. Their perseverance in the face of tremendous odds literally devastated the Nazi war machine. Lieutenant Landry and his colleagues helped assure allied victory in Europe. . . . This nation owes much to the Tom Landrys, the citizen soldiers who did their duty during wartime and returned to civilian life to engage in productive careers. The men and women of the Mighty Eighth join me in expressing our heartfelt gratitude for all you have contributed to our nation. Coach . . . sir, we present you with this plate with the best wishes from the Eighth Air Force."

Members of the media were at City Hall Plaza like locusts the day

Tom Landry was honored. Television cameras rolled, still cameras clicked constantly, and anchor persons from the three area stations told their audiences what they were seeing on the screen and continually interviewed people about Tom Landry. There were broadcasts and telecasts and specials on most every aspect of the day and his career, and he had not been interviewed so much since his team won a Super Bowl.

Some of us sat in the special section, near the speakers platform, and thought and listened. Landry had always shown a great deal of restraint and patience with the media, and even those who were especially critical of him found him to be cooperative and accessible. He was there during the good times, and he didn't disappear during the bad ones.

I'm sure Landry felt closer to some members of the media than to others, but he treated everybody equally when they were after news concerning him or his team. And because of the great success and popularity of the Cowboys over the years, Landry remained under constant scrutiny, in his own personal fishbowl. He was even criticized during the best years, the winning years, probably as much as any successful coach in modern NFL history. Sometimes no matter what you do, people expect more.

Unlike so many in his profession, Landry would not just come out and lie to you, but he was not beyond stretching the truth, underplaying things or withholding information when he believed he should. He might have covered up for a player who hadn't played well or was disciplined for breaking the rules. The great majority of the media liked Landry, even though they might point out what they considered his shortcomings or mistakes. But nobody could have accused him of not being a gentleman, unless perhaps they had a personal vendetta against him for some reason.

"I really appreciate people in the media," he once said. "I feel through the years we've had a good relationship with most of them." He'd added that there were a couple of guys he had trouble getting along with but if everything were perfect it wouldn't be that interesting.

"From my standpoint I've enjoyed the relationship. I didn't even dread the weekly press conferences on Tuesdays, whether we were winning or losing, because I believed I'd be treated fairly by most people. That's all you can ask. It's been a pleasure being with you all these years.

"I think I'll even miss those weekly press conferences . . . well, I think I will."

Although he didn't seem to care that much, Landry had once even remarked that he appreciated the publicity and respected the job Tex Schramm and his staff had done.

"The bottom line is winning as far as successful publicity," he'd said. "It certainly helps you if you are winning."

~:~

TOM LANDRY SAT RIGIDLY IN HIS CHAIR on the speakers platform, almost as if he were at attention, as Staubach continued to read the congratulatory telegrams. The day was getting hotter, especially for those sitting or standing in the sun at City Hall Plaza, and some people in the audience and near the podium had begun to stir or change positions to try to get more comfortable. Landry smiled slightly and did not seem at all aware that it was becoming warmer; nor did he stir in his chair. He was very much in control.

The telegrams had come from President George Bush and the nation's most noted evangelist, Billy Graham, and the telephone call had come from Bob Hope, and you wondered just where the next greeting would come from, just whom else Tom Landry had touched. And, sitting there and listening, you half expected Staubach to read a note that said, "Congratulations and good luck, Coach Landry . . . Mikhail Gorbachev."

Staubach read another telegram:

> *Best wishes on today's special occasion. I thoroughly regret not being able to be with you today, but my thoughts are with you as we remember your long and illustrious career. While your twenty-nine years in Dallas is a monument to excellence, there are those of us here who believe your ten years with the Giants as a player and coach are equally as memorable. Again, our very best personal regards.*
> WELLINGTON T. MARA, PRESIDENT OF
> THE NEW YORK GIANTS FOOTBALL CLUB

Staubach closed his introduction of Landry by calling him "the best coach in the NFL and a pretty darn good guy."

There was a long, standing ovation, and Landry stood before the microphone, appearing to be a little confused at the massive response. Finally, he was able to begin: "It's a great, great pleasure for me to be here today, and I'm especially thankful for all the people who have made this day what probably is the most exciting and meaningful day of my life. I never thought in my wildest imagination that something like this would happen to me, and that makes it even nicer.

"Your outpouring of love and concern, through your letters, telegrams, and all the articles that have been written, is something my family and I will never forget. We'll cherish it in years to come. I know I'm not worthy of the things that have been said about me today by any measure . . ."

People interrupted him by shouting, "Yes you are! Yes you are!"

". . . been blessed to be a part of this community and the Dallas Cowboys. This has been an experience I wouldn't trade for anything because it has meant so much to me."

He thanked the staff who put the day's program together and those who had said such nice things about him, then continued, "Personally, the Lord has meant a great deal to me. I became a Christian one year before I took over the Dallas Cowboys, and He's been with me all these days here in Dallas and meant a tremendous amount to me."

He told how families were such a major part of "our success. They're the ones who have to stand by you through the good times and the bad, and I've been blessed with a wonderful family . . . Alicia, my son, Tom, and daughters . . . Lisa and her husband Gary Childress. My oldest daughter Kitty is under the weather and couldn't get here, but her husband, Eddie Phillips, is out there with my two grandchildren, Ryan and Jennifer. If Eddie has lasted this long with those two kids, he deserves a medal.

"The Dallas Cowboys have been my life for the last twenty-nine years, and that's the reason I'm standing here today. The most important things on a football team are the players, and you've seen many of them today. There are others who operate in the organization who also have made the success possible. There was the late Clint Murchison, who brought the team to Dallas, and, of course, Tex Schramm, who had such a big part in building the Dallas Cowboys. You can't operate without good assistants, and I've had many.

"The thing that makes you are the fans. They're with you a lot and against you a lot, but they're fans. They made us America's Team. It happened not so much with what we did but because of the fans we had in so many cities across the country. We had a great twenty-nine-year run and a lot of memories. I know I have a lot. I can remember when we first became a winning team in 1966 and will never forget the speed and excitement with Bullet Bob Hayes and Don Meredith. I'll never forget the Green Bay games and . . . and that first Super Bowl we played. We'd lost those two games to Green Bay [and conference title games to Cleveland], and so everybody was saying we couldn't win the Big One. But we went to the Super Bowl, and it came down to the last play when Baltimore kicked a field goal to beat us. Bob Lilly threw his helmet the length of the football field because of the disappointment. That showed just how much it hurt us all to lose that game . . ."

Just before the festivities began, former and present Dallas Cowboy players had made their way in groups to the speakers platform, where they would take their seats adjacent to the podium. Suddenly, a man came jogging through the crowd, hurrying to catch up with them. The man was Duane Thomas, rushing to be a part of the group. The world had taken a couple of turns.

All morning Duane had warmly greeted his former teammates and members of the press and all the people he had once given the cold shoulder to, to the extent that he became known as the "Sphinx."

And Landry continued his speech, ". . . next year we came back and won the Super Bowl against Miami. Those were great memories . . . and we did it with the silent man, Duane Thomas. Is he here? [Thomas acknowledged the introduction by getting up out of his seat and raising his arms high in the air.] You know Duane called me a plastic man, and he's probably right. But we're great friends today."

It was appropriate, in an odd sort of way, that George Allen attend the celebration for Tom Landry, his major rival. Other coaches and teams would rise and fall, come and go, but during Allen's seven years in Washington the yearly meetings between the Cowboys and the Redskins became national events and the teams' rivalry is still considered, arguably, the NFL's greatest.

Allen actually received guarded applause as he rode in a red convertible in the Landry parade and drew a great deal of attention when he later would coach the former Redskins in a flag football game against former Cowboy players. The game was just for fun. Landry took it that way, but before the game ever began in Texas Stadium, Allen complained that he was outmanned and didn't have his best players present. For the record, Staubach led the ex-Cowboys to victory.

When Tom Landry was nearing the end of his speech, he mentioned that linebacker Chuck Howley had been named MVP in the Cowboys' first Super Bowl appearance and that defensive linemen Randy White and Harvey Martin were co-MVPs when Dallas beat Denver in Landry's final Super Bowl. He looked at Allen and said, "They were the first defensive players to win the MVP in the Super Bowl, George." Probably for the first time, Allen, noted for his defensive expertise in the NFL, smiled warmly at Landry.

Landry paused, looked out over the crowd, and smiled. The softness of the smile belied his strong face and the image that so many had of him. "I might not see you all again," he said. "There probably won't be any more press conferences or anything. But if I see any of you on the street, I'll sure say hello."

As he walked off the speaker's stand, it would be the last time most people would ever see him. That familiar face that seemed to be chiseled in stone with the deep-set, pale eyes that could almost become slits when he smiled or deeply concentrated, the chin that jutted out, would become a fading memory. And then Landry walked away and was gone. But he would not be forgotten.

CHAPTER 5
The Dallas Cowboys in Transition

◡⦂◠

But anybody who says time has passed Coach Landry by . . . well that's just stupid. That's what they used to say about Bear Bryant. So he put in the Wishbone and won some more national championships and was a great coach again. Coach Landry lost a lot of good assistants over the years, like Danny Reeves and Mike Ditka. That can make a difference.

—GENE STALLINGS

TOM LANDRY was making his way on crutches down the hall at the Cowboy headquarters one Saturday morning during an off-season before he lost his job, and his face seemed drawn and tired and more wrinkled than usual. He still had that slight, crooked grin and his eyes were still bright, but Tom Landry looked his age. He actually appeared to be a man in his midsixties. This was somewhat shocking because I could not remember noticing that before. I could not remember him looking his age before.

He was a man who jogged and worked out with exercise equipment, had no vices, and, some said, didn't even have evil thoughts. He was a man who, short years earlier, often appeared in as good shape as some of his players and, in fact, sometimes looked more like one of the players than their coach when you saw him from a distance walking among them.

His knee had bothered him for so long that he finally had to quit running and undergo surgery, but he still routinely rode the exercise bike and remained in good condition. No doubt the operation had taken a momentary toll on him, and he had certainly been affected by being in the throes of those losing seasons.

Watching him I felt a kind of sadness, asking myself why a man such as this didn't just walk away from all the mess, the madness. He had nothing to prove, and his reputation would only continue to diminish in the ashes. He obviously knew there were those in his own organization who wanted him to retire and that the media, at times more fair-weathered than logical or accurate, were continually taking shots at him. They were writing and saying the league had passed him by, that his system was antiquated, and that he no longer could motivate the younger players. Some even claimed he must be becoming senile because of some of the plays he was calling. And on and on it went.

"When I look at an airplane now, I say, 'Boy, wouldn't it be great if we could fly down to Austin and play golf or something,'" Landry said. "I'm getting to the age where I probably should do that a little bit, but I still have that real desire to see this team do something. I see those guys and look at them, and they're sitting there and not sure what's happening, what's going on. If I can make a difference in their lives, that's what I want to try to do. I may not do it. But I'll try until I don't think I can, and that would be the time I probably would make a change [retire]."

Of course, going through all the things he had faced would make anybody seem older, but I still could not imagine Tom Landry looking his age. It was something that would not happen. But he would go on. Lines from Robert Frost came to mind:

> And miles to go before I sleep,
> And miles to go before I sleep.

Once he was off the crutches and another season got under way and the old excitement of challenge returned, he would look younger again. But that day, that moment, he had become a kind of shadow of himself, and for his own good, I thought perhaps he should retire.

～•～

IN MANY WAYS PARITY, the NFL's plan to make the weak strong and the strong weak, had caught up with the Dallas Cowboys. They had managed to avoid what seemed inevitable for so long, but winning meant they would have low draft choices and tougher schedules. Dallas had been able to overcome that in past years by discovering players others had overlooked, such as Calvin Hill and Duane Thomas. Furthermore, the Cowboys had signed free agents like Drew Pearson and Cliff Harris. And then in the lower rounds there were choices like

Roger Staubach, who might not even have been able to play after a four-year obligation in the navy, and Bobby Hayes, a track star.

Dallas was an organization ahead of its time, but soon time not only caught up with the Cowboys, it almost ran over them. Tex Schramm had led the team into the computer age of scouting, and Gil Brandt had combed small colleges to find Jethro Pugh and Rayfield Wright and had signed basketball players such as Cornell Green and Pete Gent. But the organization then fell victim to the ultimate power of positive thinking. Drafting late, it had continually gambled, missing more than it hit, on players who seemed to be the perfect blend of size, quickness, and speed for a certain position. Potentially they might be Pro Bowl players. But they were picked on their potential, and good, solid college football players were passed over. Mike Singletary, for example, was outstanding but only 5'-10", seemingly too short for an NFL middle linebacker. He became a solid All-Pro with the Chicago Bears. Dallas also passed on players such as Dan Marino, Mark Duper, Vernon Dean, Neil Lomax, James Wilder, and Chris Collinsworth.

By 1986, Schramm had inaugurated something of a change in philosophy. He wanted Gil Brandt and his scouts to take into consideration if a guy was a good, solid football player, whether he had the attributes associated with a particular position or not. But the damage had been done. Whereas once there had been a steady ascension of good young players to replace aging ones, this was no longer true. So many replacements never realized their potential, and only fair or mediocre players were moving into the starting lineup.

Brandt headed the scouting department and, fairly or unfairly, took most of the blame for the failures. However, Schramm said, "You can't put the total blame on Gil. We're all at fault. He had the most input, using information he gets from his scouts. But remember, we all sit down and rank our choices and put them in order on the board. Landry approves the choices, and he makes the final decision on which players we pick in the early rounds, based on some oftentimes very lengthy discussions." Landry did not point a finger at anybody, or everybody.

The system worked like this: All scouting information was evaluated and run through the computer and Landry was given a list of the top one hundred players to read. The two things he enjoyed least about his job were going over the scouting reports and training camp, which kept him away from his family. Several weeks prior to the draft, Landry met with Brandt, Schramm, and members of the scouting department to rank the prospects in order of their talent, regardless of position. Everybody had input into the order, but Landry made the ultimate decision on whom the Cowboys picked in the early rounds. He would usually leave after the fifth or sixth round because, theoretically, the top prospects were gone.

So for a long period of time the draft killed the Cowboys. In 1985, only fourteen selections in an eight-year span were still on the team. Only six starters came out of five drafts going into the 1986 season, and at that time, only one first-round pick, Jim Jeffcoat, had become a regular. Jeffcoat started his career well, and it didn't hurt that he played next to Randy White. As injuries and age diminished White's talent and he stopped drawing a double-team, Jeffcoat was solid, but his performance tailed off. Kevin Brooks, the number one pick in 1985, became a starter in 1988, but his play was far from consistent and his teammates didn't particularly like him.

Dallas had some terrible misses on number one choices. Defensive lineman Larry Bethea (1978) failed to live up to his potential during his six years on the team and was cut. Rod Hill, a defensive back, was brought into Dallas for a workout before the draft and impressed everybody, especially secondary coach Gene Stallings. Hill was quick, agile, and had good moves and speed. Dallas picked him number one in 1982, but he simply was not a football player. Howard Richards (1981) and Aaron Kyle (1976) were only passable players.

Fortunately, that year Schramm & Co. did take a flyer on Herschel Walker with a fifth-round choice. Walker had a long-term contract with the New Jersey Generals of the fledgling United States Football League, but when the USFL suspended operations, Walker joined the Cowboys in 1986. And to his credit, Brandt and his staff did draft linebacker Mike Walter number two in 1983, and Gil predicted he would be a starter and Pro Bowl player. The Cowboys let Walter go because the coaches didn't think he fit into Landry's 4-3 Flex Defense. San Francisco picked him up, and he became a starter and outstanding player for the 49er Super Bowl teams. Todd Christiansen (number two, 1978) was asked by Landry to move from running back to tight end. He refused and was let go. He also failed to make it with the New York Giants as a running back. Todd ended up with the Raiders, where he agreed to move to tight end and became a Pro Bowl player.

It also should be pointed out that Dallas had rotten luck with number one picks Robert Shaw (1979), Billy Cannon (1984), and Mike Sherrard (1986). Shaw, projected as a Pro Bowl center, suffered a career-ending knee injury, and Cannon, shortly after becoming a starting linebacker his rookie season, injured his neck to such an extent that doctors told him he could no longer play football. By midseason his rookie year, Sherrard became the long threat receiver the club needed. He was outstanding but suffered a broken tibia in training camp in 1987. He ignored the advice of team physicians and began his own rehabilitation program in California; while running on the beach, he broke the same leg again. Dallas let him go because Cowboy doctors felt his leg wouldn't hold up. San Francisco picked him, and he played well but never reached his potential.

On draft day, the Cowboys were theoretically supposed to scratch the names off the list of one hundred as they were taken, then pick the next player on their list in order. If they wanted to deviate from this system, Landry was the final judge and arbiter. Landry usually did not get out and personally scout prospects, so all he had to go on was the information given him by the scouts.

Landry and his staff believed the Cowboys were so strongly set at quarterback in 1979 that, in the third round, he deviated from the list and picked Doug Cosbie over Joe Montana. He did not know 1979 would be Roger Staubach's final year, but he had great confidence in backups Danny White and Glenn Carano.

In 1983, Landry felt secure with White and Gary Hogeboom and passed on Dan Marino, whose name was next on the team's list and who was ranked higher than Jeffcoat. Other teams passed on him as well. Marino was the fifth quarterback taken in that draft. Bethea, Brooks, and Jeffcoat, to an extent, could hardly keep up the great tradition of the Cowboys' front four.

"It was obvious to everybody that we just didn't have the talent anymore," said longtime defensive line coach and coordinator Ernie Stautner. "When we were winning we had top people, but the draft was killing us and we couldn't replace them. Sure, Tom made the final choices, but all he had to go on came from Gil Brandt. Gil did a great job for a long time, but I think he should have been let go ten years ago. I'd suggest defensive linemen but they wouldn't listen to me."

During the off-season of 1989, Landry demoted Stautner to special projects and hired George Hill to take his place. Stautner admitted he felt very bitter toward Landry, who told him that he felt some changes had to be made and he wanted Hill on board because the team was going to be using more 3–2 defense.

"Tom did admit, however, that he should have listened to me five or six years ago, when I suggested we draft certain defensive linemen and questioned the people we were going to take," concluded Stautner.

Former Cowboy middle linebacker Lee Roy Jordan, who did not particularly like Schramm or Brandt, was asked about the club's decline and said, "Tom is just as good a coach as he ever was. He just doesn't have the personnel. To me, the scouting department is the poorest part of the Cowboy organization."

Lance Rentzel wrote a letter to the *Dallas Morning News* when Landry was fired. In part it said, "To understand what is wrong with the team, one has to examine Gil Brandt's performance, not the perform-ance of the coaching staff. Brandt revolutionized the art of player acquisition in the 1960s. For that he deserves a lot of credit.

"However, the rest of the league has passed him by in this area, and until he is replaced, the Cowboys will not win, no matter who is the owner and no matter who is the coach. X's and O's mean nothing if the other team has better players. That's what happens when you have ten poor drafts in a row. I cannot figure out why this simple fact has been overlooked by many of those who follow the team."

"During a ten-year period, we picked an average of twenty-second in the draft," said Brandt. "We had incredible bad luck with Cannon, Shaw, and Sherrard. We also had to reject a lot of guys because Tom didn't believe they were smart enough for his system. That certainly was his prerogative. All I've got to say is, I was with the club twenty-nine years, and believe I did a good job."

"Sometimes it can be difficult finding players who fit into Landry's system," explained Schramm. "It's very demanding. But the system has been successful, so you try to find a certain kind of player. Sometimes the intelligence factor would enter into what was done. Sometimes Tom wouldn't feel a player was smart enough for the system."

Perhaps it was because of the change in philosophy that Schramm hired Bob Ackles to scout and determine pro personnel that might ben-efit the club and placed Joe Bailey in charge of signing players. Brandt had held those duties, and Schramm wanted to free him to concentrate more on the draft. And, certainly, the fact that Dallas was picking sooner in the draft entered into it. But the final three drafts of Landry's regime were on the upswing, with thirteen picks on the final 1988 roster, including possible stars such as Danny Noonan and Michael Irvin. Thornton Chandler, Ron Francis, Jeff Zimmerman, Kevin Martin, Irvin, and Noonan had all been starters at one time or another. Landry had also personally seen Troy Aikman and planned to take him as the club's top choice in 1989. But, of course, he never got the chance.

"After twenty-five years, the pendulum swings," said Gene Stallings. "Tom is the same coach he always was. The Cowboys were better last year [1988] than people thought, but they certainly have lost a lot of talent. You know, Rafael Septien won a lot of close games for the Cowboys with his kicking. And look at all the games Roger Staubach pulled out. You might lose seventeen to fourteen, but if you have a Staubach out there you win those games twenty to seventeen. Maybe Tony Dorsett breaks three tackles and goes eighty-five yards. Is that coaching? A coach can be as good as his quarterback or field goal kicker. A head coach is like a quarterback; he might get too much credit if he wins and too much blame if he loses.

"But anybody who says time has passed Coach Landry by . . . well, that's just stupid. That's what they used to say about Bear Bryant. So he put in the Wishbone and won some more national championships and was a great coach again.

"Coach Landry lost a lot of good assistants over the years, like Danny Reeves and Mike Ditka. That can make a big difference."

⤳∴↝

THE COWBOY ASSISTANTS in those days were a closely knit group and very loyal to Landry. On the sidelines Landry would sometimes lose control momentarily, but he generally kept his poise, which couldn't always be said for his assistants, especially Ditka and to a lesser extent Stallings. Once, after a game in which his assistants had repeatedly overreacted, Landry called a meeting and said, "I tell you, sometimes I'd rather lose a game than have my assistants act like you did on the sidelines."

During a game against St. Louis in Texas Stadium, Ditka was yelling and cussing on the sidelines when an official came over and told him to cool it. Later, the same official made what Mike felt was another terrible call. Ditka calmly marched onto the field and inquired if that particular official might be a member of the Fellowship of Christian Athletes.

"Well, no, I'm not," replied the puzzled official.

"Then," said Mike, "screw you."

The official didn't know what to think. Neither did Tom Landry.

Landry used to play tennis with his assistants in training camp after practice or sometimes early in the morning. Unfortunately, Ditka was one of them. College students and fans who lived near the campus of California Lutheran in Thousand Oaks, California, would often come to watch. On a particular day Ditka was having a hard time getting his game together and, again, was letting his emotions show by yelling and screaming. Landry said nothing. Finally, Mike missed a shot, looked up at the sky, and yelled, scaring some of the fans nearby, his tennis partner, and his opponents.

Then he slammed down his racket, shattering it in numerous places. But he wasn't through. He picked it up again and threw its remains at the net. The only thing was, it went under the net and smashed into Landry's ankles. Landry didn't yell in pain, although it must have hurt a lot, but he did start hopping around.

Finally, he said to his partner, Dan Reeves, "Boy, you can get hurt playing this game."

⌣∵∼

"YOU HAVE TO HAVE THE PLAYERS," said Danny Reeves. "I look back and we had some great coaching staffs and some great players. Times just changed."

In 1986, four former Landry assistants—John Mackovich in Kansas City, Ray Berry in New England, Ditka in Chicago, and Reeves in Denver—all had teams in the playoffs. Ditka had won a Super Bowl, and Reeves had taken the Broncos to two. Berry's New England team also made the Super Bowl, and Stallings had the Cardinals in contention and missed the playoffs by one game in 1987. Reeves would go on to coach Denver into yet another Super Bowl, although the Broncos would lose as would his Atlanta Falcons, who ironically were defeated in Super Bowl XXIII by his former Denver team. Before retiring, Stallings would go back to the college ranks at Alabama and lead the Crimson Tide to the national championship.

❦

OFFICIALLY, although the signs were there as early as 1984, the fall of the Cowboys began with the first of three straight losing seasons in 1986, and the team, as far as its won-lost record, hit the bottom in Landry's last year. After what turned out to be his final year of coaching, Landry said, "God never closes a door to you that He won't open another one. That's our faith. I'm just excited to see what it is. He's carried me through a lot of tough situations. But, as far as the football team, none was tougher than last year."

Jim Myers said Landry was ready to go again in 1989. "Tom is a man more motivated by challenge than anybody I've ever known in my life. I watched him year after year and marveled how he continued to find ways to maintain the kind of enthusiasm a football coach has to have. For him, there is no past, really. What happened the season before, whether it was a Super Bowl victory or a season like 1988, was never as important as the season that was ahead. When you are able to adopt and maintain an attitude like that, the business of feeling as if you've done it all before doesn't become a problem."

Dallas Cowboy scout Dick Mansperger once commented during the club's decline, "People come up to me and are worried about the Dallas Cowboys. They want to know what it's going to take to turn the team around back to the championship level. I tell them all the same thing: As long as Tom Landry is running this show, everything will be okay. No team in history has stayed on top as long. There are those who will suggest we are long overdue for a leveling off. But, unlike some clubs who have been up and down like a yo-yo, the Cowboys have something unique. The constant that is ever present on this team is the head coach."

Assistants, on the other hand, often come and go. The fact that Landry had had so many assistants who had landed head coaching jobs in the NFL was one of a number of reasons that brought Paul Hackett in 1986. His hiring was significant too in that for the first time Tex Schramm seemed to have moved into Landry's clearly defined domain and had unprecedented input into hiring Hackett.

❦

TOM LANDRY HAD FIRST TALKED with Tex Schramm in 1984 when the Dallas Cowboys' record string of nine straight playoff appearances had been broken and the younger generation of coaches Landry had trained, including Reeves, Ditka, and Mackovich, had left the team for head coaching jobs. Landry explained he had good, respected people on his staff, but Schramm told him he believed he needed some new, younger people because they would bring in new ideas. At that time Jim Myers was sixty-four, Dick Nolan fifty-four, Ernie Stautner fifty-nine, Jerry Tubbs fifty-one, and Gene Stallings and offensive coordinator Jim Shofner both fifty.

Schramm told him he didn't want to fire anybody but, perhaps, they could be moved to other jobs in the organization and replaced by some younger people who might make more of an impact. Landry listened and agreed that some changes had to be made, but he felt that at that time of his career he didn't have the time to fully train a new coach and wanted to keep the same staff. He did, and Dallas shocked everybody by winning the NFC East and beating key rivals Washington and New York twice. But the team at times failed miserably in games it didn't have to win and was embarrassed 20–0 by Los Angeles in the first round of the playoffs. More and more, Schramm was looking over Landry's shoulder and sometimes even becoming openly critical. He said, simply, "We're not going to play with the same deck again."

"Tom Landry is an extremely intelligent man and knew some changes had to take place," said Schramm. "If we could have gone to the Super Bowl again in 1985, using the same staff and the same team, it would have been a sensational accomplishment. It's only human nature, if you've had unprecedented success, to try to keep hanging on to what you have.

"I'd been trying to take a more active interest in assistant coaches. I just don't believe Tom pays any attention to people on other staffs around the league. That's his nature. He blocks all that out, concentrating on the game and its preparation. Others had suggested people when we were looking for assistant coaches in the past."

Schramm had had his eye on Hackett, the 49ers assistant who coached quarterbacks and assisted Bill Walsh in developing the very successful 49ers passing game.

Landry had also been thinking that he might not coach more than two more years. He mentioned this to Schramm and told him he probably should start looking for a replacement.

Schramm received permission from the 49ers to talk to Hackett, and then he asked Tom to meet with him. Landry agreed to do so, and the implication in the media was that the whole thing was his idea and that he knew all about Hackett. Landry did agree to hire Hackett but was honest to a fault when he made the announcement to the media. He admitted that he knew little about Hackett and that the first time he'd met him was when they'd talked about a job with the Cowboys. It became clear then that Schramm had initiated the move. Hackett would be the coordinator of the passing game and help Landry call plays from the coaches' box; he had put himself in a position possibly to be Landry's replacement.

Although Dallas had led the NFL in passing yardage, Schramm had not been happy with Jim Shofner as head of the passing game. Dallas had the yards but had failed in key situations. Shofner was offered another job in the organization but resigned, joining Stallings at the Cardinals. Shofner became very angry with Landry, feeling Tom had tried to force him into semiretirement when he wasn't ready. Landry said nothing, accepting whatever blame or ill feelings Shofner might have toward him. The move also upset some others on the staff. Shofner was Dick Nolan's brother-in-law and was liked by the other coaches, who felt Schramm was forcing Hackett on Landry.

Obviously, Landry was aware of some of the things that were being said and written. "As far as anybody in the organization digging a tunnel under me, running in their own coaches and all, that's simply not true," he said. "I have final say on all members of my staff, and everything to do with the football aspects of the organization. I always will. No, I don't feel anybody is trying to undermine me, but I can't speak for every member of the organization.

"I've reached the point, with my longevity, that I'm not going to coach a lot longer. Therefore, Tex needs to be in a position to take an active role in looking at what is available and what will happen if I step down. There will be a transition period. I don't know how long it will be, but I'm a Cowboy and interested in what the team is going to do when I leave. It's important that Tex be in a position to do that. He hasn't interviewed or hired a coach in a long time.

"We're trying to improve ourselves in every area. After all these years, we need a fresh look. This is the first time we've taken that fresh look at our organization, and we're trying to do what's best for the future."

For the first time, Landry, who had designed and engineered the

Cowboys' very successful multiple offense and passing attack, was ready not only to listen but also to accept many of Hackett's theories . . . at least for a while.

⌣∴∾

BASICALLY, LANDRY'S PHILOSOPHY, also used by Don Shula in Miami, was that you attack a particular defense your opponent is using. A quarterback reads the defense, the coverage, and then should know which receiver will be open. The system Hackett brought in was diametrically opposed to Landry's.

Hackett is from the Don Coryell/Bill Walsh school of passing, a system Joe Gibbs also used in Washington. In this system you do not attack a particular defensive alignment or care which defense a team is using. You have certain passing plays, and you run them regardless, without adjusting to the changes in the defense. A quarterback looks for his primary receiver. If he's covered, he looks for the secondary receiver. If his second choice also is not open and he has time, then he tries to throw to a third option. If a receiver doesn't appear open or the quarterback has no more time, then he steps forward and breaks out of the pocket. When he does this, the receivers know to adjust their patterns and he often buys more time to throw.

Tom Landry believed he could gamble and infuse Paul Hackett's philosophies into the Cowboy offense in 1986 because he had a very intelligent and experienced quarterback in Danny White. Not only was White able to phase Hackett's system into the passing game, but he could also read specific defenses as Landry had taught him. So he became the leading passer in the NFC, and with the addition of Herschel Walker, Dallas had a 6–2 record at the halfway mark and seemed, once again, to be in position to make a strong move for the playoffs. But White suffered a broken wrist against the New York Giants. His replacement, Steve Pelluer, didn't have enough experience and continually had problems operating with the new system. Walker and Tony Dorsett suffered injuries, and Dallas fell apart, finishing 7–9.

"The first year Coach Landry and I would talk, and we had a blend of our philosophies on offense," recalled Hackett. "But Pelluer's ability to run the passing game really tested me. I think from that point when Danny got hurt and Pelluer came in we began to slide back to what the Cowboys had done in the past."

Even in the second year, Hackett had some input in the play calling. But his role finally diminished even more, and then Landry met with him.

"I think it's best for us to move back to what we've done and been successful with in the past," Landry suggested. "I want to go back to using what has always been the heart of our offense."

"Instead of being the guy with the ideas and the one who was going to instigate the game plans and that sort of thing," said Hackett, "I became a tutor of the quarterbacks, trying to teach them Landry's system.

"Mine was no longer a role of ideas and orchestration. It was, Hey, you've got to handle the quarterback situation and get them playing as well as you can. But there were no surprises. He was up-front with me."

Schramm also had influence in the hiring of Jim Erkenbeck to replace the retiring Jim Myers in 1987. Actually, he had tried to hire Los Angeles Rams offensive line coach Hudson Houck in 1986 to assist Myers for a year and then take over his job, but at the last minute Houck decided to stay with the Rams. Erkenbeck had done a good job with the New Orleans Saints and brought with him some new techniques for the Cowboy linemen. Certainly, with the larger linemen and new ideas, the blocking improved. Erkenbeck and Hackett were very close.

Hackett has a tremendous ego and was terribly disappointed that what had seemed a promising situation turned to dust. Landry also received a couple of phone calls from people he knew in the league warning him that the word was going around that Hackett was doing a lot of second-guessing and wasn't acting like the most loyal of assistants. Erkenbeck's name also was mentioned by one source. There was a clear division on the staff. Some of Landry's older assistants believed the rumors were fact.

After receiving one of the calls, Landry called a meeting of his assistants. Among the things he said was, "One of the best attributes of an assistant coach is loyalty."

"I think some of us didn't particularly like what had been going on," said Stautner. "Tom was the head coach and certainly had the right to do what he wanted. But for a while he'd begun to listen to Paul and Jim a lot. And here we were, the guys who had been with him so long, with loyalty that was never in question."

Stautner admitted he was very bitter when Landry demoted him after the 1988 season and hired George Hill to coach the line and be defensive coordinator, although he said he'd get over it. With a year left before retirement, Stautner was given a job in special projects.

"I should have seen it coming because he had stopped taking my suggestions during the season," continued Stautner. "When he fired me he just said he felt the team needed to go a different direction and Hill was coming in to use more of the 3–2 defense.

"I think Tom had lost some respect from some of us when he'd given up some of his authority and allowed Tex to bring in Hackett and get rid of Shofner."

Another source in the organization said that obviously both Hackett and Landry had superegos but if you did something out of your way for Tom he would thank you, whereas Hackett would often either forget or not bother to.

After the 1988 season, Landry demoted Hackett to special projects and hired Jerry Rhome to coach the quarterbacks. Again sources said Hackett was, in effect, fired from the staff. His quest for a head coaching job in the NFL was stymied. He was asked if he was bitter.

"After I recovered from the shock, I realized I wouldn't trade the three years working for Coach Landry for anything. I don't think you can compare him to anybody. I think he stands alone.

"There are very few coaches who do all that he did. He ran the whole team, the defense and the offense. It was really incredible the way he had the whole team in a meeting and could critique both the offense and the defense. He's so unique. His capacity and depth of understanding of the whole game is incredible.

"To work under Bill Walsh and Tom Landry has improved me in terms of what I have to teach and what I have to give to anyone at any level. I was fortunate. Being with Coach Landry was definitely a good learning period for me."

Schramm obviously believed bringing in Hackett to infuse new ideas was what the team needed. It looked as if it was going to work for a while, but in the end, it didn't. Some said Hackett wasn't loyal. Some thought Pelluer had been so schooled in the Landry system that he had too much trouble changing. Others suggested that in the end Landry just felt comfortable with the way he'd always done things and was too stubborn to accept change, forgetting that he had at least tried.

EARLY ON A JULY MORNING in 1985, Tom Landry greeted me in his room in the dormitory that housed the coaches and the club officials during training camp at California Lutheran in Thousand Oaks, California. He soon would go to an early meeting and then to morning practice, and so he was very busy. But I was doing a magazine story, and he took time to talk to me.

A group headed by H. R. "Bum" Bright had purchased the team from an ailing Clint Murchison Jr., and there was somewhat of a different feeling in the air. Murchison had always been the owner, and so there had been a great feeling of security. But that had changed. The same top people were still in place, with Schramm the president and general manager who ran the organization, Landry the head coach, and Gil Brandt ruling the scouting aspects.

Landry did not seem at all uneasy but, rather, just matter-of-fact as he discussed the situation and his relationship with Schramm.

Few people were more different than Tom Landry and Tex Schramm. And, yet, they worked very successfully together all those many years and the dividends were the club's great accomplishments. Landry's priorities, in order, were God, family, and football. Schramm's were football, football, and family. Landry certainly was very competitive and always wanted and tried his best to win under the rules and guidelines of his life as a Christian. He believed God wants a person to do his very best, and he always tried. But defeats did not linger with him or tear him apart inside. That is why he was able to coach in a highly pressurized, competitive situation for twenty-nine years with the Dallas Cowboys, whereas ulcers, alcohol, and other tension- and nerve-related problems took their toll on his contemporaries.

Schramm was just the opposite. To him, losses were like death, and they gnawed and lingered with him, often keeping him up half the night. Schramm was often profane and loudly vocal about his feelings, whereas Landry usually remained reserved and you could count on your fingers the number of profane words he used the last twenty years of his career. They did not think alike or feel alike, and the only time they ever socialized was during some official functions and when they used to go fishing together on Murchison's island, Spanish Cay, in the Bahamas.

"We have no relationship outside of football, but we have been able to work together successfully," Landry once commented. "Tex is obsessed with the NFL and with the Cowboys winning. Because of this,

his whole life pattern is turned in that direction. Remember, so much depends on how you see things and the life you live. I look at things differently because I'm a Christian and under God's command. Winning or losing a football game doesn't have that lingering effect on me because of this. If my life depended on the Cowboys winning and being successful, I'm sure I'd get outraged just like Tex does. Your priorities cause you to act a certain way.

"Tex has extremely strong feelings and is very outspoken about the way he feels regarding our place in history. It doesn't mean that much to me. People are always asking me how I want to be remembered, and, honestly, I have no feelings about that whatsoever. I enjoy the challenge, and I enjoy seeing young men become successful and, if I can, helping them in that direction."

Landry said he was certainly aware of and had seen Schramm's explosive temper but had not, as well as he could recall, ever been directly the target of it.

"His temper passes, and he doesn't think about it a lot after that. But the residue might be tough for some people. Sure, I'm a Christian and it [Schramm's use of profanity] bothers me, but I could say that about a lot of our players too. But being around Tex I know it's just part of his speech pattern, not meant to be taken literally much of the time. That's the pattern of speech in much of our society today. People often really don't know what they're saying, what the words mean. It's just a way for them to express things.

"God is forgiving, and everybody has the potential of going to heaven. He has to be for somebody like me to have a chance. When Jesus was on earth He didn't associate with believers but with sinners. Now, I'm not saying I do that. I'm just saying as a Christian you have to be open to any person, regardless of whether they have religious beliefs or not, because they have the possibility of becoming Christians."

⌣∴⌣

IT WAS NOT ALWAYS BEYOND Tex Schramm to play upon Tom Landry's beliefs, especially when he felt he had to make a strong point. Years ago Landry was not particularly happy with the way the Cowboy cheerleaders dressed and some of their sexy routines. He did not volunteer his feelings on the matter, but when interviewed by a magazine and asked about the cheerleaders, he did say what he thought. Landry visualized cheerleaders as they had been in his time. They did not wear such revealing outfits or do such routines.

The magazine quoted him as saying he didn't think the cheerleaders were particularly "wholesome"-looking on the sidelines and they distracted from the game. Tom did not mean to raise a fuss, but it was about that same time that the organization was mounting litigation to stop the pornographic movie *Debbie Does Dallas* from being shown in the city because the star of the movie was supposed to be a Dallas Cowboy cheerleader.

"What the other side will say is that even you admit our cheerleaders aren't wholesome, that they are pornographic-looking," Schramm told him.

Tex had a copy of the movie and asked Landry to please come to his office. When Tom got there, Schramm started showing the film. Landry watched for all of three seconds, got up, and left the room. "That," said Schramm, "is not wholesome."

"I've said all along that that was his responsibility," Landry later said. "But I can disagree and have my own moral code. Within the scope that they work, they try their best to create a good image. Everybody has to understand I love the people involved, and I'm not being critical. I never wanted to stop anything, but I just felt there might be a better way to have a good influence."

LANDRY HAD A RULE in training camp that people who were on the sidelines during practice sessions must wear their shirts. So many would take their shirts off, trying to get some sun, but Landry believed, considering all the fans who came to watch the Cowboys practice, that it would just be more proper for everybody to keep their shirts on.

One day he looked down from his coaching tower and saw a man on the sidelines with his shirt off. Landry didn't recognize the guy from a distance but used his bullhorn to remind him of the rules.

The man, embarrassed, quickly put his shirt back on. The man was Tex Schramm.

AFTER SCHRAMM had initiated the hiring of Hackett and Erkenbeck had also joined the staff, he was asked his feelings about Tom Landry at that particular stage of his career.

"His success speaks for itself," Schramm said. "Sure, over the years I've been like a lot of people. I'd look down on the field and second-guess some of his decisions. But in the long run I'd usually find out what he did was right.

"At this time I think Tom is doing the same thing I am, fighting age. I can last longer than he can because, in my job, I don't have to direct what goes on on the field, making split-second decisions like he does. But I just believe that there isn't anybody who can be as sharp in so many areas when he's in his sixties as when he was in his forties. Of course, you often can offset any shortcomings that occur with age by knowledge and experience. I suppose the great proof of that is that we have so many presidents in their sixties or, as in Reagan's case, their seventies.

"Still, there is a time when somebody in Tom's position just isn't as innovative or as pliable as when he was younger, and it becomes more difficult to devote all the time to the job that's needed. So you have to get outstanding assistants to take some of the burden off. Look at Paul ["Bear"] Bryant. He had great assistants and continued to coach well into his late sixties.

"I just believed Tom needed to bring in some young chargers to go with the more experienced guys on his staff. If you notice, that's what I do in my capacity. I try to continually bring up younger people so I can get their input, hear their ideas, and get a different perspective."

Schramm actually seemed to end up with more power when Bright took controlling ownership of the club. It had been unspoken knowledge of many in the Cowboy organization that Murchison's health was obviously on the decline in the early 1980s. As mentioned earlier, when he knew he couldn't go on, he charged Schramm to find an owner who might carry on the tradition of the Cowboys, keeping things as they were. He told Schramm that he was suffering from a degenerative nerve disease that caused speech and equilibrium problems. Pneumonia would complicate and compound the disease, and Murchison would die in May 1987. Knowing of his bad health, his creditors called in all his loans before he died, and he ended up declaring bankruptcy. However, prior to selling the team, he raised Schramm's salary to $400,000 and gave him a $2.5 million bonus. He gave Landry a $2 million bonus and Brandt $500,000. Schramm, in turn, raised Landry's salary to $650,000 and Brandt's to $225,000. Landry's salary was raised again by Schramm to nearly $1 million annually when he signed a three-year contract in 1987.

WHEN WE TALKED THAT DAY in his room at training camp, Landry recalled that stability was one of the keys to the organization's success and that it had begun with Murchison when the organization was first formed.

"Clint believed in putting people in charge and leaving them alone to do their job," he said. "Tex felt the same way after his experiences with the Rams."

(During his ten years with the Rams, Schramm had often seen players go over the head of the coach to try to talk owner Dan Reeves into firing him. There were never clear lines of authority.)

"So we always had clearly defined lines of responsibility. Nobody would go over me in regard to anything that had to do with the team we put on the field.

"Clint was a unique person. When he gave me that ten-year contract [1964] nobody had ever done anything like that before in sports. . . . Clint always knew things were going to get better, no matter how bad they looked. When you have an owner like that, it just makes you want to do a good job."

When I got up and walked to the door, Landry followed and added, "You can't tell what might have happened with the new owners. Bum Bright didn't get where he is by taking care of everybody along the way. He's a tough cookie, and I don't know what pressures might be exerted on somebody like Tex if, say, we ended up going six and ten this year. I don't think it'll happen, but it seems almost inevitable that it will sooner or later because of all the winning seasons we've had."

He then mentioned that even his job might not be safe after a string of losing years, which on that day in 1985 seemed so unlikely.

"You're not serious," I argued. "You don't really think anybody would fire you after what you've done all these years?"

"Well," he said, smiling, "if you have some losing seasons, you never know what will happen."

This certainly proved true. But no matter whether he was winning or losing, or even if he was fired, Landry's legend in a town in the Rio Grande Valley would never change.

CHAPTER 6
Mission, Texas

~:~

We value Tom Landry not just for the great success he had but for the example he set for young people here. We're proud of the kind of man he was, for his ideals, the way he conducted himself with class and dignity and his high behavioral standards. There don't seem to be many in sports that disply those characteristics now.

—JUNE BRANN
Publisher, Editor, the Mission Progress Times

SHORTLY AFTER MIDDAY Tony Guerrero was thumbing through high-school scrapbooks as he sat in the den of his home in the Sharyland section of west Mission. He was looking at clippings and pictures of his schoolboy classmate Tom Landry when he suddenly paused and looked through the glass doors onto the patio. The patio was a stone's throw to a green on the municipal golf course, where orange groves stood when he was a youngster. As he stared onto the patio, he could almost see Tom out there resting after they'd played golf. Finally, Tony said, "He sat in that chair right out there. We had an ice chest of soft drinks, but he liked lemonade so that's what he got."

Tony, seventy-five, a teacher and golf instructor, laughed and said the only thing he could beat Tom in was golf. "My handicap was two, so I tried to spot him some strokes. But he wouldn't have it. I'd make a good putt and he'd say, 'Boy, you were lucky to make that one.'"

He became quiet, chuckled at the memory of their games, and said Tom must have been on that patio five or six years ago in one of his infrequent visits to Mission. Tony then became a little sad and said, "Some people have asked me why I didn't go to Tom's funeral in Dallas. I just tell them I wanted to remember Tom sitting out there on that patio and not see him flat on his back."

WHEN TOM LANDRY DIED, local citizens attended memorial services in his honor at the First United Methodist Church. They also came to the huge, block-long mural that depicts Landry's career. It's located in the heart of downtown on Tom Landry Boulevard where it intersects Conway and has become a kind of shrine. People have left flowers and have taped cards, notes, and poems on the wall.

"Five days after his death, I counted thirty-two people across the street looking at the mural," said Gen Long. "They just needed a place to go to honor him." Gen, who serves on the city council, and her husband, Bill, commissioned artist Manuel Hinojosa to create the mural on the side of the building they owned. Bill is a pilot who got his training in Mission. Gen and Bill had lived in various places, the last of which was Vancouver, Canada. But Bill remembered how much he liked Mission, and he'd always been a Dallas Cowboy fan. So they'd moved to Mission fifteen years earlier and opened Long Enterprises.

"This country needs more heroes like Tom Landry that we use as a positive example to young people," said Bill.

"We saw a lot of murals when we were living in Vancouver," said Gen. "Unlike Bill, I'm not a very big sports fan, but I am a Tom Landry fan. We admired him as a person, the good things he'd done. So we decided to get a mural made to honor him and remind people about his life."

The mural pictures Landry's life. It shows him at Mission High School, at the University of Texas, as a U.S. Air Force pilot during World War II, and as a player with the New York Giants. Of course it mostly depicts his career with the Dallas Cowboys. Hinojosa researched the project, and then it took him almost a year to finish it in the fall of 1995. Visitors from around the country and Canada, England, and Spain have stopped to see the mural.

"A woman called from Arkansas to ask about the mural," said Gen. "We talked for a while, and she said she was only ashamed of one person from her state. I said, 'You mean President Clinton.' 'No,' she said, 'Jerry Jones for firing Tom Landry.'"

Local citizens are very protective of the mural of their favorite son. "You see a lot of graffiti around here," said Gen. "But nobody has touched the Landry mural except once. Mission beat La Joya. Kids from there threw paint on the mural. Within seconds the fire engine was cleaning it up. The police picked up the kids the next day."

In September 1995, four months after Lisa died, Tom and Alicia were in Mission for the official dedication of the mural. Bill and Tom were standing across the street admiring the mural. "There's old stone-face," said Landry. "That's what I've been told," said Bill.

⌣∴∾

MISSION MIGHT HAVE REMAINED one of those small towns philosophically tied to the past and thus overlooked by the present and future. Fifteen years before the new millennium, many downtown stores were vacant, boarded up. Some old-timers were slow to change, wondering just why they would need a new Penney's or Sears and figuring if a new airport came in, the planes would make too much noise. But the city fathers realized the future was now.

The narrow main street, Conway, was widened to four lanes in 1989. Where downtown was once the site of small family businesses like the Sam Nixon Barber Shop, now the main section of town is buzzing with banks and chain stores. Nearby U.S. 83 Freeway goes west through McAllen and Mission before veering north toward Laredo. Traffic is heavy with truckers and motorists bringing business to shopping centers, drawn magnetically toward the freeway and to the downtown district.

The snowbirds, the winter Texans, have always come to Mission, but nothing like they do now. The city has its agriculture, its citrus, but the winter Texans and the city's proximity to McAllen have been key reasons for its prosperity. Residents of McAllen, with a population of more than one hundred thousand, find it more convenient to commute the short distance from Mission than from the north side of McAllen. Winter visitors have always come to the Rio Grande Valley, and many stay in Mission. Now upward of one hundred thousand visit the Valley, with Mission getting its share. Some visitors even stay six months, meaning they can vote. The city once boasted only that it was the "Home of the Grapefruit," and now it also claims to be the "Tourist Mecca of South Texas." There are now seventy-two parks for recreational vehicles and four golf courses, and you can buy everything from what you want to what you should not have.

With the proximity of Mexico and the sister town of Reynosa, there has always been a large Hispanic migration and dominance, but never has it been more in evidence. Whereas in Tom Landry's youth the Hispanic-Anglo ratio was 50-50, now Mission, located in Hidalgo County, which is named after Miguel Hidalgo y Costillo, the famous Mexican leader, is 93 percent Hispanic.

The endless wildflowers and orchards that once dominated the area are no longer as profuse as they once were because of construction and the great influx of agriculture where farming is good on the rich, sandy loam. But the beauty is still there, if more confined—the palm trees and the Spanish daggers and multicolored wildflowers and poinsettias of spring and the bougainvillea of summer. The most ambitious project in the city's history is the six-thousand-acre development in the city's southeast city limits, including a huge sports center. The older residents won't have anything to do with Jerry Jones since he fired Tom Landry. The new blood wants the Cowboys to have training camp in the new complex.

Mission certainly has spawned its share of dignitaries and celebrities, such as Congressmen Eligio "Kiki" de la Garza and Joe Kilgore and nearby rancher Lloyd Bentsen and his son, the senator who would have been vice president had George Bush not defeated Michael Dukakis. William Jennings Bryan once had a house in Mission, and cowboy movie star Ken Maynard was born there. But the presence most felt, the name of which the city is most proud, is easily Thomas Wade Landry. The local high school football stadium is named after him, and he had many generations of friends in Mission, some with whom he grew up and perhaps others whom he had never met.

Sure, Mission has changed forever, but the old Border Theater of Landry's time is still operating, and along the main drag you can still find an elderly gentleman, sitting in a chair.

~:~

TOM LANDRY GREW UP in a small-town America that will never exist again. It was a more slow-moving time, a time when the family unit seemed more closely knit, a time of endless pickup sports games in parks or vacant lots, which always seemed to be nearby, a time of five-cent sodas and ten-cent movies and hamburgers. It was a time of iced tea and lemonade being sipped on the porch, of oscillating fans and open windows and treasuring cool breezes in hot summers. Actually, it didn't seem as hot then. But it was. You just didn't know it because you weren't addicted to air conditioning. You drove cars with big curving fenders over narrow two-lane roads and read Burma shave signs:

The Answer To . . . A Maiden's Prayer
. . . Is Not A Chin . . . Of Stubby Hair.

And there were gatherings at the corner drugstore's soda fountain and comic books and pulp magazines on the rack and Saturday-afternoon movies, preceded by serials that drew you back each week so you could keep up with the next exciting adventure. There were swimming holes and pools and a recreation building at which to gather. Movie stars were prettier, more handsome, and heroes were brave, honest, clean-cut, and fair because, if they really weren't, we willed them to be.

There was a great fascination with airplanes, the war heroes, and the trick pilots and barnstormers, personified in Mission by Slats Rogers, who was likely to drop out of the sky at just any time and do a few twists and turns for anybody who might be willing, or unwilling, to watch. Slats even got into trouble once in Dallas when he flew his plane too low on a downtown street.

People seemed to have more time to talk and listen. And a popular meeting place in Mission for friends and neighbors, and just about everybody was your friend and neighbor, was a vacant lot on Conway. You had to get there early on Saturdays to find a place to park. Everybody would sit on the fenders of their cars or bring folding chairs and talk about the citrus crop, rain, politics, the local high-school football team, and that war in Europe. But the war was so far away where the small, animated man with the funny mustache was running amok in Europe and those seeking power at all costs were gaining influence in Japan. They did not know that the war was not that far away.

Besides, things were on the upswing. The Depression had come, faded, and gone with the leadership of President Franklin Delano Roosevelt, a fuzzy picture in the newspaper and a voice mixed with static on the radio.

Ah, the radio, that magic cathedral-shaped box that made you use your imagination because you furnished your own pictures. You could hear the news, music, Amos and Andy, Fibber McGee and Molly, dramas, and soap operas and adventures for the youngsters.

Tom Mix . . . a daring crusader for justice and owner of the T–M Bar Ranch in Dobie township. Straight shooters brought you action, mystery, and mile-a-minute thrills in radio's biggest Western detective program. . . .

"Mission is a place of a lot of fond memories for me," Landry said when they named the high-school football field after him in 1984, an event for which President Ronald Reagan sent a letter of congratulations. "I was fortunate growing up here when I did and to have a coach [Bob Martin] who had such high standards and values and taught us how to compete and to play."

As the late Andy Anderson, who worked at the local hardware store, once said, "You know, you get to thinking about those old days around here when Tommy was growing up and . . . well, they don't seem so long ago."

～:～

THOMAS WADE LANDRY was born September 11, 1924, and grew up in a small frame house on Dougherty Street, a block off Conway, that had a yard in front and back and a vacant lot on one side. Now, in those days all the businesses—the grocery store, the barbershop, the clothing store, the movie theaters, the 5 & 10 cent store, the two drugstores, etc.—were lined on each side of Conway, and the residential areas began short blocks away in either direction. Mission had a population of about five thousand then, and everything seemed to be within walking distance.

This was especially true for Ray and Ruth Landry and their four children, Robert, Tommy, Ruthie, and Jack. Ray's automobile garage was on the street crossing Dougherty, and he could walk across the alley and be at work. And the First United Methodist Church, which the Landrys attended regularly, was little more than half a block away.

The house is still there, now with a greenish tint, and you can still see the room Ray built in the attic on the side of the house for Tom. The church has grown and greatly expanded from the original two-story building with the columns in front, and the place where Ray Landry had his garage has become the Mission Paint and Body Shop, operated by Ballestors and Sons.

Ray and Ruth Landry were well-liked people. He was superintendent of the Sunday school for twenty-seven years, and Ruth was always working in the church. Ray also served as chief of the town's volunteer fire department, a post he held for forty years until his retirement in

1973. People would always say if there was a drowning Ray was the first man in the boat and if there was a fire he was the first to climb up into the attic.

"He had a lot of trophies he'd won as a fireman," said Marvel Deen Rhodes, whose parents were close friends of Ray and Ruth. "After Ray and Ruth died, I had a lot of those trophies here in my house, but they wanted them for the Fireman's Hall of Fame in Arlington and I let them go."

"My father was a fine man, a great man," recalled Tom Landry. "I can remember him feeding his family on a dollar fifty a day during the Depression. But we always had enough to eat, and our parents always loved us and cared what we did. And I can't ever remember when we didn't go to church. It was something we always did, something I grew up doing.

"But I don't think I really became a true Christian until much later in my life, after I had joined the New York Giants. I just went to church because my parents always did and took us with them."

After Tom Landry had become famous, had coached his team to a Super Bowl championship, June Brann wrote in the *Progress Times*, "Tom's a fine man, but he has a way to go to fill his daddy's shoes."

⌒∴⌒

RAY LANDRY'S FATHER, Alfred, was born in Bourbonnais, Illinois, one of six children of Canadians Stanislas and Marceline (Trembley) Landrie (the spelling was later changed to Landry). The family apparently originated in France and migrated to Canada, where Stanislas, called Stani, was born in San Leon, also one of six children. Stani came to the United States and at the age of nineteen served in Company B of the Wisconsin regiment in the Civil War. He was a lumberman and farmer by trade.

Alfred, or Fred as they called him, married Lillian Celena Anderson, whose father was Scotch-Irish and whose mother was French, in 1893. At that time he spoke mostly French and was taught English by his wife. The family settled in Illinois, and the difficult winters took their toll as two of their six children died.

A family doctor advised Fred to leave Bradley, Illinois, and move his family to a warmer climate. His son Ray, born November 17, 1898, was having terrible bouts with muscular rheumatism, and fearing for the child's health, the Landrys signed on with the McColl Land and Development Company and moved to Mission in February 1912. Fred purchased a small piece of land near Mission but later moved into town and became a bricklayer.

During the train trip south, the family kept singing, "It never rains in Texas," but they arrived in Mission during a downpour, somewhat shocked. However, the weather soon cleared and stayed warm, and Ray never had any problems again with his rheumatism. The warm, healthy climate was just what he needed.

Ray's father, Fred, was a very devout Christian. Once he caught Ray, then in his teens, smoking with a friend behind the barn. Ray felt the wrath of God was about to descend on him, but his father, speaking softly, said, "If a man's going to smoke he shouldn't sneak around to do it. Come on into the house and smoke with me."

They went into the house, and Fred pulled out a box of his favorite cigars. He lit up, took a big puff, and urged his son to do the same. Ray obliged. "Take a deep, deep puff," said his father, "and then another." Ray did. "That's good," said his father. "Now once again." Ray's grin vanished and he turned gray and ran for the bathroom. He was very sick. But he never smoked again, and the example he set carried over to his son Tommy.

Ray was a good, natural athlete who distinguished himself as a fine pitcher and football player and was also an outstanding debater. He was easygoing and smiled a lot, and his classmates called him "Happy." He also managed to distinguish himself with a young girl named Ruth Coffman, who had long braids of auburn hair, ending in curls. Ruth was born January 5, 1899, in Haymaker Town, Virginia, to Benjamin and Banona Spencer Vandergrift. Her father, a farmer, moved his family from Tennessee to Oklahoma, and finally, to Mission in 1915.

Ruth was a much more serious and reserved person than Ray. She was a top student, sang in the glee club, and upon graduation, was valedictorian of her class. "Once they started dating in high school, neither of them ever dated anybody else," the late Viola Bourgeois, Ray's sister, once recalled.

Ray was graduated from Mission High in 1918 and went to Texas A&M. Ruth was graduated a year later, and her family moved to Los Angeles, California. Ray, who couldn't stand the thought of being away from her, soon went to California, where he took a mechanic's course and worked for a while. On May 8, 1920, they were married and moved back to Mission, where they would live for the remainder of their lives.

When Tommy was a child, he idolized his father and wanted to be around him constantly. He would hate to see his father leave the house and often would sit and watch for his return, running out to greet him. Once Ray Landry had just gotten back from a hunting trip and parked his car across the street from his house.

Tommy rushed out of the house and across the street without looking. He was struck by a car. "Fortunately, the driver of the car was going slow or he'd probably have killed Tommy," said Viola Bourgeois. "It did break his leg. I was outside in another car, and Ray leaped out of his car and ran to get Tommy. We rushed him to the doctor."

Things were somewhat more primitive in those days. Ray and a friend held Tommy while the doctor pulled on his leg until it snapped back into place. "Tommy would scream and Ray would just about pass out," recalled Ms. Bourgeois. "He'd have to let me take his place and go outside and lie down. But when Tommy saw his father leaving, he'd become more upset and Ray would have to come right back in. I never knew Ray to be squeamish before or after that, but he just couldn't stand to see his little boy suffering so much."

When Tommy first began to talk, he had a lisp, and the Murdock brothers, who ran the corner service station, loved to hear him talk. They had a lemon tree in back of the station and often would invite Tommy there to have lemonade. One day they were making lemonade and gave Tommy a dime and told him to go buy some sugar. Soon, he came back very upset and said the man at the store wouldn't give him any "tuga." So they wrote down the word *sugar* on a piece of paper and sent him back to the store. His parents didn't like people teasing him about the lisp, and aware of this, Tommy was very shy.

"Ruth was a beautiful woman with very striking eyes," said Wade Spillman, a lifelong friend of Tom who once dated his sister, Ruthie. "But she was the strong, silent type. She expected things to be done and done properly. I guess when Tommy and I were growing up I was over at their house every day at one time or another. The impression I had was that Ruth was the disciplinarian and Ray was the looser, more outgoing type . . . just a real friendly, lovable guy.

"There wasn't a great outward show of affection in the family, but they felt it. You could tell they loved one another."

But Ruth did let her guard down at times. "I remember after Tommy was coaching the Cowboys," said Viola Bourgeois, "that this television fellow came and interviewed Ruth. He asked her if she ever got excited watching the games. She said no, that she stayed calm.

"Well, after the feller left, I looked at Ruth and laughed. 'Why didn't you tell him how you yell and jump up and down watching the Cowboys on television?' I asked her. She just kinda grinned and blushed."

"Both those Landry women were very sweet people," said longtime Mission resident Joe Summers. "And you can't say enough about Ray. When Tommy and I were in elementary school, the schools were segregated, with the Anglos going one place and the Mexican-American kids the other. When they decided to put all the kids together, Ray Landry was one of the people for it. He had no prejudices. He worked with and for the Mexican-Americans. Those times were different, you know . . . I don't know if it was so much people were prejudiced against other races or that they were just used to things being a certain way. Some argued and discussed it, but people like Ray Landry and some other people here got it done . . . got all the kids going to the same schools. People see a lot of both his parents in Tom Landry."

All the Landry children were very popular in school and grew up loving sports and the outdoors. Ray would take the boys fishing and hunting, and Ruthie, who became a nurse, was intelligent and dependable like her mother. She also loved to play softball and swim and would later develop an interest in golf. Jack also liked sports and fishing but could never measure up in sports to his older brother Tommy.

Robert, three years older than Tommy, was the first to gain some notoriety for the Mission High Eagles. "I was probably closer to Robert than Tommy," Eddie Hedges, now deceased, once said. "Robert was just a year older than I was. Robert was an end, and I don't think he ever dropped a pass. He was a tall, lanky kid with glue on his hands. When he was little, Tommy used to hang around Robert and the older kids a lot and play ball with them, and he'd also play with the kids his own age. Everybody was always playing some game."

"Our playground was the entire town," Tom Landry recalled. "We'd get together on a vacant lot and play all the games without any organization, except what we did ourselves. We took a lot of bumps, but we learned. And there was no pressure. I think kids these days miss that type of thing. It's all so organized now, and so many of the parents and coaches of the kids put pressure on them. I was never pressured to play ball. It was just something I grew up doing."

"Tommy and some of the rest of us would meet and play football on a vacant lot," Don Albrecht, who died in 1995, once recalled. "I mean, there was no touch football. We didn't have pads, but we'd play tackle. You always got bruised and scratched up a little, but it made you tougher."

"Tommy was the leader, even then," said Joe Summers, "before we even got to high school. We'd choose up sides. There was always somebody who couldn't play much. A kid might be too little or just not very good, and nobody would pick him for their side. A lot of guys would tell that kid to go on, just leave us alone. Not Tommy. I can remember he'd say, 'Let him play on my side.' Then he'd take the kid aside and say, 'You can play. You can do it. Don't let them tell you any different. You can always play on my team.'

"After Tommy got to high school and became a big star, I was on the B-team. We were just kind of fodder for the varsity. But to this day I remember how it jarred me one time when I tackled him. It jarred me from my toes to my teeth."

Dorothy Hedges and Marvel Deen Rhodes, whose maiden name was Dooley, both remember Tommy being shy around the girls. "But he was friendly," said Dorothy. "Everybody liked him, but even after we were finishing high school, he didn't date too much. Sports were just his life. He was just quiet and reserved, but everybody liked him."

"He was shy, but he didn't mind kidding me about this boyfriend I had," said Ms. Rhodes. "And he was very competitive even when he was a little boy. I always wanted to beat him in something, but it was difficult.

"The big treat for us kids was going to the coast. It was difficult to get to South Padre Island [some seventy miles away], so we went to Boca Chica. After church our parents, who always ran around together, would pack a picnic lunch and put everybody in the car, and off we'd go. We'd go into the ocean and swim and then come out and eat fried chicken and sand. We'd go back home exhausted but happy.

"Tommy and I have remained friends all these many years. Anytime I've ever needed him he was there . . . when my husband died or anytime. One time I went to Dallas with some other teachers and Tommy met us at the airport and took us out to Cowboy headquarters. Then we went to his house for dinner.

"Once Tommy and my husband, Sonny, were playing golf and Alicia and I were watching in a separate cart. Tommy was driving his cart and looked back at us and rammed right into another one. We all had a big laugh. I think he might have laughed harder than anybody."

"You know," Don Albrecht, a high-school teammate of Landry, said, "I used to get into a little mischief now and then. Nothing serious like you hear of nowadays. But I never can remember Tommy ever getting into a fight."

"He never had to fight," said Joe Summers. "He never rubbed anybody wrong and even the bullies wouldn't pick on him. He was a pretty good-sized kid and could be very . . . well, firm."

"Tommy and I were alike in those days," remembered Wade Spillman. "We didn't take to escapades much at all. I was there, and I give you my word Tommy just wasn't the type to get into trouble. No . . . nobody had much money, but we made a little here and there, doing odd jobs. We used to pick up some money caddying. I guess that's where we learned how to play golf, caddying for those guys on the weekends. Tommy also had a job sweeping out and cleaning up this business after football practice."

"I know we dreamed a lot," recalled Landry. "Our idols were the cowboy stars and Tarzan. We lived in a fantasy world when we were very young."

"I tell you Tommy was a good swimmer," said Albrecht. "We all used to go out to Crystal Waters Pool and swim a lot."

Tommy was on the swimming team with Eddie Hedges, Dorothy's husband. His sister, Ruth, was also on the team. "He was a great swimmer and diver," said Hedges, who winked and added, "but maybe I was a little better . . . at least in that. Tommy and I could stand on the three-meter board, face-to-face, and flip and hit the water at the same time. One of us would get the board to really bouncing, and we also could do a triple together off the board. It wasn't controlled, but we could do three flips together. Yeah, he was a fine swimmer, but now in football he was something else."

"Yes . . . I knew Tommy then and now," added Ms. Rhodes. "Of course, he was such a big star, and everybody was making over him. I certainly was proud of him but didn't think that much about it because Tommy was, well, just family."

HUMPHREY BOGART, Spencer Tracy, and Errol Flynn were popular, but the biggest box-office draw was ten-year-old Shirley Temple. And there was a movie, *Hollywood Hotel*, in which Ronald Reagan had a small part as a radio announcer, a job he'd actually held until leaving to seek fame and fortune in Hollywood. Kate Smith introduced over the radio a new Irving Berlin song, "God Bless America," and Orson Welles frightened the nation with his too-realistic broadcast of H. G. Welles's "War of the Worlds," making people indeed think that the Martians were coming. Joe Louis knocked out that German, Max Schmeling, avenging the only KO defeat of his career . . . and Hitler, who once had left Austria as a penniless artist, took over the government of that country as the Third Reich marched across Europe.

And that same year, 1938, Bob Martin came to Mission, Texas, where he would build one of the all-time great high-school football teams in the Valley. The key to his success was moving young Tommy Landry from center to quarterback-tailback in his junior year.

Martin, who died in 1982, had just graduated from South Texas Teachers College in San Marcos, where he'd captained the football team. The school, which is now known as Southwest Texas State, also numbered among its graduates Lyndon Baines Johnson. After Johnson became president, Martin was given to remark, "I'm the only guy who went to that school in San Marcos who wasn't President Johnson's roommate."

Martin, whose mother was Hispanic, also helped ease any prejudice in town because he was popular with the whole community. He was hired to coach the junior varsity team, composed of freshmen and sophomores. The first time he met with the team, he looked over the group of twenty-four boys and said firmly, "Boys, the first thing I need is somebody to take this football and initiate every play we make. We need a tough, smart kid."

A tall, lean freshman with clear, gray-green eyes stood up and said, "Coach, I'll do it." His name was Tommy Landry, but Martin started calling him "Tom" because it sounded tougher. The team did well and continued to do so when its nucleus became sophomores. As juniors, they would go to the varsity and have the entire town talking about them. Among the stars of that junior team were Landry, Don Albrecht, A. B. Ward, Jimmy Mehis, Darroll and Carroll Martin, Audencio Mungia, Arnaldo Vera, and Zelmo Hinojosa. Fans were talking about them as juniors, but when they became seniors they'd set high-school football in the Valley on fire.

Teammates called Arnaldo Vera "LaGrulla" because he was from a small community of the same name near Rio Grande City. His son later played basketball for the Pan American University team, and after the team had won a big game LaGrulla went to the airport in Brownsville to meet him. Tom Landry, who had been playing in a celebrity golf tournament in the border city, was also at the airport, and LaGrulla saw him and went over to say hello.

"Tommy, I bet you don't remember me," said LaGrulla.

Landry, who had not seen him in some forty years, smiled and said, "Of course I do, LaGrulla. How are you doing?"

Don and Margie Albrecht treasured Tom Landry's friendship and were always talking about what a fine person he was. They moved to Wichita Falls for a few years in the 1980s before relocating in Mission. They had a friend there, Mary Thomas, who practically worshiped Tom Landry. She would always say the reason she never married was that she was saving herself for Tom. When Mary became ill with cancer, the Albrechts wrote Tom about her. Landry wrote a nice letter to Mary, who in turn sent a note to the Albrechts thanking them:

Dear Margie and Don,

Needless to say, I was delirious with joy on receipt of the letter. I wish I could hug all three of you—you for relating to him my longtime devotion and him for taking time to write. You made my year,

Mary F. Thomas

It would be the last year of Mary's life.

⌣∴⌣

THE VARSITY COACH had been fired, and the school board filled the vacancy by moving Martin up from the junior varsity in 1940. As fate would have it, Martin lived in a garage apartment next door to the Landrys in the summer of 1940, and he started noticing that his center, Tom Landry, could throw the football. Ray had tied a rope through a tire and hung it from a tree. Tom spent hours throwing the football through the tire and also tossing it to his younger brother, Jack. "The kid had a good arm," said Martin. "He was growing tall, had some meat on him. I figured I needed me a quarterback and decided he'd be the one. So I moved Tommy there." In those days the term *quarterback* was interchangable with *tailback*. Instead of lining up under center, Landry took the snap in a deep position. Landry was both the primary passer and runner.

Back then, Texas high schools were either classified as A, for smaller schools, or AA, for the larger ones, and no overall state champion was determined in either classification. Regional was as far as a team could advance.

When Landry was a junior, the Eagles were 6–4, playing both A and AA schools, but the team won all its district games. Landry scored forty-six points and threw for a number of touchdowns, and his thirty-four-yard run set up the only touchdown in the 7–0 victory over Pharr, giving Mission the district title. But, although the Eagles gained more yardage, they lost to Alice, 7–6, in bi-district. Landry made the All-South Texas Team. Players went both ways then, so Landry also played safety on defense. And he called his own plays on offense.

In the "Who's Who" annual that year, it was written of Landry that the junior was an "attentive, diligent student, not only with brains but brawn. Handsome Tommy is 6'-0", 165 with brown hair and gray-green eyes. He makes average grades and was a two-year first team basketball player. He was active in H-Y, track, football and won the Sophomore Service Award, the highest honor. In 1939 he was voted the cutest boy in high school." In those days, Mission didn't have a high-school baseball program, but Landry distinguished himself as an outfielder on a semipro team. His friends believed that had he not been more interested in football than in baseball, he would have had a chance to become a baseball player.

What proved somewhat of a drawback for Landry was that, in his small school, students were pressed into participating in a lot of activities. His most embarrassing time came when he had the lead in a school play and was required to kiss a girl. He managed to pull it off as his teammates hooted in the audience.

✌ ⁝ ∿

BOB MARTIN HAD HIS DISTRICT TITLE, but he wasn't satisfied. He kept urging his players to try harder, to give more. He gave them a motto, "Eleven brothers are hard to beat." That Christmas, 1940, Martin also sent each team member a card that read:

> *You are the fellow who has to decide,*
> *Whether you'll do it or toss it aside;*
> *You are the fellow who makes up your mind,*
> *Whether you'll lead or linger behind;*
> *Whether you'll strive for the goal that's far,*
> *Or just be content to stay where you are.*
> *Take it or leave it! There's something to do!*
> *Just think it over [player's name was written in]*
> *It's all up to you.*

The German blitzkrieg had invaded Denmark, Norway, the Netherlands, Luxembourg, Belgium, and Czechoslovakia and had been joined by Japan and Italy in the Rome-Berlin Axis. A scientist named Albert Einstein had written President Roosevelt, who had been elected for a third term, about the feasibility of something called the "atomic bomb." People read John Steinbeck's *The Grapes of Wrath* and Ernest Hemingway's *For Whom the Bell Tolls*, and when the baseball season ended, people were talking about Ted Williams winning the batting title with a .406 average and about Joe DiMaggio's fifty-six-game hitting streak. And Hoagy Carmichael was still singing "Stardust."

Sure, sometimes adults talked about the Germans and Japanese and the fighting going on overseas . . . but it still seemed so . . . well, far away. They also talked about another "New Deal" by Roosevelt, and Bob Martin was saying that, although the Eagles never had gone past bi-district before, the season of 1941 was going to be a "New Deal."

Martin cracked down. "He was the kind of guy who'd give you three licks if you lost a sprint and two if you won," said Dr. J. M. Baker, who was a couple of years behind Landry in school but worked out with the 1941 team. Martin told them to stop drinking Cokes and forget the girls.

"I want your complete concentration," he said. "If I see any girls wearing your letter sweaters I want it to be your mothers or sisters."

That wasn't any problem for Tom Landry. He wasn't going to break any rules, but if he did, Coach Martin probably would have seen him. From where he lived, he could look out the window and see Tom coming home. The only way Tom could get to the bedroom his father had built him in the attic was to climb the stairs outside the house.

"Coach Martin," Landry would say, "I haven't got a chance. You can't check on the other guys, but you can see for yourself if I'm breaking curfew."

Landry would often go by Martin's apartment to talk football. Then he noticed a picture of a girl that was inscribed, "Love, Dorothy."

"Hey, Coach Martin, who's that?" asked Tom. "We're not supposed to have girls during the season."

"Why, Tom, that's just my sister."

"Now, Coach Martin, that's not true. It says 'love' on it."

"Why, Tom, my sister loves me too."

"I never did tell him any different," said Martin. "Then after the season he made the high-school all-star game in Abilene and I went there with him. Dorothy was there too, and Tom kept staring at her."

"Hey, Coach Martin, that's the girl in the picture," Tom said. Bob and Dorothy were soon married.

Mission was a unanimous choice by Valley sportswriters to win the district because it had five returning players who had made all-Valley the previous year, including Landry, Mehis, Albrecht, and Carroll Martin.

The '41 season opened with Mission beating Edinburg, 12–0, as Landry threw two touchdown passes of nineteen and fifty-five yards. The Eagles then ripped San Benito, 25–0, and Landry broke loose for touchdown runs of sixty-six and twenty yards and threw eighteen- and ten-yard touchdown passes in a 28–0 win over Raymondville.

"Tommy wasn't fast," said Martin, "but he was smart. He knew how to run, giving them the limp leg, picking his way. He also started on our basketball team, swam, played tennis, and ran track. He was on our relay team but not because he was so fast. We just didn't have anybody else."

"Maybe Tommy ran an 11.5 in the hundred or something like that," said Mehis. "But he'd put on all that heavy equipment we used to wear then and he'd still run an 11.5. Those boys who ran those 10.5's would put on that heavy equipment and couldn't catch him.

"And could he ever punt! He'd really send that football up into the sky. I was the center, and one time he kicked one sky-high that must have gone forty yards. I raced down and caught it on the fly. I was real proud of myself, and then they penalized us. I didn't know it was illegal to do that."

Mission beat Mercedes, 40–0, as Landry scored on runs of fifty-five and fifty-nine yards, and he tallied four of seven touchdowns, including runs of thirty-five, thirty-six, and sixty-four yards, as the Eagles over-whelmed Weslaco, 47–0.

The area press was full of news of Tom's exploits, calling him "Terrific Tommy Landry, a 6'–0", 170-pound back who can run, pass, punt with the best of them."

Sportswriter George Wright, in his column called "In This Corner," noted one day that some people around town were saying that Tommy Landry got all the praise. "There's been too much praise for Tommy Landry and not enough for the other lads on the club, say they," wrote Wright. "Well, we'll agree with them that not enough has been said for the other boys. But we'll hold out for the belief that Tommy has deserved everything said about him. We're going on the results obtained and from remarks passed by observers who know their stuff, including other coaches.

"We've heard some complimentary stuff about the boy from nearly every coach whose team has played the Eagles. Only reason we haven't heard from all of them is because we haven't talked with all of them about this particular matter. . . . And we repeat that we still think Tommy Landry, whose head hasn't swelled a bit despite the adulation, deserves every kind word written about him."

Old-timers in Mission are still talking about the sixth game that season, which was played in Donna. They say Mission had more fans there than Donna and people were calling the Eagles the "Totem Pole Eagles" and their fans the "Missionaries."

Landry threw a pass for one touchdown, and his forty-yard run set up another touchdown as Mission led, 12–0. Landry also had a sixty-yard touchdown run called back for clipping.

"It was Albrecht who clipped," said Mehis.

"It was Mehis who clipped," said Albrecht.

But Donna moved the ball deep into Eagle territory, and on third down a pass was thrown into the end zone. Interference was called on Landry, who played safety on defense, and an official awarded Donna a touchdown instead of putting the ball on the one-yard line.

Martin charged onto the field. "Get out of here!" said the official.

"You can't award a touchdown on a penalty!" yelled Martin. "They get the ball on our one-yard line!"

"I'm calling the game! Get off the field, or I'll give you a fifteen-yard penalty!"

"You can't do much more. You already gave them a touchdown!"

"Get off!"

"All right. But you'll be apologizing to me after the meeting on Monday."

Mission went on to win, 12–7. After the area officials had their weekly meeting on Monday, Martin received a call from the official. "You were right, Bob. I apologize. It was no touchdown."

"After Tom went on to become an All-Pro defensive back with the New York Giants, some of his former teammates on that Mission squad couldn't believe it," said Martin. "He was a tremendous offensive player, but some of them said all he did on defense was stand back there at safety with his hands on his hips. They said the opposition never got that far; the only tackle he ever made that year was on the interference call."

Before Mission played McAllen, a Class AA school, the fans there were saying that the Eagles were just a mediocre team without Tom Landry. This was hardly true, but Landry ran for touchdowns of thirty-four, nineteen, and forty-eight yards, and his thirty-seven-yard pass set up still another score in the 46–0 victory.

"The mornings after the games were great times," recalled Don Albrecht. "We'd meet there at the corner drugstore and let people lay the glory on us. Tommy would be there too, talking about the game. We might have a malt. Everybody else was having a Coke."

"We got a lot of stuff in those days," said Jimmy Mehis. "One drugstore would give us a free malt if we won, the other drugstore would give us something else. We also got letter jackets and sweaters, and a local cleaners would sometimes clean our stuff." He grinned and added, "Does that mean we were on the take?"

Many felt the Eagles' winning streak would end in the game against Harlingen, also a Class AA school. Landry took a hard blow just below his right eye in the first period. He launched a forty-six-yard punt that went out of bounds at the Harlingen four, which led to a safety and, on the exchange, set up an Eagle touchdown.

But the side of his face was swelling so badly that he had to leave the game after the first period. His father came down to the bench and asked, "Can I help?"

"Yessir," said Martin. "You can put ice on the boy's face. It looks pretty bad."

Martin later recalled, "That was the only time I ever remember Ray saying or doing anything to interfere with our team. And when he did, I needed the help. As a fireman he knew first aid."

Landry's cheekbone was fractured, and there was a question as to whether he'd be able to play the following week against LaFeria. But Martin designed a special headgear using two face masks, one upside down. Teammates were kidding Tom that he looked like the Masked Marvel. Landry played only the first period against LaFeria, but by the time he left the game he had scored both touchdowns in a 14–0 victory.

He also saw only limited action the following week against Pharr, a 34–0 win, but he was stunned, shocked, as was everybody else, at what happened. A substitute running back for Mission named Billy Brown broke loose from his own twelve and was on his way to a touchdown when Harvey Risinger, who played for Pharr, came off the bench and floored him with a body block. Risinger then crawled back off the field, but an official had seen him. Pharr was given a fifteen-yard penalty.

Mission had won its fourth district title and would go to Aransas Pass for the bi-district game. Everybody in Mission was talking about the Eagles, saying how they had a chance for the first time in history to win bi-district and make the coveted regional championship game. When the Eagles played a game, the town closed down.

Students began passing around petitions and staging impromptu pep rallies to try to get school officials to turn out classes early on Friday so they could go to the game. They also wanted the businesses to close down early. They succeeded, and a special train, called the "Eagle Special," was chartered to take some three hundred fans to the game. The stands were filled.

The week of the game, the Lions Club had its annual banquet. Martin and some of his players made speeches. Landry, who had scored 111 points, stood up and talked about the team's strategy. He was named cocaptain of the team and picked by his teammates as the "Best Sport" and "Most Valuable Player." Fans gave Martin a new Chevrolet, which had a sticker price of $906.00.

～∴～

TOM LANDRY'S MAIN INTEREST was, of course, football. But he also made the National Honor Society as a senior and was president of his class. But even after football season had ended and Martin deemed it allowable, Landry didn't date that much, although he did go out with girls such as Coleen "Toodles" Bishop and Odie Dobbs.

"In the first place, it was kind of difficult to date," recalled Spillman. "None of the kids had their own cars then, and if your parents had a car, it was awfully hard to borrow. Tom was a big, good-looking guy, and so naturally all the girls were after him. When he'd go out, it usually would be with the best-looking girl. But, no, he wasn't setting the world on fire as far as girls were concerned."

Schoolmates recalled Landry would go to dances but, mostly, stand to the side and talk. He also did some singing in school, but Albrecht, who had his own group called Don Albrecht's Swingsters, noted, "Frankly, Tommy had the worst singing voice of anybody in school. Just awful. I think that's about the only thing he couldn't do well." Landry agreed, admitting he often just moved his lips without singing.

When Ruth Landry finally received the news that her son had made the National Honor Society, she asked him why he hadn't mentioned it to his parents.

"Well," said Tom, "you always taught me to do my best and not brag about it. All I was doing was my best."

His parents seldom heard him talk about his exploits on the football field either. They either saw them firsthand, heard about them from friends, or read about them in the Valley newspapers.

‿∴∾

MISSION BEAT ARANSAS PASS, 19–0, in that bi-district game, and a newspaper account of the contest noted, "The Eagles were sparked by one-hundred-seventy-pound tailback Tommy Landry, who ran and, when slowed down, passed, and whose toe kept the Eagles in good field position." Landry scored all three touchdowns, going over from the four and the thirty-eight, and, late in the game, ran through what was said to be the entire Aransas Pass team for a seventy-six-yard touchdown.

Two days after Mission had won its first bi-district game, on the morning of December 7, 1941, a chilling voice came over the radio:

WE INTERRUPT THIS BROADCAST TO BRING YOU THE FOLLOWING BULLETIN: JAPANESE AIRPLANES BOMBED

UNITED STATES MILITARY INSTALLATIONS AND SHIPS AT PEARL HARBOR, ON THE ISLAND OF OAHU, THIS MORNING IN A SNEAK ATTACK THAT RESULTED IN SERIOUS CASUALTIES AND EXTENSIVE DAMAGE. ADDITIONAL INFORMATION WILL BE REPORTED AS SOON AS AVAILABLE.

The Japanese attack killed 2,403, and that Sunday morning was a day President Roosevelt said would "live in infamy." The following day, war was declared on Japan. On December 11, Italy and Germany declared war on the United States. World War II had begun.

"Honestly, until Pearl Harbor, I don't think we were all that aware about the war, what was happening overseas," recalled Landry. "I know, personally, I wasn't. We were trying to win a championship in football and into school activities and just not conscious of what was happening. Of course, that changed when Pearl Harbor was attacked."

Suddenly, everybody was talking about the war, the enemy, about what must be done to stop the Axis. But in spite of this, of that stark reality, they were also talking about Mission playing Hondo for the regional championship. Life paused; it didn't stop.

The regional championship game was something everybody had dreamed might happen, something they hoped and planned for. Some three thousand people jammed the football stadium, then called Burnett Field, purchasing reserved seats for $1.10 and $1.50 and general admission for 75 and 30 cents.

Rain had fallen that week and the field was soggy, but nothing could stop the Eagles. Mission destroyed Hondo, 33–0, as Landry capped the first drive by scoring from the three, ran forty-five yards to set up a score, passed twenty-five yards for another, and then raced sixty-five yards for a touchdown. Mission, 12–0 for the season, had gone as far as it could. It had scored 322 points and was unscored upon, if, like the Eagle fans, you didn't count the touchdown erroneously awarded Donna on the interference call. Landry was named all-Valley, all-everything, and there was a great deal of interest shown in him by Texas, SMU, Rice, and Mississippi State.

"I went with Tommy to visit Mississippi State," recalled Mehis. "We rode the train up there and stayed four, five days. He had a scholarship offer, and I tagged along. They treated us like kings. Why, they even picked us up at the station in a 1941 limited-edition Buick. It even had a folding seat in back."

"In those days," recalled Bully Gilstrap, then an assistant under D. X. Bible at Texas, "we had two assistant coaches scouting. I had the south and east, and Blair Cherry the north and west. We kept hearing good things about Tommy Landry, what a fine player and outstanding person he was.

"He was the top player in the Valley. Maybe not what you'd consider a great blue chipper, but a fine player. I remember being a little afraid we might lose him to SMU because he was a Methodist. But in Mission we got a lot of help from an ex-Longhorn named Doc Newhouse. Doc kept talking up the Longhorns and telling us about Tommy."

"Tommy, I want you to look around you in this town, this area, this state," Gilstrap told Landry. "You note the real important people and you'll find that the majority of those come from the University of Texas. You look at the leaders in the churches, the farming industry, the citrus industry, the lawyers, the politicians . . . the majority are from Texas.

"You go to another school, say SMU, and it'll be awful far for your parents to travel to see you play. But Austin's not that far. They'll be able to come see the games."

"I was pretty sold on Texas," Landry once recalled. "In those days you just about had to have a Texas alumnus to recommend you to the school. Doc Newhouse was a big help getting me into Texas. It also helped that Jackie Fields, who was from Mission, was playing for Coach Bible at that time. I don't think the Valley was as much respected for football back then as some of the other parts of the state, but Jackie had made a good impression.

"I'd never been anywhere to speak of, and Austin was the closest place for Southwest Conference schools. That city was plenty big for me."

Although nobody would know it at the time, Mission High, like so many other schools, wouldn't play football the following year due to the war. And when Tom Landry left for Austin to attend Texas, he was much closer to the war than distance could measure, than he ever would imagine.

CHAPTER 7
The War Years

⁓⋅⁓

Tom Landry is a great American and a great patiort. . . . This nation owes much to the Tom Landrys, the citizen soldiers who did their duty during wartime and returned to civilian life to engage in productive careers.

—LT. GEN. ELLIE SHULER

THE NEWS WAS SHOCKING, devastating, and it was forever. Ray Landry was working at his garage across the alley from the house, and Ruth was washing in a small area set aside for that task in the backyard. They were told that their eldest son, Robert, was missing in action. Later they would learn that he was dead.

Robert, three years older than Tom, had joined the air force shortly after Pearl Harbor, completed his flight training, and was ferrying a plane to England when he disappeared. Finally, it was determined that as he was flying a route over Iceland, the plane exploded in midair. The cause never was determined.

Ruth Landry's best friend, Marvel Deen's mother, also named Ruth, went right over to the Landrys' home. "Ruth wasn't in shock, but she was in grief beyond words," recalled Ruth Langston, whose last name was Dooley then. "So was Ray. Ruth was such a quiet person, but if you knew her, you could see on her face how much she was suffering. It was so sad. Then she went back to her washing, and Ray went back to the garage."

Tom Landry had spent the summer of 1942 working as a roughneck in South Texas to make extra money. Then he had left Mission and gone to the University of Texas on a football scholarship. "Even then he was very mature," recalled teammate Frank Jeffers. "Tommy had a tremendous influence on other members of the freshman team. I don't believe I ever played with or against a greater competitor than Tommy Landry."

And it was while he was at Texas his freshman year that the news came. The news left an awful gnawing, hollow feeling inside Landry. He remembered so many things . . . growing up, playing catch with Robert, laughing, following him around and wanting to be like him and to play ball for Mission High as Robert had done. He remembered the fun, the talks . . . and, perhaps, the things left unsaid, feelings left unexpressed. But Robert was gone. He would not be around anymore, and the solace came when he thought of his brother being in a better place, where there was no war, no fighting, just peace.

"It's something you never expect," recalled Landry. "It shocks you, shakes you up. But he had been missing for a long time, and although you always hope, you also prepare yourself for the worst. Certainly, it was most difficult to accept and live with, but you did that better in those times because people were getting killed in the war so frequently. In normal times, it would have been more of a shock."

"The Landrys had so much inner courage," continued Ms. Langston. "There was no looking back, so they went ahead living. And they didn't put their grief on others, going around talking about it like so many would have. They handled it themselves."

~:~

LANDRY JOINED THE RESERVES when he started Texas because he wanted to, because it was the thing to do. World War II wasn't a war to protest against, to debate, as we later would the Korean War and, to an even greater extent, Vietnam. Japan had attacked Pearl Harbor, and Germany had declared war on the United States. You fought for your country, your way of life, democracy, and it was very clear that the aggressors, the enemies, were Adolf Hitler's Nazis, Mussolini's Fascisti, and Japan's warmongers.

"There was no question, really," said Landry. "If you didn't fight, there was a chance the country would be taken over by the Germans or the Japanese. We were fighting a war for our country and wanted to get into the service and help. Then, we were a country of patriots. If we hadn't been, there's no telling what might have happened."

~:~

LANDRY WAS CALLED TO ACTIVE DUTY in the spring of 1943. He was classified, sent to the college training program in Ada, Oklahoma, took preflight in San Antonio, graduated as a pilot in Lubbock, and trained in multiple-engine aircraft in Iowa. He was sent from there to Lincoln, Nebraska, where the crews were formed. In the fall of 1944 they flew overseas to England with Landry's group being stationed at Ipswich, not far from London.

Landry would fly thirty missions, five more than the required tour of duty, over Germany and occupied territory. "Tommy," Viola Bourgeois recalled, "volunteered for extra missions. He never said much about this, but he did it for his brother, Robert."

The Eighth Air Force had gone to England in the spring and summer of 1943 because from a close distance the B-17's could penetrate Hitler's Third Reich with a sustained offensive. The British would bomb Germany at night and the U.S. would do so during the day, concentrating on factories and installations, rubber and steel plants, oil fields, etc.

In fact, Landry's first mission was in a squadron of some two thousand bombers attempting to destroy or severely cripple oil fields at Mersburg, Germany. "We went in there and it was really something to see and feel the flak for the first time," he said. "They tell you about it, warn you about it, but it's like nothing you've ever experienced. It was really a scary, sinking feeling."

Flak was heavy, and Landry said the visibility was so bad and Mersburg so dark that they'd gotten in and out as fast as they could. They weren't even sure if they'd come close to the target or missed it by miles. But they returned safely, and there would be many other missions.

"They kept us awfully busy," said Landry. "We were fogged in a lot and had to be ready to go when we could. We didn't have that much time off.

"When we did, we'd go over to London to sightsee, look around. But it was a very drab city then. Very dark and gray. When they'd have the blackouts it was so dark you couldn't see your hand in front of your face. You just can't imagine how dark it was." And sometimes when they were on base they could hear the frightening, whistling sounds of German V-2 rockets heading toward London.

"But, mostly, there wasn't time for doing much of anything," he continued, "except getting ready for our missions and going on them."

❧

THE HEAVY, BULKY FLYING FORTRESS had gunners on each side and on the top, the front, the tail, and the belly. There were four large engines, and the fifteen-ton body always seemed too big to be supported by the fragile-looking wings. But it could reach speeds of 325 miles per hour, lift twenty-five thousand pounds (although payloads of six thousand pounds were more practical), and bomb accurately from twenty thousand or even twenty-five thousand feet. From the bases in England it could go four hundred miles inside Germany and take tremendous punishment. Luftwaffe officials estimated that it would take an average of twenty hits from 20 mm guns to bring the plane down.

The Eighth Air Force suffered fifty thousand casualties during the war, including twenty-six thousand who never returned from the air war over Europe.

By late 1944, the Allies had staggered the Luftwaffe, and thus the dreaded Messerschmitt and Focke-Wolf fighters no longer swept down on the bombers before and after their targets had been reached. They were still around in isolated numbers, but nothing like earlier in the war when the Fortresses would face these attacks alone, bunched in tight formations. And in 1943, the air force began using P-51 Mustangs to escort the bombers.

It they'd had time to contemplate the situation, those in Landry's group might have counted themselves more fortunate than their earlier counterparts in the war. Even with the P-51 escorts, the earlier pilots had to run the gamut of concentrated Luftwaffe attacks and avoid heavy ground fire from antiaircraft guns. On the other hand, the ground gunners had become much smarter and more accurate by the time Landry was on active duty. Earlier in the war you could make a bombing run at a certain altitude and the flak would be closer and closer as the gunners zeroed in. But the next wave of bombers could come in higher and the gunners would still be shooting below them at the former altitude of the preceding bombers. Overall, it was estimated that there was a 35 percent chance of survival for each person who completed twenty-five missions, the required tour of combat duty.

❧

THEY HAD GOTTEN UP AT 4:00 A.M. and gone to mess and did not know exactly where they were going, much less if they would be coming back. At the briefing, they were shown the target of the day, just a spot on a huge map, a spot that would become alive and real.

Their mission was to bomb a German target in occupied Czechoslovakia, but they were warned they'd be cutting it very close on gas to make it back home. They'd have to go lean on the fuel whenever they could. If they attempted to fly across the English Channel, they might have to ditch in the water, severely limiting any chance of survival. So they'd also been briefed to try to find an alternate landing field in France if they were short on gas.

Their faces were so young . . . so many were nineteen, twenty, and at twenty-four you were considered one of the older guys. Some had never been away from their hometowns until the war. It should have been a time when they were moving into adulthood, getting jobs, worrying about a grade in freshman English, a date for Saturday night. But if you were nineteen or twenty at that time and in that war, you aged very fast, saw too much too soon. To so many, World War II was a movie reel in black and white. To those who were there, it was life and death in vivid color.

"There must have been twenty-five hundred planes on that mission, and most of them were looking for a place to land," recalled copilot Tom Landry, who had just turned twenty, two years younger than the old man, pilot Ken Saenz. "Ceiling was under three hundred feet, almost zero at times, and you couldn't see anything below you. We also couldn't make radar contact.

"You didn't know what would happen, but we were in a great plane. The Flying Fortress was just a great plane. We'd get a few holes in us, but it could take so much punishment. You could get an engine, even two engines knocked out, and still fly on the other two."

As usual, flak was thick as they neared the target. It was exploding all around the squadron—swelling bursts of black, an ominous devil's flower darkening the sky as if a giant thundercloud were forming. The four engines of the Fortress made a deafening noise, so loud that a man almost had to shout to be heard by the person next to him. A person couldn't hear the shells exploding unless the plane was hit, and then it might be the last sound he ever heard.

"Sure, you'd be a little scared," recalled Landry. "You were flying into the black cloud of flak and never really sure what might happen. You made your run, tried to concentrate on what you had to do, and then you got out of there as fast as you could, any way you could."

The Flying Fortresses shook badly anyway, but with the shells going off around them they sometimes felt as if they might just come apart. It was as if you were in the middle of a storm, yanked here and there by some giant, unseen force, while trying to steady the plane and concentrate on getting over the target. That was the sole purpose: hitting the target.

When a plane was hit, fire and smoke would spurt from its engines, belly, and tail, and it would start to fall, in an awful ballet of death. And at other times a plane would disappear, exploding in midair. Death never seemed quite real until you realized some friends were gone, some familiar faces were not seen again. Some feared they would be next. They were too close to think death always happened to somebody else.

They got through the flak, dropped their bombs, turned to get out of there, then headed back. On the way back, Captain Saenz and Lieutenant Landry realized they would run out of gas over the English Channel and started down through the heavy fog looking for the base in France.

The plane literally skimmed over the tops of trees as the pilot and Landry tried to find a field, an opening, anything. They saw an opening in the trees and sat down in a farm field, hitting the ground in a violent bouncing motion, bellying along and plowing up the ground toward a cluster of trees. They hoped the plane might stop before hitting the trees, but it didn't. The plane plunged through a narrow opening as trees sheared off both wings, slowing it down enough to reduce the impact when it smashed nose first into a huge tree. The tree tore through the nose and into the cockpit. And then there was total silence, stillness . . . Were they dead or alive? Realizing they were okay, the entire crew started to shout. They walked away from the wreckage, caught a ride with allies to the French base, and were flown back to England.

"We were awfully lucky," said Landry. "So many planes were looking for a place to land and didn't make it. . . . No, as we were going down I don't remember being scared. I'm not sure why I wasn't. I guess I just hadn't had that experience before and didn't know what I faced and wasn't afraid."

ONCE AFTER THEY'D MADE A BOMBING RUN over Germany and were on the return flight to England, the engines coughed, sputtered, and died. They were fast losing altitude over Belgium and dropped to one thousand feet as fire from antiaircraft guns got closer and closer. Captain Saenz and Landry quickly went over a checklist as time was running out. The pilot told everybody to bail out. They would be bailing out over enemy territory, and if the jump didn't kill them, they would be captured and spend the remainder of the war in a German prison camp.

As everyone prepared to abandon the plane, Landry unbuckled and got out of his seat. He paused, looked back at the instrument panel, then moved the switch from lean to a full, rich mixture of gas. The engines fired up again, and the crew scrambled back to their stations. The plane regained altitude, and they made it back to England.

When Landry was asked how he could remain cool and react the way he did, he said matter-of-factly, "I guess it just occurred to me something might be wrong with the fuel mixture. I wasn't sure. It just came to me that the mixture might be off. It was just one of those things."

DEFEAT FOR GERMANY SEEMED INEVITABLE. President Roosevelt and Prime Minister Churchill had decided to try to defeat Germany before Japan because they feared the Nazis were a more imminent threat. Even in desperation, the Nazis had launched the V-1 rockets, the Vergeltungswaffe or Vengeance Weapon, on England and later the V-2, the first guided missile. They'd also put into the air the first jet-propelled fighter plane. But it was too late.

"The Germans were the greatest of military minds," said Landry, who included *The History of World War II* among his studies. "They had so many of the geniuses during the war, but the Allies, the people of the United States, were just supremely determined. We all pulled together."

President Roosevelt, who had done so much to bring the country out of the Depression and then inspire the people in war, died in April 1945, before he could experience the victory that he prayed was coming. And

Vice President Harry Truman of Missouri, the man who didn't mince words or beat around the bush, became president.

On May 1, 1945, German radio announced Hitler had died while defending Berlin against the Russian onslaught. But investigations later determined that he had committed suicide in a pact with Eva Braun, his longtime mistress who became his wife. On May 7, Germany surrendered unconditionally.

In August, President Truman gave his okay to use the atom bomb on Japan, and when the bomber, the *Enola Gay*, dropped the A-bomb August 6 on Hiroshima, some ninety-two thousand people were killed and the world was launched into the Atomic Age. Three days later, the A-bomb killed some forty thousand in Nagasaki, and Japan surrendered on September 2, 1945.

That November of 1945, Lt. Tom Landry received his discharge and returned to Mission before trying to tie his life, his education, and his football career back together. As Lt. Gen. Ellie Shuler pointed out on Tom Landry Day, Landry had been awarded the European African Middle Eastern campaign medal with three combat stars, the American Campaign medal, and the U.S. Air Force medal with four oak leaf clusters.

"Tommy and I got back to Mission from the war about the same time," recalled Wade Spillman. "We'd been to war, aged beyond our years, and returned as men of the world. We weren't kids anymore and so we decided to cut loose. We planned to go across into Mexico, to Reynosa, and, shall we say, cut a wide path. So we went over one afternoon, figuring we'd stay a few days and really have a blast.

"Well, there was no blast. We got back home about 10:30 P.M. the same day."

After the Cowboys had won a couple of Super Bowls, a reporter asked Landry about his experiences in the war. Landry thought for a minute and said, "Oh, we got a few holes in our bomber every once in a while, but nothing much happened, really."

CHAPTER 8
The University of Texas at Austin

~:~

There were some fairly rowdy boys in school back then, but Tom was just very mature. He was no kid coming to the bit city. He'd been to a war. He was older than many and acted his age. I guess, really, it's surprising to a lot of people to find a man of such character and religious intent in a rough, tough game like football. But that's the way he was. I remember him as being quiet, poised, reliable, and having just all those good American traits.

—ED PRICE
University of Texas Assistant Coach, 1947

WHEN TOM LANDRY WAS DISCHARGED from the U.S. Army Air Corps in 1946, he returned to Mission to await his fall semester at the University of Texas. He'd begun tossing the football around again and, upon discovering that his old high-school coach, Bob Martin, was coaching in Brownsville, just across the International Bridge from Matamoros, he went to see him. Martin was very surprised one afternoon when he looked over to the sideline during spring training practice and saw Tom Landry, standing there smiling.

They talked for a while and Martin said, "Tom, you've been away from the game for a while, so maybe you ought to put on a uniform and scrimmage with us."

"Sure, why not?"

"He played quarterback, and my kids really got after him," said Martin, who would eventually retire as an administrator in the Brownsville Independent School District. "Here he was a big-time college player about to go to Texas, and they wanted a chance to bust him. But Tom took it, never said a word, and I think during that spring when he worked with us it helped him get back into the swing of football again."

~:~

TOM LANDRY RETURNED to the University of Texas that fall of 1946. The most prominent landmarks in Austin then were the state capitol building, whose granite glowed pink in the early morning sun, and the Texas Tower, rising skyward like a campus beacon. There was no suburbia, as we know it today, and the movies and places of business were on and around Congress Avenue, which ran from the Colorado River, just south of downtown, right into the middle of the capitol lawn.

The population was some fifty thousand people, and the forty-acre site upon which the University of Texas was situated was actually a city within a city, a self-sufficient, self-containing place. The times were so unusual. The return of almost ten thousand servicemen, who were taking advantage of the new G.I. Bill of Rights, had swelled the enrollment to upward of seventeen thousand and caused a most unusual blend in the student population. There were the usual eighteen-year-olds beginning college, but they were mixed in with the returning servicemen, many in their mid- to late twenties and many with families. They weren't kids anymore. The war had taken their youth away, and they had a lot of catching up to do.

Landry had been in a real war, where real people had died or were maimed mentally or physically. A popular movie showing at one of the two downtown theaters was *The Best Years of Our Lives*, which depicted the complexities faced by three veterans returning home to civilian life. Fredric March and Dana Andrews starred, and in a supporting role was Harold Russell, a double amputee war veteran. He would win an Oscar for his role and never act in another movie. Styles were changing. Coeds who had worn dresses up to the knees were wearing them down to midcalf. Sweaters were in, and so were sweater girls Lana Turner and Rita Hayworth, popular pinups during the war. Women wore bobby socks, white-and-brown oxfords, and penny loafers. The guys wore baggy slacks with cuffs, loose-fitting sweaters, and short, well-trimmed hair with sideburns no lower than midear.

It would take a bit of adjustment for Landry and the other servicemen. Tom was back in an atmosphere of learning and athletics and living, where now he could really appreciate the things he had taken for granted before the war. The sky was peaceful. There was no flak. Each day could be lived without wondering if there would be another.

Although his wavy brown hair receded a little more around the part on the left side and there were a few more wrinkles, caused more by war than years, Landry's appearance had not changed that much. He had lost weight during the war but had gotten it back up to around one hundred ninety pounds. He remained very clean-cut.

At first he seemed a little quieter, a little more reflective, but those coming back from the war were either that way or loud and boisterous, letting go as if they'd held back for a long time. Landry talked very little to anyone about his war experiences. He turned his thoughts and attention to school and football, trying to recapture the competitive edge that had made him one of the brightest stars in Valley history and earned him a scholarship to the University of Texas.

~:~

D. X. BIBLE was coaching his final season when Landry returned to Texas. Bible was a thorough, somewhat low-key man who demanded excellence through repetition and hard work. But he seldom yelled at his players or raised his voice in an attempt to berate or shame them into trying harder.

"He was very efficient and a fine orator," Landry once said. "I think he became more low-key after the war because I guess the older players were coming back and he felt that approach would be better than any of the Knute Rockne–type talks he'd used before the war."

"Tom was a fine player," Bible would recall. "He was a leader, modest and quiet. He had a lot of influence without being loud or blustery. I used to tell the fellows if they would pay the premiums they would get the dividends. Tom paid them."

Those were the Bobby Layne years. Bible used the Blond Bomber at both fullback and tailback in his single-wing formation. Landry played fullback and was a defensive halfback specialist. In those days colleges played a form of platoon football in which you were allowed a limited number of substitutions on offense or defense. Many of the players had been in the armed forces, such as center Dick Harris, a friend of Landry who had returned to Texas the previous fall.

Landry had been away from football for so long that it was difficult for him, but he was very determined. Perhaps, so many years later, this experience helped him to believe, when many didn't, that a guy named Roger Staubach could regain his competitive edge after serving a four-year naval obligation and make a career for himself in the National Football League.

Landry pledged Delta Kappa Epsilon, and fraternity brother Bill Wiggins remembered, "Tom was a serious young man then, but not what you would call overly serious. He was a good sport. You could joke with him, but he wasn't the type guy to go around making a fool of himself. He stayed in control."

Landry ran around a lot with Lewis Holder and George McCall, who were ends on the football team. Bobby Coy Lee sometimes joined them, and Tom also spent a great deal of time with his fraternity brothers.

When he wasn't involved in football, Landry participated in intramural sports, not only winning the UT light heavyweight boxing championship but also helping his fraternity win the school's swimming title.

"He was so strong," recalled fraternity brother McCall, "and certainly had courage. He was weighing about one hundred ninety but got his weight down to about one hundred seventy five in order to box light heavyweight."

Landry's activities outside of football were on the opposite end of the scale from those of Bobby Layne and his running buddy, Billy M. "Rooster" Andrews. Andrews, who was slightly less than five feet tall and weighed some one hundred twenty pounds, knew Tom when he was enrolled at Texas prior to the war. Andrews had also tried to join the armed forces but was turned down because of his size. He received the nickname of Rooster one night during his freshman year when a group of seniors got him out of bed and demanded that he climb a tree to bring down their fighting rooster. They'd planned to take the bird to Elgin to enter in the cockfights. They failed, however, to tell Andrews that the bird was a fighting rooster.

So he innocently climbed the tree and reached for the rooster, which was standing on a limb. There followed one of the better fights at UT that year, which ended with both Andrews and the bird tumbling to the ground. The rooster was fine. Andrews was scratched up and had suffered a broken arm. Thereafter, he was called Rooster. He served as manager for the Longhorns but was also adept at drop-kicking. Sometimes he was used on extra points.

"With Layne out there you never knew when we'd score, so sometimes I'd carry water on the field, wearing my helmet," Andrews said. "And Tommy Landry, well, everybody liked him. He really was a nice guy, and to tell you the truth, I don't think he's changed a bit since he was in school with us. He was a gentleman, was very much respected, and well, he just didn't go around making an ass out of himself like Bobby and I did."

"Tommy," said Layne, who died in 1986, "was awfully tame by our standards, but he wasn't the type guy to put you down for what you did. Some people are one way, some people another, and he understood that then."

"Tommy wouldn't let you upset him," added Andrews, "and he wouldn't upset you."

"Yeah," added Layne, "we all liked him, but he wasn't the type of guy you'd go out with, have some beers, and make a fool of yourself with."

"Those guys," laughed Landry, "were capable of doing a lot of things."

"There were some fairly rowdy boys in school back then, but Tom was just very mature," said Ed Price, who had also returned from service to reclaim his job as assistant football coach (he would later become head coach). "He was no kid coming to the big city. He'd been to a war. He was older than many and acted his age. I guess, really, it's surprising to a lot of people to find a man of such character and religious intent in a rough, tough game like football. But that's the way he was. I remember him as being quiet, poised, reliable, and having just all those good American traits."

Texas opened the season by beating Missouri, 42–0, and newspapers reported that among the many plays that thrilled the crowd was a thirty-yard gain on a bootleg by Tom Landry. However, Landry still wasn't back in the groove, and his duties mostly involved filling in at defensive halfback. The team finished 8–2 with most of the accolades falling on the shoulders of Layne and Bible, who was ending his career at UT with a 63–31–3 record and three Southwest Conference titles.

One of the two losses was 18–13 at the hands of Jess Neely's Rice Owls. "After the game," said McCall, who would go into the insurance business in Austin, "Tommy, Lew Holder, and I took off for Galveston. There was this place at the time where they had gambling, which was illegal. We were a little curious what it was like at the place, and so we went inside.

"Well, we were looking around and I spotted this sportswriter from the *Austin American-Statesman*. It scared us to death. We weren't doing anything wrong. We weren't gambling, drinking, or anything, but if he wrote in the paper that he had seen us at the place it would have been our tails. Coach Bible was so upset about losing to Rice, and here were three of his players in a drinking, gambling place.

"So I went over to the sportswriter and asked him not to write anything, and he didn't, thank goodness. If he had, it wouldn't have mattered, I'm afraid, that we were just standing around."

BLAIR CHERRY, who had been the offensive assistant under Bible, took over the head coaching duties when his predecessor became athletic director. The previous year, Cherry, assured he'd replace Bible, had brought in Eck Curtis to help him experiment with the T formation. Curtis, coming out of the high-school coaching ranks, had been the first schoolboy coach to adapt to the Chicago Bears' T when he installed it at Breckenridge High in 1942. In 1946, Cherry had used a special freshman team of players, under Curtis, to run the T in scrimmages to get the varsity ready for opponents who used the formation. When Cherry became head coach, he decided to go all-out to make the T the major alignment for the Longhorns.

Layne, a tremendous passer, appeared the most likely candidate to become the quarterback, although Cherry also moved Tom Landry and Paul Campbell to the position. In high school, Landry's team had shifted out of the T into the box formation, and he'd been a good passer. But this was his first actual experience as the man under center in a formation.

Tex Schramm, who'd also been at Texas before the war and returned there to finish his education, was a journalism student but also worked full-time for the *Austin American-Statesman*.

"I knew of Tom, of course, but never remember actually talking to him while we were at Texas. I do recall, however, that when he came to Texas everybody was talking about what a fine passer he was."

But Layne, who of course went on to become a top NFL quarterback, was an outstanding passer and appeared the most likely candidate to become quarterback. He wasn't overly sold on the idea of the T, so Cherry took Bobby and his wife, the former Carol Krueger, to the college all-star game to see how the pros used the formation. They also visited the Chicago Cardinals, later to move to St. Louis and finally to Phoenix, and the Chicago Bears, where Sid Luckman was one of the best at operating the formation. Layne was sold. He adapted well, becoming the starting quarterback, and Landry would be a backup and also come in for Bobby on defense and play some at fullback.

Cherry was a tough, more emotional coach than Bible. It was the practice of many during those days not to allow the players to drink water during practice, although, of course, now water breaks are common and known to be necessary. But Cherry adhered to the practice of the times, and when a player fell out and became sick, trainer Frank Medina administered cold towels to revive him. Cherry worked his team so hard that observers were calling it the best-conditioned ball club in school history. And some felt it also might be the best team in the Southwest Conference, although sportswriters in Dallas were predicting big things for the SMU Mustangs under Rusty Russell, a team featuring Layne's old teammate at Highland Park High, Doak Walker.

The Longhorns opened the season by overpowering Texas Tech, 33–0, and then crushed Oregon and its sophomore quarterback, Norm Van Brocklin, 34–13, with Landry playing mostly on defense. "Tom could have played any position except guard or tackle," recalled Bully Gilstrap, an assistant first to Bible and then to Cherry. "He studied and listened, and he knew all the assignments."

Ray Jones was the starting fullback, but a lot of talk centered around the prospects of two-hundred-pound Ray Borneman from Houston. One day Borneman was having problems on his timing, and Cherry shouted to Landry, who was on defense:

"Tommy, get over here and show him how to run this play!"

Landry responded and ran the play correctly. "Even in those days," said Layne, "Tommy was as smart as they come."

The third week of the season, national attention was focused on the game between the Longhorns and the powerful North Carolina Tarheels, featuring all-American halfback "Choo-Choo" Charlie Justice. An injury had forced a position change. Landry had suffered a broken thumb and no longer could take snaps or pass, so on offense he was moved to fullback.

"I remember being very apprehensive," said Landry. "But the way it turned out, maybe that was good."

Justice was held to only eighteen yards rushing. The running star of the game was Tom Landry, who netted ninety-one yards on twelve carries as the Longhorn juggernaut crushed North Carolina, 34–0.

"Well," said Landry, "you have to remember that Bobby was such a tremendous passer that it opened up things for me. I think I must have gained a lot of those yards on draws."

~•~

THAT YEAR A STRIKING YOUNG LADY enrolled at the University of Texas. Raised in Dallas, she then moved to Houston with her family, living there for a short time before entering UT. She was trim, had beautiful eyes and reddish blonde hair, and was to become one of the campus beauties, a Bluebonnet Belle. Her name was Alicia Wiggs, and her father, Herbert Wiggs, was chairman of the board of a Houston insurance company. Alicia was majoring in child psychology. And, in common with Tom Landry, she had practically been raised in church. Alicia had attended Highland Park High School during the time Layne and Walker were playing there, and she'd become a football fan. She would soon become an even stronger one.

At that time George McCall was dating a girl named Ann Tynan, the Sweetheart at UT, and through Ann he introduced both Lew Holder and Bobby Coy Lee to girls they later married. Holder began dating Gloria Newhaws, a Delta Delta Delta sorority friend of Alicia. Gloria wanted Alicia to double date with them and suggested she have a blind date with one of the football players, Tommy Landry. Alicia declined.

"I didn't particularly like the idea of a blind date," she recalled. "But Gloria kept after me, and I finally went just because I thought so much of her and didn't want to disappoint her."

"You might say the first time I saw Tommy I was a little surprised."

Landry had played a game the day before and was very battered. He had bruises on his face, a black eye, and a bandaged thumb.

"I suppose he was a little shy, as everybody says, but I was so shy then myself that I wouldn't have noticed," said Alicia. "But he was so polite and very handsome, and we continued going out. After I got to know him, I knew that he was exactly what I was looking for in a man. He had manners, and we'd go to church on Sundays, and he seemed just perfect for me." Tom felt the same way.

"Alicia and I would go to the movies or down to New Braunfels where they had the rapids or to San Marcos," said Landry. "For a long time there it was a little difficult to get around. There weren't many of us who had cars. But I finally did buy a car, a convertible, from Frank Guest [a halfback on the team], and that made it easier."

"Sometimes I remember that Tommy came back from the war when I started to attend Texas," said Alicia. "Otherwise, had things gone normally in those times, I suppose we'd never have met because he'd have graduated and been gone before I ever got to Texas.

"I just *thought* I was a big football fan, but after I started going with Tommy, I really became an avid one."

❖

IN AUSTIN, football does not just happen. The city literally vibrates with the sport all the way from the snack shops on campus to the Texas Tower to the capitol. In a larger city, such as Dallas or Houston, so many other things detract from the game, but Austin is just the right size to become completely caught up in the Texas Longhorns.

Texas followed the thumping of North Carolina with a 34–14 victory over Oklahoma, which in those days had a fine halfback-punter by the name of Darrell Royal. By that time Landry was the starting fullback, dividing time with Ray Jones, and also played full-time on defense.

"As a player," recalled Ed Price, "Tommy didn't have the breakaway speed. He wasn't flashy, but he was strong and tough. And he could get the tough yardage for you."

"Tommy was a tremendous punter," said Layne. "We had two fine punters in those days in Tommy and Frank Guest."

The Longhorns beat Rice and Arkansas, and then they headed into the Cotton Bowl in Dallas for the showdown with Southern Methodist and its epitome of Saturday's hero, Doak Walker, who made the covers of *Time, Life, Look,* and *Sport* magazines. A crowd of forty-five thousand came to the stadium that afternoon to watch the number-three-ranked Longhorns face the number-eight-ranked Mustangs in a game that would decide the Southwest Conference title. Others all over the state, from Mission to North Texas, tuned in over the Humble Network to hear the colorful radio coverage of legendary sportscaster Kern Tipps:

. . . And the Blond Bomber Bobby Layne puts the ball into the belly of Tommy Landry, who bucks into the Mustang line for a few hard-fought yards and tries to bull his way forward when Dick McKissack comes up and says, "No you don't, that's the end of the line." . . .

Known for its trickery, SMU ran a reverse on the opening kickoff when Walker took Harris's boot then handed off to Paul Page, who sped to the Texas nineteen, setting up an SMU touchdown, which was scored when Walker handed to Page on the old Statue of Liberty play. Walker kicked the extra point, but Texas came back to tie the score after Byron Gillory's forty-yard punt return and Landry's plunge into the end zone, followed by Guest's extra point.

The Ponies scored again as Walker slipped across the middle and took Gil Johnson's pass on a play that covered fifty-four yards and carried to the Texas one, from where McKissack scored. Landry was covering another receiver near the sidelines when he saw Walker break free and Johnson loft him the ball.

"Walker caught it right in front of me and took off," said Landry. "We chased him down and finally knocked him out of bounds at the one. He was just a tremendous player, could do it all."

Again, Walker kicked the extra point, giving the Mustangs a 14–7 lead, but Layne, Walker's old Highland Park teammate, got hot and passed Texas on another touchdown drive with twelve minutes remaining. This time Guest's extra-point try was wide, and SMU led by a single point, 14–13.

Texas made one last drive, moving to what appeared to be a first down at the SMU fifteen, only to have the play wiped out with a penalty. When another play failed, the Longhorns found themselves facing a fourth and one at the SMU thirty-two. If they made it, they still had time to score, perhaps get close enough for a field goal. Needing the toughest yardage, they called on Landry, who said he'd never forget the play as long as he lived.

"We lined up, and Bobby took the snap and turned to give me the ball," recalled Landry. "But I had slipped and fallen. I can still see the funny look on his face, standing there with nobody to give the ball to. I regained my balance, but it was too late. There was no chance, and SMU took over."

"It was such a freaky thing," said Price. "If Tommy had been anywhere else on the field, he'd probably have made it. But there was a mud puddle near him, and that's what made him slip."

Texas went through the remainder of its schedule undefeated, but so did SMU, and the Mustangs became SWC champions. The Longhorns finished fifth in the final Associated Press rankings, and SMU was third.

"We really had a fine team that year," said Landry. "A fine team. We shouldn't have lost a game."

"Football was such a big part of our lives," recalled Alicia. "Tommy talked a lot about it. Of course, we were getting pretty serious, although we had a little disagreement.

"I'd never smoked before in my life, but it was something I'd thought about. So I told Tommy I believed I'd give it a try."

Landry, who had never smoked, looked at her and said, "If you do, I won't kiss you anymore."

"So," said Alicia, laughing, "I never did smoke. But if I had . . . he'd still have kissed me."

SMU was to beat Oregon in the Cotton Bowl, a team Texas had beaten 38–13 during the regular season, by 21–13, and the Longhorns were invited to the Sugar Bowl in New Orleans to play the sixth-ranked Crimson Tide of Alabama, featuring new passing sensation Harry Gilmer. Although Layne had better statistics, most of the talk around the game concerned Gilmer, about whom Grantland Rice wrote, "Gilmer is the best college passer I ever saw, barring neither Sammy Baugh nor Sid Luckman." Nevertheless, Texas was established as a seven-point favorite.

"Everybody was so proud of Tom," said Bob Martin. "He'd gone through the war, was away from the game so long, and had come back and become an outstanding player again through real dedication. I went to New Orleans to see the Sugar Bowl game that year because I was so excited about him. The Longhorns were staying in a dorm on the campus of Tulane there, and I went looking for Tom.

"A bunch of Texas players were sitting around on the grass outside the dorm, watching all the pretty coeds go past. You know, they'd whistle or holler at them. I asked one of the players if he'd seen Tom Landry."

"Oh, he's probably up in his room, concentrating on the game and studying the game plans," said the player.

"Sure enough, that's where I found him," reported Martin. "I knocked, went in, and he was sure surprised to see me."

"What are you doing here, Coach?" asked Tom.

"Well, I've come all the way to see the game, and I expect you to be superb," replied Martin. They chatted for a while, and Landry went back to studying the game plan.

Texas easily beat Alabama, 27–7, before seventy-three thousand fans on a bright, chilly day in the Sugar Bowl. The Longhorns limited Gilmer, the best college passer Grantland Rice ever saw, to 41 yards on four completions while Layne hit ten of twenty-four passes for 183 yards and was named the game's Most Valuable Player. It had been a banner year for the Longhorns, who finished 10–1, with Layne, Harris (who had been moved from center to tackle that year), and end Max Bumgardner making all-SWC and Harris and Layne being named all-American. Landry was the all-SWC second-team fullback. It was still one-platoon football, with only a few specialists such as Landry also playing on defense, so no mythical defensive unit was named.

The Longhorns had a banner celebration in the French Quarter after the Sugar Bowl victory. "A bunch of us went to dinner at Antoine's restaurant," said Rooster Andrews. "I remember Dr. Krueger, Layne's father-in-law, was with us. Whenever they'd make a crepe suzette, you know, they'd turn down the lights and strike a match to it. It kept happening, and Dr. Krueger said, 'This might be a great restaurant, but the electricity sure is bad.'"

"One thing led to another," said Layne. "You know, everybody kept talking about our million-dollar marching band. Well, we decided we'd form our own million-dollar band. So we got some brooms, mops, plungers and took off, marching up and down the streets of the French Quarter. I don't know. I think Tommy might have been with us."

"No," said Landry, "I wasn't. Ray Jones had gotten hurt, and so I had had to play full-time on offense and defense. I played fifty-eight minutes of that game and was so dead tired when it was over that I went back to my room and rested."

Dick Harris did recall that both he and Landry were having a little trouble in a particular course in school that year. It was letter writing, of all things.

"Oh, Tommy was a fine student," said Harris, "but we were all having problems in that course. This prof who taught the course was busting all of us. So Tommy went home with me that summer to Wichita Falls, and we took the course over again at Midwestern."

The teacher who taught the course at Midwestern was a big football fan and badly wanted to see the UT–Texas A&M game the following year. Harris confided to her that he would be able to secure her tickets to the game. Both Harris and Landry passed the writing course.

"So you could say, for example, that Tommy might have helped me pass a statistics course at Texas but I helped him pass that letter writing course," said Harris.

～:～

AS SCHOOL BEGAN in the fall of 1948, Landry was having problems with impacted wisdom teeth. They were bothering him a great deal and hindering him in football, although he seldom talked about the problem and just tried to ignore it. Layne had graduated and gone into pro football, where he would one day make the Pro Football Hall of Fame, but the Longhorns were still strong. Harris was returned to center and was named with Landry as cocaptain. There was also a newcomer named Bud McFadin, who would make his mark in both college and professional football.

The big problem, of course, was replacing Layne, and that duty went to Paul Campbell, a slim 174-pounder who was a fine ball handler but at times an indecisive passer.

"Paul was a fine person and turned out to be a good quarterback for us after a while," said Harris. "However, I still think Tommy would have been a better quarterback. But even that last year he still couldn't take snaps or throw the ball as he once had because of the broken thumb. So he stayed at fullback and defensive right halfback."

Because of the constant problems with his wisdom teeth (even after he'd had them taken out), Landry felt weak. His playing weight stayed almost ten pounds below normal.

"I still had the poison in my body from the wisdom teeth problem, and I didn't regain my full strength and stamina until the last couple of games of the season," said Landry. "So I wasn't able to play as much my senior year as I had as a junior."

Campbell had begun to find himself after a slow start, but his early problems contributed to Texas losses to North Carolina, Oklahoma, and SMU, which again claimed the SWC title and had found still another star in Kyle Rote. Furthermore, the Longhorns tied Texas A&M, 14–14, which was considered a major disaster among the Orange and White supporters. And naturally the 6–3–1 record was very disappointing after Texas had been projected as a contender for the SWC title. Cherry became the center of a great deal of criticism. So it was a great surprise when the Orange Bowl committee picked the Longhorns to play highly ranked Georgia in the Miami game. The Bulldogs of

Wally Butts had lost only one game, 21–14, to a North Carolina team that had shattered Texas, 34–7. The natives were restless in Miami; there were threats of forming another bowl game. Critics called Texas a third-rate team and said the Orange Bowl had scraped the bottom of the barrel to come up with the Longhorns.

"Everybody was talking and writing about what a poor opponent we were for Georgia," said Landry. "But we noted this and really geared up for the game."

⌣∙∿

AND PEOPLE WERE ALSO TALKING and writing about shocking events that were taking place. There was the newly established State of Israel . . . the Berlin airlift, which thwarted the Soviet blockade aimed at forcing the Allies out of Berlin . . . the Kinsey Report, which told Americans about their sex habits . . . the assassination of Mahatma Gandhi . . . that shocking book by Alan Paton, *Cry, the Beloved Country*, which depicted the evils of apartheid . . . and a mounting communist spy mania.

Those were shocking times, all right, and perhaps a period for upsets. The polls had predicted that New York's Thomas Dewey, the famed fighter of organized crime, would easily defeat President Harry Truman. Columnists noted Truman never would have been president in the first place had Roosevelt not died in office. On election night, the *Chicago Tribune* printed a screaming headline that said, "Dewey Defeats Truman." The next morning when the votes were all counted, Truman had won. . . .

Why would anyone ever match Texas against Georgia in a major bowl game? "Coach Cherry really impressed me before the game," recalled Harris. "He told us flatly that the Bulldogs would use a 4–4 defense, and we prepared for it, adjusting our plans. It never was clear whether he picked up the fact they might use it in watching films or what. There were some rumors that somebody had tipped him off. But, sure enough, that's the defense Georgia used."

After a slow start, Campbell had a good day, and Landry, as he'd had to do in the bowl game the previous year, ended up playing the entire game at fullback and defensive halfback, this time because Ray Borneman, the other fullback, injured a knee. The game was evenly matched for three periods, and Georgia led 28–27 with 11:15 to play. But Landry, running hard and tough like his old self, led Texas on an eleven-play, seventy-yard touchdown drive, and then, breaking tackles and running over other tacklers, he crashed twenty-one yards to set up still another touchdown as Texas won going away, 41–28. Landry had perhaps his best day in his final game as a Longhorn, finishing as the Bowl's top rusher with 117 yards on seventeen carries and playing a fine, rugged defensive game.

In the jubilant Longhorn dressing room, players were yelling, "Who's third rate?" And Butts told a group of writers, "Next time you writers call a team third rate, you're going to have to play them yourselves . . . that bottom of the barrel was full of snakes."

~:~

LANDRY HAD BEEN DRAFTED AS A SOPHOMORE by both the New York Giants and the New York Yankees of the All-American Football Conference, which was dominated by Paul Brown's Cleveland Browns.

As Tom walked off the field at the Orange Bowl that day, he was met by Jack White, an assistant coach for the football Yankees. "I had the contract in my pocket, and he signed it," said White. "He wasn't hard to deal with. He was very fair, and we just made him a better offer than the Giants."

"We knew he was a class guy. He was a big, raw-boned kid and a tremendous punter too. He could turn and back-pedal and seemed a natural on defense. He had a lot of courage and would really come up and bust the ball carrier.

"I remember when we first began checking on him. I talked to Dutch Meyer at TCU, and he said, 'He's a hoss. Landry's a hoss.'"

White recalled that at the Orange Bowl that day Landry also caught the eye of other teams. "Paul Brown came over to me at the winter meetings and asked if I'd trade him Landry," continued White. "I told him there was no way."

Tom and Alicia had bigger plans that January of 1949. They had so much in common and had the blessing of each other's parents. Tom gave Alicia an engagement ring on her birthday, January 12, and they were married January 28 in Houston, where Alicia's parents lived. The Yankees had given him a five-hundred-dollar bonus and a six-thousand-dollar yearly salary. With the five hundred dollars, the couple was able not only to honeymoon in Mexico but also to pay the first month's rent on an apartment near the UT campus in Austin.

After their wedding, Tom and Alicia returned to Austin, where he received his B.A. degree in business. He had decided to become an industrial engineer and to study engineering at the University of Houston.

"Pro football was such an unknown thing then," said Alicia, who left school as a sophomore to go with her husband. "Tommy was going to go ahead and get his degree, but neither of us had been up East and it was kind of like an adventure for us. So we talked about the future and decided that he'd play in New York for a couple of years, get his degree in engineering during the off-season, and then go into that field. It was all a big adventure for us."

CHAPTER 9
New York

~:~

*While Tom Landry's twenty-nine years in Dallas is a monument to
excellence, there are those of us here who believe his ten years with the
Giants as a player and coach are equally memorable.*

—WELLINGTON T. MARA
President, the New York Giants

THE 1950S WERE AMERICA in summertime. They were Hula-Hoops
and penny loafers, flattop and ducktail haircuts, bobby socks and the
beginning of the great migration to suburbia, with its barbecue pits in
the backyard and gas-powered lawn mowers, and Edward R. Murrow
and Jonas Salk, who'd developed a vaccine that would combat the disease we feared most, polio. It was a decade of excitement and change, a
time when we would get more and more household appliances, when
married women, more and more, would join the work force and the Big
Band sounds would be replaced by rock-'n'-roll. It was a time when we
broke ties with the past, enjoyed the present, but still connected with
the future.

Certainly, there were fears of the Red Menace, especially when
Russia launched *Sputnik* into orbit around the earth, and of the Bomb,
radioactivity, the Cold War, and the apocalypse, but we went on, perhaps putting our fears and the dark side of the moon of our society aside
until tomorrow . . . and tomorrow.

A war in Korea would begin and end, and there would be almost as
many casualties as there later would be in Vietnam. But the country still
held together. A power-hungry egotist named Joseph McCarthy would
ruin scores of lives by simply hinting that a person might be a communist. And the 1950s were a time for Eisenhower ("We Like Ike") to

become president and young Richard Nixon, a lawyer from California, to be his vice president and the Republican Party's rising star. We would begin to use the term *sex symbol* for people such as Marilyn Monroe and to loosen the collars of what we felt to be the proper morality, on the one hand, and tighten them on the other. Elvis Presley would twist his torso in such a shameful way that Ed Sullivan would televise him only from the waist up.

Herman Wouk, the man who in future decades would write *The Winds of War*, would emerge with *The Caine Mutiny*, and James Jones would shock us with *From Here to Eternity*. But books with a religious background, such as Thomas B. Costain's *The Silver Chalice* and Lloyd Douglas's *The Robe*, would also be very popular. The heroes were clear cut, such as Gary Cooper in *High Noon* and Alan Ladd in *Shane*, and that new medium, television, would gradually come into our homes and begin to change the entertainment habits of a nation.

As the 1950s began, baseball and college football were the most popular sports, and the players were bigger-than-life heroes. But in the final part of the decade, vows would be taken on the perfect marriage of television and professional football, and a nation of sportsmen would come to totally embrace the National Football League. Tom Landry would be a very important part of that league, the league that got the country's undivided attention and whetted its appetite for the professional game.

~:~

NEW YORK CITY has always been alive in and of itself. When Tom and Alicia went there, the city buzzed with the great Broadway musicals *South Pacific* and *Peter Pan*. There were all-time sports heroes such as Joltin' Joe DiMaggio and fine places to go such as Toots Shor's, where you might bump into a movie star or even Rocky Marciano, who had knocked out the great Joe Louis when he was making a comeback try in 1951. And also there were El Morocco and the Stork Club, and you could send your kids to play in Central Park and go there yourself without fear of being mugged or worse. New York had always been a city to which successful people migrated, a place that author Willie Morris, a southerner, once called the "City of Finalists."

"We loved New York when we were there in the 1950s," said Alicia.

"The kids and I could go all over town back then without worrying because it was much safer there then. Tommy and I would meet at Toots Shor's once a week to have lunch, and then we'd spend the rest of the afternoon going to the shops.

"It was just a good place to be then. But all our children were born in Texas. We wanted them to be Texans, although the people we knew when we were in New York were so nice. Oh, sometimes people at stores would be a little rude, but you'd play this game with them. You'd just keep being nice to them and see how long they could go before smiling and being nice to you."

"It was just a great experience being in New York in those days," recalled Landry. "The game of professional football really caught on. It grew up during those days, and, I suppose, those of us who were there felt a part of what was happening.

"I remember that television wasn't a dominant force at all and the newspapers didn't carry that much about pro football around the country. When I started playing, pro football was less than a six-month-a-year job, and we'd go back to Texas each year during the off-season and I'd have a regular job. When we'd go back, nobody would come up and ask me about pro football.

"Things were a lot more low-key then. Pro football people were a pretty closely knit group. The game didn't have the sophistication, the big salaries, and the media exposure. Heck, none of us knew anything about big business. We were Depression babies, just happy to be playing football and getting paid for it. There just wasn't much money talk, and nobody knew what the other guy was making."

⌣∴⌣

TOM LANDRY HAD BEGUN HIS CAREER with the New York Yankees, who merged with the Brooklyn team in the All-American Football Conference in 1949 and became the Brooklyn/New York Yankees. The AAFC was in its fourth and final year before being absorbed by the National Football League. So, including the Giants and Bulldogs of the NFL, New York City had three professional football teams that year.

"The All-American Football Conference wasn't solid," said Landry, "but actually we [the Yankees] were owned by the baseball Yankees and were probably more stable than the Giants and even might have out-drawn them."

As they would one day observe about the American Football League, the purists, the Establishment, chuckled about the AAFC, saying its teams were inferior, a point that the Cleveland Browns of the very innovative and intelligent Paul Brown soon would prove ridiculous.

Landry, the rookie from the University of Texas, was the Yankees' punter, averaging 44.1 for the season, second only to Frankie Albert of San Francisco. He returned three punts for a 17.3 average and intercepted a single pass, which he ran back forty-four yards. On October 31 of that year, he had become a father. In Houston, the Landry's off-season home where he was working on an industrial engineering degree at the University of Houston, Alicia had given birth to Thomas Wade Landry Jr. Tom phoned a number of times but didn't get to see the baby for more than six weeks, until the season ended. The Landrys were learning early that you could not live what was considered a normal life when you played professional football.

Cleveland won that final AAFC championship, as it had each of the previous four, with San Francisco finishing second and Brooklyn/New York third. Cleveland beat Buffalo in the playoffs, San Francisco toppled Brooklyn/New York in the semifinals, and the Browns whipped San Francisco, 21–7, in the title game. In the NFL, the Philadelphia Eagles beat the Los Angeles Rams, 14–10, for the championship.

"To begin with I played offensive halfback behind Buddy Young, but I didn't do a very good job," said Landry. "Then we lost our cornerback Harmon Rowe, and they sent me in to play. Man, Otto Graham went crazy when he saw me. That game I'll never forget. I've never seen so many passes caught in my life. They killed me, but I learned how I'd have to play the game, that I'd have to use my head rather than any great physical talents, which I just didn't have."

The game in question was played November 20, 1949, and Graham, picking on the inexperienced Landry, mostly threw to Mac Speedie, who set an AAFC record with eleven receptions for 228 yards as Cleveland won, 31–0. The experience would have destroyed many before they ever really began. But, of course, it did not destroy Landry. He would go on to become the biggest obstacle Paul Brown and his team would face in the ensuing years.

AFTER A GREAT DEAL OF HASSLING, remindful of things to come in later years between the AFL and the NFL, the National Football League finally agreed to take three AAFC franchises in their entirety, including the champion Browns, the San Francisco 49ers, and the Baltimore Colts. Players from the other teams would be drafted, with the proximity of locales given preference. The Giants, as an example, were allowed to choose five players from the nearby Yankees.

Steve Owen, who had played for the Giants in the formative years then became head coach in 1931, conferred with those in the organization. Then from the Yankees he picked Landry, mostly because of his punting ability, defensive backs Rowe and Otto Schnellbacher, tackle Arnie Weinmeister, and guard John Mastrangelo. Unlimited substitution had been installed in the NFL in 1950, and Landry, Rowe, and Schnellbacher were to become mainstays of a tremendous New York secondary and Weinmeister, a fine tackle.

"I suppose the fastest I'd ever run the hundred was about 10.3," said Landry. "I'm sure the only reason the Giants picked me was for my punting ability. Steve Owen told me I might play some on defense too.

"I was just too slow to play cornerback in the league, so in order to keep my job I had to study a lot. I had to try to figure out what the other team was going to do. I watched films, picked up tendencies."

And Landry was extremely competitive; he would find a way. So he would analyze an opponent to such an extent that he would be there waiting long before the receiver concluded his route. Landry, even then, was picking up the keys that would unlock the secrets of the offensive huddle.

The first year of the merger, Commissioner Bert Bell wasted no time in getting the immediate and undivided attention of those who followed pro football. On Saturday before the regular season began on Sunday, he scheduled a contest between the AAFC champion Cleveland Browns and the defending NFL champion Philadelphia Eagles, featuring Steve Van Buren. Fans of the AAFC rubbed their hands together in anticipation, and NFL followers wondered just who were those guys named Graham, Marion Motley, Speedie, Dante Lavelli, Lou Groza, and a so-called innovative coach, Paul Brown. The question was explicitly answered. Cleveland crushed Philadelphia, 35–10, before 71,237 fans in the City of Brotherly Love.

In attendance that day was Steve Owen. That day Brown had made a popular NFL defense, the Eagle Defense, created by Philadelphia coach Earle "Greasy" Neale, look obsolete. The predominant defense before and during the war years was the 5–3–3 (five linemen, three linebackers, three defensive backs). Neale was tired of seeing fast backs outrun the linebacker on passing plays, so he conceived the Eagle Defense, a 5–2–4 alignment, putting in another defensive back for the linebacker.

The Eagle Defense was quite vulnerable up the middle when an offensive team sent its backs into the flat, occupying the linebackers, and then moved the ends back across the uncovered middle. Brown had done this and had also introduced to the Eagles that day, and to the NFL, the comeback patterns in which Speedie and Lavelli would run downfield toward the backs, then turn and come back a couple of yards to take the ball from Graham on timing.

Owen, a defensive innovator in his own right, was very much aware of what he had seen. Many NFL observers watching the Browns and Eagles that day would talk about how their players must try harder, hustle more against the Browns' receivers, but Owen saw that help come from another direction, a new defense.

The Giants were to play the Browns the following game, and so as the week's preparations began, Owen walked into the team meeting and went to the blackboard. "Gentlemen," he said, "this week we will make changes. This week we will use the 6–1 [six linemen, one linebacker, four defensive backs] against the Cleveland Browns." He then diagramed the alignment and added, "Sometimes we'll be dropping off the ends into the hook zones, the flare zones, and at other times, we'll let them rush Graham. Gentlemen, this is how we'll beat the Cleveland Browns this week."

With that statement, Owen walked out of the room. The players and coaches looked at one another. "Steve Owen was not a great detail man," said Landry. "He'd just do things like that and figure you would work out the details for yourself on the field. I learned much of my coaching by playing under him because I had to work out the details of what he meant.

"The day he drew the 6–1 on the blackboard and walked out of the room, there was some confusion. We had never played that defense before, and I knew somebody had to get up and explain it. Somebody had to exert leadership. I'd never done anything like that before, but I just got up, went to the blackboard, and began to explain in detail what he meant."

Landry explained that the defense would fan out in a semicircle downfield with the middle linebacker as a kind of stem. Sometimes, he told them, the ends would be standing up and dropping off (into pass coverage), and sometimes they would get down in a lineman's stance and rush. The idea was to keep the Browns off balance, never letting them know what was coming. What Owen had devised and Landry had helped explain was what came to be known as the Umbrella Defense, which would replace the Eagle Defense as the most used alignment in the NFL.

When Tom Landry got up that day and explained to the team what Owen meant, he was twenty-five years old. One day he would take the Eagle Defense and the Umbrella Defense and go a step further.

"I was a personnel guy then for the team," recalled Wellington Mara, who became president of the Giants when his father, Timothy Mara, died. "But I can remember being in training camp and Owen would be up at the chalkboard, going over a defense. Suddenly, he'd just stop and say, 'Tom, come up and do this. You know more about it than I do.' It was during those times when he was still playing that he also was becoming a coach, whether he knew it or not."

"We had a great game against the Browns that day," said Landry. "Graham didn't complete a pass in the first half. Certainly, that's one of the games I'll never forget."

When Graham walked under center for the first time, he thought he was looking at a straight 6-1 defense. But as he faded to pass, ends Jim Duncan and Ray Poole dropped off with the receivers. Speedie and Lavelli were, in effect, double covered. Graham not only didn't complete a pass, but he had three passes intercepted.

Paul Brown made adjustments at halftime, telling Graham to throw short passes or run wide, toward the retreating New York ends. But Owen countered, having Poole and Duncan charge the passer most of the time and sending Landry and Em Tunnell, both big for defensive backs, up to make the tackles. The Giants won, 6-0, the beginning of what was to become a fabled rivalry. No matter when or where the Giants and Browns played, it was always like a championship game.

New York also won the second meeting between the two teams, 17-13, and finished with a 10-2 record, tying the Browns for what was then called the American Conference of the National Football League. However, the playoff game to determine the conference's representative in the NFL championship game was another matter. The winner would play the flashy Los Angeles Rams of Elroy Hirsch, Norm Van Brocklin, and Bob Waterfield. They were champions of the National Conference and had an up-and-coming young assistant to president Dan Reeves by the name of Tex Schramm.

"Even then," said Mara, "that plastic-man image was totally false. Tom had a very painful shoulder injury, and it appeared the only way he could participate in the playoff game against Cleveland was to get an injection to deaden the pain. Our team doctor wouldn't give it to him, fearing it might further damage the shoulder. Tom just kept pleading with him to no avail. So Tom played anyway. He wasn't about to miss that game."

Mara recalled standing by the Giants' bench and watching Landry. "He was hollering and yelling and screaming when the offense was on the field," said Mara. "And he had tears in his eyes. When a Cleveland tackler hit one of our players who appeared to be out of bounds and Tom interpreted this as a 'cheap shot,' he rushed over and was all over the guy and ready to fight before they separated them."

In a magnificent defensive battle on a frozen field, Cleveland won, 8–3, making only two field goals and scoring a safety near the end of the game. The Browns would go on to win the NFL title, beating Los Angeles, 30–28, on Groza's field goal with twenty-eight seconds left to play.

To this day, Schramm, who went on to become general manager for the Rams, considers the game one of the toughest defeats he's ever experienced, not only because of what it meant but also because, even then, he was such a strong NFL man and Cleveland had come over from a rival league. And Landry couldn't forget the loss to the Browns either, because he strongly believed those 1950 Giants were one of the best teams New York ever had.

"I still think," Tunnell once said, "that the 1950 team was the best the Giants ever had. Imagine, holding a team like Cleveland to a single touchdown in three games."

Some experts, even today, agree that this was indeed one of the great accomplishments in NFL defensive history.

In 1951, the Giants finished second to Cleveland in the conference, although this time the Browns lost the NFL championship to the Rams. Cleveland beat the Giants twice, 14–13 and 10–0. Landry intercepted a pass in the first week of the season and returned it for a touchdown. He duplicated that feat the following week against the Eagles. Landry also served as the Giants' punter from 1950 to 1955, ranking first in team history in total punts and yardage until Don Chandler came along and broke his records.

"In those early years we lived in a resort hotel on Long Island," recalled Alicia Landry. "It was almost vacant during the season, the winter months, and so it was a nice thing for us. Tommy would commute to work at the Polo Grounds. I loved it there then. We'd have some nice snows, and it was so much cleaner than now."

Tom was at training camp in 1952 when Kitty was born on August 25 in Houston. Again, he phoned but was unable to see Alicia or his daughter until the Giants played an exhibition game in Dallas.

The 1952 season was one in which Tom Landry would begin to assert himself as one of the NFL's top defensive backs. It was also a year in which Dallas, ever so briefly, would have a professional football team. The chain of events had begun in 1949, the final year of the AAFC-NFL war. The Boston Yanks left that city and moved to New York, becoming the Bulldogs. When the leagues merged, the Bulldogs became the Yankees of the NFL, being given the same name as the AAFC team with which Landry had begun his career.

But in 1952, Yankees owner Ted Collins sold his club back to the NFL, which, in turn, allowed it to be bought by a group of Texas businessmen headed by Giles Miller. The team played in the Cotton Bowl, but the talent was inferior, the losses almost sure, and nobody came to watch. So at midseason the franchise was given back to the league and became a "traveling" team, playing the remainder of its games on the road. The Dallas Texans were the last NFL team to fail. The following year the team was purchased by Carroll Rosenbloom and moved to Baltimore, becoming the Colts and soon an NFL power. It would be eight years before another NFL team, the Cowboys, appeared in Dallas.

Landry was superb that season, leading his team with eight interceptions, punting well, and officially becoming a coach on the field. He also was getting a reputation of being able to back up his brain with brawn.

"Tom," recalled Pat Summerall, a place-kicker for the Giants who later became a prominent sportscaster on national television, "was big [198 pounds] for a defensive back and a hard hitter, even a late hitter at times in his enthusiasm. He was just aggressive, and I also remember what a tremendous punter he was."

Dick Nolan was a defensive back for the Giants in 1954. He later would serve two tenures as a Landry assistant between head coaching jobs in San Francisco and New Orleans. It was while he was coaching the 49ers that they suffered narrow defeats to Landry's Cowboys, 14–3 in the 1971 NFC title game and again in the conference championship in 1972, 30–28.

When asked what kind of a player Landry had been, Nolan said, "Tom was such a tough competitor. I guarantee you he'd knock your block off. He was so smart, just amazingly so. The Rams used to have a sprinter named Bobby Boyd. The guy could fly and would just take off and run past the defensive back. Not Tom. Tom would study the guy thoroughly and give him fits. Tom knew when Boyd was going deep and would be there, waiting for him."

One night years ago, a group of writers covering the Dallas Cowboys in their training camp in Thousand Oaks, California, had gone into Encino to eat at the Rams' Horn, a fine restaurant that at the time was owned and operated by former Los Angeles linebacker Don Paul. Paul was reputed to have been one of the toughest players in the league. He began talking about Landry and told a story about a time when Tom chased Mr. Outside of West Point fame, Glenn Davis, all the way back to the Ram bench. Davis, a fine halfback-receiver for the Rams, had beaten Landry for a touchdown.

Davis later agreed that the story as told by Paul was fairly accurate. "I caught a pass about ten yards behind Tom and scored," Davis recalled. "But I could still hear Tom coming after me. I knew he was going to punish me for what I'd done, and, sure enough, he really crashed into me in the end zone. I got up and said, 'If you want the ball that bad, here.' I threw it at his head, and then I took off for the bench. He came after me. Fortunately, I had friends over there."

~:~

AGAIN, AS IN THE TWO PREVIOUS SEASONS, the Giants were battling the Browns for the conference title. New York was improving and had added SMU all-American Kyle Rote in 1951 and Southern California glamor boy halfback Frank Gifford in 1952. The conference title came down to the last three games, the first of which pitted the Giants against the Pittsburgh Steelers, featuring one of the best, toughest, and meanest men ever to play the game, Ernie Stautner. Stautner, a Hall-of-Famer who served as defensive line coach and later defensive coordinator for the Dallas Cowboys, had wanted to play for the Giants, although the Steelers had drafted him. It appeared something might be worked out, if the Giants were interested.

"I was a defensive tackle and weighed only about two hundred thirteen pounds when I got out of college," said Stautner. "I went to talk to Steve Owen, and he took one look at me and said I was too small to play in the line for his Umbrella Defense."

Stautner's famous temper boiled. "I tell you something, Mr. Owen," said Ernie, "I'll play in this league and you'll rue the day you refused me."

Obviously, he did. Stautner carried on a personal vendetta against the Giants, and, although the Steelers had poor records during the '50s, they held their own with the Giants, becoming a major reason New York kept finishing behind Cleveland, as they did in 1952.

"When we played the Giants near the end of that season we could do nothing wrong," said Stautner. "First we knocked out Charlie Conerly, then got their second-string quarterback [Fred Benners, of SMU], and they had nobody to play quarterback. Tom had had a little experience at the position at Texas, and so they put him in there."

"We were lucky to be playing in Pittsburgh," said Landry. "The ground was soft there . . . I could draw plays in the dirt."

"I was rushing Tom when he went back to pass," said Stautner. "You know like always, foaming at the mouth, hellbent-for-leather. I broke through, doubled up my fist, and smashed him in the face, right through his face mask. The blow broke his nose, bloodied him up, knocked him over.

"I just casually started walking back to the defensive side when Tom jumped up and pounded me on the back. I kept going. I knew I'd done a bad thing, but I hated the Giants so much because they'd told me I was too little to play."

Pittsburgh beat the Giants that day, 63–7. It was the last time Landry ever played quarterback, and after the game, Owen, originator of the Umbrella Defense, remarked, "It's a good thing I'm known as a defensive genius or the score would have been one hundred to seven."

The Giants then lost to Washington, but they beat Cleveland in the final game, 37–34. They'd also beaten the Browns, 17–9, in an initial meeting that season, but because of the loss to Pittsburgh as much as anything else, they finished a game behind Cleveland for the conference title.

"Tom never forgot that game and that I'd broken his nose," said Stautner. "After I went to work for him in 1966, he just looked at me one day and said, 'Ernie, I remember you breaking my nose that day in Pittsburgh.'"

It came as a shock for most everybody concerned that the Giants fell apart in 1953, finishing with a 3–9 record and twice losing to Cleveland, including once by the humiliating score of 62–14. There were key injuries to Rote and Ed Price, the fine running backs, and so Owen asked Frank Gifford to move to offense. Gifford went on to become one of the all-time stars at halfback, a man who not only could run but also could catch and throw passes, adding a new dimension.

"Most of us in those days just played the game," said Gifford. "Not Tom. He studied it, studied everything. When I was playing on the defensive unit with Tom in 1952 and before moving to offense in 1953, defense was just hit or miss with most everybody in those days. Not with Tom. He put the same kind of discipline in the defense that the offense had. He had begun to create pro defense as we play it today.

"He had begun to give us keys, although we didn't call them that in those days. But you had to be disciplined. One time I remember I intercepted a pass. I'd just gone for the ball, but I was out of position. Tom didn't say nice play. He just said, 'Frank, you know you were out of position on that play.'"

When the season ended, the rumors circulating in football circles around New York became fact: Timothy Mara fired Steve Owen. Owen had been a loyal Giant all his pro career, playing for the team for ten years and then coaching for twenty-three seasons, in which he won two NFL titles (in 1934 and 1938), took nine conference or divisional championships, and tied for still another. His critics said that the game had passed him by but that he was a stubborn man who resisted change. Certainly, the NFL offenses had begun to exploit his Umbrella Defense. But Owen was hurt deeply when the ax fell, and he refused a job in the organization. Jim Lee Howell, a soft-spoken 6'-4", 250-pound man from Arkansas who had once played end for the Giants, was given the job as head coach.

Two major steps were taken. First, Mara told Howell he wanted him to talk to a young assistant at West Point under Earl "Red" Blaik. If the young man met Howell's requirements, he should hire him. So Howell hired Vince Lombardi to handle his offense. The next step he took was to ask Tom Landry to become a player-coach, to assume responsibility for the defense, something he had already taken upon himself to a degree. Landry, at twenty-nine, became the youngest assistant in the NFL.

"I hadn't planned on a coaching career at all," said Landry. "It just happened. I had my work during the off-season and planned to pursue a career in another profession when I retired as a player. I had been working in real estate and insurance. Then, of course, I retired [in 1956] and became a full-time assistant, but even then, football only lasted half the year and I could pursue other interests.

"When the Giants made me a player-coach, they raised my salary to twelve thousand dollars a year. I was playing left cornerback, coaching the entire defense by myself, and had made All-Pro. When I went into Wellington's office to ask for a raise, he said, 'I don't know if you had a good enough year.' He's been picking up the tab on my meals ever since."

During the season, the Giffords, the Landrys, and some of the other players moved to a hotel on 81st Street. "It was a lot of fun," recalled Gifford. "My family spent a lot of time with Tom's. We'd play cards, go out together."

"I can still remember going to Yankee Stadium and seeing Ted Williams and the Red Sox play the Yankees and Joe DiMaggio," said Landry. "That was quite a thrill."

"I think we saw every Broadway show that came to town," recalled Alicia. "Sometimes the wives would go. We'd spend a lot of time together, maybe getting together to prepare dinner for our husbands and things like that. Oh, we saw shows such as *Call Me Madam*, *South Pacific*, *Peter Pan*, and *Harvey* with Ray Bolger. We saw Mary Martin a number of times and Ethel Merman. Tommy liked the musicals all right. But sometimes he'd just say he wished they'd quit singing so they could get on with the plot. But, of course, the plot was there because of the singing."

Once they went to see a popular drama on Broadway, Eugene O'Neill's *Long Day's Journey into Night*. Alicia recalled, "It depressed us so much we tried to stay away from things such as that.

"And it was also during those days that Tommy and I established a tradition we carried on even when he was so busy with the Cowboys. We'd go out to dinner at least once a week, no matter what was happening."

The 1954 season would be Tom Landry's best as a player, and a suggestion he made one day in practice would not only prolong but add even more stardom to the career of Kyle Rote. Rote, as a halfback, was continually having knee problems. His knee simply could not stand the pounding from the position.

"Oh, I'd run patterns against Tom in practice from my position, which, basically, was a halfback split out wide. I suppose I'd run pretty good patterns and catch the ball fairly well, so one day in practice Tom stopped me."

"Hey," said Landry to Rote, "why don't you try it at end? I think you'd do a good job there."

Rote took the suggestion and became one of the great NFL ends of his time. "Tom knew I couldn't run out of the backfield anymore because of my knees," said Rote. "I just couldn't do it. When I moved to end, it was the biggest break of my football career." Rote played end for the Giants until his retirement in 1961.

The Giants finished third in what then was called the Eastern Conference. Landry not only coached the defense but also intercepted eight passes, tying Tunnell for the team lead, finished fourth in the NFL in punting with a 42.5 average, and had a long kick of sixty-one yards. His hairline was receding on both sides, just as his father's had, but some of the Giants joked that he lost his hair because he was hitting opponents so hard. Years later, others would say the same thing about Cowboy free safety Cliff Harris.

"We'd get into the defensive huddle," said Nolan, a rookie then, "and Tom would call the defense. He'd look over at me and say, 'Dick, if they put the flanker out in front of you, then you key the fullback, and if the fullback swings out, the flanker will run a down-and-in, so be ready.' He was usually right."

Landry was always at his best against the Browns, perhaps because deeply embedded in his mind was the time as a rookie in 1949 when Otto Graham had picked him apart. One day he caught Graham in the open field, running with the ball, and crashed into the Browns' quarterback with a shot that could be heard around the stadium. It was the final play of a particular series, and as Landry started off the field, the usually calm Paul Brown charged a few steps on the field and yelled, "Cheap shot, Landry! Cheap shot!"

Calmly, Landry turned toward Brown and said, "You know better than that, Paul."

Tunnell, the first black man to play for the Giants, an NFL Hall-of-Famer, and a man many believe to be their greatest safety to play the game, once said, "Landry was real smart. He never said much, really. But he always knew what was going on. We didn't have words like they do now, keying or something like that. Tom would make up his own keys and teach them to us.

"But socially . . . he seemed kind of weird to me sometimes. We played alongside each other and played great for all those years, but outside of football we didn't communicate much at all. Tom was his own person, going his own way, and I was mine. Some of us would go out for a beer, but Tom, mostly, would just disappear, go off with his family. But I say this, I had a lot of respect for him."

"Tom was so strong-minded and such a stickler for the way things should be done," recalled Nolan, a grin creeping across his face. "We were playing Detroit, I believe it was, when John Henry Johnson, a big, mean sonuvagun of a fullback, headed in my direction. He had all three guys leading interference for him, and it seemed like they all were coming at me. Anyway, I do know they all hit me, leaving me all in pieces on the ground. My shoulder was separated, and I just lay there, trying to figure out whether or not I was dead. The first thing I see when I open my eyes is Tom, standing over me.

"'I know,' I told him, 'you want me to stay in the game.'"

"'No,' he said, 'you had bad technique on that play.'"

The Giants' defensive unit had a slogan on the blackboard: "What if?" Landry would be explaining a situation, what would happen and what a particular player was supposed to do, and somebody would continually ask, "What if he doesn't? What if?"

"He will," Landry would answer.

"Geeze," said Nolan, "one time he drove me crazy. He said a certain thing would happen and I said, 'But what if the guy does this instead of that?'"

"He won't," said Landry.

"Okay, but let's say he does. Then what?"

"He won't."

"But what if he did!"

Landry, looking at Nolan calmly, repeated, "He won't."

"And, like I said before, he was right most of the time," said Nolan, who then grinned again and added, "And if he wasn't, he wouldn't admit it."

"Very early in his career Tom had such tremendous self-confidence," said Mara. "That carried over to our defensive players. They were hard, tough people, but Tom would win them over by a force of intellect. He would tell them things and be right, and he gained a lot of respect from them. He knew if they did what he told them they'd be fine."

Mara recalled the time a particular player, whose name he wouldn't mention, became available to the Giants. The guy had never played that well against the Giants, but Mara asked Landry what he thought.

"Oh, he's a good player," said Landry.

"But he didn't do anything against us."

Landry thought for a second and added, "Haphazard coaching."

Landry was very serious about his football, and although there were often times when he was amused or would chuckle at what happened, he just wasn't a guy from whom you'd expect a great belly laugh. Well, Nolan did recall one time . . .

During the final stages of that 1954 season, the Giants were hosting the Los Angeles Rams in the rickety old Polo Grounds in Coogan's Bluff. The game meant nothing as far as the standings because Detroit and Cleveland were on their way to a showdown as the conference winners. But there occurred that day a particular play that caused Tom Landry to crack up every time he thought of it.

Now, in those days the Rams were still the glamor team with Van Brocklin, Hirsch, Tom Fears, and a pair of bull-like running backs nicknamed by Van Brocklin "Deacon" and "Tank." The former was Dan Towler and the latter Paul Younger.

Deacon and Tank had rattled the rib cages of more than one defender, especially a defensive back who might have the ill fortune to be in their paths once they cleared the line of scrimmage and got up a head of steam. Dick Nolan was a rookie and played the right corner; Landry, as player-coach, played the left side.

In those days Nolan weighed about 175 to 180 pounds, giving up some 30 to 40 pounds to running backs such as Deacon and Tank. Dick

The Landry family (Tom sitting), around 1930

Landry at the University of Texas

Tom Landry, assistant coach, the New York Giants (Bill Winfrey photo)

The Landry Family (1970s)

Craig Morton, Landry, and Roger Staubach (John Mazziotta photo)

Danny White, Landry, and Mike Ditka

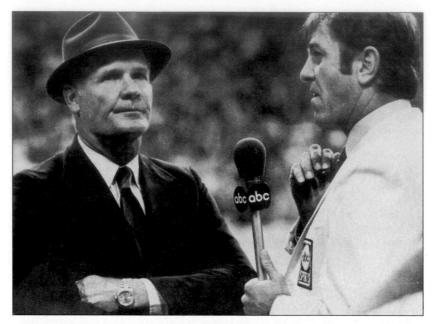

Landry and Don Meredith

Tom Landry, Jr. and Sr.

Coach Landry in Texas Stadium

Landry and Bob Hayes

Landry and Danny White (Brian Williams photo)

Tom and Alicia at home

Tom with grandson Ryan

Tom supported the Fellowship of Christian Athletes

An excited coach

A real cowboy

Coach Landry with current Cowboys' owner Jerry Jones

Quarterback reunion: (left to right) Danny White, Troy Aikman, Don Meredith, Eddie LeBaron, Craig Morton, Coach Landry, and Roger Staubach

Good-bye to a legend

did, however, have a great deal of nerve and was very aggressive, although he did not particularly want to see the likes of the Ram runners breaking into the secondary and thus requiring him to face them head-on.

At that time goalposts were situated on the actual goal line, not at the back of the end zone as they are today, and they were not even padded. In fact, it was often smart strategy for runners to use the uprights to shield off would-be tacklers as they plunged for the end zone.

During the course of the game, which the Rams would win, 17–16, Los Angeles drove inside the New York five-yard line. The Giants tightened, preparing to meet another bullish charge by Towler or Younger. Deacon's number was called, and as he lined up, his face became stern, grim, but inside he was smiling because he liked the contact, to feel defenders crumble against his awesome power. He set and on the snap lunged forth to take the hand-off from Van Brocklin. It was the right play at the right time, and a huge hole opened over guard. Deacon was unchallenged at the line of scrimmage as he charged forward in all his fury, his head lowered and his helmet set to butt anything in his way. So he gained momentum and drove with all his might to the end zone without any of the expected opposition. Only thing, he ran smack into the goalpost with his head.

There was a bone-rattling collision, muscle and power against steel set solidly into the ground with concrete. Nolan later recalled looking at films and said you could actually see the goalpost give, bend a little, and then catapult Deacon backward some four, five yards, sending the ball flying out of his hand as though it had been dynamited loose.

"The goalpost," said Nolan, "went shooooooshhhh."

Deacon, thrown on his back, sat up, stunned, his eyes blank, looking like Orphan Annie, his helmet askew, slightly cracked, a man having no idea what great force had hit him. He tried to shake cobwebs loose in his head, the stars dancing madly in front of his eyes.

"I just stood there for a while," said Landry, "looking at him to see if he'd ever move again."

Emlen Tunnell was very concerned and said, "Deac! Deac! You all right? You okay, Deac?"

Nolan, never one to miss a chance, sashayed over to Deacon, bent over, and stuck a finger right into the Ram running back's face.

"Yeah, Deac," barked Nolan, "you come through there again, you sonuvagun, and the next time I'll really hit you!" Deacon stared up at Nolan in disbelief.

Landry laughed aloud again as he recalled the story, then said, "I couldn't look at either of them. I ran off the field and got to the sidelines before I really broke up laughing.

"Those were great years, and that Nolan could be crazy at times."

Landry went on to make All-Pro at cornerback that year, 1954, along with such players as Otto Graham, Doak Walker, Ollie Matson, Lou Groza, Leo Nomellini, Les Bingaman, Chuck Bednarik, and Bucko Kilroy, the feared Chicago Bear lineman who would one day become a scout for the Cowboys.

༺ : ༻

IN 1955 THE GIANTS finished third again in the NFL Eastern Conference with a 6–5–1 record, but they did so in a different arena, Yankee Stadium, to which they had moved from the old Polo Grounds. It was a much better place, with improved dressing facilities, but Yankee Stadium still was the "House That Ruth Built" and baseball was still king. It also marked the year that Landry retired as an active player, becoming a full-time assistant defensive coach for Howell.

Former longtime Giants publicity director Don Smith once recalled the year and the transition by saying, "When Tom became a full-time coach, it was as if he had been doing it for twenty years. There was no sense of time passing. Even today when you see him, you get the feeling no time has passed. It's just like you wake up, pull a shade, and all the wisdom of a lifetime is under the pillow."

Although the record didn't reveal what was happening, the Giants were getting awfully close to becoming a power in 1954 and 1955, with the credit going not only to the fine array of talent being assembled but also to Howell's young assistants, Landry and Lombardi.

"In the early years Vince was a fine coach but not the great coach he later became," Landry said. "When he came into pro football with us it was his first time in the game [he hadn't played professional football], so he was not only doing the job but also learning.

"But it was pretty obvious to all of us that one day Vince would be a really great coach. He was very basic in his approach and was a master of knowing how to utilize, to get the most out of personnel.

"Vince was a very emotional man. If the offense didn't look good, sometimes it'd be two, three days before you could talk to him. He really hated to look bad. He was that sensitive. But that was just Vince, and we understood him. We got along very well, were friends. It was just if the offense played well and won, he was very outgoing, emotional, and if not, the opposite."

"Tom and Vince were both tremendous coaches and people," said Mara. "On the surface Vince was a warmer person than Tom. He went from warm to red hot. You could hear him laughing or shouting for five blocks. You couldn't hear Landry sometimes if he was in the next chair. Lombardi was more of a teacher, whereas Landry seemed like a professor. It was as though Tom lectured the top 40 percent of the class and Vince the lower 10 percent.

"When they looked at films, one got as much out of them as the other, but Tom would do it more quickly. He absorbed things more quickly."

"There's no doubt," said Nolan, "that Landry and Lombardi were the main guys. Vince was gregarious, and, you know, he was the type guy to get you to jump through a hoop for him. He would get a guy to play above his capabilities. Tom would tell you exactly what to do, and if you did it you were successful. It was that simple."

Howell gave Landry and Lombardi the reins, then let them go. "I just pump up the footballs and keep curfew," he once said. "With those two around, I have very little to do.

"Vince was very aggressive, sometimes to the point of being abrasive, but that was just his personality. On the field he would walk guys through plays before there was contact. He wanted every player to understand his assignment before the play was carried out. And he was daring, which I liked.

"Tom was the best defensive coach in the business, brilliant, a great organizer. His manner was very different. Vince was a yeller, a shouting type guy. Tom never raised his voice; he was very quiet and got his point across just as effectively as Vince. Tom was extremely talented at analyzing films. It would take him, maybe, twenty minutes to dissect a team's performance, whereas it might take somebody else hours. He was also outstanding at evaluating players, which later helped him so much at Dallas.

"It was a wonderful situation. They were friends, competitive, and each had a fire in him to win."

"They were good friends," said Nolan, "but Tom knew more football."

Rote remembered once walking down the hall at the Giants' training camp at St. Michael's, Vermont. "I looked on one side of the hall and there was Lombardi looking at films," said Rote. "I looked on the other side and there was Landry looking at films. I continued on down the hall and saw Jim Lee reading a newspaper."

"I doubt there ever will be a situation like that again," said Landry. "I mean one where you have three men like that working together and a head coach just turning things over to his assistants like Jim Lee did Vince and myself.

"Jim Lee was a very soft-spoken man. But I'm sure if we'd messed up he'd have said something to us. But as long as we were doing the job, he just let us handle it. Vince and I ran our units during the week and during the games."

"It was extremely competitive," said Nolan. "You can't imagine how competitive it could be. But it just happened . . . the offense and defensive units separated. The toughest competition either ever faced was when one scrimmaged the other."

"The defensive unit in those years was very close," said Landry. "As I look back on those times in the mid- and late 1950s, I think of them as some of the best experiences of my time in football. It was as close as any team with which I've been associated. I didn't have any help coaching the defense. I coached everybody . . . the line, the linebackers, the secondary [he also coached the kickers], and it was a great time.

"We all worked hard. It seemed like we worked until we were about ready to drop, and then we'd work some more."

Of course, Lombardi would always want the offense on the field, and Landry would want the defense out there. Nolan remembered seeing Howell run up and down the sidelines, yelling at Landry, "What should we do? What should we do?"

"Punt," said Landry. "Give them the ball."

Lombardi had installed the power sweep with the fullback blocking, the two guards pulling, and the halfback following with the ball. It was perfect for Gifford, a fine runner who was also a threat as a passer. This was the same setup Lombardi later exploited at Green Bay with Paul Hornung.

And Landry had taken the defense a step further. He began using a

4–3 alignment (four linemen, three linebackers, two cornerbacks, two safeties) when he was a player-coach. The unit was solid, but something was lacking. In 1956 he found that ingredient in Sam Huff, a man who was to become the epitome of middle linebackers of his era, and the Giants took steps to establish a dynasty in the Eastern Conference and to head on a collision course with the Baltimore Colts two years later. That game would change the nation's television viewing habits, making pro football the national game, television's game.

⌣∴⌣

WHEN THE NEW YORK GIANTS began training camp in 1956 at St. Michael's, Vermont, a baby-faced lineman from West Virginia was among the rookie crop. He had an innocent, easygoing air about him, but at times when he was on the field, he could become overly aggressive or, as some put it, "downright mean." But he was only 6'-1" and about 225 pounds, and he was trying to make it as a guard. The times were changing, and so the pros were beginning to look for taller and heavier blockers to withstand such huge rushers as Baltimore's "Big Daddy" Lipscomb, who weighed 280 pounds. The kid was also too small to play in the defensive line. The only guy about his size who could do that was Ernie Stautner, and the Giants didn't even like to think about him getting away to Pittsburgh.

The kid and his roommate, Don Chandler, a punter who the coaches hoped would take Landry's spot as the team's punter, became very disenchanted in camp. The kid kept hearing talk that he was a man without a position, and he figured he was going to get cut anyway and there just were too many sacrifices to be made for nothing. So the pair packed their bags, sneaked out of camp, and headed for home, where the kid planned to become a schoolteacher.

One story has it that Vince Lombardi stopped them before they left the dorm at training camp. Another says Lombardi roared up in a car before they boarded their train and put an end to their idea of going AWOL.

With the fury he could show so well, Lombardi mesmerized the deserters, saying, "Listen, you two might not make this club, but nobody runs out on me! Nobody!"

So they came back, their heads lowered. And Tom Landry, then the full-time defensive coach, began to get some ideas about the baby-faced kid named Robert E. Lee "Sam" Huff. He would become the epitome of a position called middle linebacker, and his violent world would be talked about by pro football fans from New York to Texas as he became a part of the defensive renaissance.

~:~

LANDRY HAD ALREADY EXPERIMENTED with the 4–3 and by that year had begun, more and more, to explore all the aspects of the alignment. Other teams around the league had also begun to drop off their ends from a six-man line to defend against the end sweep, but Landry was still ahead of his time.

Wellington Mara recalled, "What everybody was doing was forcing the play back inside. But Tom came up with the idea of defensing the end run inside-out, stopping opponents up the middle with the idea that pursuit would take care of the outside. Simply, Tom was talking about today's 4–3 defense, where the four defensive linemen are charged with the responsibility of keeping the five offensive linemen from getting a clear shot at the middle linebacker. Jim Lee Howell accepted this theory, and the rest is history: the 4–3 defense."

"Even during the days I was playing offense, I felt defense was the most challenging part of the game," recalled Landry. "The offense has its plays diagramed for it and knows ahead of time what to do. The defense must constantly anticipate and react. On defense you have to accept the fact that you're going to give the other guy the first shot. The initial advantage is his. I just always have had an analytical mind, and this was most intriguing for me.

"Again, the 4–3 was a combination of the Eagle Defense and the Umbrella. The Eagle Defense had begun taking on a 4–3 look because they'd put an extra back in for the linebacker to help on passing downs. He'd be standing up. It was just becoming obvious to me that the thing to do was keep the ends dropped off, covering the flare areas, making them linebackers.

"But what I needed was a guy in the middle who was pretty quick, pretty active, and could key. Sam seemed like he might be that guy. We tried him, and it worked out well for all concerned."

"Ray Beck got hurt in an exhibition game," said Huff. "And they stuck me in there. By early season I was the starting middle linebacker."

"Well, it was obvious he ought to be tried at middle linebacker,"

182

continued Landry. "In those days, we kept things very simple, easy to make the adjustments. I gave him a couple of keys, and that's what he looked for.

"Actually, when we got Randy White with the Cowboys, I felt the same way about him, that he should be tried at middle linebacker and could be tremendous due to his size and ability. But the game had become so much more complicated. It would have taken a much, much longer time for Randy. Had Randy been around during the days when Sam came up, he'd have moved in and done extremely well at middle linebacker too.

"But Sam . . . he just was excellent at following instructions. He was very disciplined and would listen. He also had a mean streak, which is nice to have in a middle linebacker.

"Our defense was coordinated, and you had to have discipline to play it, sometimes sacrificing individual plays for the betterment of the overall defense. It's based on the ability of a unit to react together. Most defensive players get hit and fight through the block. We hold. We do not fight through a block. We control an area. That's based on my engineering background, coordinating people."

"I don't know who takes credit for the 4–3," said Frank Gifford, "but it was Tom . . . he exploited it, coordinated it, made it work. Few people outside football realized what a great coach he was, what a great innovator he was. Most coaches should have been worshiping at his feet."

Dick Nolan remembered the 4–3 and Huff. "Sam was perfect, but Tom made him what he became with the defense. If the right defense hadn't been there for him, if Tom hadn't been there, I don't know what would have happened to him.

"But against some of those big fullbacks, Tom would tell him exactly what they'd do. If they line up like this, and he's here, then he'll do this. Tom could look at an opponent's films, even in those days, and know what they'd do. He was so far ahead of his time . . . you just can't imagine how far. You realize, the 4–3 is still being used in the NFL today."

Andy Robustelli, an NFL Hall of Fame defensive end, recalled when he was traded from the Los Angeles Rams to the Giants in 1956. "When I was with the Rams, they used a very active type defense, one where they would just turn you loose," he said. "When I got to New

York, I didn't know what was happening. Landry had this methodical defensive scheme in which you read the offense and used techniques. It was completely coordinated, and everybody had a job.

"I didn't understand what was happening at first, but Tom would just say do it . . . do this or that in a certain situation. Then I did understand the defense, and it was amazing, so far ahead of its time that it was incredible.

"But you had to concentrate and do your job, not worrying about anybody else. You take two steps too many and a runner might break for a sixty-yard touchdown run on you.

"Those were great days with the Giants. The country was different then. There was so much more tradition for the country, the family, and religion. We needed each other to be successful, and we loved the game and each other. Now a guy makes millions a year and even if his team loses he considers himself successful. We enjoyed playing. It was a lot of work, but some funny things would go on too . . ."

As the story goes, before the Giants played Philadelphia in 1956, two reporters slipped into the meeting room while Landry was giving a rundown on the Eagles. "He's too slow to react." . . . "You can take advantage of him because he loses his concentration." . . . "This guy will sometimes quit on you if you take him on physically."

They wrote about what he said in the newspapers the next morning, and of course, it was also picked up by the papers in the City of Brotherly Love. Head coach Jim Lee Howell was worried and told his team, "Those guys read what was said and they're going to come in here Sunday with fire in their eyes, ready to draw blood. Now what are you going to do about it!"

Roosevelt Grier had come to the Giants in a trade in 1955, and he would later gain fame as one of the Fearsome Foursome for the Los Angeles Rams. He was a fine football player, but he didn't have a mean bone in his body. When Howell asked the team what they were going to do, he looked right at Rosey Grier.

"Uh, maybe it isn't too late, Coach," Grier is reputed to have said. "Maybe we could write an apology."

⌣∴⌣

WHEN THE GIANTS BROKE TRAINING CAMP, eighteen players and coaches moved that year to the Concourse Plaza, near Yankee Stadium, not far from Central Park. Kyle Rote Jr. remembered that he used to go to Central Park and play games with Tom Landry Jr. and Jeff Gifford. And when the team would go through a light workout on Saturday morning before it played a home game, the boys would go to Yankee Stadium and wear Giants T-shirts or old jerseys and run around, throwing the football.

Huff, the rookie, moved into the Concourse Plaza in 1956. "You might say I learned to play middle linebacker while sitting in the Landry suite at the hotel," Huff said. "I'd be there in my room, you know, after practice, relaxing, and the phone would ring. It would be Tom."

"Sam," Landry would say, "what are you doing?"

"Oh, hello, Coach. Just resting, sitting here watching television. Kinda caught up in this show."

"Good, I'm glad you aren't doing anything. Why don't you come up to my room and look at some football films with me? There's some things I want to show you."

Huff recalled, "Tom had this projector in his apartment, and we'd go over the team we'd be playing that week, over and over . . . tendencies, what to look for, keys. I didn't get to finish watching a lot of interesting television programs that year, but I learned more football in that one season in Tom's apartment than I'd learned throughout high school and college."

"It was good to get out of the Polo Grounds," admitted Landry. "Yankee Stadium had a great deal of tradition and it was an exciting place to play, to be. Of course, it seated a lot more people [sixty-two thousand] too, and we were going to draw the crowds."

"One time in the Polo Grounds," said Nolan, "we played before eight thousand fans." He said he thought he'd never experience anything like that again and he didn't, until he got to Dallas.

❧

THERE WAS NO DOUBT the Giants had something special going in 1956, especially on defense. The club had a fine new defensive lineman in Jim Katcavage, who soon would join Andy Robustelli, Rosey Grier, and Dick Modzelewski in the front four, linebackers Huff, Harland Svare, Bill Svoboda, and Cliff Livingston, and a secondary of guys such as Nolan, Tunnell, Jim Patton, Ed Hughes, and Lindon Crow. Before the 1950s had ended, they would have fans cheering for the defense as much as, if not more than, the offense. They would become the heroes, almost cultlike, and fans who previously had only watched the ball suddenly would chant throughout Yankee Stadium, "Defense! Defense!" and then, "Huff-Huff-Huff-Huff!" until it sounded almost like a locomotive gaining speed.

There had been great defensive players in the past and great defensive coaches, but because of the attention Landry and his unit were to receive in the nation's largest city, its largest media market, the defense in all sports would take on new proportions as far as the general public was concerned. The defenders would begin to reach the same stardom, the same status as those on offense.

The Giants would one day hold an opponent to zero yards passing, and the confrontations with the explosive Cleveland Browns and Jimmy Brown would get the nation's attention.

"We really did have an exceptional football team," said Landry. "I think by 1958 and the great championship game with Baltimore that our defense was catalystic in giving the defense in professional football recognition as a unit. It was the beginning of the change that has carried through all these years."

But the Giants also had great offensive stars in Conerly, Gifford, Rote, Alex Webster, Roosevelt Brown, Bill Austin, and young Don Heinrich. They had outstanding kickers first in Ben Agajanian and later in Pat Summerall and a tremendous punter in Don Chandler.

In 1956 changes had come and were coming. The Western Conference Los Angeles Rams dropped from the top to the bottom, and the Baltimore Colts were on the rise when a free agent named Johnny Unitas, cut by Pittsburgh, took over for injured quarterback George Shaw. The always potent Cleveland Browns took a step backward when Otto Graham retired, and Paul Brown tried to find an adequate replacement. The times were right for the New York Giants.

"Everybody worked so hard," recalled Howell. "Landry would be in my office one minute, asking for more time in practice for his defense, and Lombardi would walk in the next minute, wanting more time for the offense."

"It hadn't been that way before, but it finally got to where the offensive and defensive units were separated, in meetings and otherwise," said Landry. "But, of course, one depended on the other."

Conerly had been through some lean years in New York, and then

Howell used the theory of starting Heinrich to probe the defense, see what was happening, discuss it with Conerly on the sidelines, and then send him in, usually after about a period or less.

"A lot of the fans were on Charlie," recalled Landry. "They'd boo him pretty badly at times. They wanted the young guy in there, you know. But Vince was a strong supporter of Charlie, whom he called the 'Pro.' Everybody called him that."

When Landry took over the Cowboys, he would often experience the same situation. At first, fans wanted Don Meredith to replace Eddie LeBaron, and then, Jerry Rhome or Craig Morton to replace Meredith. Then they would react negatively when Landry did not immediately put in Roger Staubach for Morton. Then they would want Gary Hogeboom to step in, and finally, Steve Pelluer to take over for Danny White. It would go on and on. The Conerly situation just gave Landry another experience upon which to draw later.

In 1956, Ike was in office, Debbie Reynolds and Eddie Fisher were married, and the New York Yankees beat the Brooklyn Dodgers in the World Series.

And the New York Giants defense limited famed Chicago Bear fullback Rich Casares, who was to lead the NFL in rushing with 1,126 yards, to a mere 13 yards rushing. The teams had tied 17–17 in late season, and many felt it was a preview of the NFL title game. It was. With the fine defense and Gifford having an outstanding year offensively, rushing for 819 yards and catching fifty-two passes for 603, the Giants took the East with a 7–5 mark. The Bears won the West with a 9–2 mark, beating out Detroit by a single game.

On December 30, 1956, they met in Yankee Stadium before fifty-six thousand fans for the NFL championship. Temperatures were near eighteen degrees and dropping by midafternoon, ironically reminding some old-timers of the weather in 1934 when the Giants had beaten the Bears, 30–13, in the NFL title game. That day the Giants had played on the hard, frozen field with sneakers instead of cleated shoes and they'd been able to maneuver much better than the Bears. Howell said they would use sneakers in this one also, to get better footing. The move paid off again.

Rookie Gene Filipski returned the opening kickoff from George Blanda fifty-four yards to the Bears' five, and the rout was on. The Giants led, 34–7, at halftime and won the championship, 47–7.

"The way our defense and offense played was a great tribute to two men," said Howell, "Landry and Lombardi."

George McCall, Landry's old fraternity brother from the University of Texas, recalled being in New York after the Giants won the championship game. "The whole team was at Toots Shor's and celebrating like crazy," he said. "Gifford was there, and Rote too. We left Shor's, went somewhere else, and celebrated until 4:00 A.M. I was there for an insurance school and missed it the next day. I imagine a lot of other people were having trouble too. But I bet Tom jumped right up and went about his business."

In the early 1960s Landry sometimes would have a martini. Once during training camp the coaches were relaxing and Jimmy Parker, a teetotaler who was the Cowboys' business manager at the time, was fixing drinks. Tom said he'd take a martini, and when Jimmy asked him how he liked it, Landry said, "Oh, four to one."

Parker shrugged and put four parts vermouth and one part gin. Landry took a sip and almost gagged. A joke in the organization was that that was when Tom stopped drinking.

～:～

MOST FELT THE GIANTS would repeat their championship win in 1957, but something happened beyond their control. Paul Brown drafted the big running back from Syracuse, Jim Brown. It wasn't that Cleveland could handle the Giants, but with Brown running wild and Tommy O'Connell having a good year at quarterback, Paul Brown's team beat practically everybody else.

The Browns won the first meeting of the two clubs, 6–3, on Lou Groza's two field goals, but obvious from the score, Landry's defense couldn't have played much better. Cleveland also won the second meeting, 34–28, as the defense didn't play so well, but Landry still got in a word.

Brown was on his way to leading the league in rushing with 942 yards, a 4.7 average per carry, but before the final game with the Giants, Landry chided Giant running back Mel Triplett.

"Mel," said Landry, "how is it Brown makes more yards in one game than you do the entire season? Is he that much better than you are? Is that what it is?"

Jimmy Brown rushed for 114 yards that day. Mel Triplett rushed for 116.

Cleveland won the Eastern title with a 9–2–1 record, while the Giants finished second at 7–5. Detroit claimed the West and routed the Browns, 59–14, for the NFL title.

Studying and working during the off-season, Landry had gotten his industrial engineering degree at the University of Houston to go along with the B.A. he had received at the University of Texas. He moved his family in 1955 from Houston to Dallas, where he worked during the off-season in real estate and insurance. On March 4, 1958, a third child, Lisa, was born. This time Tom was there.

"He was working but took off and stayed at home and helped me with the baby and the other kids," said Alicia. "He really worked hard, taking care of the baby. But Tommy always has been a good father, and the fact that he was there with me just made up for the other two times when he was away and couldn't be with me."

⌣∶⌣

PRIOR TO THE 1958 SEASON, everybody was talking about Jimmy Brown and just what he might accomplish, about ageless George Halas reinstating himself as coach of the Chicago Bears, about Texan Buddy Parker abruptly walking out on the Detroit Lions and going to the Pittsburgh Steelers, where he quickly traded for Bobby Layne, and about Norm Van Brocklin moving from the Rams to the Eagles.

But nobody had any idea then what great significance the end of the 1958 season would hold. There would be a title game that would become legendary, one that would turn the eyes of the nation to professional football and unite the game with television, once and for all. Professional football would become the television sport, and the New York Giants and Tom Landry would be very much a part of it all.

Most were picking the Giants behind Cleveland and, perhaps, the Eagles because of the addition of Van Brocklin. The Landrys had moved away from New York City to Stamford, Connecticut, from where Tom commuted to Yankee Stadium with Ed Hughes, who had taken Landry's place at right cornerback when he'd retired as a player in 1956. Andy Robustelli, Cliff Livingston, and a lawyer-turned-sports-caster named Howard Cosell also lived in Stamford.

"Howard," remarked Landry, "wasn't as caustic in those days. He was doing mostly boxing."

When reminded that Cosell, a strong Lombardi and Don Shula

apostle, had been critical of Landry on *Monday Night Football*, often saying his team was overrated, Landry just smiled and said nothing.

"Oh," said Alicia when it was pointed out that Cosell had knocked her husband, "we didn't pay much attention to things such as that then. When people got very critical or attacked Tommy, we just considered the source."

Alicia also has fond memories of the years in Connecticut. "The times I enjoyed most were when I'd go into the City and meet Tommy for lunch," she said. "It was lovely there."

Hughes, who also became a Landry assistant in Dallas, recalled, "In those days Tom used to have a saying. He had just about everything figured out, but of course, there's always a gray area. So if it came to that gray area, Tom would say, 'Well, then you react like a football player.'

"It was funny, but years later when I was into coaching I wrote Tom and asked him how to handle a certain situation. I got a thirteen-page reply back from him, explaining all aspects. 'But, of course,' he said at the end of the letter, 'there's a gray area; not black or white, so in this case you must react like a football player.'"

Cleveland, with the great Jimmy Brown running rampant, got off to a 5–0 start. Brown was averaging 163 yards per game and a 6.9 average per carry and had scored fourteen touchdowns. The Giants, losing Gifford temporarily to injury, were 3–2 but got back into the race by beating Cleveland, 21–17.

Almost like it had been scripted, it all came down to the final game with the Giants hanging on by their fingernails. They had to beat the Browns in order to tie Cleveland for the NFL Eastern Conference title and cause a playoff.

Snow had been falling in New York, making it look somewhat like a Christmas card on that Sunday in mid-December. The game was a typical fierce battle between the two teams, with the Giants trailing 10–3 at halftime but tying the game 10–10 when Gifford twice completed halfback passes. Jimmy Brown had opened the game by bursting through the Giants' defense on a sixty-five-yard touchdown run but thereafter was almost shut completely down by Huff and the defense. Many believed that Landry had Huff following Brown on each and every play, but this wasn't true. Landry had discovered a tendency used by Paul Brown, who called the Cleveland plays. Most of the time, if Jim Brown lined up in such a way in a certain formation, he very likely would run a certain play. Landry had unlocked the Browns' offense by watching films.

All Cleveland needed was a 10–10 tie, and it seemed it would get this when Summerall missed a thirty-seven-yard field goal with less than five minutes to play. Cleveland wanted to kill the clock, but Landry's defense held and the Giants moved to the Browns' forty-two-yard line with 2:07 remaining. They faced a fourth and ten.

Howell had planned to pass on fourth down, but at the last second he turned to Summerall and told him to go in and try the impossible, a forty-nine-yard field goal in the snow. "You always have hopes," said Landry, "but with the snow and all, Pat couldn't even see the goalpost."

When the Giants lined up, the yells and screams in Yankee Stadium became muffled emotions, murmurs. Conerly cleared a spot in the snow and put down the snap from Ray Wietecha. Summerall, in picture form, moved forward, locked his ankle, kept his head down, and met the ball solidly, sending it soaring toward the goalposts. It split the uprights, and the Giants won, 13–10, forcing a rematch between the teams for the NFL Eastern Conference championship.

When they played again, the Giants' defense—Landry's 4–3, his keys, his game plan, his analysis of what Cleveland would do, especially what Jimmy Brown would do, and a fine array of players—completely dominated the Cleveland offense as Brown was held to eight yards rushing and the Giants won, 10–0.

After the game, a stunned Lou Groza remarked, "There's only one man who could have done this to us: Tom Landry. Nobody else."

The game ball was handed to Robustelli, who said, "This doesn't belong to me," and gave it to Landry. Jim Lee Howell said, "Tom Landry is the best coach in football."

The Giants had survived a season and won a title by depending on a great defense and doing the things offensively that they had to do, a field goal here, a big play there. Meanwhile, Baltimore had swept the Western Conference behind Unitas. Players such as Ray Berry, Lenny Moore, Jim Parker, Gene "Big Daddy" Lipscomb, and Gino Marchetti were soon to become household words. The stage was set for the historic meeting, a classic match-up of the best offense (the Colts had scored 381 points in twelve games) against the best defense (the Giants had allowed but 183 points in thirteen games). The Giants had already won a regular-season meeting between the two teams, 24–21, but

Unitas had missed the game with injured ribs and Johnny U., as fans were calling him, made a lot of difference, all the difference. So the oddsmakers made Baltimore a three-and-a-half-point favorite.

⌣∴∾

SEVEN DAYS AFTER THE GIANTS had beaten Cleveland for the NFL Eastern title, they met the Colts in Yankee Stadium in what many have called the greatest game ever played. This, of course, is only one's perspective, an opinion, but there is no doubt it was a game that would be replayed by the critics many times. Those who participated became a part of pro football nostalgia. The game had the media's undivided attention because of the great success of the Giants in the nation's largest city and became a focal point of that particular Sunday's television viewing around the country. The game was televised into 10,820,000 homes. People watched it and became intrigued by it, excited by what was happening. America was hooked on professional football.

Some sixty-four thousand fans watched on a mild wintry day as the Colts dominated the first half when Unitas led an offense that gained two hundred yards and Landry struggled for the answers to stop the onslaught. Baltimore took advantage of Rote's fumble at his own twenty to score one touchdown and then drove eighty-eight yards for another score to take a 14–3 halftime lead. Landry talked to the defensive players at halftime and told them what they must do or they'd be blown out of the stadium.

The Colts moved to the Giants' three-yard line as the second half started, and Landry walked the sidelines and yelled at the defense to hold, that they must hold. Ameche got a yard to the two but was slammed back and Landry screamed, "That's the way! That's the way!" Unitas made another yard, but on third down Ameche was stopped for no gain and the crowd began chanting, "Defense! Defense!"

Coach Weeb Ewbank and Unitas discussed the situation, fourth and one at the New York one, and decided to go for it. They felt the Giants had shut off the middle but they might get Ameche wide on a play in which he would first draw back his arm, as if to throw, and then run for the flag. But this time the 4–3 and the people who played it performed flawlessly. Ameche was hit first by Katcavage, then Modzelewski and Huff came over to finish him off. He'd lost four yards. The crowd was wild over what their heroes were doing, and the momentum switched.

With Gifford hurt much of the year and Conerly reaching the end of his career, Lombardi's offense was not what it had been in 1956. The 246 points the offense had scored was bettered by eight of the twelve NFL teams. But the Giants still had what it takes to make the big plays, planned and unplanned, that are part of football.

After Baltimore was stopped, Conerly launched a long pass from his own nineteen to Rote, who gathered it in and took off. After covering sixty-two yards, he fumbled. But Alex Webster, racing downfield to block, picked up the ball and raced to the Colt one, from where the Giants scored to get back into the game. In the final period the New York team went ahead, 17–14, when Conerly found Gifford on a fifteen-yard touchdown pass. The Colts had been silenced, shut out in the third and most of the fourth period, and the game was in the grasp of the Giants, who were trying to run out the clock.

But then an unfortunate turn of events followed, typical of the kind Landry was to become so familiar with as coach of the Cowboys. Needing four yards for a first down, which would perhaps give them time to run out the clock, Gifford got the ball and swept wide, cutting back inside. Marchetti hit him, and Lipscomb came over to finish him off. Gifford seemed to have made the four yards, a little more, but confusion erupted as Marchetti began to scream for people to get off him. His leg had been badly broken, and when the bodies were cleared, official Ronnie Gibbs marked the ball a few inches short of the first down.

Years later Gifford recalled, "I know I made the first down. You know things like that. I asked Gibbs about it later and he said, 'I blew it.' But there was so much confusion with Marchetti getting hurt that I can understand what happened."

At any rate, Chandler got off a beautiful punt that went out of bounds at the Colt twelve, the clock was running out, and the Giants' defense had dominated the second half. Then it began to happen and couldn't be stopped. The rest is pro football folklore, faded photos in our minds, pictures that will be there always.

Landry, desperate, had decided to double with Ray Berry and Lenny Moore. But when you are magic, when you have a date with destiny, it makes no difference what anyone else does. Unitas went to work, taking his team downfield against the clock in what would be a classic two-minute offense, one that would forever characterize the excitement that can be the NFL. He threw to Berry, who took the ball just as he stepped out of bounds, stopping the clock. He found Berry, who was doubled, at the Giants' thirty-five with forty-three seconds left and then again for twenty-two yards as the Colt split end made a diving catch, saving the reception just inches off the ground. The Colts were at the Giants' three with twenty-five seconds left. Steve Myhra came in and kicked a field goal to tie the game, 17–17, with nine seconds remaining. Professional football went into its first sudden-death overtime.

"There was such a big psychological factor involved," said Landry. "We were just inches away from winning a championship, and then they kicked that field goal to tie the game. There was a big letdown. All of a sudden, you've let go of what you seemed to have had, what seemed a victory and it wasn't. From a psychological standpoint it ruins you. Now, Baltimore had its second chance.

"When Frank missed the first down by inches, the momentum had completely changed. Defensively, when something like that changes the momentum, something happens to you psychologically. You're going to get penetrated, no matter how good you are.

"And, remember, the Colts were the best offensive team in the league."

The Giants won the toss, but again on a crucial play Conerly was inches short for a first down and Chandler had to punt. The crowd and some of the players, sensing the Colts had become unstoppable on offense, wanted to try to make the first down, but Howell played the percentages and Chandler punted the Colts back to their twenty. With the same faces, the same attack, Unitas moved his club seventy-nine yards to the Giants' one, the big play being a twenty-one-yard completion to Berry on third and fifteen.

For the Colts, there would be no easy field goal. What followed is a play that will remain indelibly etched in the minds of those who saw the game. In the gray darkness of late afternoon, which seemed hardly brightened by the flood lights, Ameche took a hand-off from Unitas and bore up the middle into the end zone to give the Colts a 23–17 victory in 8:15 of sudden-death overtime.

"I'm not sure whether it was the greatest game ever played," said Landry, "but there's no question in my mind that it marked the time, the game, and the place where pro football really caught on, where the public attention caught on and brought the game into the spotlight it enjoys today."

No. Perhaps it isn't the best game ever played, but it is the one that still holds the most significant place in NFL history because it is a game, a day, that will always be remembered by those touched by it. People watching across the nation would remember the names, the place, where they were, what they ate, what they said and thought—and that is what legends are made of.

~:~

ALTHOUGH THE SAME TEAMS would meet again for the 1959 NFL championship, they would do so with a different cast. Prior to the opening of the season, Timothy J. Mara, founder of the Giants, died at seventy-one years of age. Vince Lombardi took over the head coaching job at Green Bay, a team that in 1958 had lost ten games with players such as Paul Hornung, Jim Ringo, and Jimmy Taylor. Allie Sherman took Lombardi's place with the Giants' offense, and Em Tunnell retired.

Plans were also being made that would again change the face of professional football. Becoming extremely disenchanted and frustrated in his dealings with the NFL to bring a franchise, especially the failing Chicago Cardinals, to Dallas, Dallas millionaire Lamar Hunt announced he would form another league. Hunt led a group that included Denver's Bob Howsam, Houston's Bud Adams, Los Angeles's Barron Hilton, New York's Harry Wismer, and Max Winter and William Boyer of Minneapolis-St. Paul and formed the American Football League. It would begin competition in 1960 and be headquartered in Dallas.

The NFL had planned an expansion in 1961 with Dallas and Minnesota being mentioned as the likely candidates. NFL officials, behind closed doors, noted Hunt's intentions, his power and money, and decided to expand to Dallas in 1960 and Minnesota a year later. But Dallas definitely was the key, a city in which the NFL hoped to fight the AFL and perhaps bury it.

As the season began, Texas E. Schramm, former PR director and general manager of the Los Angeles Rams who had spent the last three years as assistant director of sports for CBS, was put in touch with another Dallas millionaire, Clint Murchison Jr., who was very much interested in an expansion team he might bring to his city. George Halas, remembering Schramm's work with the Rams, where he was one of the innovators in a scouting system after which all others one day would be modeled, told Murchison that Schramm would make a fine choice to lead a team in Dallas, if indeed the city got enough votes at the NFL owners meeting in January of 1960. He strongly hinted this probably would happen.

Landry's New York defense was better than ever in 1959, allowing opponents just 170 points, which truly is amazing when you consider that in the second game of the season the Norm Van Brocklin–led Eagles scored forty-nine points in beating the Giants, 49–21, in Philadelphia's Franklin Field. Van Brocklin and his understudy, Sonny Jurgensen, had a field day throwing to former Oklahoma all-American Tommy McDonald.

Nolan, who had the ill luck to be swapped to the Cardinals in a deal for Summerall and Crow in 1958, was brought back to New York in 1959 and remembered that Eagle game.

"Tom was livid," said Nolan. "If you knew him you could look at him and tell, but all he actually said was, 'That'll never happen again.'"

Ed Hughes recalled, "You know, in those days, we were taking turns driving from Connecticut. Well, for the Eagle game we drove a car into New York, left it at Yankee Stadium, and caught a subway to the train to take us to Philly.

"We got our butts kicked, and, I think, Robustelli and Livingston were with us coming back after the game. With the train ride, the subway ride, then the drive back home, we were together maybe three and a half, four hours.

"Tom was really upset about the way the defense played. Lombardi had screamed and yelled and cut guys to pieces. Tom could do the same thing with just a look, making you feel about two inches tall.

"Anyway, he wouldn't talk to any of us all the way back home. We even stopped for coffee, and I bet he didn't say two words."

When the teams met two weeks later in Yankee Stadium, the Giants won, 24–7. Landry had devised a plan to double McDonald in which Crow picked him up short and Patton covered him deep. "We knew we had to stop McDonald to win, and that's what we did," said Landry after the game.

Conerly had his best year, to the surprise of most, leading the league in passing, but although the offense had its moments, the main scoring punch was Summerall's kicking. He had come from the Cardinals as a mediocre kicker. He showed improvement in 1958, hitting twelve of twenty-three field goals, but in 1959 he led the league, connecting on twenty of twenty-nine.

"The big difference was Tom Landry," said Summerall. "He was the kicking coach too and would watch films of me kicking and pick up any flaws I had. He also studied Wietecha and Conerly, the center and holder, to see if they were doing anything wrong. He put it all together so we all had a good year kicking—together."

The Giants twice beat the rival Cleveland Browns to finish with a 10-2 mark, best in the entire NFL. Cleveland and Philadelphia tied for second. New York beat Cleveland, 10–6, in the first meeting and 48–7 the second time, ending all hopes for Paul Brown's club to catch it in the championship race.

"That Landry," said Nolan, "here we were forty points ahead of the Browns and he'd be out there yelling, 'Don't let them score! Hold 'em! Hold 'em!'"

The Colts won the NFL Western Conference title with a 9–3 mark, a game ahead of the Bears and two in front of the vastly improved Packers under Lombardi. In the title game, the Giants' defense dominated the game for three periods as New York held a 9–7 lead. But Conerly was off, losing three interceptions, one of which was returned for a touchdown. And Unitas rallied Baltimore for twenty-four final-period points and a 31–17 victory in a game watched by, among others, Vice President Richard Nixon, who would soon become the Republican Party's nominee to oppose John Kennedy for president.

A month prior to the NFL title game in November, Murchison hired Schramm to head what he hoped would be a pro football team in Dallas. Schramm attempted to get standard NFL contracts from acting commissioner Austin Gunsel, who had taken office when Bert Bell died while watching an Eagles game in October. Gunsel refused to accommodate him, so Schramm duplicated the standard NFL contract and hired Gil Brandt, a former baby-photographer and self-made talent expert who had done some work for him in L.A. He also hired Hamp Pool, who had been one of the head coaches of the Rams when Tex was assistant to president Dan Reeves. Schramm sent them out to sign all the free agents they could to the counterfeit contracts. If Dallas didn't get a team, the contracts would be voided. If it did, the Cowboys would at least have some players under contract. Schramm also worked out a deal with Pete Rozelle, who had taken his place as general manager of the Rams, to use L.A.'s scouting information on players who wouldn't be drafted, paying five thousand dollars for its use.

Landry wasn't sure what he'd do. Jim Lee Howell had tired of the rigors and pressures of coaching and moved over as director of the Giants' personnel department. Landry had also been approached by Bud Adams to coach the Houston Oilers of the new AFL. Landry was only thirty-five at the time, but his reputation as a defensive coach was unmatched. Wellington Mara called Landry into his office.

"I offered him the head coaching job for the Giants," said Mara.

Landry told him he believed he was ready to become a head coach. "I know what it takes to win," Mara recalled Landry told him. "I learned a lot about that from Lombardi."

Landry said he admired NFL coaches such as Buddy Parker and Jim Timble but he especially was impressed by Paul Brown, a man with somewhat the same demeanor as Landry and, of course, one of the game's great innovators.

Tom told Mara how he loved his years with the Giants but had a firm offer from the Houston team of the new AFL and thought he'd just go back to Texas.

"Being an NFL man, this worried me," said Mara. "I was very aware of Tom's capabilities, and if he wasn't going to coach our team, I certainly didn't want him going to the AFL. So I got in touch with Tex Schramm and strongly recommended he hire Tom for the Dallas expansion team."

"I lived in New York at that time [he was still with CBS while also working for the possible franchise in Dallas]," said Schramm. "And I kept hearing about a Giants assistant named Tom Landry. People were calling him a young genius for what he'd done with the Giants' defense. For the first time anybody could remember, the crowds were giving the defense a standing ovation, instead of the offense."

Paul Corley, a prominent sports figure in Dallas, knew Landry and also was a friend of Murchison. He recommended Landry to Clint, who asked Schramm what he thought. Schramm also had some interest in Sid Gillman, a man he had once hired as head coach of the Rams, but he settled on Landry.

"Tom was an NFL man, first and foremost," said Schramm. "He'd had the offer from Houston and New York, but he wanted to live in

Dallas. I never actually talked to Gillman because I became so sold on Landry."

"Even when I was coaching for the Giants, I don't think I actually thought of myself as a coach," said Landry. "I still leaned a little toward a career in business. During the off-season I was constantly getting ready for a career in business when I finished what I thought would be only a job as an assistant coach.

"I'd worked in Houston until I'd gotten my degree, and we'd then been living in Dallas for a number of years during the off-season. I'd heard from Adams about the Houston job and that Jim Lee Howell was stepping down and that I might get the Giants job.

"But then Tex approached me about the Dallas position. It just seemed ideal. It was where we were living, we liked the city and the area, and the idea of such a big challenge intrigued me."

CHAPTER 10
Living the Christian Faith

~:~

Tom Landry was one of the greatest Christian gentlemen I ever knew.

—DR. BILLY GRAHAM

WHEN THE 1958 FOOTBALL SEASON ENDED and Tom Landry returned to Dallas, a friend, Frank Phillips, invited him to join a group of men who would often meet at the Melrose Hotel for a breakfast during which they'd discuss the Scriptures. Landry was somewhat skeptical, but when he agreed to attend the meeting that morning, it would be the beginning of the biggest change ever to take place in his life.

"I had been in and about the church all my life," Landry recalled. "But, really, it was only half-heartedly. I considered myself a church-goer and a pretty good guy. Certainly, I thought of myself as a Christian but found out I really wasn't. I was just a church-goer, which is a lot different. If you just go to church, it's like going to the Lions Club or something like that. Oh, man, there's no comparison.

"Anyway, I wasn't sure Bible discussion was for me, since my scientific approach made it difficult to accept certain parts of the Scripture."

Nevertheless, he arrived at 7:30 A.M. and found four tables of eight to ten men each. After breakfast, men at each table chose a moderator to begin discussion of the Bible. Landry's analytical mind was properly challenged, and so he kept going back each week to the informal sessions in which the men searched for answers in the Bible. He listened and began to question things about his life, and then he asked himself a most critical question: "Is not life more important than football?"

His football accomplishments were stacked high. The loss to Baltimore in the NFL championship game had been disappointing, but he knew there would be other seasons and he had already played an important part when the Giants won the NFL title in 1956. That had been the ultimate achievement in pro football for a player or a coach. He had had success before. At Mission High School his sole goal had been to help the Eagles go as far as they could and win the regional title while playing as well as he possibly could. He had accomplished this. He had been a big part of the University of Texas teams, which one year beat Alabama in the Sugar Bowl and the following season defeated Georgia in the Orange Bowl. He had found great success at Texas and been named cocaptain. He had been blessed with a fine, beautiful wife and three children. So what was wrong? Why was there emptiness, dissatisfaction? What was lacking? He wasn't sure but was more than willing to search for the unknown factor that would complete the equation to happiness, to fulfillment. To do so, he was compelled to turn his thoughts in a more serious manner toward Christ. He had read about Him throughout his life, but who was this man, really? Did he actually accept Him? If he did, then he must accept what He said. If he accepted what He said, then the way he had been living his life was not right.

"At that point I nearly stopped going to those Bible sessions," Landry admitted. "For my whole life had been carefully structured throughout the year, and I was almost convinced that my future lay in being a coach. That was no time to become confused about my goals in life."

Yet the challenge was there, and he continued to attend the Bible-study breakfasts regularly until he was convinced that Jesus Christ was the missing link in his life. "I find it difficult to pick out any one specific turning point for me," said Landry. "I can't pinpoint it by a time or place. There was no emotional experience. As with the Galilean we talked about during one of those Bible sessions, I found myself attracted to Christ."

Landry remembered that his earliest urge to accept Christ was drawn from two Bible passages, both from the Gospel of Matthew.

"Therefore I say unto you, Take no thought for your life, what ye shall eat, or what ye shall drink; nor yet for your body, what ye shall put on. Is not the life more than meat [food], and the body more than raiment [clothing]? . . . But seek ye first the kingdom of God, and his righteousness; and all these things shall be added unto you. Take therefore no thought for the morrow; for the morrow shall take thought for the things of itself" [Matthew 6:25, 33–34].

"Therefore whosoever heareth these sayings of mine, and doeth them, I will liken him unto a wise man, which built his house upon a rock. And the rain descended, and the floods came, and the winds blew, and beat upon that house; and it fell not; for it was founded upon a rock" [Matthew 7:24–25].

He read the passages over and over and began to wonder if, indeed, his house was founded on rock. Certainly, he and Alicia and the children went to church, but what did it really mean to them? What kind of foundation was he building for his family? What kind of real foundation?

"For a self-centered person, those can be disconcerting questions," said Landry. "For the first time, I began to feel a quickening desire to get to know this man, Jesus Christ. At the next meeting I asked, 'How can we be sure Jesus is who He says He is?' Nobody there could answer the question in a way that satisfied me."

So Landry spent a great deal of time analyzing what he had been thinking about and researching the man, Jesus Christ. Football had taught him to measure things in terms of results. Players are trained to accomplish certain objectives, such as a kicking specialist putting three points on the scoreboard when the ball is in his range and a passer throwing the ball so a receiver can catch it a high percentage of the time. Landry began thinking about Jesus in terms of what He did and the results of His life. In doing this, he discovered Christ's compelling impact on the lives of countless millions of people down through the years.

"At some period during the spring of 1959, all my so-called intellectual questions no longer seemed important, and I had a joyous feeling inside," said Landry. "Internally, the decision had been made. Now, while the process had been slow and gradual, once made, the decision has been the most important one of my life. It was a commitment of my life to Jesus Christ and a willingness to do what He wanted me to do as best I could by seeking His will through prayer and reading His Word."

This in no way meant that he would have to give up football or trying to be the best at his profession. "I simply believed that Christ wanted me to bring Him into my daily life, including football. I also began trying more and more to think a little less about football systems and a little more about the people involved, although the adjustment took time. I had a lot of maturing to do as a Christian."

Because it was his nature, Landry continued to strive for perfection, but as the years passed with the Dallas Cowboys, his somewhat dictatorial approach began to lessen. He became more capable of understanding the different, more individually oriented players and also those who, unlike Landry, would give less than 100 percent. His faith certainly was a factor in helping him try to understand players such as the much-troubled Duane Thomas and be more fair and understanding of a person such as Thomas "Hollywood" Henderson or the sometimes erratic behavior of someone such as Tony Dorsett.

Landry became much more tolerant of players who broke the mold, beginning in the early 1970s and carrying over until the end of his career. "I give everybody a full opportunity to make a change," he said. But when he later recalled what happened to Thomas, who had only two productive years before becoming a victim of the culture he sought, and Henderson, whose involvement in the drug culture Landry overlooked so many times before giving up, he added, "If I have a weakness, it may be that I'm too compassionate. I give people a chance to see whether they can turn it around. It didn't work out for me too often."

"Tom Landry is probably the fairest guy I've ever been around," said Mike Ditka. "He let a lot of players push him to the limit. But when they did, that was it."

Relating his thoughts to the *Dallas Morning News* at the time of his firing, Landry reflected on Thomas and Henderson and the drug culture:

"My disappointment in the case of Duane Thomas is that I had no idea what he was doing. At the end of the 1960s, the drug culture came in and everybody wanted to do their own thing. I knew something was different with Duane, but I didn't know what it was. Boy, it's a shame to see a guy's career being ruined.

"My feeling is if Duane had continued to play the way he had for the two years we had him, it would have been very hard for Pittsburgh to beat us [in Super Bowls X and XIII]. If we had had Duane and Calvin Hill together, they would have made a tremendous impact.

"Thomas Henderson was such a showman, I couldn't tell whether he was serious or not. He was another great talent wasted. The most disappointing thing is I just couldn't help them enough. I feel guilty that I couldn't get them back on the right track. Once you get on coke or crack, you're destined for trouble. Nobody is going to change you either."

Landry never did try to push his faith onto his players, but he always told them exactly how he felt. "I didn't want them to feel pressured or obligated to be a part of it," he explained. "I didn't want to come across as a pious-type person. We always had players who were strong Christians. A lot of people thought we had only a Christianlike atmosphere on our team. That wasn't correct. The atmosphere we tried to create was one in which we hoped to develop good character, although we knew not everybody was a Christian.

"I always hoped the influence was such that whether we were out in public or on the field, we conducted ourselves in such a way to show Christian traits. If we had a player who had no values at all, then I wouldn't tolerate this. When a guy has good character he's at least pointed in the right direction."

Landry would, on occasion, directly share his faith with his players and at times reassure them with words from the Scriptures when they were going through difficult times. "God does not give us fear, but power and love and self-control," he told them. "The thing that eats you up is fear and anxiety. Once you commit your life to Christ, it's in God's hands. He has a direction He wants to take you which isn't based on winning or losing. The more you dwell on your own power, the more anxious you become."

Randy White said he always enjoyed when Landry would give the players a small bit of Scripture or share his feelings with them. And Charlie Waters recalled, "Nobody resented it when he told us something from the Bible or about his faith. He never tried to force it on us. I always appreciated hearing what had guided a man as wise as he was."

"He shows you by example what a Christian life is all about," said Danny Reeves. "That's more impressive than any words can be."

Under Landry, the Cowboys had a team prayer session before each game and an early-morning nondenominational service before road games. Attendance was optional. Players were encouraged to attend a service of their own faith, but of course, that was also optional.

Once I told Landry about an argument I'd had with a well-known college coach who asked God to give his team the strength to win. I had voiced the opinion that God did not care who won a football game. Landry commented, "God doesn't interfere in games. We have great Christian friends all around the league. What God does is give you the courage to excel and the confidence to perform to the best of your ability. So many players don't do that; they don't use the talent they have."

Landry didn't believe a person must be a Christian to become a great athlete, although he did feel it helps. "I put some emphasis on a religious commitment in relation to everything," he said. "I feel a man who is not committed to Christ is handicapped in almost anything he does. A person who is committed to Christ has more freedom and is, therefore, able to develop himself to the fullest. He doesn't need to have the fears and the anxieties that can hold him back. I always found our Christian players seemed to get more out of their jobs. I believe they enjoyed them more and reached higher levels than they would have had they not been committed.

"I'm not saying that you will become a great athlete by receiving Christ, but I do believe that if you have the natural ability, your commitment to Him will enable you to achieve a greater degree of excellence. The most unfortunate thing in my life was that I did not discover Christ until I was coaching. I didn't have the pleasure and enjoyment of knowing Him while I was a player. If you have a positive attitude, good things will happen. Why has positive thinking become a multimillion-dollar industry? They're just teaching what God gives us in the Bible.

"When I first started coaching, I thought mostly of physical ability such as quickness, agility, control, strength, and explosiveness. Then, as we developed into a stronger team, character became more important. The character and competitiveness of a player become the more controlling factors. When you reach a championship level, what separates you is basically the character on your team. If you have enough character, it'll usually pull you out of tough situations.

"I think that's why Roger Staubach and Drew Pearson pulled out the Minnesota playoff game in 1975 with that long pass in the last seconds. It wasn't so much the play but the quality of the players involved and their attitude in the situation. The player without character usually finds excuses for why he shouldn't produce with everything he has. A player with character looks at the best side in every situation. There's always hope for him even though the clock is running out. He's looking for a play to win the game. That's the difference, and it has won a lot of games for us."

On the surface, which is where so many people look, there seems to be a conflict between the image of a Christian as passive and the violence associated with professional football. One appears the antithesis of the other.

"This is a misconception," said Landry. "Religion is anything but passive. Every man must have his correct relationship with God, and if he has certain talents, he must demonstrate them. No matter what a man does, God expects him to be at his best. Some of the greatest competitors I've seen in pro football are Christians. If there is any conflict from a religious point of view, it would be playing on Sunday. The occupation causes this, so most Christian athletes feel all right about doing it."

One of the most admirable traits of Tom Landry, especially from the perspective of those who were around him a great deal, was his ability to bounce back so quickly from painful setbacks and disappointments. The worst, of course, was the death of his daughter Lisa, but there were other soul-searching setbacks in his life: when he was diagnosed with leukemia, when Jerry Jones fired him, and gut-wrenching, narrow losses on the football field. Landry would feel hurt by a football defeat, but he'd be able to put what happened in perspective more quickly than others, especially other head coaches. This is why he was able to keep his health and perspective so long in a profession that made nervous wrecks out of so many fine men: for example, Allie Sherman with the Giants, Don Coryell when he was with the Cardinals, Tommy Prothro in Los Angeles, Dick Vermeil in Philadelphia, and John Madden at Oakland. Madden was on the top of his profession but had to retire because of bleeding ulcers. The pressures of coaching in the NFL have had adverse mental and physical effects on the majority of coaches in the profession. But Landry did not drink to excess, chain smoke, or take pills to relax or perk himself up. Nor did he have ulcers or trouble sleeping.

"I suffer after losses, but fortunately do recover quickly," he said. "My relationship with Christ gives me a source of power I would not have otherwise.

"As a Christian, I know my life is in God's hands. He has a plan for me. Therefore, I never worry about tomorrow and try to keep winning and losing and the good and bad things that happen in my life in perspective. The knowledge that my life is in God's hands helps me keep my composure or regain it in tough situations."

After Landry was fired from the Cowboys, Dr. Leighton Farrell, then pastor of the Highland Park United Methodist Church, said, "During all the turmoil, with his dismissal and everything, I was close to Tom, and it certainly bothered me a great deal what was happening to him. I expressed my feelings to Tom, and he said, 'Leighton, it's all right. I'm not worried about it, really, because God just has something else planned for me.'

"I honestly think Tom was less concerned than I was. But he would have been the same no matter what happened because it was a part of God's plan.

"I have met few people like Tom Landry, who are so strong and sincere in their faith and let God lead them in everything they do. Tom [he laughed] just doesn't seem to care a whole lot about what others might think of him. If he believes God wants him to do something, he does it."

Landry also had a great tolerance for those who did not have beliefs as strong as his or adhere to his lifestyle. "I think I can understand the nonbeliever's attitude because I've been there," he explained. "It's probably more difficult for him to understand mine."

In conjunction with its sponsorship of a yearly charity exhibition game in Dallas, the Salesmanship Club used to hold an annual fishing trip for Cowboy officials and the media at an exclusive wilderness retreat about seventy-five miles from Dallas. One evening a group of beer-drinking writers decided it would be amusing to have their annual all-night poker game in Landry's cabin. There would be drinking, gambling, and cussing, and some of the older members of the group wanted to see what Landry's reaction might be when he returned from the day's fishing to find them in his cabin.

When Landry walked in, he didn't blink an eye, although he politely declined to take part in the game or in the consumption of alcoholic beverages.

One of the writers suggested in a joking manner, "That's all right, Coach. If you're not drinking, would you mind tending bar?" To everybody's amazement, Landry proceeded to do just that. He proved a perfect host until the wee hours of the morning when he caught a quick nap prior to attacking another fishing location. The writers talked for days about what a good sport Landry was. He had shocked them more than they had shocked him.

Alicia Landry shared her husband's faith. One of the first things they did when they moved from Houston to Dallas was join the Highland Park United Methodist Church. It had been her church when she was growing up in Highland Park. It was where she was baptized and had one of the largest congregations of any church of its denomination in the country. Tom Landry became a very active member of the church.

Landry began each day with a prayer, asking the Lord to help him make fair decisions and give him the proper words to use. His day ended similarly when he privately took inventory of himself with prayer, asking the Lord if he handled situations properly. But he once said the main evaluation at the end of the day was whether he had brought the Lord into the situations he faced or barged ahead on his own.

Few people, regardless of profession, can come to grips with themselves on such a daily basis. That can only come, Landry believed, through a strong faith in Jesus Christ. And he felt that sometimes the church does not challenge the young people of this country to truly discover Christ.

Commenting on this situation, he said, "Young people want Christianity to help them solve their problems, but we're failing to show it to them. You've got to show young people."

He recalled a story in which Paul Anderson was speaking in front of a group of young people. He took a twenty-penny nail and drove it into a two-by-four with his bare hand. Then he asked eight kids to come up onto the stage and get onto a table. Then he lifted the table high into the air. He put it down and went back to the microphone and said, "It takes courage to be a Christian; it's no sissy game."

"I'm a Christian," said Landry. "It's where I live."

Landry believed God wanted him to be a football coach and use a high-profile platform to influence others, whether it was by the way he conducted himself with his players, or speaking to FCA groups or churches, or going into prisons, or in conjunction with the Billy Graham crusades. There is no doubt he had a great influence.

He was a churchgoer all his life, but at the age of thirty-three he became a true Christian. There would be shaky times, frustrating times, that would follow, some that would have deeply scarred those with less faith. But Landry's faith helped sustain him. It sustained him through personal tragedy and disappointment and sometimes helped him be incredibly patient. He certainly had patience with his players, something that was never more needed than in the formative years of the Dallas Cowboys.

CHAPTER 11
The Dallas Cowboys: The Early Years

~:~

He [Landry] wasn't a yeller or a hard-sell guy, but I don't think he ever lacked confidence. I mean, you had the feeling he knew what he was doing. He had a terrific way of selling a game plan. You knew it would work because Tom said it would work. It was that simple. It was just that . . . well, our talent was so inferior. We didn't have much of a chance to win any games, but we'd go out there and use everything we had trying.

—EDDIE LEBARON
Quarterback, 1960–1963

AFTER THE GIANTS LOST to Baltimore in the title game, Tom Landry, thirty-five, was announced as the coach for the proposed expansion team in Dallas, which at that time Schramm planned to call the Rangers. Landry, then the youngest head coach in NFL history, was given a five-year contract calling for $34,500 annually. At the owners meeting in Miami Beach on January 28, 1960, Clint Murchison Jr., Bedford Wynne, and John Murchison, Clint's brother, were awarded an NFL franchise. Everybody concerned breathed much easier when it became official that Dallas would indeed get the team.

Jim Lee Howell, the New York Giants coach, said the Dallas team had hired the best coach in the business but was also quoted as saying, "Tom is a warm person but not so much with his players. Sometimes he gets impatient with them, doesn't pat them on the back. He expects them to go out there and do their jobs. One thing is that he's so much smarter than most of them. Maybe he should be more of a dope like me. He's like Paul Brown, a perfectionist. But he's smarter than anybody."

At first the actual starting date for the team to play was 1961. But in what was an obvious attempt to hurt the AFL and Lamar Hunt's Dallas Texans, NFL owners decided the club would begin playing that 1960 season, with its record counting in the Western Conference. It had a schedule that included all NFL teams, giving the fans of Dallas a chance to see the league from top to bottom.

And unlike any team before or after, Dallas didn't have the benefit of the draft because the draft had already been held. Fortunately, however, with a big assist from Halas, Murchison was able to sign SMU all-American Don Meredith to a personal services contract. Halas had drafted Meredith, but sympathetic to the Dallas plight and angered by the AFL, Halas asked only a future third-round draft pick from the team that Schramm finally talked Murchison into calling the Cowboys.

Murchison also had a friend, New Mexico senator Clint Anderson, sign New Mexico University running back Don Perkins to a personal services contract. Both Meredith's and Perkins's contracts had been contingent on Dallas getting a team, making it look on the surface like the Cowboys were forced to scramble for unwanted rookies and try to lure old veteran players out of nursing homes or wherever else they might find them.

The situation could have been even worse if Landry hadn't gone before the NFL owners and made a plea for help. He pointed out that his team was going into Dallas and would be fighting Lamar Hunt's Texans of the AFL and that the Cowboys just had to have some players. It was then that the owners came up with the idea that Dallas could draft veteran players from other clubs . . . mostly unwanted ones.

"I think I was at my best that day," said Landry. "They did help us some. Each team could protect eight players, and we could pick three off each club. But every time we'd pick one, the team could protect him and we'd have to go down the list to get somebody else. That's the way we started, with just about nothing."

Dallas was allowed to stock its franchise by selecting thirty-six veterans from existing NFL teams. Each team was allowed to freeze twenty-five names on their roster of thirty-six, and Dallas could pick no more than three from each existing club. The league gave the Cowboys only twenty-four hours to make their selections.

Prior to the announcement of the process by which the Cowboys would get players, Landry had made a whistle-stop tour of the NFL, looking at films of each team. He'd also made a deal with the Giants in which New York could freeze more players if Landry were able to sign Don Heinrich as a player-coach.

Schramm was also able to trade a future draft choice for Eddie

LeBaron, the 5'-8" Washington Redskins quarterback who had once led the league in passing but had retired. LeBaron said the only reason he came out of retirement was his respect for Landry. He wanted to be a part of what was happening in Dallas as the 1960s began.

The early 1960s were a time when the Freedom Riders attempted to end segregation, when an actor named Paul Newman emerged as one of the all-time box-office favorites in *The Hustler*, when Ernest Hemingway, a physical and mental shadow of himself, would take his own life with a shotgun. And it was a time when a group from England called the Beatles would drive adults up the wall and send young women into screaming frenzies. It was also a time in Dallas when water fountains in the downtown area were clearly marked "White" and "Colored" and when John F. Kennedy would die that awful day from an assassin's bullets.

~:~

MOST OF THE ORIGINAL PLAYERS who reported to the Cowboys' first training camp in July 1960 were, frankly, the dregs of the league. The team was formed too late to take part in the draft and was only able to get the players the other dozen teams felt most expendable, plus a vast number of free agents whom Gil Brandt and his helpers had found after scouring the country looking, figuratively, under every rug.

So the first team was made up mostly of nonentities, malcontents, the injury-prone, clubhouse lawyers, and only a handful of good athletes such as Frank Clarke, Jerry Tubbs, Eddie LeBaron, Don Perkins, and of course, Don "Call me Dandy" Meredith.

Landry's first lineups were written on Magic-Slates. Each game was more survival than competition, with a sparkling moment here and there and, perhaps, a clear sign of what was to come. Those players reporting were asked to run the "Landry Mile," which backs and receivers were expected to do in under six minutes and linemen in under six and a half minutes. Not one made it.

When the team got to Dallas it worked out at Burnett Field, a minor-league baseball stadium. Rats roamed the locker rooms and gnawed at the players' shoes. The training room was set up in what had been the ladies' rest room, where the walls were painted pink. The executive and coaches' offices were in a single room in the Automobile Club Building on Central Expressway.

When Bob Lilly was drafted number one in 1961, the second year of the team, he said he expected this plush place with his name on his own locker, something like Yankee Stadium. "Burnett was a condemned baseball field," he recalled. "There were no doors, just openings. Lighting was thirty-watt bulbs. You could barely see. In one so-called room I could hear this voice, which turned out to be Coach Landry. Something squeaked. It turned out to be Coach Landry writing with chalk on this backboard of green slate. I was a few minutes late, and the first thing he said to me was, 'Lilly, that'll cost you fifty dollars.'

"At that first team meeting he told us his priorities . . . God, family, and football, in that order. I thought he was kidding, that he had them all backward."

The team was hardly glamorous, on or off the field, except for Don Meredith in his own way. If it had been possible to design a working model of an NFL quarterback whose temperament and attitude were radically different from Landry's, one who at the beginning was so ill-suited for what Landry planned, then off the drawing board would have popped a walking, talking Don Meredith.

And it was the irrepressible Meredith who left the lasting impression of those early teams because, more than anyone, he typified the splendor and, more often, the sorrow. Yet Landry stuck by him, for better or worse.

They were the Odd Couple. Whereas Landry was studious and pensive, Meredith was finger-snapping flip; while Tom looked at the game as an intensely serious business, Don came into pro football with the notion that the game was just another chance to go out and have a little fun. Landry had developed his skills through exhaustive repetition, painstaking analysis, and an almost mystifying devotion to the game. Meredith had come by his skills naturally. It was as if one day they were just dumped in his lap and he accepted them with an easy grace. "Why do they call you Dandy?" he would be asked, and he would reply, "Because I am."

Yet Meredith had another side he seldom showed. Like Landry, who controlled his feelings behind a stone face, sometimes Meredith hid his real emotions behind flippancy and clever remarks. Both men likewise had a strong desire to win and suffered greatly after defeats. So perhaps, outside appearances notwithstanding, these decidedly different men were not exactly worlds apart, as we painted them in those days.

In those days Meredith came with strings attached. At times his talents would desert him as if yanked by some unseen hand or force that pulled the strings. For years he suffered from awful to nonexistent blocking. Some of the brutal hits he took should have carried an X rating. But Landry felt Meredith could overcome his shortcomings as a quarterback through devotion and hard work. To Don, football was still a game. And in his early years he was known to have come into the huddle singing lines from a country-western song, a favorite being, "It Wasn't God Who Made Honky-Tonk Angels." Sometimes others would sing along with him. Meredith was later to remark, "But when we started winning, I was the only one still singing."

"Meredith had tremendous talent," said Dan Reeves, who came to the team as a free agent in 1965. "But he played the game for the fun of it. If he had been as dedicated as John Elway, no telling what he might have accomplished. Of course, that always led to friction with Coach Landry, who just couldn't understand that kind of thinking."

Meredith had come to the Cowboys after a great deal of personal success at SMU. Twice he made all-American and established an NCAA record for passing accuracy of 61 percent. Yet, the best the Mustangs ever did when he was there was a 6–4 record in 1958. He would do great things, but he would also appear to have lapses at times, such as when he stepped across the line of scrimmage before he threw what would have been the winning pass against Rice. On the field, SMU had been almost an extension of his football days at Mount Vernon High School. The point was to give Meredith the ball and let him do something and not be burdened with the technical aspects of the game.

When Landry first met Meredith, he knew Don had the talent. But he was somewhat shocked about the rookie's lack of knowledge about the basic technical aspects of football. It wasn't until he'd gone through a few blackboard sessions with Landry, Meredith was later to admit, that he learned that an offense was predicated on what the defense presented to it.

With the help of Don Heinrich and, especially, Eddie LeBaron, Landry nursed Meredith through some very frustrating early times. Often they would be almost at wit's end with each other, but the bond was there. In later years Landry, certainly, began to understand Meredith better, knowing that under the flippant exterior, Meredith hurt and felt as much as anybody, probably more. The humor was often just his way of hiding his emotions. Landry also let his emotions hide, under the weight of his tremendous concentration on the job at hand.

⁓∴⁓

MANY OF THE PLAYERS didn't know what to think of Landry. Landry, thirty-five, was the same age as many of his players. But he was detached, all business, seldom even exchanging pleasantries.

"Tom was closer to Don than he was the rest of us in the early years," recalled defensive end Larry Stephens. "At least they seemed to be. Don always seemed to have some idea what Landry felt about the team, what was happening. Tom never said much to the rest of us."

"I felt if Tom had been more personable with his players in those early days he might have gotten more out of them," recalled Tom Franckhauser, a defensive back who later became a successful stockbroker. "A lot of us didn't particularly like his standoffish attitude."

L. G. Dupre, who had played for Baltimore in the 1958 championship game against the Giants, came in the expansion pool to Dallas during the twilight of his career. He said, "I could understand what Tom was doing. He was concentrating so hard on trying to build a winner and he had to be shifting people around all the time, constantly trying to find the players who could fill the gaps."

It just seemed to many that Landry was aloof, as though he thought he was smarter than everybody else. "Well," said Jerry Tubbs, one of the few truly outstanding defensive players in the early days and later a Cowboys assistant coach, "the fact is that Tom *was* smarter than everybody else."

"Some of the other guys didn't see eye-to-eye with Tom," recalled LeBaron, who pursued a law career after he quit playing and for a while was general manager of the Atlanta Falcons. "They had been around the league and were pretty set in their ways. But I never bought the idea that he was cold and detached. To me he's always just been very intense, yet where I've been concerned, he's been a warm person. In practice he didn't have a great sense of humor because it was a serious business for him. But off the field, even in the early days, I saw the warm side of him.

"I was going into law, but when Tom got in touch with me I decided to play again. He's probably the only person I'd have done that for. He always had a lot of respect in the league when he was with the Giants."

"The worst thing I ever did for Eddie was talking him into playing for us," said Landry. "He was going to become a lawyer in Midland in those days. I guarantee you those guys took a great beating. I hate to say those early teams were awful, because it would be a discredit to so many of those great guys, but we were weak. We just didn't have the personnel."

～∴～

THE COWBOY ORGANIZATION knew it had little chance of winning, but it was locked in a battle for the sports dollar with Hunt's Dallas Texans. It was hoped Landry could at least field an exciting team. Landry knew immediately that, outside of Tubbs, who was to become a Pro Bowl player, he had few defenders to stop the opposition. He would try to outscore his opponents . . . or at least score points and maintain the interest of the fans.

So Landry devised the multiple offensive concept with its phone-book of plays, its motion, false direction, and continual shifting. The Cowboys didn't just run the two basic formations of football, they ran practically all formations. What Landry did, in effect, was try to destroy the 4–3 defense he had nurtured while with the Giants.

"I felt the best way to attack the 4–3 we'd established in New York was the multiple offense," he said. "I knew that defense so well that I had a good idea of the best way to beat it. Remember, the 4–3 was based on formation recognition with man-for-man basic pass coverage. To be effective, the defense had to have a jump by first recognizing the formation, then knowing what plays could be run from it. I felt if we used multiple sets, shifting from one to the other, we could confuse the defensive players. After all, they had worked all week on perfecting certain keys, and if we could destroy those keys we might be able to move the ball and even have a chance to win."

By the time Landry's career with the Cowboys came to an end, the multiple offense had evolved into some dozen sets, and the team would also line up in one formation and shift into another. There were, perhaps, forty to forty-five basic plays in the offense with numerous variations from the different sets.

LeBaron at first called his own plays and then became part of a quarterback shuttle in which he would alternate on each down with Meredith while Landry told each one the next play he wanted run.

He recalled, "Tom and I often talked about the theory of what we were trying to accomplish. The shifting and moving was necessary because we just didn't have the personnel to blow anybody out. We had to do things differently, so we basically relied on deception. I was never concerned about who called the plays, really. What happens is that your thinking becomes so similar that it really doesn't matter. I understood pretty well what Tom was trying to do. He wasn't a yeller or a hard-sell guy, but I don't think he ever lacked confidence. I mean, you had the feeling he knew what he was doing. He had a terrific way of selling a game plan. You knew it would work because Tom said it would work. It was that simple. It was just that . . . well, our talent was so inferior. We didn't have much of a chance to win any games, but we'd go out there and use everything we had trying."

LeBaron, of course, was an NFL-class quarterback. Tubbs was a fine linebacker who had planned an early retirement after a great deal of frustration in San Francisco. But Landry talked him into playing, and he enjoyed many fine seasons as the club's first middle linebacker. And then there was Frank Clarke, who came from Cleveland in the expansion draft and was going nowhere until he got to Dallas. Before he was through, Clarke would become one of the NFL's premier receivers, twice ranking third in the NFL in receiving, once catching sixty-five passes in a single season and scoring fourteen touchdowns.

"People would question what Tom did at first, but, soon, they would learn he was right," recalled Clarke. "I was just fortunate to end up in Dallas." Clarke had been a high draft choice of Cleveland in 1957, but he quickly got on Paul Brown's bad side. Frank recalled that during one particular game he missed a block, taking a bad angle, and when he came off the field Brown told him he couldn't play, not only for the Browns, but for any team in the NFL.

"During 1963 with the Cowboys, we were driving for a touchdown and Meredith threw a pass high for me in the end zone," said Clarke. "Sure, the pass was high, and I jumped, but I just didn't go after it with much intensity. When I went to the sidelines, all Coach Landry said was, 'Frank, do you think you could have made a better effort on that pass?' I remembered how Paul Brown had treated me and then how Coach Landry treated me and I was determined I would make a better effort, for my own sake and for that of Coach Landry."

Dallas played its first game in history against San Francisco in preseason, losing 16–10. Overall, Dallas was 1–5 that first preseason, beating only Landry's old team, the Giants, 14–3, as Clarke caught a seventy-three-yard touchdown pass from the rookie Don Meredith.

Meredith had other game-stoppers as well. Mostly operating in a state of confusion, Don had gone back to his natural instincts for the touchdown to Clarke. However, earlier in the day he was faced with the menacing figure of Sam Huff, looking him right in the eye as he set up to bark signals. Meredith would start his count and Huff would adjust the defense. Meredith then would remember an audible. Huff moved accordingly and seemed to know exactly where the play was going.

Meredith's signal calling went something like this, with appropriate stares into Huff's eyes: "Four-three Set! . . . uh, Red Right . . . uh, twenty-two. . . . Ah, shoot [editor's translation]! Time out!" Huff, the entire New York defense, plus the Cowboy offense broke into laughter. Landry only managed a smile.

In later years, Meredith would get some revenge. Once he had torn stomach muscles and trainer Larry Gardner fitted him with a special heating pad filled with a red liquid that would keep the muscles warm. During the game, Huff blitzed and hit Meredith so hard that the bag burst, the red liquid covering his jersey.

Huff, thinking he'd inflicted a mortal wound and that Don was bleeding to death, said, "Oh, no. What have I done?"

"Oh, it's all right, Sam," said Meredith. "But do me a favor. Write my mother."

"Yeah, sure. I will. I promise," said Huff, almost in tears.

Trainers Gardner and Don Cochren, who had come onto the field to see if Don was all right, broke out laughing. Huff never thought it was very funny.

During the regular season, Dallas, as expected, generally could put up points but couldn't stop any opponents, losing ten straight games before going into Yankee Stadium to play the Giants on December 5 with 55,033 fans in attendance. The fans remembered what Landry had done in New York and gave him a tremendous ovation as he came on the field with his team.

Dallas was a two-touchdown underdog, but LeBaron, the Little General, hit three touchdown passes and the game was tied 24–24. New York scored again, and it looked like another day at the office for Dallas. Then Joe Morrison lost a fumble at the Giants' forty with 2:27 to play. LeBaron guided Dallas to the New York eleven, from which he found

Billy Howton with a touchdown pass, tying the game 31–31. This marked the first game Dallas did not lose.

Jim Lee Howell, in his final year of coaching the Giants, was amazed at the performance of Landry's band of misfits. He had called Landry the best defensive coach in football when he was with the Giants, but after the tie he went a step further and said, "Tom Landry is the best coach in all of football."

Following LeBaron's heroics in New York, Meredith, who had been in and out of the lineup, was certain he wouldn't see action in the season's finale in Detroit. "So," recalled Dandy, "I picked the night before the game to go and acquaint myself with the Motor City." Meredith's only consolation for the hangover he had as he dressed the next day for the game was the thought that he wouldn't have to play. An assistant coach ambled over to Meredith in the locker room and said, "My God, you look like you're dead."

"I'm fine, sir, just fine," said Meredith, deep, dark bags under his eyes.

"Well, you better be. Coach Landry said you're starting today."

Dandy dragged himself off the locker-room bench, got a second wind, cursed his fate, warmed up, and then returned to the locker room for a final word before the kickoff. Something in his demeanor, his hangdog look, must have tipped Landry, who changed his mind and said, "I'm going to start LeBaron. But Don, you stay warm. You'll be going in."

"The rest was kind of hazy," said Meredith. "Eddie got his hand stepped on and Tom said, 'Warm up.' I stood on the sideline with my jacket off, warming up the entire first half. At halftime, Tom told me I'd be starting the second half. I tried to look concerned . . . well, I *was* concerned but not for the reasons he thought."

But again Landry chose to stick with LeBaron, although constantly telling his rookie to stay warm. By the middle of the fourth period, Meredith still had not played. Finally, he walked to the bench, put on his warmup jacket, and sat down.

Presently, Landry came over to him, and it seemed certain he was going to tell him to warm up, that he was going in. But before Landry could speak, Meredith said, "Coach, I ain't warming up again." Dallas lost that final game in 1960, and Meredith remarked, "I could tell Tom and I were going to have a real fun time together."

Dallas was finally able to draft in 1961 and picked Bob Lilly, the giant defensive lineman from TCU. Lilly was to flounder at defensive end until 1963 when Landry would move him to tackle.

"Lilly," said Nolan, "just wasn't a very good defensive end. He didn't have the long-range speed. He'd have ended up being just a mediocre defensive end, but Tom saw some traits in him that seemed to lend themselves to making a tackle. So Tom moved him to tackle, I guess, in 1963. And he was great, maybe the greatest ever to play the game at that position."

"It was just becoming pretty obvious as I watched him that Lilly had all the attributes of a tackle," said Landry. "He was so very quick, had strength, short-range speed to make it at tackle. He was just tremendous. In Lilly, we had a guy we could start building our defense around."

It was also during that 1961 season that Tom Landry would get his first victory as a head coach. This came in the league opener against the Pittsburgh Steelers before some fifty thousand empty seats (23,500 fans) in the Cotton Bowl. Landry had said he planned to use both Meredith and LeBaron as starting quarterbacks, depending on his feeling the particular week and the circumstances. Meredith started and did all right until throwing an interception to Johnny Sample, who ran it back thirty-nine yards for a touchdown to give Pittsburgh a 24–17 lead. Landry then put in LeBaron for Meredith, who retired quietly to the bench, joked with those around him, and then sat down by himself and cried.

LeBaron took the club seventy-five yards to tie the score, 24–24, and in the waning seconds Jerry Tubbs intercepted a Bobby Layne pass at the Dallas thirty-eight with only seconds left. Meredith, although he didn't know it at the time, would have appreciated what happened next. LeBaron dispensed with the regular offense, turned to Billy Howton, and said, "Just take off deep. Everybody else block." LeBaron found Howton on a forty-yard completion, the Cowboy receiver stepping out of bounds at the Steeler twenty-two with one second left. Rookie Allen Green, who had missed two earlier field goals and had a punt blocked, then kicked a twenty-seven-yard field goal to give Dallas a 27–24 victory.

"I think," recalled Landry, "we all stood there stunned for a while, not believing. And then it was great, just great."

Dallas went on to win three other games, including a 28–0 victory over Minnesota, after Landry began to employ his quarterback shuttle in which he could call the plays and also give Meredith needed experience.

A highlight was the 17–16 victory in New York over the Giants, a team that had beaten Dallas earlier, 31–10. In those days the Giants still had Huff, Gifford, Rote, and Y. A. Tittle, and they were on their way to the NFL Eastern Conference title.

"I was involved in a lot of exciting, satisfying victories in my days as a player," said former Rice all-American Dick Maegle, a defensive back for Dallas in those days. "But that day in New York was something else. Shoot, even Landry was jumping around, yelling in the dressing room afterward. To beat a great team like that, with the bunch we had, and do it in the final minute was like having your childhood fantasies come true."

This time Green won the game on a thirty-two-yard field goal with 1:32 left. Landry told the players, "I want you to know that regardless of what happens from here on out, I'm proud of you, proud of what you've accomplished this season." Dallas finished 4–9–1 in 1961 and then 5–8–1 in 1962, under Landry's quarterback shuttle system. It was then Meredith casually pointed out that Landry had a mind like an IBM, which probably was the beginning of the metaphor generally used in referring to the Cowboys coach.

Nineteen sixty-two was a very trying year. In the second regular-season game, Pittsburgh beat Dallas, 30–28, on a play that nobody would ever forget and sent Landry onto the field to argue with officials to no avail. In the third period, LeBaron faded into his end zone to pass with the line of scrimmage the Dallas one. He caught a glimpse of Clarke flying down the sidelines and threw the ball as far as he could. Frank caught the ball and apparently scored on a ninety-nine-yard play.

But back in the end zone there was a flag. Official Emil Heintz said Cowboys guard Andy Cvercko was holding in the end zone and cited long-forgotten Rule 9, Sec. 5, Art. 2. It stated that a safety would be awarded if an offensive team was guilty of a penalty in its own end zone. The touchdown was taken away from Dallas, and Pittsburgh was awarded a safety, which turned out to be the winning margin. The rule was removed from the books the next year.

There were other trying periods as well, such as the life and times of one Samuel Baker, occupation, place kicker–punter, man about town. Baker was one of the league's better kickers but just wasn't overly serious about rules and did like his beverage now and then. He once showed up for a Cowboys game in Pittsburgh carrying a potted orange plant and wearing a silly grin.

Another time the team flew to an exhibition game and then returned to training camp. But Baker was AWOL. He arrived on a commercial flight at 3:30 A.M. and phoned training camp, asking for Gil Brandt.

"I imagine the Man wants to talk to you, Sam," said Brandt.

"Now?" asked Baker, slurring his words. "Right this minute?"

When Baker arrived in camp he marched to Landry's door and knocked as though he were trying to break down the door. When Landry finally woke up and opened the door, Baker swung to attention, clicking his heels and giving a *Sieg heil.*

"Sam Baker reporting for duty, sir," he said.

"Good," said Landry, blinking. "That'll cost you one thousand dollars." Landry closed the door and went back to sleep.

Once on a road trip Landry had returned from dinner and was on the elevator at the hotel when Baker came staggering in. He got on the elevator, leaned up against the wall, and then looked over and saw Landry.

"Drunk again, huh, Sam?" said Landry.

"You too, Coach?" replied Baker.

Baker lasted two seasons with the Cowboys then went to Philadelphia, where he continued to be one of the league's better kickers. Years later when the Cowboys staff was coaching in the Pro Bowl game, Landry needed a kicker for his all-stars. He conferred with special assistant Ermal Allen, who scouted and rated all players in the league.

"Ermal, who's the best kicker available?"

"Tom, Sam Baker's the best."

There was a long pause. And then Landry said, "Ermal, who's the second-best kicker?"

"I don't think," Baker once recalled, "that Tom really disliked me, but it is probably safe to say he doesn't have the respect for me that I do for him."

❦

LANDRY ALWAYS SEEMED to have problems with kickers, those football players from another world. He did have great hopes for a transplanted Australian, Colin Ridgway, nicknamed "Boomer" because of his long, high punts in practice. Ridgway had been a high jumper at Lamar Tech, but Gil Brandt figured he'd had some success with basketball players so why not try a high jumper as a punter? Boomer caught everybody's eye, and Landry had visions of grandeur. After a year, Boomer's promising career ended abruptly in a preseason game in San Francisco, where a small gale was blowing as usual. Dallas was backed up to its fifteen when Landry charged Boomer with the true test, sending him in to boot the team out of trouble. Boomer, a fresh wind in his face, rushed onto the field and really got his foot into the ball, which went up, up, up.

"That sonuvagun's hit pretty darn good," Boomer recalled telling himself.

Harold Hays was among those who took off on punt coverage. He started looking up to find the punt. Films showed him bending slowly backward, almost doing a flip, as the ball, caught in the wind, began heading back toward its origin.

What could Boomer do? Nobody had taught him how to signal for a fair catch. He stood there, frozen, as a 49er lineman got the ball at the Dallas twenty, five yards downfield. Boomer was cut before the regular season started.

Toni Fritsch came along in the early '70s and drove Landry up the wall. He had been a soccer player in Austria and knew nothing about football, but he could, as he said, "keek." Toni was a little spacey, like Boomer, but for a different reason. He did like his beer. He was 5'-8", 185 pounds, and with his stomach sticking out, looked like anything but a football player. He had some fine moments for the Cowboys but also some, well, unusual ones.

As a rookie, the veterans sent him out for pizza one night during training camp in Thousand Oaks. He'd had a few and was pulled over for speeding. The officer asked him what his profession was, and Toni, in broken German-English, said he was a football player for the Cowboys. The officer looked at him and felt he'd heard everything. Toni was taken off to jail, where Brandt went to get him out.

One day at practice Toni had had a few and, not knowing Landry was near, started telling everybody to get back, that he was going to keek the ball a mile. He ran up to the ball and missed it, digging his toe into the ground. Toni let out a few words and did it again.

"Toni," said Landry, "this isn't funny. We take *practice* seriously too."

Toni listened and then clicked his heels and yelled, "Heil Hitler!" Landry didn't cut him on the spot. As Tex Schramm once said, "Tom has the patience of a saint."

~:~

DICK NOLAN was having a lot of trouble with his shoulder and decided he'd retire from the Giants in 1961. Then Landry phoned him.

"He asked me if I'd like to coach in Dallas," said Nolan. "By February fifteenth [1962], I was in Dallas. He turned the defense over to me. I knew the system, what he was trying to do, because that was what he installed with the Giants. At one time I was the only defensive coach he had.

"My weight had gone up to about one ninety-five, maybe twenty pounds over my playing weight, but I had come to Dallas to coach. Right? So, jeez, before a game I'm out there on Saturday at practice. I'm just throwing the ball around and Tom walked over to me and said, 'Dick, how would you like to play again?' I said I didn't know, hadn't even thought about it but I didn't think I could. Tom said, 'Good, I've activated you and you're playing tomorrow.' So we kept playing catch, and I threw the ball and dislocated my shoulder again. Tom rushed me to the team doctor to put it back in place so I could play. They wrapped it, and I played . . . what? About all the games that season. My shoulder was knocked out four more times."

Nolan recalled that after he had again become a full-time assistant coach, "Tom called me up one night and said that there had been an article in the *Washington Post* about us having a fight on the sidelines, that we were on the outs with each other.

"'What are you talking about?' I asked Tom.

" 'Well,' said Landry, 'the *Washington Post* said you and I were arguing on the sidelines.'

"'I don't know what they're talking about.'

"'Well, Dick, I thought I'd call and let you know what the paper said.'

"So, the next week we played the Cardinals and Tom told me, 'We'll have to be careful what we do on the sidelines.' I told him, sure, okay. Anyway, Cornell Green got beat on a thirty-yard pass and here comes Tom storming down the sidelines and he gets right in my ear and says, 'Did you see that? Did you see that?'

"'Yeah, I saw it. I saw it. What the heck do you want me to do? I can't do anything about it now.'"

Landry kept on questioning Nolan about the play, and, remembering what Landry had cautioned him about, Nolan just kept walking on down the sidelines, trying to get away. "I'm looking up the field toward the open-tunnel side of the Cotton Bowl. He keeps talking, and I just keep staring at the tunnel. So, anyway, Tom had had Alicia watch him on the sidelines and she told him that people had interpreted what was happening as a fight between us on the sidelines."

After the game, Landry came over to Nolan at a party and said, "Dick, I'm sorry about what happened on the sidelines."

"What happened?" asked Nolan.

"Well," said Landry, "you know, I'm sorry about arguing with you out there."

"Heck, nothing to be sorry about. You've been doing the same thing ever since I met you in New York."

THE COWBOYS were 5–8–1 in 1962, but the rivalry with the Dallas Texans ended as Lamar Hunt moved his team to more lucrative ground in Kansas City. Hunt's team had been more competitive in the weaker AFL, posting a 25–17 record and winning the league title in 1962, whereas the Cowboys were 9–28–2. Attendance figures were close, but both teams were losing money. Hunt once had proposed a "Loser Leave Town" game, but the Cowboys refused.

After that, the joke going around town was that the teams were indeed going to play and the loser would have to stay in town. But prior to the 1963 season, the Texans were gone and the Cowboys were improving.

Paul Brown remarked that Landry was building a fine team, and *Sports Illustrated*'s Tex Maule, caught up in the moment, predicted the Cowboys would win the NFL Eastern title. Landry knew this wasn't true and that it would only put more pressure on his team. However, he did say, "Dallas will be a great team when it jells. I don't know when this will be, but it will come. We're going to be the next great team, eventually, I think, reaching the status Green Bay has now."

But 1963 just wasn't a good year in Dallas. President John F. Kennedy, moving in a motorcade through downtown, was shot and killed by a hidden assassin, believed to be Lee Harvey Oswald. This would leave a stigma on the city for years to come, a stigma that, to a great degree, the Dallas Cowboys would help erase because of the great popularity they would achieve in the late 1960s and 1970s.

At times the Cowboys would almost put it together, but then they would fall apart at inopportune moments, when inopportune things would happen. Amos Marsh, another one of the club's phenoms, was big and had great speed, but he would also often drop the ball on such things as pitchouts. Once during a game Marsh circled under a high, spiraling punt. The ball came down and hit him right on top of the head. (Dallas did retain possession, and Marsh wasn't seriously injured on the play.) "That was just Amos's way of doing things," said Ermal Allen.

But there were highlights, and it was obvious Bob Lilly was taking to his new position at tackle. George Mira of San Francisco faded to pass, spotted a receiver, and threw the ball with all his might as Lilly rushed after him. There was a hush over the crowd. The ball had not appeared downfield. Nobody knew where it was . . . except Bob Lilly. Lilly had charged in with his arms held high, and the ball, almost point blank, had stuck in his hands. Lilly, almost nonchalantly, jogged forty-two yards for a touchdown.

But the team finished 4–10–0 in 1963, with one less victory than the previous year, and some element of fans began howling for Landry's job. Clint Murchison Jr. responded by awarding Landry a ten-year contract, the longest in sports at that time, which would begin when Landry's contract expired in 1965.

"I thought Tom was a darn good football coach and had what it would take to make us a winner," recalled Schramm. "I talked to Clint, and he decided we should make a strong commitment and let everybody—the fans, the press, the players—know how we felt."

"That was one of the most significant things that ever happened to me," said Landry. "I'm sure it shocked a lot of reporters. Everybody thought they were going to make a change. From then on, I decided to dedicate myself even more to being a good coach. Clint was always so important. He never pressured any of us and was always so positive when we'd have a losing streak. We'd be in a slump and he'd write us some clever note.

"Today, everybody panics after a few bad years. . . . When Clint gave me that contract, I realized God wanted me to serve Him in the capacity of a coach."

"We were getting a lot of criticism," said LeBaron, who retired and turned the reins over to Meredith after 1963. "If it had happened somewhere else, they might have fired the coach and later regretted it. We'd had some lean years and there would be others, but Tom kept the faith in his system, went down the road with it, and the club kept faith with him. Tom had his mind set on things he wanted, and as time went by, the players improved and the system became more believable to them."

After Dallas had gone into a tailspin again in 1964, Murchison noted, "I was having lunch with this friend of mine and he noted the team had been losing and said, 'Well, one good thing, Landry's only got nine years left on his contract.'"

"We were playing the Chicago Bears in 1994," said assistant coach Jim Myers. "They were the Monsters of the Midway back then. Coach Landry was walking on the field with Coach George Halas right before the game started. These big ol' Bears came lumbering out there. They just kind of jogged over to the sideline. Then, the Cowboys came roaring out of the tunnel and sprinted to the bench. Coach Halas said, 'Tom, how'd you ever get your guys to do that?' Tom looked at him and said, 'Coach, I just told the squad that the last ones to the bench had to start the game against the Bears.'"

The Cowboys beat the Bears that day, 24–10, as one of the highlights of a disappointing 5–8–2 season. By then the defense had begun to come together. Lilly continued to develop, and the club had added Lee Roy Jordan and Chuck Howley at linebacker, George Andrie at end, and Mel Renfro in the secondary. By that time, Landry also had installed a new twist in the standard 4–3 defense, calling it the 4–3 Flex. The defense, which he employed with variations until he was fired, got its name because one or more defensive linemen are a few feet off the line of scrimmage, flexed, so to speak.

Basically, after Landry refined the original 4–3 defense, he installed in his multiple offense a "run to daylight" theory of his friend and rival at Green Bay, Vince Lombardi. Lombardi's reasoning was to have a blocker hit a man and let the defender react to the block, moving one way or another against the pressure. A running back would then go to the hole created as the defender reacted to the pressure of the block. The specific hole varied, depending on the easiest direction the blocker would take the defender. Certainly, this made it easier to block because you'd just take a defender the direction he was trying to go. The back would then adjust to the available hole.

Landry sought something in which the defender would not react to pressure. Thus, in theory, Cowboy defenders would not react to false keys and pressure, and no holes would be created. Each had a gap responsibility and would simply go to that gap, no matter what appeared to be happening. A defender for Dallas, such as the defensive lineman, would first hold his gap, wait, and then react. The natural instinct of an athlete is to react immediately to what he sees, so it took two, three years to teach a player to wait and then react.

The "Flex" theory was added to give certain linemen an easier path to the particular gap for which he was responsible. For instance, the weakside end might be on the line of scrimmage, whereas the tackle would be "flexed," or back a few steps. The tackle would have an extra instant to step into his gap at the snap of the ball before being blocked. Over the years, Landry ran variations and change-ups off the 4–3 Flex to disguise it, to try to confuse opponents. Perhaps one variation might change the particular gap for a player and another would not.

The "Flex" also proved successful for Nolan, who used it when he won two NFC Western titles as head coach of the 49ers. He also installed it as head coach of the New Orleans Saints when the usually disastrous team reached .500 at 8–8 for the first time in 1980.

~:~

EARLY IN THE 1960s, Landry needed the players. Still, by using the 4–3 Flex, the Cowboys trimmed almost one hundred points off opponents' scoring totals from 1963 to 1964. Tex Schramm tried to help the offense by trading for two of the top receivers in football, Buddy Dial and Tommy McDonald. Tom Landry wanted to give Don Meredith, who would be on his own at quarterback, the best receiving cast available. But it didn't work out. Dial faded beneath a wave of injuries, and Meredith just had problems connecting with McDonald. Tommy asked to be traded and was.

He later admitted being disappointed with his year in Dallas but did say Tom Landry "was one of the finest men ever to coach the game."

Don Meredith, the man upon whom the franchise had based its future, suffered in 1964 and 1965 through more injuries than most players sustained during an entire career, but he courageously hung in there when others would not have attempted to play. Much of his courage was lost amid the boos from the fans in the Cotton Bowl and a great deal of criticism in the press. Meredith was still Meredith. Once during a meeting Landry was talking about the importance of intelligence, and

Meredith volunteered, "I can take C students and beat your A students in football every time."

Sometimes when Landry was calling the plays, Meredith would audibilize when there was no need. "Every once in a while I just had to show him who had the last word," said Don.

In 1965, when Meredith was calling his own plays, he would sometimes drive Landry up the wall. Against St. Louis with the ball on the Cowboy five-yard line, Meredith called for a bomb and faded into the end zone. It fell incomplete. "You guys held them out pretty good," he told the line in the huddle. "Let's do it again." The pass again fell incomplete, but Meredith, fading each time into his end zone, had time to throw. So he called the play a third time. And again it fell incomplete.

"This," recalled former Cowboy trainer Larry Gardner, "drove Tom nuts. But the players loved Don. They'd do anything for him."

Tom Landry's plan to make the Cowboys a winner by no later than their fifth year went down the drain in 1964 when the team finished 5–8–1. But 1965 looked promising. He had some top athletes, his defense was playing well, and the Cowboys had won their first two games by impressive scores over New York and Washington. Then the club went into a tailspin, losing four in a row by ten points or less, including a very tough one to Lombardi's Packers, 13–3, in a game in which the Cowboys defense held Green Bay to a net gain of minus ten yards, one of the most incredible performances against a good team in NFL history.

Meredith was in a slump and Landry had benched him and gone with Craig Morton and Jerry Rhome, the much-heralded rookie duo. Sometimes Landry would use one of them, sometimes the other, and sometimes both, shuttling them on each down while he called the plays, as he once had done with Meredith and LeBaron.

Meredith seemed to be coming back strong, however, and he looked good in practice as Dallas prepared to travel to Pittsburgh to play the struggling Steelers. Landry felt certain his team would turn the season around. And he put Meredith back in the lineup. Landry worked hard, knew the Steelers well, and even with a few backfires, felt strongly Dallas would win. But the game got away. Meredith was miserable, hitting just twelve of thrity-four passes for 187 yards, and Pittsburgh won, 22–13. Don had tried, Landry had tried, but it just hadn't worked. As Landry got up to talk to the team after the game, his words seemed to come very slowly, his voice almost shaking. He said that this was the first time he truly had been ashamed. Perhaps, he went on, the fault did lie in his system, in his approach. He coughed softly, and tears came into his eyes. The man they said had a stone face, the man they said had no emotion, was crying.

"He told us we had done all he asked, given that hundred and ten percent," recalled Lilly. "He said he believed in the system but had let us down. . . . Then he cried. He was right about the system, everything. The only problem was the players. *We* had let *him* down."

"It was so unexpected, we didn't know what to think," said flanker Pete Gent. "It just wasn't something, well, you'd associate with him."

"I felt a little ashamed and then disappointed because I just didn't expect him to do something like that," said center Dave Manders.

Meredith said he felt awful, that he'd never tried so hard and done so badly. Landry didn't say anything else. He walked into the coaches' locker room and closed the door. When he came out again, he hinted to the press that, certainly, he had to seriously consider going with Morton or Rhome. Those present agreed it was the only thing he could do. After that game in Pittsburgh, Meredith's popularity rating in the Dallas area would have been zero.

On Wednesday, December 3, 1965, Tom Landry's weekly press conference was filled with speculation as to exactly what he'd do. Would he go with Morton? Would he go with Rhome? Or would he shuttle Morton and Rhome on each play? Everyone had his opinion with, perhaps, Morton being the consensus favorite.

Landry had done a great deal of soul-searching before the press conference, weighing each player, each thing involved. He had prayed that God would help him make the correct decision.

"Our offensive team is very young," he told the press, his voice strong, his appearance unruffled. "We have three rookies starting. Leon Donohue [a guard] is a veteran but has been with us only two months. The only veterans with experience on our offensive team are Jim Boeke, Don Perkins, and Frank Clarke. We need a quarterback to lift us to our potential, and that's why I have made the decision . . . Don Meredith will start the next seven games this season."

You could have heard a pin drop. Landry continued, "After five straight losses, a decision of this nature is difficult, but I had to go with the man I felt everyone on the team had the most confidence in, the man I felt could make the team rise up and play well enough to make up the seven to ten points we've been losing by all season."

Radio men ran to the phones, reporters hurried downtown to tell of the decision and write their stories. Most everybody disagreed with Landry's call, but Landry was the man, he made the decision.

Reflecting on various decisions he'd had to make over the years with the Cowboys, Landry said, "The Meredith decision I made that year was the most difficult I've ever had to make. Everything seemed to be going against Meredith. The press, the fans were down on him, and he was getting booed something awful. But I felt strongly he was the right choice. It was more difficult than when I was faced with the Morton-Staubach decisions. The team, the town was divided over Morton and Staubach, and they both were doing well. But that time in 1965, Meredith wasn't doing so well."

Explaining his feeling more in depth, Landry said, "A lot of people had just forgotten what Don had done for us in 1964. It's hard for me to forget. He quarterbacked for us when no other man could have stood on the field with the injuries he had. When he was healthy for one short span in 1964, he won three straight games for us. I'm not foolish enough to put a quarterback out there . . . if I don't think he can win. I have no doubt Don can win."

It was the correct decision, one that launched the Cowboys into a winning era, a far cry from the beginning in 1960 when each day for Landry seemed more trying than the day before and players nobody else wanted appeared and disappeared as if they were going through a swinging door.

The Cowboys won five of their final seven games, finishing 7–7, and, as runners-up to Cleveland in the NFL Eastern Conference, were invited to the Playoff Bowl to play the Baltimore Colts, second-place finishers in the NFL Western Conference. Lombardi's Green Bay Packers and the Colts had tied with 10–3–1 records during the regular season, but the Packers won a playoff game, 13–10, and then beat Cleveland, 23–12, for the title.

Most felt the Colts would have won the title, but they lost first Johnny Unitas and then backup quarterback Gary Cuozzo to injuries. At the end of the season, the Colts had to play halfback Tom Matte at quarterback. Matte, who hadn't played quarterback since his college days, wrote his assignments on tape wrapped around his wrists. Dallas, reaching .500 for the first time, appeared ready. Some two thousand Dallas fans, caught up in the excitement, made the trip to Miami for the game. But Matte looked very polished, offensive tackle Jim Parker got the best of Lilly, and the Colts humiliated the Cowboys 35–3.

It was after the game that Landry, philosophically, uttered his immortal words when asked which players had faltered for the Cowboys. "It was," said Landry, "a team effort."

But Landry knew the Cowboys were growing up. They would show just how grown up the next season, launching the team into an unprecedented era.

CHAPTER 12
The 1966 and 1967 Seasons

‿∴∽

Tom has the great ability to recognize potential in a player. We have kept players who would not have been around on other contending teams. Tom can see something worth keeping in a mass of humanity. Tactics dwindle in importance to that. What a coach can contribute to a team, in my opinion, is 10 percent inspiration, 10 percent motivation, 20 to 30 percent tactics, and 50 to 60 percent player recognition.

—CLINT MURCHISON JR.
Former Dallas Cowboys Owner

THE LATE '60S were a staggering, eventful time. Neil Armstrong would become the first man to walk on the moon. President Lyndon Baines Johnson, a Texan who strongly pulled for the Cowboys, would continue to persevere and have a great deal of success pushing civil rights issues at home but, like those before and after him, would find Vietnam an unsolvable puzzle. There would be movement and movements. The city proper of Dallas, like other metropolitan areas, would sit still as the populace continued to migrate to the suburbs, eventually making area towns such as Plano, which once seemed so far away, become almost an extension of Dallas. The young would begin to speak out against Vietnam and anything else they didn't like. They would burn property, lock themselves in the offices of presidents of universities, say this was wrong, or that was wrong. And some would let their hair grow long, drop out, be called hippies, and make their surrogate capital the Haight-Asbury section of San Francisco. What they would do would upset us. But it would get our attention.

Most newsworthy in sports, the NFL and AFL had reached peace. The leagues had reached a financial peak as teams spent a combined total of seven hundred thousand dollars to sign 1966 draft choices, each trying to outbid the other. So after Tex Schramm and Lamar Hunt had been negotiating in secret for months, a merger was announced on June 8,

1966. Champions of the two leagues would meet in what Hunt named a "Super Bowl" game.

This added some extra excitement to the season, and for so many fans around the country, the Cowboys had become a great escape, from themselves, from what was happening. By that season of 1966, watching the Cowboys had become the thing to do in Dallas. It had always been said that Dallas only loves a winner, and as fans flocked to and filled up the Cotton Bowl, this proved to be true.

The great patience of Tom Landry had paid off. As late as 1964, some of the veteran Cowboys were saying his system was too complicated, that it just wouldn't work. Critics said his 4–3 Flex Defense, in which players were in a holding pattern before reacting, just wouldn't cut it because it went against human nature. But the Cowboy defense led the NFL in fewest yards given up rushing. When he installed the multiple offense, which became standard procedure among many NFL teams, detractors noted it would self-destruct, dissolve in its complexities. But the Cowboy offense led the NFL in scoring with 445 points and ran up single-game totals of 52, 47, 56, and 52 points. Jokes were still being made about the system, only by this time Landry could laugh too.

Don Smith, the New York publicity director who had known Landry when he was with the Giants, came to Dallas to advance a game and remarked, "I took a page from Landry's playbook to a Chinese laundry. They gave me three shirts and a lace pillowcase."

Cowboy flanker Pete Gent, who one day would find success as an author but served in those days as somewhat of a team cynic, a rebel with long hair, watched a rookie poring over Landry's playbook in training camp. "Don't bother reading it, kid," quipped Pete. "Everybody gets killed at the end."

But Ernie Stautner, the all-time NFL great who joined Landry's staff for the 1966 season, said, "I almost fainted when I saw Tom's playbook. It was all there, things that had taken me sixteen years to figure out for myself in the NFL. I mean things that just weren't taught in most places, such as keys. All the keys for the defensive linemen are down in black and white. There's no guesswork to it. Maybe I'm dumb, but I didn't realize anyone taught keys to defensive linemen." Few did then. Everybody does now.

Landry had been patient, however, and the players had learned his playbooks. And Dallas had won. Landry got dividends as well for the patience he displayed toward his players. Cornell Green, a basketball player signed as a free agent, complained after a few days' practice that his hip was sore. It was discovered that he had been wearing his hip pads backward. When this was corrected, he was obviously much more comfortable, although he continually struggled to adapt to football with its many frustrations. Landry saw something in him, however, and felt he might develop. By 1966, Green was rated as one of the two or three best cornerbacks in the NFL. Landry also watched and waited for Mike Gaechter, a gifted, moody athlete who was known mostly for track and had very little college football experience, to come around. The same goes for Gent, who had been an all–Big Ten basketball player but had not played football in college. Landry also saw football potential in Bobby Hayes, the world's fastest man, and the list goes on and on.

"Take a guy like Cornell," said Gil Brandt. "So many would have given up on him, but Tom just saw something he liked and waited. It paid off. The man just has a great ability to see something in a player that maybe somebody else wouldn't see. And he's patient enough to watch that trait develop and the guy become a good football player."

Clint Murchison Jr. noted, "Tom has the great ability to recognize potential in a player. We have kept players who would not have been around on other contending teams. Tom can see something worth keeping in a mass of humanity. Tactics dwindle in importance to that. What a coach can contribute to a team, in my opinion, is 10 percent inspiration, 10 percent motivation, 20 to 30 percent tactics, and 50 to 60 percent player recognition."

This never was more evident than on the 1966 team, although a great deal of credit must go to Brandt and the scouting system for finding overlooked and unwanted players in the first place. But no less than eight free agents started for the 1966 Eastern Conference champions, including Green, Gaechter, linebacker Dave Edwards, and cornerback Warren Livingston on defense. Gent, Danny Reeves, center Dave Manders, and tight end Pettis Norman started on offense. The draft had also brought in Hayes, Bob Lilly, Mel Renfro, Ralph Neely, and Lee Roy Jordan to go with already established stars such as Chuck Howley, Don Perkins, and Don Meredith. Meredith was 29, Lilly 28, Jordan 26, Hayes 24, Green 27, Renfro 25, and Neely 23. It was the youngest team ever to play for the NFL title.

Landry's faith in Meredith in 1965 paid big dividends in 1966. Don enjoyed an outstanding season, winning both the Bert Bell and Maxwell Club awards as the NFL's MVP.

"The confidence came from Tom," Meredith said. "He worked with me closer than he'd ever had time to do. We'd meet during the week, when we were on the field. He told me I was great, and you know [he grinned] Tom's never wrong. He drilled details into me. He had everything all spelled out. He said I could complete 51 percent, which would be outstanding. I hit 51.5." He also threw for 2,805 yards and twenty-four touchdowns, a club record for a fourteen-game regular season.

"Championship quarterbacks," said Landry, "are the ones who can make the big play and turn a game in your favor. I'm convinced Don can do that." At a banquet in Philadelphia where Meredith was to receive the Maxwell Award, Landry told the audience, "You people in Philadelphia compare all quarterbacks to Norm Van Brocklin. Sure, Dutch had great leadership, but remember, he had ten years in the pros before he won a championship here in 1960. Don's getting that kind of command. He will have it." Don Meredith would not in fact complete his ten years in the pros, although in 1966 there seemed to be no doubt that he would.

Landry had put more emphasis that season on winning in preseason, a time he ordinarily used to test new players and to work on techniques with the veterans.

"The basic problem you face is developing a losing pattern," said Landry, recalling that his team did not reach .500 until 1965. "The most difficult thing in coaching is to overcome that feeling you're going to lose. You only can do it by bringing in new blood. We brought them in in 1965, people like Hayes, Neely, Morton, Pugh, Reeves, and we became more solid, began turning things around, including the feeling that we would lose. This culminated in 1966."

Dallas won all preseason games, and after beating Green Bay, 21–3, Lombardi met Landry at midfield in the Cotton Bowl and said, "Tom, you have a damn good football team."

"Thank you," said Landry. "I hope you're right."

Landry had tried one of his great experiments in preseason, which both worked and failed. A great weakness of the 1965 team had been that it couldn't run wide, causing the opposition to gang up on Don Perkins, trying to work the middle. So Landry decided to move Mel Renfro, a Pro Bowl free safety and fine kick returner, to halfback.

Renfro, who had played offense at Oregon, had always wanted a shot at either halfback or wide receiver, and he got it. His tremendous speed and acceleration gave Dallas a new dimension. He averaged some seven yards per carry in preseason but suffered a hip-pointer. When the regular season began, Mel had eight carries for 6.5 yards per try and caught four passes for 65 yards. But he badly sprained his ankle.

Landry replaced the injured Renfro with one of the free agents, a little-known quarterback from South Carolina named Danny Reeves. Danny was not fast, didn't seem all that quick, but continually did the things necessary to win. He went on that season to rush for 757 yards, catch forty-one passes for 557 yards, and score sixteen touchdowns. With his ability to throw the halfback pass, he also proved a tremendous asset, as Frank Gifford had been. Reeves was an even better passer than Gifford or Paul Hornung. He turned out to be perhaps the best passer from the halfback position in modern-day football.

Reeves had not exactly gotten off to an auspicious start with the team. During training camp, the rookies always have to put on a show for the veterans. They sing, dance, do whatever, and when Reeves was a rookie he ended the show by mooning the audience, which he believed to be only players and coaches. Certainly women weren't usually allowed in the audience. What Reeves didn't know was that Alicia Landry, who was visiting camp, had attended the show. Reeves almost had a heart attack when, after the show, Alicia walked up to him and said, "Danny, I enjoyed that closing number." When Renfro returned, Landry moved him back to defense, fearing he might be prone to more injuries.

Dallas averaged an amazing 45.7 points in winning its first four games, then faltered when it faced contenders St. Louis and Cleveland. The Cowboys bounced back to beat Pittsburgh and then lost to the Eagles, a team it had beaten earlier in the year, 56–7, by the score of 24–23. The offense and defense were fine, but the specialty teams were lacking as Timmy Brown returned kickoffs for ninety-three and ninety yards for touchdowns and Aaron Martin ran a punt back sixty-seven yards for a score. Even then, Dallas appeared to be moving for the winning score near the end of the game, but Reeves had the ball stolen out of his hands by an Eagle defender. The next week, Danny opened his locker and found a football with handles taped on it, courtesy of equipment manager Jack Eskridge.

Writers covering the team asked Landry if they could come to his office to see films of the kick returns by the Eagles, but he said no. When told this, Alicia remarked, "Oh, just come over to the house any night. Tommy has the projector running every night anyway."

Landry was feeling more and more at ease around the writers. Early that year the Cowboys had flown in prop-propelled DC-7's. When an overload of fuel delayed their arrival in Atlanta, causing a workout prior to the game to be canceled, Landry suggested a switch to Electra jets. This enabled him to hold Saturday workouts in Dallas and still get to road games in plenty of time for the players to rest. After switching to the jets, however, the Cowboys tied one and lost two road games. Asked before the next road game in Washington if he planned any changes, Landry deadpanned, "Well, we might go back to DC-7's."

The 1966 Dallas-Washington game was just one of many high-scoring classics the Cowboys and Redskins, led by Sonny Jurgensen, would play. Dallas was trailing Washington, 31–30, with 1:10 left to play and the ball at its own three-yard line with no time-outs left. Then, in a game that Landry considered one of the club's most memorable comebacks, Meredith took control. Using a rollout series in which he could throw or run out of bounds to stop the clock, Don took Dallas to the Redskins' thirteen in six plays. Danny Villanueva then kicked a winning twenty-yard field goal with twenty-five seconds left.

"That just doesn't happen," said Landry. "You just don't pull a game like that out when you have no time-outs left. It was a great performance by Meredith."

The showdown for the Eastern Conference title game came on Thanksgiving Day in the Cotton Bowl before a crowd of 80,259, the largest ever to witness a sporting event in Dallas.

"As long as I've been in the NFL, dating back to my days with the Giants, the Cleveland Browns have personified the best in the league," said Landry. "Cleveland always has been the team to beat to win the title.

"Before this season [1966] we just weren't good enough to cause clubs preparing to play us to go all out. The result of this is that we don't have that many big games, big game experiences from which to draw. Cleveland has. It's just tough to crack that nut, but once you've done it, you're a better team. So we've got to prove we can do it."

But, with the press not around, he told his players, "I have all the confidence in the world you'll win this game."

The Cowboys overcame a 14–13 halftime deficit to win, 26–14, as Meredith and Perkins led a fourth-period touchdown push that put the contest away. Landry called the victory the biggest in the club's history at the time because the winning team would win the Eastern Conference title.

Perkins was a serious, intelligent, astute gentleman who would threaten to retire before the 1968 season because of racial difficulties in finding equal housing for his family and schools for his children. He also displayed a sense of humor when you least expected it.

Once Reeves was knocked out of bounds near the Cowboys' bench in a game against St. Louis. The Cardinals had the reputation of being one of the meanest teams in football. Danny was still on the ground when a tackler suddenly reached over and clamped down on the soft, inside part of Reeves's leg.

"Ouch! Ouch! OUCH!" yelled Danny, who started kicking at the tackler. Landry heard the commotion and walked over.

"What's the matter, Danny?" asked Landry. "You're going to get us penalized."

"Coach," said Reeves, "I just got pinched."

"Oh," said Landry, shaking his head and walking away.

When Reeves got back to the huddle, his teammates asked what had happened and Danny said, "That sonuvabuck pinched me." Perkins, never looking up, replied, "Oh, that's all right, Danny. I'll goose him on the next play." The players broke up, and it almost cost Dallas a time-out.

Dallas beat St. Louis 31–17, but Meredith suffered a concussion and second-year men Craig Morton and Jerry Rhome quarterbacked the final two games of the season as the club coasted to a 10–3–1 record and the Eastern Conference title.

～∶～

IT HAD FINALLY HAPPENED, and all of Dallas was caught up in the excitement of the time, the event. The city in its entirety was more up for this game than for any sporting event since Doak Walker's days as the Great American Hero at SMU. In the vernacular that was creeping into the times, the city of Dallas was on a "natural high" because the Cowboys had gone through a storybook season in which they had done to opponents what opponents had been doing to them for so many years. They had won the National Football League Eastern

Conference title and would play the legendary Green Bay Packers, Western Conference champions, defending NFL champions, for the league's championship in the Cotton Bowl on the first day of 1967.

The game was a match for the times. The youthful, exciting Cowboys were the team that could explode from any place on the field, the team that had gone against the grain and one that counted among its stars so many players who had been overlooked or forgotten by other clubs. And they were going against the time-tested Packers, the team of Starr and Nitschke and Taylor and Adderley, a club that did things simply, played in the trenches, and personified the NFL Establishment. Most fans around the nation felt strongly, as did the oddsmakers, that the Packers would win. But in their hearts they were pulling for the exciting, brash underdogs, the Dallas Cowboys.

On the final day of 1966, fog shadowed the city. But it lifted the morning of the game, and the day turned out to be sunny and brisk. Landry had dissected films of the Packers and reached a somewhat astonishing conclusion that his team could move the ball on Green Bay, something nobody else had done effectively all season. "I'm confident of this if you'll just execute," he told the team.

For the second time in his career, Landry was involved in what people were calling the "Game of the Decade." It did not begin as if it would be, because the Packers moved the opening kickoff seventy-six yards for a touchdown and then scored again as Mel Renfro fumbled the ensuing kickoff and Jim Grabowski picked up the ball and raced into the end zone. Green Bay led 14–0 and the Cowboy offense had not touched the ball.

"Even then," said Meredith, "Landry had us convinced that we could move the ball on them." Meredith brought the Cowboys back for two touchdowns to tie the game, 14–14, before the first period had ended.

Green Bay scored twice more on Starr's passes, and Villanueva countered with two field goals. In the final period, Starr found Max McGee with a nineteen-yard scoring pass and the Packers seemed out of reach, 34–20, with just 5:20 left to play. Certainly, the all-important extra point by Don Chandler would put the game out of reach, would place the Packers more than two touchdowns ahead. Lombardi was screaming, "Watch it! Watch it! Don't let them block it!" But Lilly rushed through to block the kick. The man who missed the block came off the field and walked clear around the Packers' bench, trying to avoid Lombardi, who looked ready to take his head off.

Dallas needed two touchdowns to send the game into overtime, but it had to get a quick score to have a chance. Meredith called his own plays but got a great deal of advice from Landry, who gave him the right play at the right time. Frank Clarke, the club's premier receiver during its formative years, was then used as a replacement for Pettis Norman at tight end on obvious passing downs. Clarke still had good speed and could get past a strongside linebacker and, more times than not, just outrun a strong safety. Hayes had done little, a pattern that was to repeat itself in the next championship game, by catching only a single pass for one yard, but with his speed, he was still the man Meredith could use to get the Cowboys back into the game. Lombardi had duly noted this.

So when Dallas faced third and twenty at its own thirty, cornerback Bob Jeter and safety Willie Wood both drifted with Hayes as he ran a route to the right sideline, opening up the middle. Suddenly, Clarke, who had delayed slightly, shot up the middle full speed ahead and was past strong safety Tom Brown before he knew what was happening. Meredith laid the ball into his arms, and Clarke raced in for a touchdown to pull Dallas within seven with 4:08 remaining.

"That was Landry," Lombardi said later. "We had it all figured, everything covered, and he springs that on us."

The momentum had changed. Edwards blitzed and threw Starr for an eight-yard loss. Willie Townes batted down a pass, and Lee Roy Jordan roped Jim Taylor for a loss of seven yards on a sweep. Chandler, under a big rush, flubbed the punt off the side of his foot, and the ball traveled just sixteen yards, going out of bounds at the Packer forty-seven with 2:11 left.

Meredith went to his hot receiver, Clarke. He found him for twenty-one yards, and two plays later Frank had again sprinted by Brown and was running under a ball for what seemed a certain touchdown. At the last instant, Brown grabbed his jersey and jerked him out of the way. Interference was called and the ball was placed at the Packer two, but it should have been a score.

There then began a series of events, unusual happenings, that would almost become a trademark, an inexplicable pattern when Dallas played in title games.

Reeves made a yard on first down on the one, but something else was happening, unnoticed by those who should have seen it. All year Hayes had been taken out on goal-line situations and replaced by Clarke because Frank was bigger and a much better blocker. With Clarke replacing Hayes at split end, Norman, a fine blocker, would remain in the game at tight end. But with Dallas on the brink of keeping itself in the biggest game in the club's history, Hayes was still in the game. Clarke had run off the field after the interference call, but Hayes had stayed in. Meredith should have noticed, sending him to the bench. Hayes knew full well he wasn't supposed to be in the game and should have taken himself out. And Landry or an offensive assistant should have noticed and sent Clarke back in.

On second down, tackle Jim Boeke jumped offsides, costing Dallas a five-yard penalty back to the seven. Boeke, a good tackle, would always be remembered for the time when he jumped offsides. But Meredith threw a swing pass at Reeves, who had enough daylight in front of him to score. However, on a previous play Reeves had gotten a finger in his eye and had blurred vision. He couldn't follow the flight of the short pass, and he dropped it. Reeves should have mentioned the eye problem when it happened.

Facing third and six at the six, Meredith threw short to Norman near the goal line. Pettis had to come back and dive to catch the ball at the two. "If there is one thing, one slogan, Landry pounds into us, it's never give the defense more credit than it deserves," said Meredith. "The pass to Pettis is designed on the premise that the outside linebacker [Dave Robinson] would not react quickly enough to cover Pettis. I guess I just couldn't believe that. Surely, I was thinking, Robinson would be on him.

"So I hesitated before I threw the ball. That's why it was low. If I'd just had the confidence I should have had in what Tom told us, I'd have thrown the ball chest-high and Pettis would have waltzed in for the score."

Meredith called a rollout on the final play, a good call. He could throw if the defensive backs came up on the play or perhaps run the ball over if they dropped back. Meredith took the snap and faked inside to Perkins. Ordinarily, Robinson would have taken the fake, delaying his reaction to Meredith moving outside. Robinson slanted out with Meredith, however, and then shot inside to get him. Had Clarke been in the game, he might have blocked Robinson, delayed him for a needed second. Hayes was there, however, and could only brush the much larger man. Robinson was all over Meredith before he had time to do anything. As Robinson grabbed his left arm, Meredith did the only thing he could—loft the ball up for grabs in the end zone. Brown grabbed it. The game was over.

"We had the momentum," said Landry. "We would have beaten the Packers in overtime."

But Green Bay had won. Lombardi's team had beaten his, and it left a hollow feeling inside after fighting for all those years to gain respectability, to field a winning team then have it all fall short by less than twenty-four inches.

The Packers went on to smash Kansas City, 35–10, in the first Super Bowl in Los Angeles. But it was the young, exciting Dallas Cowboys about whom everybody was talking. "We were," said Schramm, "the heroes of the country. We had gone up against a poised old machine called the Packers and almost won. We were still riding on that crest the next season."

Tom Landry won more honors that year than he would ever win again. He was named "Coach of the Year" by the Associated Press, by United Press International, and by his peers in a poll by the *Sporting News*. The Texas Sportswriters Association also honored him as "Pro Coach of the Year." He was very proud of his team and of Meredith, who after all those years finally believed, with a lapse every now and then, in his system. But before the next season began, Landry was heard to remark, "The only caution I have about Don becoming one of the very best is that he's had a lot of injuries. They've plagued him every year, and so he's always faced with the prospect of it happening again." In hindsight, we know that what Landry said foreshadowed what was to come.

~:~

DURING TRAINING CAMP in the summer of 1967, Dallas seemed more than able to take up where it had left off at the end of the 1966 season, and there definitely were signs that the club would be improved with the addition of Lance Rentzel, who came from Minnesota for a third-round draft pick. Rentzel had tremendous ability but had never gotten along with Vikings coach Norm Van Brocklin. The club also noted that he had once been picked up in Minnesota for indecent exposure, although charges were dropped. But Landry realized everybody made mistakes and believed Lance's problems would remain in the past.

Landry had not been satisfied with the production at flanker, and Rentzel quickly took over for Gent at that position. Dial, who had never achieved much success after coming from Pittsburgh, retired after suffering back trouble. Gent became bitter with Landry over Dial and after Rentzel moved in. He was also disenchanted with club officials and would later voice his feelings in a novel, *North Dallas Forty*, an account of the dehumanization of an athlete.

"I was mostly a survivor," Gent would say years later. "When I first joined the club in 1964, everybody just kept saying I was a basketball player, and I was very determined to prove I could make it in football. It became obvious from the first that Coach Landry was very religious. When he first met the team he said something like, 'Gentlemen, I've given my life to Christ and I find answers to my problems in the Bible.' He didn't come on that strong, but it was like he just wanted us to know where he stood.

"But, heck, that first year I went to church with Tom and his son, who was visiting camp. I did it a couple of times, figuring, quite honestly, that it wouldn't hurt my chances.

"The Dial thing bothered me. He'd come in as a big star and was making all that money, but I was doing a better job. One time Tom started him and told me, 'You have better moves, better hands, and run better routes, but Buddy has proven he can make the big play. It's just a feeling I have that Buddy will make the big play for us.'"

Gent finally won the starting job, which he held until Rentzel came on the scene in 1967. Pete then backed up at flanker, played some at tight end, and became more than ever the club's caustic humorist-in-residence to the delight of the writers covering the team and to the chagrin of Landry.

Once Hayes had been injured during a road game, and on the return flight, Landry decided he'd move Gent from flanker to the other side, split end, where he'd start against Philadelphia in place of the injured Hayes. Landry walked to the back of the plane, the players section, and found Gent.

"Pete," said Landry, "you'll be moving to the other side this week."

"You mean, Coach," said Pete, "that I'm going to play for Philadelphia?"

Landry, as he would in such moments, took a semideep breath and walked away. It was as difficult for him to understand Gent, who had become the first of the Cowboys to grow his hair long, as it was for Gent to truly understand him. Landry probably thought only briefly about the situation and then continued to reflect and think about Gent as he did most all his players, only in regard to their effect on his football team.

"Landry was so far ahead of his time in the technical aspects of football that it was amazing," recalled Gent. "He was doing things people wouldn't begin to do for years. It was as if everybody else, his peers, were picking up chips here and there and Tom already was well into practical innovations of the overall structure of the game. But he was a computer. He was like the head of some giant corporation. He's there, you know he's there, making the plans, but he is humanly untouchable. I was on the team for five years and I never got to know the man at all. I imagine some guys who were on the team ten years would tell you the same thing."

After Gent's book became a bestseller, his popularity around the Cowboys offices dropped somewhere below zero. As said earlier, Landry had heard about the book, the sex and violence, etc., it depicted, and he refused to read it. Publicly, he said little about the book.

"Pete and I just were never on the same wavelength," Landry did say. "Pete was just different. I don't know how to describe him." He paused, smiled, and added, "Of course, he went on to describe us in a different fashion too."

Ironically, years after his book had come out, Pete was assigned to do a story on Landry for *Sport* magazine. "Most people would have felt that he wouldn't talk to me, and I'm sure a lot of the club's officials wouldn't have," said Pete. "But I knew, in the final analysis, Landry would be fair. I felt he'd talk to me because it was the fair thing to do. And he did."

Some of the other players had noticed Landry was loosening up toward them, often not only being more courteous but also at times listening to what they had to say about football. In the early years he had been a closed book.

"One day during the early years I went to see Tom in his office," said Chuck Howley. "He was by the window, looking out. I must have waited for five minutes before he was aware that I was there. You used to pass him in the hall at the Cowboys offices and he'd walk right by without speaking. I don't think he ever saw you. But in the later 1960s he started speaking to you when he passed you in the hall."

Nolan mentioned that Landry was preoccupied with decisions and game plans, more so in the early days of the team, but pointed out how fair he was with the players. "Tom is probably one of the most fair people anywhere."

Landry did not particularly take to nonsense in regard to football and, unlike most of us, didn't particularly find it funny when Meredith threw an interception to Cornell Green in a controlled scrimmage then took off his helmet and started chasing Green as though he were going to beat him with it. Landry said, "Gentlemen, nothing funny ever happens on the football field." Then he added, "If we can help it." And then he smiled.

~:~

PERHAPS THE OFF-FIELD SHENANIGANS of Sam Baker had prepared him for Lance Rentzel. Certainly in regard to football Rentzel was a paradox. When he was on the field, whether in a game or for an unimportant workout, nobody tried harder than Lance. But off the field he was something else. Rentzel liked to be around the shiny people, and the proximity of Los Angeles and Hollywood to the club's training camp in Thousand Oaks was just too much for him. Often he would sneak off into the night to head down Highway 101 to L.A., not just bending curfew but shattering it.

There was the time Rentzel was out on the town in Los Angeles long after curfew. On the way back to camp he ran out of gas and didn't get back until the next morning. "I cooked up a number of very convincing stories to tell Coach Landry," Rentzel said. "I thought of things that would get his sympathy. Then I tried to decide which one to use."

As Rentzel walked to Landry's room, he rehearsed a story in which he had been detained in Los Angeles because he was trying to talk his younger brother, who had run away from home, into going back. Landry opened the door, let him in, and said, "Well, Lance?" Rentzel looked at him, into his clear eyes, his almost angelic face, and said, "Uh, Coach, no excuse."

"That'll cost you eight hundred dollars," said Landry.

But Landry liked Rentzel and admired his courage on the field. He would be very disappointed when Lance's problem resurfaced in 1969 and he had to leave the team.

⌣:⌣

DON MEREDITH SUFFERED TWO CRACKED RIBS in the second preseason game in 1967, and Craig Morton, in his fourth year, came in and pulled out a victory against San Francisco. Morton looked great the remainder of preseason, and it became obvious to everybody that he had beaten out Jerry Rhome for the number two quarterback spot. Meredith detractors, hiding in the shadows of Don's fine 1966 season, resurfaced and said Craig should replace him.

"Meredith is my quarterback," Landry said. "And I'm not taking anything away from Morton, who has done a fine job."

It would be that kind of season for Meredith, who would also suffer a twisted knee and a busted nose and be hospitalized with a severe case of pneumonia. He did make it through the first four regular-season games, three wins and a loss, but barely survived, as did Dallas, the fifth game in Washington.

With 1:10 left to play, Dallas set up at its own twenty-nine-yard line, trailing 14–10. Meredith hadn't felt well but played the entire game. On that final series, he was hit and suffered a mild concussion, although nobody knew it at the time. He seemed to be a little out of it, but everybody figured that was just the way he acted sometimes. He moved the Cowboys to the Redskins' thirty-six, and on a pass play, weakside linebacker Chris Hanburger, an All-Pro, made a fatal mistake. He forgot to pick up Danny Reeves coming out of the backfield. So Reeves just turned and took off for the goal line, all alone and yelling back at Meredith. Meredith, in a haze, reacted and threw what looked like a dying quail toward Reeves. Danny waited, caught the ball, and took off for the winning touchdown.

Later, with Meredith standing within hearing distance, Landry was asked why he hadn't noticed his quarterback was woozy and taken him out of the game. Looking at Meredith, Landry quipped, "Well, I couldn't tell the difference."

When the club returned to Dallas, Meredith went into the hospital with pneumonia and lost twenty pounds within a week. He would miss three games, but Morton would step in and perform well. Craig showed a flair for final-minute dramatics when Pittsburgh had Dallas, 21–14, with 1:12 remaining and the Cowboys were at their own twenty-three-yard line. Rentzel faked a sideline pattern as cornerback Brady Keys bit, and then raced downfield. Morton threw the ball as far as he could, and Rentzel ran under it, caught it, and took off. But safety Paul Martha hit him at about the fifteen and he fumbled, the ball bouncing crazily to his right. Reeves, the alternate receiver, had run downfield to block, and he tried to pick up the ball. He bobbled it, dribbled it, and nudged it toward the goal line, where he finally gave up and fell on it at the Steeler five. Morton threw the winning touchdown pass to Norman from there.

Ermal Allen, the Cowboys special assistant who had joined Landry's staff in 1962, explained the intricacies of the play: "Rentzel, you see, had an option of fumbling out of bounds to stop the clock, or toward the end zone to the alternate receiver, who had the option of running to Lance's left or right. Carefully reading his keys, he went to the right and there was the ball. As you see, Tom has all avenues figured. We call that play 'Vaudeville Right.'"

Meredith returned as Dallas won four of its final five games, losing to the Baltimore Colts, 23–17. Dallas then split its final two games, finishing with a 9–5 record and what was then called the Capitol Division title of the Eastern Conference. The Colts were one of the league's strongest teams, and Landry was disappointed with the loss, especially considering his team had led at halftime, 14–10, then allowed the Colts to score thirteen final-period points.

"There used to be a joke among coaches," said Landry. "It was, 'What did you tell 'em at halftime to make them come back out and play so bad?'"

Meredith had suffered a broken nose in the final regular-season game but was expected to be ready for the Eastern Conference title game against Cleveland, champions of the Century Division. The game was amazing, Dandy's finest hour. He connected on ten of twelve passes (one was dropped) as Dallas took a 24–0 lead and went on to crush the Browns, 52–14. Meredith departed at the beginning of the final period to a standing ovation from the Cotton Bowl crowd of 70,786. Before he left the field, he shook hands with each of his offensive linemen.

"It was our best game," said Landry, "because so much was at stake and we did everything well." He did not know that lopsided victory would come back to haunt him.

Green Bay, like Dallas, had struggled through an injury-ridden season but had won the Central Division with a 9–4–1 record and beaten Los Angeles, the Coastal Division champion, 28–7. After many problems and narrow escapes, both teams seemed to be at their best, and it was the match-up the nation wanted for the NFL title. They had met for the NFL title on the first day of 1967, and now they would meet again for it on the final day of 1967.

◡∴◠

BACK THEN GREEN BAY, WISCONSIN, was a city of some one hundred thousand straddling the Fox River. It is unique in the NFL because of its size and because its townspeople constitute all the stockholders. The team was shooting for its fifth NFL title, its third straight, in the last seven years, and the town had another name, more popular with the natives. It was called Titletown, USA.

Dallas was still very young. The Packers had a fine defense, but age was beginning to show. It was a matter of whether Lombardi could get them "up" one more time, because most felt age wouldn't allow the Packers to repeat the following year.

"I don't think there was any doubt," said Nolan, "that we had the better team. Tom knew it. I think everybody did. Something really unusual had to happen for us to lose."

And so it did. After the Cowboys had arrived in Wisconsin, they went to Lambeau Stadium to work out. Temperatures hovered around fourteen degrees above zero, which worried the players and coaches. But the sun was out, and after the workout Meredith said, "It's not bad. If it gets no worse, we'll be fine."

Talking to the Dallas–Fort Worth press, Lombardi said predictions were that the weather would get no worse but, if it did, the field would still be in great shape because of the eighty-thousand-dollar electric heating wire apparatus he had had installed under the turf.

"Gentlemen," he said, "the field will not be frozen."

That night the entire Cowboy entourage went to bed assured, and then the wake-up calls came from the operator. "Good morning. It's 8:00 A.M. and the temperature is sixteen degrees below zero."

George Andrie, rooming with Bob Lilly, had already gotten up and gone outside. He returned to the room just as Lilly answered the wake-up call. Andrie watched as Lilly opened the curtains and heard him say, "It doesn't look that bad." Andrie calmly got a glass of water, pulled the blinds, and tossed the water onto the window. It froze before it ran down. "My God!" said Lilly.

248

"I remember going to bed and getting up for breakfast the next morning and just not believing it," said Landry. "Everything was ice, like on the North Pole. You can't imagine the shock. I think we were in shock most of the game."

Landry did all he could to keep the players' minds on the game. But it was impossible. "The Packers," he told the team, "are playing in the same weather as we are." Nobody believed him. The Packers were much more used to frigid temperatures. Five hours later, at kickoff time, the temperature had warmed to thirteen degrees below, but a strong wind caused the chill factor to be thirty below. Equipment manager Jack Eskridge gave the players extra sweat socks and sweatshirts, and then noticed Landry. Eskridge, the team doctor, and the trainers knew Landry would be too preoccupied to dress warmly, so they put a fur-lined coat and hunter's cap on him.

It was the coldest December 31 in Green Bay history. Meredith couldn't throw the ball normally and watched Bart Starr warm up to see if he could pick up the trick. Receivers had trouble holding the ball, and Bobby Hayes seldom, before or during the game, took his hands out of the warmth of his waistband. You couldn't blame him, but he caught only three passes for sixteen yards. They had butane blowers on the sidelines and stoves in the press box. But the coffee they served in the press box would freeze before you could get it to your mouth.

Fans huddled in the stadium in arctic dress. Some built small fires. There was no way the game should ever have been played, but nobody seemed to know what had to be done to stop it. National television, the world, was ready. It had to be played. The NFL felt it must march on.

The Packers struck for the first two touchdowns, driving eighty-two yards and then scoring as Starr hit Boyd Dowler on a forty-three-yard touchdown throw. As in the previous title game, Dallas trailed 14–0.

"It was all so odd, really weird," Landry said. "In the awful cold, everything was so confused. You couldn't find anybody on the sidelines to keep up communications. You just don't play football in temperatures like that." But they did.

Andrie got Dallas back into contention after Willie Townes tackled Starr, causing him to fumble. Andrie picked up the loose ball and skidded and skated into the end zone. Villanueva kicked a field goal and Dallas trailed, 14–10, at the half.

By the second half most of the field was frozen, more suited for hockey than football. Lombardi's heating wire system had failed. The game did not look real. The players became gray, ghostlike figures who seemed to be moving in a painful, slow motion.

Dallas drove eighty-three yards to the Packer thirteen. Meredith ran nine yards to the five but fumbled when hit, and Green Bay recovered. At best this cost Dallas a field goal. Landry, however, had devised a special play for the Packers. Actually, it was an old play with a new twist. Reeves had had great success with the halfback pass. He'd go to his right with the option of running or throwing. But, for the Packers, who knew Reeves's pattern well, Landry had decided to send Danny sweeping to his left. Green Bay wouldn't expect him to throw the ball going to his left. He'd have to stop and turn to throw, and it would be unnatural. As the final period began, Dallas was at the fifty-yard line, and Reeves told Meredith he felt it was time.

Reeves took the ball from Meredith and headed to his left. Cornerback Bob Jeter came up to stop the sweep, and Willie Woods also moved in. Rentzel faked as though he were going to block Jeter, then turned and took off for the end zone. Reeves suddenly stopped and threw the ball. Rentzel slowed down, caught the ball, and high-tailed it into the end zone. Dallas led 17–14.

It seemed in the cards, at last, that the Cowboys would win as Green Bay took over at its own thirty-two with 4:50 left to play. But Starr was at his best. He continually tossed short passes to running backs Donny Anderson and Chuck Mercein. They'd take the ball, fake as the Cowboy linebackers would slip on the frozen field, and make valuable yardage.

Finally, Mercein rambled eleven yards to the Dallas one-yard line when Edwards, in position to make the tackle, slipped down. Anderson got a foot, and the Packers called their final time-out with sixteen seconds remaining. Starr went to the sidelines to talk to Lombardi. Lombardi told Starr to try to sneak the ball across. If the play failed, Dallas would win the game. But of course it didn't, and the Packers won, 21–17.

"That game," Landry would later recall, "hurt more than the loss to Green Bay the year before. That first time we really weren't in their league. But in the Ice Bowl we were the better team."

On the flight back to Dallas, the plane was like a hearse. Landry, patient as always, talked to the press, answering questions the best he could. Andrie, Townes, and safety Dick Daniels had frostbite, and Pugh and Renfro also had to be treated because of problems from the extreme cold. Some NFL officials were saying no game would ever again be played in such terrible temperatures.

The physical damage to Landry's team was great, but the mental damage was even worse. The long-range effects of another championship loss at the very end of the game would eventually cause critics to claim that the Cowboys couldn't win the Big One and that Landry should alter his approach, should cut out the cuteness and field a more physical team like Lombardi's. Fans would also say Landry needed to be more emotional like Lombardi. The Packers beat Oakland, 33–14, in Super Bowl II, and shortly thereafter, Lombardi stepped down as coach and became general manager. But the Packers' era was over. It was almost, in fact, the Cowboys' era, but there would be an unexpected obstacle to overcome.

CHAPTER 13
The 1968 and 1969 Seasons: Don Meredith Retires

~·:~

You've got to remember that Don [Meredith] was way ahead of his time as far as attitudes of players were concerned and the way they acted. He was free-spirited and all that, which a lot of guys were later. And maybe Tom was just a little behind his time in that regard. But, you know, to his credit, Tom changed.

—RALPH NEELY
Offensive Tackle, 1956–1977

NO MATTER WHO YOU WERE, where you were, or what you did or thought, everything paled under the devastating magnitude of the events that took place during a sixty-four-day period in 1968. The madness of assassination engulfed us as first Martin Luther King Jr., the catalyst of the Civil Rights movement, and then Senator Robert Kennedy, the man who might have been president, were senselessly gunned down.

We were saddened as pictures in still life and scenes that were too real flashed across our minds . . . King, the advocate of peaceful demonstrations, standing there before huge throngs and saying, "We shall overcome! We shall overcome!" as the earth around him seemed to move, and Kennedy, the United States attorney general under his brother President John F. Kennedy, reaching out to shake hands with young people on college campuses, where other politicians would not go. (Kennedy seemed to be able to touch the college crowd, to give them an alternative to rebellion against everything that even hinted of Establishment.) King's life was taken as he stood on the balcony of a Memphis motel, and Kennedy was killed in the lobby of a Los Angeles hotel. These places were Anywhere, U.S.A.

The killings seemed to be part of a chain reaction that shook the very roots of a country already disturbed by the murder of President

Kennedy and the Watts riots in Los Angeles in August 1965 during which thirty-four people were killed and more than one thousand injured. People were saddened, afraid, and searching for answers as the year 1968 moved into the hot summer months, so prone to violence.

Tom Landry was busy, as usual, during the off-season, traveling around the country making speeches and attending various functions for the Fellowship of Christian Athletes. He too wondered just what was happening in this country and voiced his thoughts and opinions in late June of that year as the featured speaker at the FCA Coaches banquet in Atlanta, Georgia, prior to the all-American (College All-Star) football game.

Landry, a quiet and dignified air about him, moved to the speaker's stand amid a long and loud ovation. The narrow losses by his young Cowboys to Green Bay in the NFL title games had made his name and face most familiar to those there. After the usual formalities, he became very somber and said:

"I had planned to tell several jokes, but with the events of recent weeks they don't seem appropriate now. I believe that every American who lives in these United States is genuinely concerned about the direction America is going. Every time we pick up a paper or magazine, writers are asking the question, 'What is wrong with the United States?' Billy Graham, at the HemisFair Crusade in San Antonio, made the statement that there has been the rise and fall of twenty-six nations that followed the same path the United States is following today. Will God make an exception of us? Ruth Graham said, 'If He does, He is going to have to go back and apologize to Sodom and Gomorrah.'

"In the past few years, we have seen a president assassinated. We have watched the Watts area of Los Angeles burn, snipers stalk, and looters run rampant. The Dallas Cowboys were scheduled to open the 1965 preseason against the Rams in the Times Charity game during the height of the Watts riot. We had to postpone the game on a day-to-day basis until we finally played after four days. There was nothing to do but watch television coverage and observe people trying to carry off television sets, furniture really too heavy to carry. It would have been comical if it had not been so tragic to see the disregard of law and order and, yes, the rights of others.

"Several months ago, Martin Luther King was struck down by an assassin's bullet. Riots were touched off in many cities, the worst being in our nation's capital. Men in government and education were fearful of the next step that might be taken. A team of athletes was invited to Washington, D.C., to speak to the high-school and junior-high assemblies. The theme was 'Fitness: mental, physical, and spiritual.' The officials were hopeful the athletes could influence the young students.

"You can appreciate our concern when you imagine walking on a stage of an auditorium and observing the fire damage where the drapes had been set to flames . . . and watching the principal sit on the edge of his chair and, while the athletes spoke, getting up three times to eject students from the assembly.

"The murders of King and Robert Kennedy finally have awakened the American public to the fact that there must be something wrong with us. Immediately, there was a furious rush to pass gun-control legislation. This is okay, if it makes anybody feel better, but it is more of a conscience-easer than an anti-toxin. Until a man changes what is in his heart, the solution to our problems won't be found. Christ says a wise man builds his house on rock if he wants it to withstand a storm. Murder, rioting, and looting are evidence of a society that is sick.

"Not only in the area of violence is our nation decaying, but in other areas as well. There is an atmosphere of getting something for nothing. Paul Anderson spoke last week at Estes Park, Colorado, at one of our FCA conferences. He did a wonderful job of dispelling the idea that you can get something for nothing when he launched into a dramatic message on what it means to be free. He said a price must be paid. He said, 'You ask about free love? It destroys you physically and mentally. You ask about our free country? It was paid for by the lives of men. Free? Being free? Me? Yes. But it was purchased by Christ on Calvary.' So you see, there is nothing really free . . . someone has to pay.

"The Supreme Court confuses me; the Constitution says that this country was established under God, and yet you can't pray in schools because an atheist says you can't. The Supreme Court says a prospective member of a jury can be disqualified because she or he does not believe in capital punishment. Yet, the law says for first-degree murder the penalty is death—capital punishment. I must admit that I am confused. Where is the rule book you're supposed to play the game by?

"I know our only lasting hope lies in Jesus Christ." Landry went on to quote UCLA basketball coach John Wooden, who said, "There is only one kind of life that truly wins, and that is the one that places our faith in the hands of our Savior. Until that is done, we are on an aimless course that runs in circles and goes nowhere."

"For this country to survive as a powerful nation with freedom and opportunity, the hearts of men must change," Landry continued. "Only Christ can change men so drastically. At no time in history has the athlete wielded so much influence. This is what prompted a high-school coach by the name of Don McClaren to conceive of the idea of FCA thirteen years ago. James Jeffrey, the executive director of the FCA, uses a quotation from Shakespeare to express the urgency of the hour. It goes like this: 'There is a tide in the affairs of men which if taken at the crest will lead on to fame and fortune, but if missed, will return to the shallows.' What Jeff is saying to us, tonight, is to use this great influence we have to challenge our young people to follow Christ, which in time will save our country.

"Within the framework of competitive athletics, we have important values that we have learned as athletes—values that are on the decline in almost every facet of American life, namely, competitive spirit, character, and discipline.

"When a rookie reports to the Dallas Cowboys training camp, our staff knows an awful lot about him—his quickness and control, strength and explosion, mental alertness and character have been evaluated closely. The only thing we are not sure about is his competitiveness, which we define as will to win or determination to be the best. So, to me, this is the most important trait an athlete can possess because it determines whether he stays or goes.

"In our country, we are destroying man's competitive spirit in so many ways. It has become fashionable to expect the government to guarantee almost anything. No longer are our young men asking for an opportunity to prove themselves, but they only ask, 'What are the benefits?'

"I am starting my twentieth year in professional football, and I have seen a change in the athlete coming into pro ball. In 1949, all the athletes were a product of the Depression years and World War II. Coaches could treat them any way they wanted and the athletes would respond, because to them success was important. The alternatives they had seen had not been attractive.

"In the midfifties, the athletes entering pro football were the products of the postwar era—plenty of everything—and we observed more independence, and motivation became an important factor. Job opportunities were plentiful in other lines of work.

"In the sixties, I have seen the decay so prevalent in other areas of American life start to take its toll on the athlete. Competitiveness is being eroded; the will to win, determination to be the best, is not so important anymore. There are easier ways to get by. Now is the time we must reestablish the competitive spirit in America that has made it the greatest nation on earth with the highest standard of living."

Landry paused, then quoted Knute Rockne, who said, "Some of you may say this will to win is a bad thing. In what way is it bad? Education is supposed to prepare a young man for life. Life is competition. Success in life goes only to the man who competes successfully. A successful lawyer is a man who goes out and wins law cases. A successful physician is one who goes out and wins—saves lives and restores people to good health. A successful executive is a man who can make money and stay out of bankruptcy court. There is no reward for a loser. There is nothing wrong with the will to win. The only penalty should be that the man who wins unfairly should be set down."

Then, attempting to put winning in proper perspective, Landry quoted Bart Starr, who said, "Vince Lombardi taught me that winning is not everything but making the effort to win is. It not only made me a better quarterback but a bigger and better person."

"We must never lose the competitive spirit," Landry told the audience, "that enabled Pettis Norman to come from a tenant farm to a recent appointment as vice president of a bank in Dallas. We must never lose the competitive spirit that enabled Lee Trevino to hit one thousand to fifteen hundred golf balls a day because he knew if he became good enough he would be given the opportunity to win a national Open.

"The old cliché that 'We're building character' after a losing season is still valid. Only Christ can build character faster than the athletic field. When all is said and done, character is probably the most important value of all. Horace Greeley said, 'Fame is vapor, popularity an accident, riches take wins, those who cheer today will curse tomorrow, only one thing endures—character.' Mr. Greeley was talking about the type of character that was revealed in Jesus Christ. The apostle Paul wrote to the Romans, 'If you love your neighbor as much as you love yourself, you will not want to harm or cheat him, or kill him or steal from him.' If we would all do that, it would take care of everything else. But until that happens, we need a third value that may be the most pressing at the moment. That is discipline."

Landry made an analogy between the rules in sports and the laws of the country. He said if the rules were broken in football, you received a penalty or might even be thrown out of the game. He said you either learned to play by the rules or suffered the consequences. "Apparently," said Landry, "the sentiment in the U.S. today is that if you don't like the rules or laws, forget them. He then cited Police Chief William Parker of Los Angeles, who said during the Watts riots, "I don't care what color they are or what cause they represent. They're breaking the law, and there's only one place for them, in jail."

"He was soundly chastised, but his words made some sense to me because I am used to watching people play by the rules," said Landry. He quoted Darrell Royal, who said, "Athletics seems to be the last place where we have discipline, and sometimes you wonder how long it is gonna last."

And then he cited a piece written by Blackie Sherrod, nationally known columnist of the *Dallas Times-Herald* and later of the *Dallas Morning News*, who recalled something Vince Lombardi had said after Robert Kennedy was murdered: "It is beyond belief. We have suffered a complete breakdown of mental discipline in this country. Something has happened to our moral fabric. We confuse freedom with license. We don't have any understanding of freedom. Before you can understand freedom, you have to understand duty and respect."

Landry continued to quote from Sherrod's column. "The other day, when a March on Poverty group sent a delegation to call on Ramsey Clark, the attorney general, they pounded on the doors and broke windows in the Justice Department. Broke windows, honey, right there in the USA grounds. Gentlemen, this is where I would have loved to have seen a door open and a stocky man walk out and say, 'My name is Vince Lombardi. I am the attorney general of this country. Now what was it you wanted to see me about?'"

The audience applauded, imagining Lombardi, the man whose countenance could strike fear in a 6'-5", 260-pound athlete.

"It is high time we define clearly the rules for playing the game in the U.S.A.," continued Landry. "And it is high time we have the intestinal fortitude to make them stick. You might be thinking, 'Yeah,

Coach, I agree. We need to reverse this trend. We need to renew our competitive spirit, reestablish character, and apply discipline. But, heck, what can I do?'

"Don't ever underestimate your influence as an athlete. Every red-blooded American boy knows more about athletes and sports than he does about anything else. He is looking to be like you. There is a poem entitled 'To Any Athlete,' and one of the three verses goes like this:

> There's a wide-eyed little fellow
> Who believes you're always right,
> And his ears are always open,
> And he watches day and night;
> You are setting an example
> Every day in all you do,
> For the little boy who's watching
> To grow up to be like you.

"It is not only the little guy who listens to you. When the athletes gathered in Washington, D.C., that day to speak to students, there were doubts in many officials' minds whether we would be received properly in the schools. I was asked to speak at a breakfast of local dignitaries preceding our appearance in the high schools. I could see the worried expressions on the faces of the athletic directors and school officials. I told them without reservation that the athletes would be received without incident."

Landry told how the athletes were given a standing ovation from more than thirty thousand students. He said the athletes told the students, some of whom were from the toughest schools in the city, that they had to get off the seats of their pants and get an education, that the United States was the greatest country, and that they had to have respect for law and order.

"I'm not sure whether the students wanted to hear what was said or not," continued Landry, "but they listened and respected the athletes for what they said."

He related a story Maxie Baughan, then a linebacker for the Los Angeles Rams, had told him. Baughan had recalled being upset at a call that went against the Rams in a 24–24 tie with Baltimore. As he left the field, Baughan threw his helmet to the ground and kicked it. When he got home, his six-year-old son met him, wearing a Rams uniform. The boy asked him to come outside. When they got outside, the kid threw his helmet down and kicked it. "Look, Dad, just like you," said the kid.

"So you can see, fellows, as athletes we can influence so many people," continued Landry. "This is what the Fellowship of Christian Athletes is all about. It is the greatest organization in the U.S. because its purpose is to confront athletes and coaches and through them the youth of America with the challenge and adventure of following Jesus Christ in the fellowship of the church and in their vocation. It is not an organization of saints. FCA is made up of athletes, coaches, and businessmen who love Jesus Christ and are willing to stand up for Him. The Bible tells us, 'For God so loved the world that He gave His only Son, that whosoever believes in Him should not perish but have everlasting life' [John 3:16]. That is the life that wins."

In later years, after experiencing the aftermath of the '60s, including the various protests, Landry softened his view somewhat and came to believe that the period, although destructive, had some positive ramifications because it made the older generation look upon people more as individuals and in the process take a closer look at themselves. But he continued to believe that the violent protests contributed strongly to the negativism of the country and the destruction of necessary discipline.

~:~

WHAT HAPPENED AGAINST THE BROWNS that season of 1968 would repeat itself in 1969, magnifying the losses to Green Bay in big games the previous two seasons and forming a mental barrier that Landry, the players, and the organization would have a terrible time overcoming. The Cowboys would become known as the team that couldn't win the so-called Big One.

Landry knew as training camp was about to open in the summer of 1968 that, physically, he had his best team. It was solid at every position, and Meredith, going into his ninth season, seemed to be showing more maturity. He certainly had the knowledge and ability to be among the best at his position. What Landry did not know, but perhaps subconsciously feared, was the extent of psychological problems in the wake of two close and frustrating losses to Green Bay in the NFL title games of 1967 and 1968.

Meredith had prepared himself more than ever for the season and actually said, "I'm becoming more and more oriented to Landry's way of thinking. I fought it for several years, but he's got the best thing going in the pros. He's right in his approach, and I'm glad I finally realized it."

One morning during off-season, Meredith appeared at the Cowboy offices. His hair was tousled, and he was wearing loafers with no socks, blue jeans, and a wrinkled sweater. It was obvious that he had just gotten out of bed.

Al Ward, then the team's vice president, asked Meredith what he was doing there, and Don said, "Well, the man called and said he had some things he wanted me to look at."

"How long ago did he call?"

"About three minutes."

Meredith was feeling a little mischievous during a session Landry was having with his quarterbacks. The coach was at the blackboard, with his back to them. Meredith took a cigar out of his mouth and began twirling it around, as though he were a symphony conductor controlling Landry's movements. Jerry Rhome and Craig Morton covered their mouths to keep from laughing. Suddenly, Landry turned around, and Meredith quickly put the cigar in his mouth—the lighted end first. Don started coughing and spitting tobacco everywhere, and Landry asked, "Are you getting this, Don?"

"Yessir," said Meredith, still choking.

~:~

DALLAS WON ITS FIRST SIX GAMES in 1968. They opened by beating Detroit, 59–13, in the Cotton Bowl. During an interview on the radio, a local broadcaster talked to Landry:

"Just a great game, Coach Landry. And now, can you tell us if there were any defensive problems?"

"No, not really. I thought we played very well."

"Okay, Coach, now can you tell us the problems we had on offense?"

Landry, ever polite, said he felt his team had performed very well on offense.

The Cowboys, 6–0, felt they'd finally get a measure of revenge on Green Bay, which had slipped to a 2–4 record and, obviously, was fading with age. Lombardi had named longtime assistant Phil Bengston to replace him, but the dynasty was over. Yet Green Bay won, 28–17. Landry, reminded at a postgame press conference that his team still couldn't beat the Packers, bristled a little and snapped back, "I'm making no apologies for this team. The whole idea is that someday it will grow to the point where it can beat the Packers. Right now, I'll certainly take a 6–1 record."

Landry knew what was coming, and he was trying to soften the blow for his players. He knew people would write once again that the Cowboys couldn't win the big game. He was right.

The Cowboys remained a little sluggish for two weeks following the Packer loss. One reason was they lost Danny Reeves to a knee injury. Reeves's replacements, Craig Baynham and Les Shy, were inconsistent the remainder of the year, and if the club lacked anything physically, it was at the halfback position. It won five of its next six games, however, and it had already taken the Capitol Division as it traveled to New York to end the regular season against the Giants in Yankee Stadium.

Meredith had been superb, throwing to Lance Rentzel and Bobby Hayes. Don Perkins was finishing his final season by rushing for 836 yards and a 4.4 average. Roughly, all Meredith needed to win the NFL passing title over Baltimore's Earl Morrell was to hit two of ten passes. But Dallas already had the division title and would play Cleveland for the Eastern Conference crown. Don and some of his teammates just didn't feel too intense as they attended a long party held by author George Plimpton the night before the game. When Meredith showed up in Yankee Stadium the next day, he couldn't, in his own words, "hit the ground with the ball." He completed just one of nine passes, told Landry he didn't have a "feel" for the game, and was replaced by Craig Morton, who saved the day by quarterbacking Dallas to its twelfth victory of the season. The 12–2 mark was the best the club was to post in regular season until 1977.

Snow had begun to fall in late afternoon, and after a two-hour delay, the 747 lifted the team out of New York. All at once, there was a loud explosion and the plane rocked abruptly in its climb.

A stewardess screamed. Bob Lilly said, "That's it! That's it!" D. D. Lewis, a rookie, sat next to Meredith. "Dandy, aren't you scared!" Meredith noted casually, "Naw, D. D., it's been a good 'un."

The plane straightened in its climb, gained altitude, and leveled out, and the remainder of the flight was uneventful. One of the engines had sucked in ice, and while the nose of the aircraft was pointed upward, it became locked in low-altitude mode. Dave Manders and George

Andrie said they'd never fly again. Landry sat through the entire episode looking extremely calm and unruffled.

The expected win over Cleveland would put the Cowboys into the NFL title game against the Minnesota-Baltimore winner. The Cowboys remembered how they had stomped the Browns, 52–14, in the 1967 Eastern title game and had beaten them, 28–7, in the second game of that 1968 season.

Landry cautioned his team that the previous games with Cleveland were misleading. "There is no way we were thirty-eight points better than Cleveland last year," he said. "In a championship game like this, there aren't two inches separating the teams. Because it's such a mental thing, a big game like this, sometimes the scores become lopsided because a team will get behind and see things slipping away and start making mistakes."

Meredith had an off day, and also rotten luck. But the defense was playing well, and Chuck Howley picked up a fumble and raced forty-four yards to give Dallas a 10–3 lead. However, Leroy Kelly then slipped past Howley, who went with the wrong man, on a pass route. He gathered in a forty-five-yard touchdown pass thrown from Bill Nelsen to tie the game at halftime, 10–10.

The second half blew up in Meredith's, and the team's, face. On the first play, Meredith threw a sideline pass to Hayes, who was open. But linebacker Dale Lindsey batted up the ball, caught it, and ran twenty-seven yards for a score. Meredith's keys told him Lindsey wouldn't be in the area, but he was. The next time Dallas got the ball, Meredith threw for Rentzel, who batted the ball into the surprised hands of defensive back Ben Davis, whose interception put the ball in position for Kelly's thirty-five-yard touchdown run. Some two minutes into the second half, Cleveland led 24–10. Landry benched Meredith, replacing him with Craig Morton.

"We needed a psychological lift," explained Landry. "Morton was the only thing I had that I could use. I took Meredith out not so much for what he was doing but to try to shake things up. I told him I thought I'd go with Morton, and he agreed."

Meredith was angry for a long time that Landry pulled him, but he said, "I could never argue with Tom. That's because it's Tom I'm talking to. I won't second-guess the call because Tom's job is bigger than mine, and mine is big enough."

Dallas got behind 31–13 with 2:09 left, but Morton, who hit only nine of twenty-three passes, did rally the team to a final deficit of 31–20. The game had begun on a dark, gray afternoon in Cleveland's Municipal Stadium, and as it ended, snowflakes had begun to fall on nearby Lake Erie.

Meredith boarded the return charter back to Dallas, then abruptly got off, taking Pete Gent with him. They went to New York to try to forget what had happened, and Landry didn't fine either of them.

Later, Landry was to say, "All I know is Meredith was a better quarterback this season than he has ever been and this is the best team we've ever had." Some on the club felt Landry had been unfair pulling Meredith. They knew Meredith had not thrown well, but they also believed that other circumstances had gone against him, such as Rentzel tipping one of the interceptions. But it didn't matter. Tom Landry was not a man who second-guessed himself on decisions. Something I wrote about after the loss always reminds me of Landry.

~:~

His head, bent low, was resting in his hands for what seemed a long time, although there was no real gauge of seconds or minutes because it was one of those periods of time when there is no clock. The dream for which Tom Landry had worked, planned, and used all his energies had blown up in his face, leaving the entire Dallas Cowboy organization in ashes. The heavily favored Cowboys had gone to Cleveland to play the Browns for the 1968 Eastern Conference championship in a game that appeared to be only a formality to get the Cowboys into a third straight NFL championship contest.

Certainly, this was Landry's best team, better and more mature than the ones that had gotten to an NFL title game before losing twice to the veteran clubs of Vince Lombardi in the twilight hour. It was to be the year, the time, the place, to end the frustrations of the Packer games, the narrow misses. But when the time came, the machine malfunctioned and Landry's blueprint for a championship crumbled before his very eyes. It must have seemed an infinity of disappointment and frustration.

The shock, the reality of unexpected failure, was thick, stifling. Until that time, the organization had progressed, although sometimes painfully, from an expansion team of castoffs to contenders in 1968, the year it all seemed to be there for the taking. But it had not been. Inside the charter going back to Dallas that evening, it was dead quiet, even for those who tried to blunt feelings with a few drinks.

Landry had not done so, and when he raised his head, turning slightly in his seat by the aisle, he looked like a defrocked priest. His eyes were glassy, faded watercolors. When a proud man, one with such control, is devastated, it seems to go much deeper. Landry would say years later that there had been times when he had felt worse about losing, but it was difficult to imagine this because the hurt never seemed to have shown through so vividly, and he never had seemed to have been such a defeated man.

The jet landed at Love Field, and the slow procession of players, coaches, and club officials filed off the plane, walking slowly with their heads down or dragging the weight of what had happened as they made their way down some psychological tunnel of no purpose, of what seemed so hopeless. Football is supposed to be a game, no more and no less, but it was much more then.

Then, suddenly, Landry came off the plane, his wife, Alicia, beside him. His head was high, his eyes were clear, and he almost seemed to be marching to a beat that only he heard. Soon, others, from the crowd and from among those who had gotten off the plane, began to watch him. He looked neither right nor left but marched right through the terminal. Landry was already back from where he had been and was ready for another step, another challenge, another tomorrow. That scene, as much as any, was Tom Landry.

⌣⋮∾

BALTIMORE BEAT FIRST MINNESOTA and then Cleveland to win the NFL title and earn the dubious distinction of losing Super Bowl III to the New York Jets, led by brash Joe Namath. Dallas and Minnesota had to play in Miami in the Playoff Bowl game, and Meredith hit eleven of thirteen passes during one stretch to lead Dallas to a 17–13 victory. He was named MVP of the game and received a trophy with the figure of a football player on top. As he carried the trophy to the charter flight back to Dallas, it was noticed that the head of the figure of the football player had been knocked off.

"Figures," said Meredith.

⌣∶∼

IN EARLY JULY OF 1969, before training camp began, Don Meredith was doing a lot of soul-searching. He was disappointed and hurt that Landry had pulled him in the Cleveland game. He was also getting tired of being booed in the Cotton Bowl. He had some family problems and, after nine years, just wasn't sure he wanted to play football anymore. He went to see Landry to tell him his feelings. Many believed that if Landry had strongly tried to talk him out of retirement Don would have continued to play. But Meredith was to say later that after he told Landry the reasons for retiring, Landry remarked, "If that's the way you feel, then it's probably the right decision."

At the July press conference when he announced his retirement, Meredith said, "Coach Landry and I have worked very hard these past nine seasons, and I'm sure he has worked a lot harder than I have. If I have any regrets in retiring, it's that I won't be around to play an active part in a championship for this team. And I'm sure it'll come. I have come [he looked over at Landry] to love this man."

"Don and I were very close during the years of building the team," Landry said. "Don was a very important part of the success of the team. It certainly is a deep personal loss to see him step down. I know many people still disagree, but I firmly believe my decision in 1965 to stick with Don was the most important one made in this club's history and that it led directly to our conference championship games in 1966 and 1967."

Asked how he would like to be remembered, Meredith replied, "I won't be remembered as a great passer, a great signal caller, but I hope I'll be remembered as a nice guy."

He was remembered as much more. Roger Staubach said, "I followed a guy who took all the punishment and did such a tremendous job to help bring the Dallas Cowboys to a high level. I mean Don Meredith."

People singled out Meredith when the team faltered. They booed. Once I remember Meredith throwing a long pass in the direction of Bobby Hayes, the ball falling incomplete near the sideline. Bobby had broken his pattern and had headed upfield after the ball was thrown. Fans seemed almost to shake the stadium booing Meredith. They did not know that Hayes had made the wrong adjustment.

"Don retired when I joined the team," continued Staubach, "and, if he hadn't, I might have ended up somewhere else. When I look at the films when he was playing I appreciate what a really fine player he was. He was a great quarterback who did a lot to make the Cowboys a great team."

Ralph Neely was one of the best linemen the team ever had and also was and is a close friend of Meredith. "You've got to remember that Don was way ahead of his time as far as attitudes of players were concerned and the way they acted," he said. "He was free-spirited and all that, which a lot of guys were later. And maybe Tom was just a little behind his time in that regard. But, you know, to his credit, Tom changed.

"Even when we got good and something would go wrong, the fans would get after him. One time we were on the field and the crowd let out this big cheer when he got his ribs busted."

Meredith's retirement was very premature. He would only have been thirty-one in the 1969 season, a time when a quarterback is into his prime years. Meredith later would have second thoughts and talk to Tex Schramm about returning in 1970, but he didn't want to have to compete with Morton for the starting job and Schramm told him it would have to be that way.

"I've always liked Don, probably better than he did me," said Landry. "Yet we didn't always get along well. I think we were just a little different in our outlook on life. I think Don would rather have had a good time and didn't really discipline himself like I believed you have to do to become a top quarterback. But there's no doubt he performed extremely well. He was probably the toughest guy I've ever seen at quarterback. He would be badly hurt and still play. He took an awful beating in those early years."

After Meredith became a star as a commentator on ABC's *Monday Night Football*, he was critical of Landry, who had gone back to calling plays for Craig Morton, and called him "Old Stoneface," noting Minnesota coach Bud Grant was also very stoic. "In a personality contest between Tom Landry and Bud Grant, there would be no winner," said Don.

But his best line was during the heat of a Monday-night game when the cameras zoomed in on a fan. The guy responded with the universal sign. Nobody knew what to say except Meredith, who responded, "Aw, that's just his way of saying, 'We're number one.'"

Meredith also became an actor and did a number of commercials before eventually retiring in Santa Fe, New Mexico, and dropping out of the spotlight that had glorified and at times burned him unfairly.

Long after he retired, Meredith would comment on his relationship with Landry. He said he expected too much from Landry, that when he was in high school and college his coaches were close, like fathers to him. Don said that a couple of times when he was having problems, "I expected him to flip on the light for me but he never did."

After the Cowboys lost to Cleveland that second time in 1969 with Meredith's successor Craig Morton at quarterback, Don knew Landry's great disappointment, whether he showed it or not. So he went to the Landrys' home and told Tom and Alicia how sorry he was for what happened. Don now plays each year in the charity golf tournament for the Lisa Landry Childress Foundation.

CHAPTER 14
Craig Morton

~·:·~

I think that Landry's great strength, along with the great faith we have in him, enabled this team to pull itself off the floor after all those disheartening blows and come back with renewed purpose.

—TEX SCHRAMM
1970

CRAIG MORTON was different from Don Meredith around Tom Landry. Craig was attentive and serious. He was twenty-six and had served a four-year apprenticeship, and Tom Landry decided to let him call the plays in 1969.

In another somewhat surprising move, Landry announced that a twenty-seven-year-old rookie named Roger Staubach would, despite his lack of experience, be Morton's backup. Roger had been drafted as a future in 1964, was graduated from the naval academy, and then spent four years fulfilling his obligation of active duty. No one who had been away from football that long had made a successful pro career. But by the time training camp had ended, Landry knew Staubach was someone special, if he could just curtail his impatience.

Whereas it took most quarterbacks four or five years to get into a position to start, Landry said he believed Staubach, due to his maturity and hard work, could challenge in three. For Roger, that was about three years too long. He certainly was establishing new curves on dedication and hard work. Staubach had even arranged his leaves from the navy so he could spend time in training camp going through two-a-days. He *wanted* to go through two-a-days.

In the 1970 training camp, trainer Don Cochren watched Staubach continue to work out after most everybody else had already gone in.

268

"I'd hate to have him after my job. You'd begin to hear footsteps after a while. He'd be out there working while you were playing or sleeping."

Landry thought he'd seen everything when, during a preseason game against Baltimore, Staubach scrambled thirty-one seconds on a single play as he completely wore out the Colt front four, who had been chasing him on the hot summer night.

At first, neither Morton nor Landry took Staubach's challenge seriously. Morton remembered how he'd had to wait four years while Meredith ran the team, but it would not take long before everybody took Staubach seriously.

Don Perkins had joined Meredith in retirement, and thus Dallas was a different-looking team, bearing the stamp of Morton and rookie sensation Calvin Hill. In spite of glowing reports from his scouts, Landry had been reluctant to pick Hill as the club's number one draft choice. Calvin was 6'-4", 220 to 225 pounds, and had speed and a lot of ability. But he was from Yale, the Ivy League, and you just didn't make a guy from there your number one pick. Landry thought, however, that he might make Calvin a tight end or a linebacker. But when Reeves injured a knee in preseason, Calvin was tried at halfback and became an immediate sensation, a running mate for Walt Garrison, who had replaced Perkins.

Morton worked hard, but Landry still worried about the changes. Prior to the first game, he walked over to Morton's locker, and Craig said, "I can do it. I'm ready, Coach."

"Yes," said Landry, "I know you can, Craig."

Morton was outstanding, but he would also become a tragic figure. He would do well, but things beyond his control would seem to transpire at times to cause him to fail. Those same forces would work for Staubach. Such things can't be defined, but they're there.

Morton was spectacular, although he dislocated a finger on his passing hand in the final exhibition game and Landry had to play his rookie, Staubach, in the league opener against St. Louis. But Landry simplified the game plan, and Staubach hit a long touchdown pass as Dallas won, 24–3. Morton returned after that and was unbelievable. He was completing 73 percent of his passes as Dallas went into Atlanta seeking its fourth straight victory. On a delayed screen, end Claude Humphrey crashed into Morton, who had just released the ball. Craig fell on his right shoulder and immediately left the game. His shoulder was slightly separated. He might be out for the season, and Landry felt there was no way, at that stage, that Staubach could take over the team.

Landry and club officials huddled with team doctors. Doctors said Morton would be in pain but could continue to play without causing further damage to the shoulder. Surgery, if needed, could wait until after the season. Morton had waited too long to be number one and wasn't about to quit. He insisted he could play.

The following week, Landry, after talking to doctors a final time, asked Morton his feelings. "Coach, it's going to be this way the rest of the season," said Morton. "I've waited a long time, and I'd like to give it a shot." For some inexplicable reason, Morton threw extremely well on his return, perhaps camouflaging the seriousness of the injury. He played the remainder of the season, but his shoulder grew worse. He was unable to throw much at all during the week, and by the final part of the season he would often lose his feel for throwing the ball and the zing and power had left his passes. But Morton was calling a fine game, utilizing Hill and Garrison behind an excellent line of tackles Ralph Neely, Tony Liscio, and Rayfield Wright, guards John Niland and John Wilbur, and centers Malcolm Walker and Dave Manders.

Dallas was 6–0 as it went into the scene of the previous disaster, Cleveland's Municipal Stadium, to face Bill Nelsen, Leroy Kelly, and the Browns. Nelsen, who seemed to gear his entire season toward playing Dallas, completed eighteen of twenty-five passes for 255 yards and five touchdowns as the Browns took a 28–3 halftime lead and won, 42–10. Dallas came completely apart.

"All our previous games built up to the match with Cleveland," explained Landry. "We were hopeful of a different outcome, but the results were not there. We played a game totally uncharacteristic of our team." But secretly, Landry had begun to realize that there were underlying problems in his club that seemed to show up against the Browns. These were forgotten as Dallas followed Hill's lead to an 11–2–1 record, the Capitol Division title, and another meeting with the Browns for the Eastern Conference championship.

This game was in the Cotton Bowl, but strangely enough, the day was gray and cloudy and almost seemed to be Cleveland weather. In the ramp before going out for the kickoff, some of the Cowboy players began griping about the rain. This might have been an indication that some were already searching for an excuse, if needed. Hill, because of a toe injury, had missed two games and been hobbled in others the final part of the year. He still tied Jim Brown's rookie rushing total of 942 yards. But for Cleveland, he was far from the back he had been, and Morton simply was not physically able to take up the slack.

On Cleveland's first possession, Lilly led the Cowboys in smothering the Browns, and the crowd and the Cowboys became excited. But the ensuing punt by Dale Cockroft bounced off Rayfield Wright's leg. The Browns recovered and went on to score. They padded the margin to 24–0, and then Walt Sumner intercepted a Morton pass and returned it eighty-eight yards for a touchdown in the final period. The Browns won, 38–14, to take the Eastern Conference and send the entire Cowboy organization spinning, second-guessing.

"Those two championship losses to Cleveland were particularly disappointing to me because I feel we didn't accomplish one thing," said Landry. "It can happen to you once. But when it happened again, I was even lower than the first time. It caused us all to start second-guessing ourselves. Once again, some people were saying it was the system, but I never thought that was it. I wondered about our mental approach to the game. We just had some problems, and we had to find them."

Landry had spoken to the players and the press, and then he went into the coaches' dressing quarters, talked to his assistants, then asked them if they'd please leave for a while, giving him a few moments to himself. He sat there, alone and quiet. He realized that what happened against Cleveland in the Eastern Conference championship games might occur once, but twice . . . It was too much, really. Just too much. So he left the dressing room, walked out of the Cotton Bowl, got into his car, and began the long drive to his home in North Dallas. He was later to recall his experience in *Lenten Guideposts*, where he wrote:

I drove home with an overwhelming sense of disappointment. Before going to bed that night, I sat down in my bedroom chair to review the whole day. Not a pragmatic review, but a spiritual assessment. "Lord, what went wrong today?" I asked Him. As almost always happens during these sessions with Him, I soon found perspective. A crushing setback today, yes, but I've learned that something constructive comes from every defeat. I thought over my relationships that day with the players, coaches, officials, friends, family. Nothing wrong there. No bad injuries, either. "Thank You, Lord, for being with me out there," I said. And with that prayer the bitter sting of defeat drained away. Disappointment remained, but I've found that it doesn't sap energy and creativity. One football game, after all, is quite a small fragment of one's total life.

But in the wake of the loss to Cleveland, the entire Cowboy organization was spinning. Club officials, coaches, players were first in the depths of depression and consternation and then began questioning themselves and those around them. When some normalcy returned with time, those in charge began looking for answers.

"We reevaluated our entire organization," said Tex Schramm, "and our system of operation. This did not, however, include a reevaluation of our head coach."

Landry knew in retrospect that even with Morton hurting and unable to throw the ball well and Hill hobbled, the Cowboys should have had enough. Perhaps it was entirely mental—perhaps it was their approach to the game. After meeting with his staff, Landry sent out questionnaires to each player, asking them their opinions about all aspects of the club—the approach, the system, the coaches, their teammates. This was a revolutionary move and something he would not have done in the earlier years, but now it was his team, not a makeshift bunch of stopgap players. The players would not be required to sign the questionnaires; in exchange for candor, they received anonymity.

Some players said the team was overly prepared for games, that there were too many cliques on the club, too many prima donnas. They felt tired of trying to finesse opponents and wanted to physically blow them out. Some criticized what was termed Landry's "puritanism" and voiced their opinions about some of the assistant coaches. Landry weighed what the players said, as did his assistants, some of whom became angry.

Bob Lilly summed up the feeling of the majority when he said, "There was nothing wrong with Landry's system, nor his approach to the game. He's a great coach, but the team just needed some shaking up."

Landry concluded that he must take a tougher approach. He hired Alvin Roy, a former Olympic weightlifting coach who'd had a great deal of success in helping the Kansas City Chiefs, to start an off-season weight and conditioning program. It would be voluntary in a mandatory sort of way. Players did not have to attend the sessions, but roll was taken and the coaches knew who wasn't there. Bob Ward would join the Cowboys in 1975 and implement the program with a more scientific approach to conditioning and strength. Variations of off-season conditioning programs would become common in the NFL. In his original setup, Roy included weightlifting, running, and ability drills. It interfered with some of the player's off-season jobs, but Landry had reached the conclusion that, in order to win a championship, professional football had become a year-round job.

Landry also believed the team had been relying too much on the big play to score and planned to use more of a power attack, featuring Calvin Hill behind a good, veteran offensive line. Backfield coach Ermal Allen was moved to a newly created position in which he would scout and rate all teams and players, including the Cowboys. This position too would become commonplace, not only with Dallas, but around the league. Danny Reeves, who was popular with the players, took over Allen's backfield duties and became a player-coach. Furthermore, all players, whether starters or backups, would be judged by performance levels, and those who didn't measure up could lose their spots.

Landry was taking a gamble but believed he must in order to shake up the team and make it stronger for the future. He knew some of the regulars would be upset because they wouldn't be starting at the first of the year. "We'll sink to a lower level than we have been in several years," he explained. "But eventually it'll pay off. There will be confusion for a while, but I just believe we have to shake things up if we're going to progress to a real championship team."

⌣∶∾

CALVIN HILL, OF COURSE, loomed large in Landry's offensive plans for 1970, and so it came as somewhat of a surprise to him when Gil Brandt and the scouting department kept recommending that the club use its top draft pick on a running back from West Texas State named Duane Thomas. The computer had rated Thomas among the top three players in the country, and the Cowboys, who wouldn't pick until twenty-third in the twenty-six-team draft, had him ranked third. There was some question about his attitude. Dallas, generally, will pick the top-rated player remaining when its time comes, regardless of position, but Landry kept thinking that he already had a fine halfback in Hill.

On the morning of the draft, Landry sat at a table with his scouts and watched the board as teams made their picks before the Cowboys' turn came. Landry had read and reread the report on Thomas and was sitting by Red Hickey, former San Francisco head coach who had been an assistant for the Cowboys before joining the scouting department.

Thomas was 6'-2", 220 pounds, had run a 4.6 forty-yard sprint, and was intelligent, agile, and quick. "I told Tom," recalled Hickey, "all about Duane's ability, his positives and negatives. I told him I had seen him taken out of a college game, walk to the bench, throw his helmet down, and then curse his coach. But I also told him that when Duane went back into the game he continued to rip off yardage. I told Tom that Duane worked very hard in practice, knew the assignments of all positions, but had had trouble with the trainer in college over treatment of injuries. Tom would say, tell me about Duane again, and I would. Our time to pick kept getting closer."

Finally, Hickey turned to Landry and said, "Thomas is the best running back in the country, bar none."

"Does that mean," asked Landry, "that he's better than Calvin Hill?"

"If he comes here, Tom," said Hickey, "he'll be your halfback."

"Hmm."

"Tom, I'm telling you, if Thomas is still there when our pick comes, take him, if you think you can handle him."

"You say he's better than Calvin?"

"Yes, he'll be your halfback."

"Then, Red, I think I'll try to handle him."

This turned out to be a bigger job than Landry had anticipated, but it would pay off—for a while. Thomas became the club's number one pick, and the draft proved to be the best in the club's history to that time. That year Dallas drafted Thomas, Bob Asher, Charlie Waters, Steve Kiner, John Fitzgerald, Pat Toomay, and Mark Washington and signed Cliff Harris as a free agent.

Before training camp, Landry discussed the criticisms his team had received. He had obviously found some answers:

"The most difficult championship to win is the first one. After a club knows it is capable of winning, it gains a great deal of confidence in important games. Success breeds success. If we had won that first game against the Packers for the championship, there's a pretty good chance we would have won our next three. But the Packers were at the height of their game in 1966 and 1967. If they hadn't been around in those years, we probably would have dominated the league then. But they were a great team with a lot of maturity and a lot of winning tradition behind them when we hit the scene in 1966. And even though we played two great games against them, people started talking about our not winning the Big One.

"When that happens to you, you begin to have a negative attitude about whether or not you're ever going to win the Big One. Even though we had great overall success, we remained the team that couldn't come through in important games.

"Failure, like success, has a carry-over effect. After we lost the second title game to Green Bay, our chances of winning the third were much less than they had been before the second. After the third loss to Cleveland, we continued to be at a big psychological disadvantage in the playoffs and lost again.

"So to a great extent I think our problems all go back to the Ice Game. That year we had a team capable of beating Green Bay for the championship. But when we lost near the end, it triggered and set in motion things that were to cause us to get beat in the Cleveland games. It's psychological because football is mostly a mental game. Our situation now is tough. Once we break the spell in the big games, we'll start to win our share of them."

For a while, the 1970 season looked like the same old story, but then it would all change. Before training camp Landry had planned to tighten up his system; he would use a new style of attack and also move former All-Pro tackle Ralph Neely to right guard because Rayfield Wright had become a premier tackle and Tony Liscio was also solid at tackle. Landry also traded for Herb Adderley, hoping to get at least a couple more years out of the former Green Bay great and shore up one of the team's glaring weak spots at cornerback. He was moving Cornell Green to strong safety and believed that in Adderley and Mel Renfro the Cowboys could hold their own at cornerback with anybody. A good, solid training camp was important to fit in new people at new positions, to begin a new style of attack. But the National Football League Players Association called a strike and delayed for two weeks the veterans' reporting to camp. This severely hindered Landry's plans for change.

CRAIG MORTON WAS STILL HAVING PROBLEMS throwing the ball. Off-season surgery had corrected his shoulder problem, but now his elbow was bothering him. Later it was learned that he had injured his elbow while trying to compensate for his shoulder problem. When the 1970 season was over, Morton would undergo surgery on the elbow, but the seriousness of the new problem didn't come to light until, once again, he had played a season in pain. On the other hand, Roger Staubach, twenty-eight-year-old second-year quarterback, was most anxious to play, and unlike Morton, he was very outspoken.

During a quarterback meeting, Landry was explaining, "There is no quarterback in the league with less than three years' experience who has won a championship. Joe Namath was unusual in that respect. He was the only quarterback to win a title after playing three years."

Staubach, fuming, blurted out, "Namath was only in his third year [in reality Namath was in his fourth year]. Besides, how can you judge every individual by the same yardstick? If you do that, I don't have a chance because I'm only in my second year. You've got to judge each individual separately."

"Roger," said Landry, "see me after the meeting."

When the others had left, Landry told Staubach, "You've got to understand my feelings about the development of a quarterback. The mental process is very important. A lot of quarterbacks have been ruined, lost their confidence, because they've been stuck out there before they were ready, before they had the proper knowledge. You must be able to read and understand the defense and utilize our offense to its fullest potential."

"Coach, I know that, but I feel I can physically make up for any mental shortcomings."

Landry knew Staubach had all the physical tools and was more devoted to the game and worked harder than any quarterback he'd ever had. But Roger was having trouble reading keys, and at the slightest confusion or provocation, he would tuck the ball and take off running. Outside of Fran Tarkenton, NFL quarterbacks just didn't do that. That left them open for shots by the defense, and they just wouldn't last very long. Landry remembered how, in an exhibition game against Baltimore in 1969, Staubach ran twelve times for 118 yards and kept the team and the crowd very excited. But he had also thrown four interceptions. When Landry later showed films of the game, the players laughed at Staubach's escapades as a runner, how he'd faked tacklers off their feet, but Landry didn't think it was very funny. He had runners in Calvin Hill and Walt Garrison. He wanted a quarterback.

Morton was a classic dropback passer, but injuries had delayed his development, and at times Landry wondered if they had shaken his confidence. Discussing his quarterbacks, Landry said, "Craig takes a more serious approach than Don did to the game. Don had his serious moments but not all the time. Of course, due to injuries, it still hasn't been determined if Craig will be able to perform on a steady keel.

"I think Craig's knowledge of the game is comparable to Don's. In that aspect he was more ready to play after four years than Meredith had been at the same stage. Don didn't apply himself as well as early as Craig has. But of course when Don did start applying himself the last four years of his career he became a fine quarterback.

"Personality-wise, I'd say Craig is somewhere between Meredith and Staubach. He's not in the real serious mold of Staubach but not as loose as Meredith. Before the injury to Craig's shoulder, his arm was very strong, and I'm sure it will be again. In those early years with the club, I remember he sometimes would throw the ball too hard on short patterns and split a receiver's hands. If he regains the strength in his arm, if it becomes as it once was, he potentially can throw the deep routes and sideline patterns with more force than Don.

"Last year [1969] Craig surprised me a little. He had an excellent knack of calling plays. He moved the plays and the formations around and kept the defense off-balance. But . . . nobody works harder than Roger Staubach. He's very rare, and with his maturity, he certainly could challenge, possibly in three years."

It took Landry almost the entire preseason to put in the various changes he had planned, moving to more of a power, run-oriented attack. He was also continuing to develop in his repertoire the Flip Formation, with the wide receivers on the same side, that he had put in during the preseason of 1968. It was becoming a widely used formation in the NFL. He said he had first seen it used by Houston in the AFL, but he was the first NFL coach to employ it. (The Washington Redskins began to use the formation a year after Landry, and a wire service story out of the Capital wrongly credited that club with coming up with the formation.)

Landry had also added an innovation to his defense that would be picked up by other clubs. A strongside linebacker was utilized for his ability to handle the tight end (always on the strong side of the formation). He had to have the strength to fight off blockers and penetrate an opponent's running game, which came to his side the majority of time. A weakside linebacker had to be more agile, faster, and able to cover a back coming out of the backfield on passing patterns. Ordinarily, teams are right-handed, with the tight end or strong side being to the right. But some clubs had begun putting the tight end on the left side, causing the weakside linebacker to have to play off the tight end, which he wasn't used to doing.

Landry decided to flip-flop his linebackers. For instance, the strongside linebacker would always go to the side the tight end was lined up on, and the weakside linebacker would move on the weak side, no matter whether it was on the left or on the right. Today, practically all NFL teams use this tactic.

Due to the delay in camp opening and to Landry's changes, Dallas did not look good in preseason, losing five of six games. True to his word, Landry shocked just about everybody by actually benching starters Morton, Neely, and Bobby Hayes as the regular season opened. They were replaced by Staubach, Blaine Nye, and Dennis Homan. Landry said the benched players simply had not reached their performance levels. Of course, Neely was trying to learn a new position at guard, and soon he would be moved back to weakside tackle. He had spent his entire career playing strongside tackle but agreed to switch, at Landry's urging, because Rayfield Wright could not play weakside tackle.

Hayes was especially surprised. He was still doing the same things he'd always done, but with the emphasis on the power running game, Landry also expected his wide receivers to block and felt Bobby hadn't done an adequate job. It would take Morton, Neely, and Hayes a few games to regain their starting positions.

The Cowboys opened by beating the Eagles but then fell behind the Giants, 10–0, at halftime of the second game. Staubach had not played well in the first half, and all indications were that Landry would go with Morton in the second. But as the teams were walking to the dressing room at halftime, Landry might have been influenced by Staubach's competitiveness. "Coach, I can do it," Staubach told him. "I know I can do it. Please don't take me out in the second half." Landry left him in, and Dallas won the game, 28–10, as Rentzel, on a flanker-around pass he had talked Landry into using, pulled up and threw a forty-three-yard touchdown pass to Hayes, who had entered the game to sub for Dennis Homan.

Against St. Louis the following week, Staubach threw two early interceptions to safety Larry Wilson, once badly misreading the defense, and Landry, who all along had wanted to get Morton in there, made his move. When he told Morton to go in, Craig literally jumped into the air on the sidelines and Staubach, his head down, went to a corner of the bench and sat by himself. Dallas lost anyway, 20–6. It beat Atlanta and traveled to Bloomington, Minnesota, to play the Vikings, one of the toughest and strongest NFL teams, but also one that had lost Super Bowl IV to Kansas City, 23–7. The Cowboys were destroyed, 54–13, and Landry didn't even bother to show game films to the team.

"Cornell Green, Lee Roy Jordan, and I were tri-captains," recalled center Dave Manders. "After the loss to the Vikings, we were meeting on Monday and Coach Landry's opening remark was, 'I knew we weren't ready to play the game by the way our tri-captains came off the field after the coin toss.' I tell you, after that, we literally sprinted off the field after a coin toss."

The Cardinals, tired of playing in the shadow of Dallas, had a tremendous start and brought a 7–1 record into the Cotton Bowl to play the Cowboys on a featured game of ABC's *Monday Night Football*. Don Meredith, well on his way to becoming a star of the show, would do the color. The Cowboys, 5–3, knew they must win to stay in the race for what was now called the Eastern Division title (the NFL and AFL were each aligned into three divisions, Eastern, Central, and Western). It had become obvious by this time that the Cowboys should start Duane Thomas at halfback. Thomas had ridden the bench early, but although Hill had started strong, injuries had slowed him down. In fact, Thomas had led the Cowboys to a 27–16 victory over Super Bowl champion Kansas City by rushing twenty times for 134 yards and scoring two touchdowns, one on a forty-seven-yard run in which he burst through a hole and outran the secondary. But nobody could do anything against the Cardinals, who beat Dallas for the second straight time, 38–0.

The crowd booed Morton mercilessly and then began to look toward the broadcast booth and chant, "We want Meredith! We want

Meredith!" But Dandy, remembering they had done the same thing to him, said, "No way you're getting me out there."

It was over. The Cowboys, with a 5–4 record, appeared to have lost the divisional title with five games to play. Landry told the team, "Well, I've never been through anything like this. It was embarrassing to all of us. You guys didn't really want to win. Maybe it was my fault. I don't know, but it was the worst performance I've seen."

Ordinarily the day after a game the team goes through a light but formal workout. But Landry said, "Just go out and let's play touch football." It was madness, with centers playing quarterback and tackles playing wide receiver. But soon everybody was laughing and having a good time, including Landry.

The team became very loose. One day there was a heavy downpour before practice. The coaches have designated parking spaces against the field house, but rookie Steve Kiner, feeling he didn't want to get wet, pulled his 1964 Volkswagen into Landry's parking spot and went inside. Later, Landry came in soaking wet, looked over at Kiner, and said, "I admire a man with courage."

Landry did, however, insist on punctuality. Once a number of players and assistant head coach Jim Myers were late for an 8:00 A.M. meeting because a truck had overturned on Central Expressway and they were delayed by a traffic jam. Landry fined them each $150, including Myers, who said, "You shouldn't fine those guys, or me either. We couldn't help it if that truck turned over."

"You gotta plan for that," said Landry, never changing his expression.

Landry had taken a lighter approach in practice, and something else was happening. "The fans, the press, everybody was down on us," said Lee Roy Jordan. "Tom seemed to indicate to us that if we did anything the rest of the year we'd have to do it ourselves. So we got together, really got together, and decided everybody was against us and all we had was ourselves. It brought the team closer together, and what happened was one of the most amazing things I've ever experienced in my career." The Dallas Cowboys turned the season around.

Landry did have one big decision to make. Morton had been feeling the pressure. Either Landry could start calling plays for Craig, taking that burden off him, or turn to Staubach. Many players at the time felt Landry had given up on the team winning a division and had decided to go ahead and give the inexperienced and younger players more work.

The fact that he decided to stick with Morton disproved this. But he began calling plays for Craig by shuttling tight ends Pettis Norman and Mike Ditka.

Landry would not relinquish the play-calling again. He was often criticized for this, but today it is common practice in the NFL.

Led by Thomas, Dallas stormed the Redskins, 45–21. But the next week they were hit by another trauma, another note of sobriety. Upset and despondent after the loss to the Cardinals and bothered by personal problems, Lance Rentzel had exposed himself to a ten-year-old girl on November 19, three days after the game. The club had kept the news quiet as it prepared for a November 26 Thanksgiving Day game against the Packers and had hoped to keep it out of the papers and get Rentzel psychological help.

"Lance," Landry said at practice, "I'm sorry about what happened. I hope it can be kept out of the papers so you can continue to play. Is that what you want?" That's what he wanted.

The story broke, however, and Rentzel played what turned out to be his final game for the Cowboys, a 16–3 victory over Green Bay.

Nobody knew until later the burden carried during the Packer game. The night before the game, Landry told the team, "Something has happened which is difficult to talk about. Lance will tell you about it."

"I've made a mistake in my life before [at Minnesota] and now I've made a second one, and Green Bay will be my last game," Lance said, then broke down. The players rallied behind him and said they wanted him to continue to play. In the long run, it was decided that it would put too much pressure on Lance and the team for him to continue playing, and so he was placed on the reserve list. Before the next season, he was traded to Los Angeles. Charges of indecent exposure were filed on November 30. He pleaded guilty at his trial on April 8 and was given a five-year probated sentence with the understanding that he receive regular medical and psychiatric care.

Rentzel had been an outstanding receiver and blocker for Dallas, easily having his best years in the NFL. He would play for the Rams but never again perform as well as he had during his three and a half seasons with Dallas.

Landry once said that Rentzel had a very keen mind and was an exceptionally gifted athlete but tended to become very frustrated with himself when he didn't reach the high standards he sought. He recalled that Rentzel needed to have recognition and was very sensitive about how others felt about him.

Rentzel prepared for a game but was sometimes a distraction to teammates because he'd always be the last to show up at meetings and practices. Landry discussed Rentzel's problems and frustrations with him and felt, at times, that Lance would misread his thinking and become quiet and moody. But they would talk again and the air would clear and Lance would be his old self and certainly perform well on the field.

"When I made the decision to trade him to Los Angeles, I was confident this was the best thing for him," said Landry. "He would have the opportunity to start fresh, while seeking professional help for his problems. My prayer for Lance was that he would be able to enjoy the greatest victory of all, that being his own peace of mind."

Public sentiment was against Rentzel, but some of his teammates were sympathetic to his problems and wanted him to stay on the team. Not knowing how Landry felt, they believed he had been cold and detached in dealing with Lance.

After the episode, Landry was fishing with a group headed by Paul Wiggins, his old friend from the University of Texas. Landry became very quiet and reflective during the trip, and when pressed about what was troubling him, he said, "I guess I'm just very concerned and worried about Lance."

⌣∶⌣

DALLAS WAS ABLE TO RIDE an amazing defensive performance and the running of Duane Thomas to victories in its final five regular-season games, whereas the Cardinals fell apart. The defense had a string of games reaching into the playoffs in which it didn't allow a touchdown for twenty-three quarters, an unprecedented performance in Dallas history. Morton was still having arm trouble, but the Cowboys beat Detroit, 5–0, in the first round of the playoffs and Dick Nolan's San Francisco 49ers, 17–10, for the NFC title to advance to Super Bowl V and a meeting with AFC champion Baltimore.

The game on January 17, 1971, was the first in a series of Super Bowls played in Miami's Orange Bowl in which Dallas would have rotten luck. Morton's arm was bothering him, and he was ill and had lost his voice. *Sports Illustrated* called Dallas the "team without a quarterback."

Morton had sought help from a hypnotist, and that story was circulating around Fort Lauderdale, where the team was headquartered. Thomas had yet to withdraw into himself and was very popular with the media. He made reflective statements such as, when asked if the Super Bowl was the ultimate, "If it was the ultimate, then they wouldn't play it again." Once when he was walking on the beach and stopped to stare out across the water, Duane was asked what he was thinking about and said, "Denmark. I'm thinking about Denmark and maybe retiring there."

Landry knew the Cowboys had finally won the Big One, taking two playoff games and breaking Cleveland's jinx in the regular season, 6–2. He indicated to his aides that he believed Dallas could win a low-scoring game. "We knew we could handle their offense," he said. "Their defense was the best we'd played against, but I felt we could hold them and win. Even during the game, with the breaks going against us, at no time did I feel we weren't in control and wouldn't win."

Super Bowl V was a series of freak plays, all of which went against the Cowboys. Dallas led 6–0 as the defense completely destroyed Johnny Unitas, sending him to the bench with an injury after he had completed just three of nine passes and suffered two interceptions. Baltimore tied the game 6–6 (Dallas blocked the extra point) on a fluke play. Unitas had thrown badly for tight end John Mackey up the middle. The ball had been tipped by another Colt receiver. Mel Renfro leaped for the ball as it settled into the hands of a startled Mackey, who raced for a touchdown to complete a seventy-five-yard play. (An official said Renfro had also touched the ball. Mel said he had not. If the official had agreed that he hadn't, the throw would have been an illegal pass and would have been called back.) Dallas took a 13–6 halftime lead, and when the Colts fumbled away the second-half kickoff, Landry's team faced a second down at the Colt one, ready to put the game away for all practical purposes. As Thomas fought for the goal line, linebacker Mike Curtis hooked the ball out of his hands. There was a huge mix-up, and official Jack Fette's view of the ball was obstructed. As films and still pictures later showed, the ball bounced right to Dallas center Dave Manders, who easily recovered. But Colt tackle Billy Ray Smith began shouting, "Our ball! Our ball!" and pointing upfield. Fette, under pressure, pointed upfield too, giving the ball to the Colts. The recovery officially was credited to defensive back Jim Duncan, who was not even close enough to have had a chance to recover.

Manders actually got up holding the ball and handed it to the referee. Landry, seeing what had happened, went ten, fifteen yards down the sidelines, yelling that Dallas, not Baltimore, had recovered.

"We go ahead at that time 20–6, and the way we were playing defense, I don't see how they could have caught us," he said.

Colt defensive end Bubba Smith later said, "We ought to give the game ball to Billy Ray. He conned that official right out of the Super Bowl." Billy Ray Smith would later admit to friends that there was no way the Colts recovered. Instead of seven points, three at the very least, Dallas had nothing.

But with the game tied 13–13, Morton was moving the Cowboys into position for what could have been the winning field goal, until a holding penalty against Neely, plus a loss, left the Cowboys in a position of second and thirty-five at their own twenty-seven with 1:09 to play. Morton threw for Danny Reeves downfield. The ball was high but certainly catchable. It glanced off the fingertips of Reeves and into the arms of Curtis, who ran back to the Dallas twenty-eight, where moments later Jim O'Brien kicked a thirty-two-yard field goal with five seconds left to give Baltimore a 16–13 victory. It was then, when the ball crossed through the uprights, that Bob Lilly jerked off his helmet and slung it thirty, forty yards downfield, vividly illustrating the frustration of the Cowboys.

"We're disappointed but not ashamed," said Landry. "You just can't play better defense than we did. Three tipped passes gave them all their points [Mackey's catch, another tipped pass in the Colts' second touchdown drive, and Reeves's tip of Morton's pass]."

There were eleven turnovers in the game, and for the first time a player from a losing team, Chuck Howley, won the MVP award. Most of the writers were saying that with all the turnovers it was a sloppy game, but Landry noted, "Very few people understand what happened in the game. The reports were colored by writers' pre-conceived notions. I think it was the greatest Super Bowl game ever played, even though we lost. The close calls the officials were forced to make seemed to work against us. Whether our luck ran out or not, I don't know."

Landry later commented that Manders had, indeed, recovered Thomas's fumble near the goal line. But he realized what a great turn-around the 1970 team, once 5–4 and seeming to be hopelessly out of the championship race, had made.

"The lowest point in the existence of our team came when St. Louis wiped us out that Monday night," Landry explained years later. "There had been tremendous pressure on us to win, and we had sunk to the depths. But we came back and made it all the way to the Super Bowl. That was due to the character of the players we have, and it had a lasting effect, showing future teams that we could come back during difficult times."

"I think," said Tex Schramm, "that Landry's great strength, along with the great faith we have in him, enabled this team to pull itself off the floor after all those disheartening blows and come back with renewed purpose."

The Cowboys had come back from great adversity, from lingering psychological problems, to make the Super Bowl. There would be other setbacks the next season, but nothing would stand in their way to do even more as that guy from the naval academy asserted himself. Landry would, for the first time, deal differently with a very unusual individual than with the rest of the team.

CHAPTER 15
A Super Bowl Win

~:~

As long as I played and coached in the NFL, I can't think of any other coach who could handle both defense and offense. You'll search long and hard to find someone who put together a unique defense and then an offense, which changed offensive football in the NFL with the use of motion, shifting, and multiple formations. I defy you to come up with someone else who had that much football knowledge.

—RAY BERRY
Hall of Fame Receiver, Former Landry Assistant, and Head Coach of the New England Patriots

THE 1970S HAD BEGUN much as the 1960s had ended, with an epidemic of violence and rampant dissent. Arab commandos hijacked three planes leaving Europe for the United States, and four students, protesting Vietnam, were killed by National Guardsmen at Kent State. Lt. William Calley Jr. was found guilty of premeditated murder in the My Lai massacre. By mid-decade there would be Watergate and the fall of Richard Nixon, and eighteen-year-olds, whose duty it was to fight and perhaps die in war, would be given the right to vote. And yet, some of the old ideas would creep back into our culture. Americana would be in vogue again, with the slower-paced music of Burt Bacharach, and a popular movie would be *True Grit*, starring that hero of the '40s, John Wayne.

And it certainly did not seem as training camp opened in July 1971 that the Dallas Cowboys were headed for a Super Bowl championship. The acquisition of Lance Alworth to fill the void created by the departure of Lance Rentzel, who was traded to Los Angeles for tight end Billy Truax, had seemed to strengthen the team. Still, Tom Landry did not enjoy the fact that he'd had to trade Tony Liscio, Ron East, and Pettis Norman, for whom he had tremendous respect, to get Truax.

Landry was very proud of Norman and had often referred to him in speeches, explaining how he'd had the fortitude, drive, and character to

286

work his way up from very humble beginnings to gain a college degree and become successful not only in professional football but also in the community. He had joined the Cowboys in 1962 and helped them bridge the gap between being an immature expansion team and becoming one of the NFL's elite.

Landry had actually called Pettis and driven out to the Oak Cliff Bank, where Norman was vice president, to tell him of the trade. "I tell you," recalled Norman, "maybe the man isn't very emotional, like they say, but he cares. He certainly cares about you."

Alworth would be a great addition, and Truax, alternating with Mike Ditka, would help. But Landry had no idea that he would have to deal with the dark side of Duane Thomas, the rookie sensation of 1970 who had been the main thrust of the offense as Dallas made its first Super Bowl appearance.

Duane had had problems with the agents who helped sign him to his three-year contract with the Cowboys. The agents had taken a greater percentage of his contract than they should have; additionally, it had cost him to buy out of an agreement with them. Duane was in debt and needed money badly. After his sensational rookie season, he'd wanted the Cowboys to tear up the remaining two years of his contract and give him a new one, at least doubling his base salary.

Schramm told him no, that the Cowboys had not done that for Calvin Hill after his great rookie year and they wouldn't do it for him.

"But," said Duane, "I'm not Calvin Hill." Duane brooded, became very angry, and went to visit friends in the Los Angeles area, some of whom had rebelled or dropped out of society and now urged him to do the same. He said he wouldn't report to training camp without a new contract.

So Duane didn't report to Thousand Oaks in mid-July, but Calvin Hill looked extremely good and seemed capable of taking up where he'd left off before being hampered by injuries. Later in the month Duane showed up at camp, with an unusual friend who wore a dashiki and said his name was Ali ha ka Khabir. Duane announced not only that he wanted Khabir to stay in his room in the players' dorm but also that he wanted Khabir to be given a tryout. Refusals on all accounts were given in record time, and Duane and Khabir, whose name had previously been Mansfield Collins, left camp.

Thomas next surfaced in Dallas, where he called a press conference and rambled almost incoherently at times. Basically, he wanted an eighty-thousand-dollar base salary and said Dallas had never made the Super Bowl without him and never would do so again unless he returned. He indicated that he was being treated badly because he was black and that Texas Schramm was "sick, demented, and dishonest." (Schramm would reply, "That's not bad. He got two out of three.") And Thomas would say Gil Brandt was "a liar" and Tom Landry "was a plastic man, actually no man at all."

Thomas Henderson, by his own admission on cocaine, would also accuse Landry of being against him because he was black. This was a ridiculous charge, and Harvey Martin would later say, "Tom Landry doesn't have a racist bone in his body. All he sees is a player's ability, never his color."

Landry said Duane was entitled to his opinion but added that he did not see whether a player was black or white and, when asked at the time about Duane and any other enemies he had made, replied, "I don't think I make enemies. I don't consider people enemies or look at them that way. Players are like other people in that they sometimes react to a situation they're in. They say things on the spur of the moment that many of them usually regret or apologize for later. It's just the nature of the game. I don't think it's a lasting thing. In football you have responsibilities and you have to make decisions that affect people's lives. Therefore, you can't avoid situations where players might dislike you for decisions you had to make. And they might dislike you even though the decision you made might have been the right one."

When it became obvious that Duane wasn't going to report to camp, Landry consented to a trade that sent Thomas and two other backup players to New England for running back Carl Garrett and a number one draft pick. Garrett loved the trade and immediately after joining the Cowboys said how glad he was to get away from the Patriots' interior offensive line. Shortly thereafter, the trade was nullified and Garrett had to go back to the Patriots, where his popularity with those who would block for him wasn't running very high.

Thomas had caused the trade to fall through. When he reported to the Patriots, he refused to take the blood test and urinalysis required as part of his physical exam, fanning rumors that he might be on drugs. On the practice field he refused to get in a three-point stance, as suggested by Coach John Mazur, saying the Cowboy running backs lined up in a stance, where their hands were just above their knees so they could see more clearly. When he asked why he should use the three-point stance, Mazur told him, "Because I say so." When Duane still refused, Mazur told him to get off the field. Thomas again disappeared.

~:~

ONE OF LANDRY'S PRIORITIES was to settle the number one quarterback issue between Craig Morton and Roger Staubach. After the Super Bowl V loss, Landry began to think more seriously that, perhaps, Staubach might indeed be able to do the job, might be able to give the Cowboys a winner. In fact, on a charter taking some of the players and their wives from Miami to Dallas after the loss to Baltimore, Landry approached Staubach and said, "I think you can make your move this coming year, if you're ever going to make it." Staubach had indicated that if he wasn't given a shot at number one he wanted to be traded. At twenty-nine years of age, he felt he had no more time to waste on the bench.

Morton, coming off his second straight off-season operation on his throwing arm, was throwing well again after surgery on his elbow. He was quietly upset about the situation, recalling how Landry had once handed Meredith the number one quarterback job regardless of what he did. But Craig said if he had to go out and prove again he was the top quarterback, he'd do it. There will always be a question as to what Landry might have done had Craig been the winning quarterback in Super Bowl V. Had Dallas beaten Baltimore, there certainly is a possibility that Landry would have left Morton at quarterback, and if he had done so, Staubach would have demanded to be traded.

Landry made plans to let Staubach and Morton play equally during preseason and let them call their own plays. Before the regular season began, he would get with his offensive coaches and evaluate their performances, with the number one job going to the man who had the edge. Both Staubach and Morton were superb in preseason as the Cowboys won all six games. When it was over, Staubach had a slight edge in statistics, but Landry also liked some intangible things that Morton had done. Landry wasn't sure what to do. Things were just that close. He made his decision early in the week before the regular-season opener and, generally, kept his own counsel about it.

He announced it at his weekly press conference:

"When we opened training camp, each quarterback had something to accomplish. Morton had taken a lot of criticism last year because he couldn't throw [due to a bad elbow]. He had to reestablish his confidence, and I'm very satisfied that he has. On the basis of the confidence he regained and the way he's throwing, his production has been excellent, certainly good enough for us to win. I couldn't be more satisfied with Morton.

"Staubach had to make great strides in experience and know-how to offset Morton's experience. He doesn't have Morton's overall grasp, but he has enough for us to win. He can read a defense, doesn't scramble as much, and shows poise.

"On a competitive basis, Roger has a slight edge in the categories we consider most important. This is not a put-down of Morton but an acknowledgment that Roger is slightly ahead. But he does not have a clear-cut advantage, and so this is why we're going with the two-quarterback situation.

"I just feel this is the best thing for the Cowboys at this time. It is, certainly, important that we establish a number one quarterback for the future, but at this point, it can't be done because they're so close. So at this time, anyway, we'll go with them on an equal basis. One will start one game and the other, the next one.

"I don't like to do this because I know there will be a lot of criticism and people always will be second-guessing. But it's just something that must be done before we can establish a number one quarterback for the future. Sometimes a quarterback doesn't play well and I know I'll be criticized, but that's just the way things must be at this time."

Other positions had solidified, including Lance Alworth at flanker. Everybody had marveled at his great concentration, a trait Drew Pearson would also have. Landry had always felt that concentration was a big part of success on the football field.

"Concentration," he once said, "is when you're completely unaware of the crowd, the field, the score, other than how it might affect strategy. You're concerned only with your performance, playing well at your position. Golf is an excellent example of concentration. You see a golfer blow a hole, then go bogey on the next two holes. You know his concentration has been broken. When my concentration [as a play-caller, a head coach] isn't broken, I'm never on the defensive. When you start thinking defensively, you think such things as, 'Gee, this field's bad, and we're behind and we're not gonna be in the championship game.' It's difficult to recover then.

"Most people don't realize it, but a great measure of a football player is his ability to concentrate. This is why any team in the NFL can win any game if a superior team isn't concentrating, and this is why Vince Lombardi's teams at Green Bay did so well. Lombardi was a driver who kept his teams concentrating.

"For instance, concentration is what we lacked when we lost to Cleveland in 1968 and 1969. But when we made the Super Bowl against Baltimore and had a chance of winning it, we concentrated very well as a team."

Morton and Staubach did alternate, but then at midseason Landry shocked everybody—the players, the media, and perhaps most of all, his quarterbacks—by announcing that he would begin calling plays for his team by shuttling Craig and Roger, using each one on alternate plays. Secretly, Landry believed this was the perfect system if you had two talented quarterbacks. He could talk to the quarterback before he went in to run a play and explain exactly what to look for and explore what his options might be. He had used the tactic before with Eddie LeBaron and Don Meredith and, later, with Morton and Jerry Rhome when they were rookies. The thing he overlooked was that he would be making the players little more than his personal robots and that the team needed a quarterback, not two quarterbacks, as a leader.

Dallas did indeed move the ball with great success against Chicago that week, totaling 480 yards on offense. But the club had problems putting the ball across the goal line once it got inside the twenty and lost, 23–19, putting itself in a terrible hole with a 4–3 record. There was a great deal of panic among the press and Cowboy fans, and some were even calling for Landry to be fired, a fairly consistent theme during difficult times.

"His job was never in jeopardy and will never be as long as I have control, or as long as Clint Murchison is the owner of the club," said Tex Schramm.

Landry was probably less worried than anybody else. There was a feeling that he wasn't overly concerned if his team didn't play particularly well the first half of the season, if it was one or two games behind the divisional leader. He believed that races are won or lost in the final half of the season and that it was impossible for a team to stay at a top-level performance for the entire year. Often a club that started out strong tended to tail off at the end, as Dallas teams had done in 1968 and 1969. But if a team streaked during the final half of the season, reaching its peak, then its momentum would usually carry it through the playoffs. In four of its five Super Bowl seasons under Landry, Dallas had not been in good shape around the halfway mark. The team had been 5–4 in 1970, 4–3 in 1971, and 5–3 in 1975. In 1978 with the expanded sixteen-game schedule, it had been 6–4 and trailed the division-leading Redskins by two full games.

"Sometimes," admitted Cliff Harris, "I think he wants us to play bad at first and get ourselves into a corner because he knows we'll get mad and fight our way out. I think the reason that we always seem to come on strong when we get our backs to the wall is that it presents a personal challenge to Coach Landry. He's at his best when he's challenged. Sometimes I don't think he calls as good a game when we're 9–1 and way ahead of the other teams. He becomes more conservative."

Although he continued to defend the quarterback-shuttling system, Landry realized that to quiet the situation he must pick a number one quarterback.

He spent restless hours trying to do so. Because he had turned to Morton during crucial times even though the quarterbacks had basically split time, most believed Craig would be his choice. This was probably true even of Staubach, who had lost his temper after being pulled during the first game against the Giants, with Dallas leading just 13–6 at halftime and the offense sputtering. With Morton, Dallas had gone on to win, 20–13, and Landry, knowing how Roger felt, approached him after the game. But before Landry could speak, Roger said, "Coach, don't say anything. Whatever you say, you'll never understand me. What you just did by pulling me out there wasn't called for. You'll just never understand me."

Meredith would have been hurt in the same situation, but he might have hidden his feelings in a flippant way. Morton would have felt he'd been treated unfairly but remained silent. But the great fire within Staubach, the restlessness to start a meaningful career and his competitive desire, caused him to speak out. Landry liked his fire, felt it could be a positive factor when properly channeled, but he also wished Roger would let him run the quarterback situation without reacting so vocally when a decision went against him.

The team was divided. Some of the coaches, including Danny Reeves, wanted Morton to run the team. Most of the offensive players also wanted Morton because they believed he was steadier and operated better within the team concept. But, oddly enough, most of the defensive players opted for Staubach, feeling he just had a knack for getting something done, whether it was by Landry's book or not.

Finally, Landry reached his decision, during the week before the game against the Cardinals in St. Louis. His choice was Roger Staubach. Staubach was a tremendous competitor and also a catalyst, a guy who could turn a game around on individual effort. He might not play according to the book, but he had the great ability to find a way to win. Landry felt bad about Morton. He thought about the great disappointment Craig would feel after being groomed all those years to replace Meredith and then having the job go to somebody else. But Landry had examined all angles and believed that if a decision had to be made, as had become apparent, Staubach should be the quarterback.

"Both our quarterbacks have played well," said Landry. "They've been a strong part of our team, which I've said before. But I will go with Roger just in case some of the indecisiveness about the situation is, truly, upsetting to our team. Roger will make mistakes, but I'm confident he'll do the job we need and keep improving."

On Tuesday of that week, Landry phoned Staubach at home and said, "Roger, I've made a decision. I've decided you're going to be the starting quarterback for the rest of the season."

"Coach," said Staubach, "I really appreciate that. I won't let you down."

But Staubach later recalled, "You could tell he felt bad for Craig. I did too. It's tremendous the way the man came back off those two operations. But I think Coach Landry made sure Craig had every opportunity to keep the number one job. Craig couldn't have been nicer to me. He's a class act and a great quarterback."

"Sure, I'm disappointed," said Morton, ever the diplomat. "I'm sure it was a difficult decision for Coach Landry, but it's his decision to make. All I can do now is be ready and help the team in any way I can."

Immediately, Landry's decision came under scrutiny. "I don't second-guess myself," said Landry. "I take all the facts available and make decisions on what I think is right at the time. I think the real mistake is to look back. It's already done . . . there's not much you can do about it. I'm never one to replay things."

Landry's decision proved to be the right one, and something else had happened earlier in the season, before the Cowboys played the New York Giants in mid-October in the game that would be the club's final appearance in the Cotton Bowl. It would be both a great distraction and a great benefit to the team. Duane Thomas had quietly reported to the team and begun to practice. Landry wasn't sure when Duane would be ready to play but pointed out it might be sooner than most expected because he was such a natural. It came a lot sooner than even Landry imagined. Against the Giants, Hill suffered a knee injury early in the second half and Thomas entered the game. He had missed all of training camp, all the preseason games, and three regular-season games. He had worked out only a few times, and yet it was as if he'd never been away. Thomas got the ball nine times and rushed for sixty yards.

"Duane," said Landry, "is just an amazing fellow. He is a great natural runner and doesn't make mistakes."

In later years Landry would repeatedly give what the players would call the "Duane Thomas Speech." At team meetings Landry would say, "Duane Thomas used to sit in the meeting room and never look up. He'd never open his playbook. But when Sunday came around, he was perfect. He never made a mistake. He knew his assignments and, it seemed, those of everybody else too."

When the Cowboys officially opened Texas Stadium October 24 against the New England Patriots, Thomas was at his best when he scored the first touchdown on a beautiful, darting, yet fluid fifty-seven-yard run. Dallas won, 44–21. Duane had once described his running in abstract, "When you run out there you see shadows," he had said. "Then there's a flash of daylight and you move through it, like in a dream. I look at running as being like an art design. You can create anything you want. It can be a beautiful thing. Like life, appreciate the beauty of it."

When Duane returned to the club, the only way he communicated was through his running. He refused to talk to any of the media and almost all his teammates. It was a bad situation, which grew worse for the Cowboys. The media began calling Duane the "Sphinx."

Landry had a rule that players had to wear a coat and tie on charter flights. So Thomas would do such things as wear a regular jacket, with his shirt unbuttoned, and a tie, untied, thrown over his shoulder. Landry let this pass. Duane also refused to answer roll call, which greatly angered Reeves, who had the duty of calling it. Once when he called Duane's name three times and there was no answer, some of the players began to chuckle, and Reeves stormed out and went to see Landry.

"Coach, Duane won't answer roll call."

Landry thought for a second and said, "Just get on with it. We have a game to get ready to play." When he later questioned Thomas, he said, "He sees me. He knows I'm there."

Duane's only constant companion was a toboggan cap, pulled down tightly over his head. He'd wear it on all the road trips and just sit and stare, silently.

Landry tried repeatedly to talk to him, to reach him, and when this failed, he tolerated Duane's actions, something he had not done for anybody else. At times, he even defended him. Once Walt Garrison had run a play in practice and it was Duane's time to step in for him. After Walt ran the play again, he asked Landry, "What's wrong with Duane? He's over there screwing around!"

"It's your turn to run," Landry said. "Get in there."

Garrison later said he understood what Landry was trying to do but that anybody else would have cut Duane right away. At that time, in 1971, the players were griping a lot about the double standards but accepted Duane's quirks and the tolerance of Landry as long as Thomas helped the team win, which he did.

Mike Ditka, then a tight end, reflected on the situation after he became head coach of the Chicago Bears. "The Duane Thomas situation was the worst anguish Tom ever went through. I've never seen a man suffer so much in trying to do what he thought was best for the team and for an individual. He did it, but it was pure hell for everybody."

"To me," said center Dave Manders, "the best job Tom ever did was in his handling of Duane Thomas. It was like a powder keg."

"Some of the things that went on in the late 1960s and the Duane Thomas situation went against most everything Tom was brought up to believe," said Tex Schramm. "I tell you, he was more tolerant of Duane than nine-tenths of the coaches would have been. He really made every effort possible to help straighten up Duane. But, in the long run, I think his dealings with Duane also helped him get a broader perspective in his relationship with players in later years."

"It was a unique situation," said Landry. "I varied my treatment toward Duane because I felt I could help him and because of what I felt the other players were thinking. They seemed to be saying, 'Yeah, we'll tolerate something different like that for the best interests of the team.' Winning the Super Bowl that year was our only goal. All of us were willing to put up with anything to achieve that goal. But once we had won the Super Bowl you couldn't expect a team to go through that again.

"It took a team like the Cowboys, who had been through so much adversity, to get through something like that. Adversity is what builds character. If the team hadn't had a great deal of character, it would have been 3–11 instead of 11–3.

"I believe in people. My job is more than just winning but also dealing, in a way, with people's lives. My main hope in the Duane Thomas case was that I could have found some way to save an individual. I strongly believed in him, and that caused a lot of criticism. But I didn't listen to the critics. I've always tried to take a player who is not of my mold and hope he changes his character or personality. This is because of my background as a Christian. I guess I haven't been very successful because, at times, I really don't believe you can change a person's character. But I'm always willing to try because I know the only one who can change a person's character is Jesus Christ. As coaches, we're really not successful in changing character, just in molding it. Heaven knows, I've tried hard with a lot of players, probably at my own expense as a coach."

~:~

AFTER TOM LANDRY PICKED Roger Staubach, the team began to jell and didn't lose a game the remainder of the year. But there were other problems besides Duane Thomas.

In early November, Landry felt the team needed a boost at kicking and replaced Mike Clark with Toni Fritsch. An unexpected hurdle developed when starting tackle Ralph Neely, who had taken up motorcycle riding as a hobby, was in a bike accident, suffering a badly broken ankle. Backups Don Talbert and Forrest Gregg were also sidelined, and the Cowboys had nobody to play left tackle against the Redskins in the crucial last meeting between the clubs. Landry got an idea, however, as far-fetched as it may have seemed.

After being traded to San Diego, Tony Liscio was shipped to Miami and then retired. He was back in Dallas in the real estate business. The Monday before the Redskins game, he answered the phone, and to his surprise, it was Tom Landry.

"Tony, how would you like to play this weekend and block Verlon Biggs for us?"

"Uh . . . Coach, I don't think my legs would hold up. I'm completely out of shape. I . . ."

"Tony, I think you can do the job, and we need you."

"Let me think about it a couple of days."

"Tony, I'll give you thirty minutes. I have to make a decision."

Liscio agreed to try, and although he spent many days in the whirlpool, he probably had his best season with the Cowboys and, certainly, was a key factor in the Super Bowl drive.

Dallas beat Washington, 13–0, with Staubach doing the usual to put the game away. Roger set the club up at the Redskins' twenty-nine to run a deep in-route to Alworth, a play Landry had called. But Roger, noticing the left sideline open, tucked the ball and took off on a touchdown run that won the game.

"No," said Landry afterward, "we don't have any plays where Roger is supposed to run. Gosh, he runs enough as it is."

Dallas beat Los Angeles, 28–21, and the following week Calvin Hill was ready to play again. Landry had envisioned for a long time a big backfield, featuring Hill and Thomas. Thomas had played fullback in the past, so Landry told backfield coach Danny Reeves to work him there too in practice.

"Duane," said Reeves, "we want you to get in some work at fullback this week."

"No, I'm not going to play fullback," said Duane.

"Duane, go ahead," said Staubach.

"You shut up," Duane told him.

But Duane and Hill played in the same backfield and were tremendous as Dallas crushed the Jets, 52–10, and the Giants, 42–14, and finished the regular season by beating the Cardinals, 31–12. Both Thomas and Hill were big, fast, and could catch the ball well. Unlike Herschel Walker and Tony Dorsett in later years, they also worked well together. It was a dream backfield, but the dream would never again become reality. Landry would later reflect that, if it had, he believed Dallas, not Pittsburgh, would have been the team of the 1980s.

Hill was injured again prior to the playoffs, and Walt Garrison moved back in at fullback. Asked how he had felt watching Duane and Hill as he sat on the bench, Garrison remarked, "Like the bastard son at a family picnic."

~:~

PERHAPS IN EARLIER YEARS it would have made a difference, but when the Cowboys went to Bloomington, Minnesota, to play the Vikings in the divisional playoffs and found temperatures hovering around ten degrees, they didn't seem to mind. The team had become determined, almost clinical, and crushed the Vikings, 20–9, after taking a 20–5 lead late in the final period.

Dick Nolan's San Francisco 49ers beat the Redskins, the wildcard team, in the other divisional playoff game, 24–20, and moved into Texas Stadium to once again play Dallas for the NFC title and a Super Bowl berth. It would turn out to be the toughest playoff game yet for the Cowboys. Nolan had geared his Flex Defense, a system he'd learned from Landry, to stop Duane Thomas and was very successful, holding him to forty-four yards on fifteen carries. But 49er quarterback John Brodie experienced an off day and made a crucial mistake in the second period, trying to dump off a screen pass deep in San Francisco territory. He failed to see Cowboy defensive end George Andrie, who intercepted and returned nine yards to the 49er two, setting up the Cowboys' first touchdown.

By the final period, San Francisco, trailing 7–3, seemed to have regained momentum. Dallas, facing third and seven at its own twenty-seven, needed a big play, so Landry called a pass play in which Staubach was supposed to drop the ball off to running back Danny Reeves. A big rush, led by end Cedrick Hardman, was on, and as Staubach faded he had little time to do anything but scramble. He ducked a tackler, dodged another one, and retreated all the way to his three-yard line before starting back upfield. He ran toward Reeves, who was covered by linebacker Dave Wilcox. Dave wasn't sure what to do. If he stayed on Reeves, Staubach would run for the first down. If he went after Staubach, Roger would drop the ball off to Reeves. Wilcox came after Staubach, who passed to Reeves for nine yards and a first down. This was the highlight of an eighty-yard drive that won the game for Dallas, 14–3, and put them into Super Bowl VI against AFC champions the Miami Dolphins.

"The big play for us was that third and seven," said Landry. "If Roger hadn't made the first down, we would have had to punt and San Francisco could have gotten the ball and won the game." And on Staubach's running, he added, "Roger will keep running until he keeps getting hit, and then he'll slow down. The more he learns, the less he'll run."

The attitude of the Cowboys was strange after they beat Minnesota and San Francisco. There was no celebration, no cheering in the dressing room. The Cowboys were like a surgeon who had just completed a successful major operation. As much as anything, the team seemed to reflect the composure of Tom Landry. But there were other reasons. From the first day of training camp, winning the Super Bowl was the major goal, the only goal. The club didn't think about winning divisional or conference titles because it had done that before, the footsteps already were there. It wasn't interested in going to the Super Bowl but only in winning it. The disappointments, narrow losses, bad calls by officials, nothing would stand in their way because an almost cold-blooded approach would eliminate variables that had hurt them in the past. They were not emotional on the field, and they were not emotional after winning the playoff games.

But Landry never had felt a player should be overly emotional on the field. Discussing the subject, Landry once said, "If you are prepared, then you will be confident and you will do the job. Emotion can cover up a lot of inadequacies, but in the end it also gets in the way of performance. An emotional team cannot stay that way consistently over a full season or even a few games.

"Of course, a defensive player not motivated like an offensive player. An offensive player's motivation may be what he hears, reads, or feels. A defensive player has a certain temperament. He faces a challenge, and this motivates him accordingly. If he doesn't have this, then he won't be a good defensive player.

"But at these times you don't let the emotional factor overrule your style of play. We play a coordinated, disciplined style, so we've had more success with less emotional types of players. Our success proves that you don't have to have a guy who tees off every time the ball is snapped. Nor does it mean the type of player we use is any less motivated to succeed.

"For one thing, I don't believe in team motivation. I believe in getting a team prepared so it knows it will have the necessary confidence when it steps on a field and be prepared to play a good game. Players can sense this, and they respond to it.

"It's a long year, and there are a lot of highs and lows. Sometimes it's difficult to get ready to play, but if they are not ready, they know it. If you can cause them to be ready, and be prepared for all situations they'll have to face, they'll be motivated."

Landry never prepared a team better than he did the Cowboys for Super Bowl VI on January 16, 1972. The club had two weeks in which to get ready, one in Dallas and one in New Orleans, the site of the game. Landry worked hard before the club left for New Orleans because he knew that he had to make his plans and solidify them before facing Super Bowl week. There would be too many distractions then. Of course, there was a distraction in Dallas that he hadn't planned on facing. Duane Thomas didn't show up for a practice session, and nobody knew where he was. There were rumors that his new adviser, Jim Brown, the former Cleveland Browns All-Pro, might feel the ultimate in rebellion would be for Duane to skip the Super Bowl game. But Duane had apparently been sick or something because he was at practice the following day. He huddled with Landry, who said when questioned that he had no reason to believe Duane wouldn't play in the Super Bowl.

There had been some amusement prior to the game. President Richard Nixon, whom Landry had strongly supported, had suggested plays that might work against Dallas to Washington Redskins coach George Allen. He had strongly recommended a flanker around, which lost yardage when Allen tried it against the Cowboys. President Nixon had also phoned Miami coach Don Shula and said, "I'm a Washington Redskins fan, but I'm a part-time resident of Miami and I've been following the Dolphins real close. I think if you use [Paul] Warfield on down-and-in patterns in the Super Bowl it'll be very successful against the Cowboys."

"I think the president hedged a little on Coach Shula," said Landry. "He gave them a play they've been running all year."

Before the club boarded a flight for New Orleans, Landry received

a telegram from former president Lyndon Baines Johnson, who had
seen the club beat San Francisco in the NFL title game. Johnson said in
the telegram, "My prayers and my presence will be with you in New
Orleans, although I have no plans to send in any plays."

"At least," said Landry, "we have one president on our side."

~:~

THERE IS NO PLACE MORE UNLIKE Tom Landry than New Orleans,
and yet it is a town where Landry won two Super Bowls. So although he
could not relate to many aspects of life in that city, some of his fondest
memories are there.

It has been called the "Fun City of the South" or the "Sin City of the
South," and when the Super Bowl is held there, it takes on a carnival
atmosphere with loose banjo strings playing and a high-pitched voice
singing, "Ohhh, way down yonder in New Oreleceans, that's the land of
the dreamy dreams. There's a Garden of Eden there . . . ohhh, you
know what I meannnnnn. . . ."

More than fifty thousand visitors were lured to the city for Super Bowl
week, and many made the French Quarter their nightly mecca of celebration. Bourbon Street literally shook with jazz coming from a brassy
horn that might or might not have belonged to Al Hirt. Passersby paused
to listen to the blue, soulful sounds filtering onto the street from
Preservation Hall. Behind doors on the main drag of the Quarter, strip-
pers shimmied in dark, smoky rooms, their mouths grinding gum in
rhythm to the music, while spielers stood just outside and called to those
going past, "Come in! Come in! Seeeee the amazing Miz Brandy . . . a
Super Body for the Super Bowl! Haw! Haw!"

Girls of the night walked the streets and stood around hotel lobbies,
and magic names abounded: restaurants such as Tujague's and Arnaud's
. . . Hurricanes at Pat O'Brien's, Ramos Gin Fizzes . . . shrimp
rémoulade, bouillabaisse, seafood gumbo . . . and hangovers, with a shot
of whiskey taken as an antidote. When the Super Bowl is in New
Orleans, it becomes an early Mardi Gras. But it also becomes the sports
capital of the nation.

Whereas the Miami Dolphins were housed at the storied
Fontainebleau Hotel, which was several miles from the Quarter but
sparked with an Old New Orleans atmosphere, the Cowboys stayed at
the Hilton Inn directly across from the airport. It was twenty-five miles

from downtown, and jets passing over made it difficult to sleep at times. Chuck Howley probably summed up the feeling of the team as it arrived Sunday afternoon, a week before the Super Bowl, when he said, "This is a crummy place, a crummy hotel, and by game time we'll be so mad we'll beat the devil out of Miami."

Landry gave the team the first night off, and most went to the Quarter. But thereafter it was all business. Apparently that first night trouble developed between Walt Garrison and Margene Adkins, because in the dressing room the next day at practice they exchanged words and a scuffle started. It was quickly broken up, but it angered Landry, who told the team, "If something like this happens again or anything else occurs which might disgrace this team, I'll fine those involved five thousand dollars."

Adkins was also subject to a Landry scolding once during the season. After failing to make a tough catch, Margene came off the field and remarked, "That would have been hard to catch." Landry, never changing his expression, said, "We don't pay you to do the ordinary. When the times come, you'd better make the catch."

Forty-five minutes were set aside Monday through Thursday for the press to interview the players. Thomas worked hard but refused to speak to the press, his only words being, "What time is it?" A number of people printed that in-depth quote. Mike Ditka, obviously referring to the double standards concerning Thomas, once said, "There's a lot of BS around here, but it'll all be worth it if we win the Super Bowl."

The team practiced in the afternoon, and each night Landry called his quarterbacks, Roger Staubach and Craig Morton, into his room to look at films and go over the plans already made in Dallas.

"Miami is a zone team," he kept telling them, "and you've got to hit the backs. Notice how the linebackers drop back pretty deep. So this leaves our backs open short. Hit them. Let them make the yardage."

~:~

SEVEN YEARS BEFORE Super Bowl VI, there had been no Miami Dolphins. But in six seasons the team had made the biggest of games, becoming the youngest franchise ever to do so, even younger than the 1966 Cowboys who had challenged Green Bay for NFL supremacy. The Dolphins were reminiscent of those 1966 Cowboys, full of young, good talent but without championship experience from which to draw.

Certainly Don Shula's team had not experienced anything like the atmosphere surrounding the Super Bowl game and the pressure it caused.

"Well," said Miami quarterback Bob Griese, "I feel we're even with Dallas. We haven't won a Super Bowl, and neither have the Cowboys."

But veteran Herb Adderley, who had been to two Super Bowls with Green Bay and was in his second with the Cowboys, cautioned, "The Dolphins have never known pressure like this week, with all the press around and everything. When you get to the city where the Super Bowl game is held, the atmosphere is so different than in the regular season, and it gets worse the closer you get to the kickoff. We've been here before. Miami hasn't."

Landry had a masterful game plan. He knew that the Dolphins, because they were young, would have trouble coping with his multiple system.

Larry Csonka and Jim Kiick had had fine seasons running the ball, but Landry felt Bob Lilly and the Flex Defense could stop any runners. He worried about Warfield but devised a plan to stop him. At times he would use both cornerback Mel Renfro and strong safety Cornell Green to double Warfield inside-out, and at other times he would let Renfro, one of the league's best athletes, take him man-to-man. Landry had also picked up a consistency pattern. When the wide receiver lined up six, seven yards closer to the ball, it ordinarily meant the Dolphins were going to run. Shula felt the wide receiver could get a better shot at blocking the defensive end or linebacker in close. But Landry wanted his outside linebackers, when the wide receiver came in, to shoot into the Miami backfield.

Offensively, he wanted Staubach and Morton to throw short into the spaces left vacant by Miami's retreating linebackers. The key to any running game against Miami, he knew, was neutralizing middle line-backer Nick Buoniconti. Buoniconti was quick and had tremendous pursuit. The Dolphin defensive linemen tried to keep the blockers off him so he would be free to go for the ball carrier.

Landry decided he could counter this, actually take advantage of Buoniconti's aggressiveness in pursuit, by having his running backs—Thomas, Garrison, and Calvin Hill—make a false step as though they were going wide and then cut back up the middle. Guards Blaine Nye and John Niland and center Dave Manders (especially Niland and

Manders) would contain the defensive tackles at the snap, then slip off their blocks and butt Buoniconti into the direction he'd already started. By the time Buoniconti recovered, the running backs would already be through the hole in the middle he'd vacated. Landry figured Buoniconti would take a step and start toward the outside when the Cowboy running backs made a false move in that direction, and when he'd try to come back as they veered back toward the middle, Niland or Manders would be there to hit him.

Before the game, Landry said, "We're just very calm and taking a very businesslike approach to the game. We are not as excited or tense as we were last year when we played the Colts. The players seem to be taking a matter-of-fact approach. But don't misinterpret this. We're up for the game, maybe even more so than last year. It's just that we've been here before [to the Super Bowl]. If we win, you'll see some excitement."

Some people talked that week about how the Cowboys "couldn't win the Big Game." Of course, in 1970 and 1971 they had won many big playoff games to get to the Super Bowl. But the stigma still hung in the air. It was always there, somewhere, although at times obscured by the cool, almost clinical confidence the Cowboys displayed in their preparation. It would not be dispelled until the team won the National Football League championship.

Yet no ghosts of championship games past crept into the minds of Landry or the Cowboys as they boarded the team buses and joined the early crowds slowly moving toward the early afternoon Super Bowl kickoff. Landry was deeply aware this wasn't the youthful Cowboy team that had submitted to Green Bay on a brisk day in Dallas, nor the team that had lost an Ice Bowl game to the Packers in Green Bay, nor the one that had finally been edged by Baltimore in Super Bowl V. It was a new team, a new dawn, and although he did not admit it until later, Landry knew, just knew, the Cowboys would win. He had never had more confidence in a victory and later said, "The team had a chip-on-the-shoulder attitude. The players were very short tempered. They were ready, and you knew then that they were going to do it."

A couple of days before the Super Bowl game, rains had fallen on New Orleans in the early morning hours, chilling what had been a sluggish, humid atmosphere. The weatherman had said there was a possibility of rain on game day, but the rains never came. On Super Bowl Sunday, temperatures stayed in the high thirties, with a little wind, and a bright sunshine shone on the throngs that converged on the Super Bowl like armies of ants.

The game began slowly, as though the teams were two boxers, feeling each other out. Staubach's first few passes went high, causing some alarm among Cowboy fans, but Landry had hoped to stay even with the Dolphins the first half and win the game after halftime, that is, unless the Cowboys got a break. On Miami's second possession, they got one. Kiick and Csonka had fumbled only once the entire season, but Csonka lost the ball and Howley recovered at the Dallas forty-eight. Methodically, Dallas moved to a third and two at the Dolphin two. Landry called a play in which Staubach was supposed to go to tight end Mike Ditka if both the safety and outside linebacker moved toward Thomas, who would swing out of the backfield. Staubach missed the key and threw to Thomas, who was smothered. Mike Clark, who had become the kicker again after an injury to Toni Fritsch, put Dallas on the scoreboard with a nine-yard field goal.

Midway through the second period, Landry's plans for Buoniconti began to work, and the Cowboy ground game started grinding out the yardage in bursts up the middle. Before the day ended, Thomas, Garrison, and Hill would amass a Super Bowl record of 252 net yards rushing and a tremendous 5.3 per try, Thomas would get ninety-five on nineteen carries, and Garrison seventy-four on fourteen. Hill, who rushed for twenty-five yards, explained the situation: "My knee was so sore I couldn't cut sharply, but the linemen were doing such a good job on Buoniconti and there were such big holes that anybody could have gotten through."

Dallas controlled the ball a full five minutes before the half and scored as Staubach found Alworth, who cut just inside cornerback Curtis Johnson for a nine-yard touchdown pass with 1:15 left in the half.

The frustration of Bob Griese and the Miami offense was personified by a play in the first half. Griese was supposed to pass to a wide receiver but saw penetration into the pocket and began to retreat because he knew he wouldn't have time to get the ball off. He kept going backward, then tried to come back up field. He started one way and then the other but saw his paths cut off by George Andrie and Larry Cole. Finally, Bob Lilly smacked him down for a twenty-nine-yard loss.

Just before the half, Griese finally found Paul Warfield for a twenty-three-yard pass that set up Garo Yepremian's thirty-one-yard field goal. Those would be the only points scored by Miami and also the only big pass Warfield would catch all day as the defensive plan blanketed him with Mel Renfro, having one of his best days ever. Outside of the twenty-three-yard completion, Warfield would make only three other catches, totaling sixteen yards.

At halftime, Don Shula told his defensive tackles to pinch in closer to the middle, hoping to shut down the freeway that was opening up for the Cowboy runners. Expecting this, Landry told his offense that it would begin running wide in the second half.

On the second-half kickoff, Staubach, who would complete twelve of nineteen passes for 119 yards and two touchdowns and receive the game's MVP award, guided the Cowboys seventy-one yards in eight plays for a touchdown, completely blunting the spirit of the Dolphins.

As the final period began, Dallas led, 17–3, and Chuck Howley, the team's oldest player at thirty-six, made a tremendous play, again showing why he was one of the game's best linebackers and why Landry, unlike many, preferred the smaller, quicker linebackers to the bigger and stronger ones. Miami faced third and four at its own forty-nine, and Griese attempted to throw to Kiick on the right sideline. Howley had tried to knock down wide receiver Howard Twilley and was on the ground as Griese released the ball to a wide-open Kiick. But Chuck leaped up, intercepted the ball, and ran all the way to the Miami nine before he tripped and fell. Three plays later Staubach threw a seven-yard touchdown pass to Ditka, on the same pass play he'd misread earlier, making the score 24–3 with 11:42 to play. The Cowboys could have scored another touchdown, but Hill, diving for the end zone from the one, lost the ball and Miami recovered. It didn't matter. Dallas had left no doubts, no room for second-guessing, by registering the most thorough Super Bowl victory to date.

As the game was ending, Craig Morton, the man Landry had benched, walked over to the Cowboy coach, shook his hand, and said, "Coach, I'm very happy for you." John Niland and Rayfield Wright raced to Landry, lifted him on their shoulders, and began carrying him off the field. Landry broke into the biggest smile anybody could remember, and Bob Lilly, who had experienced all the frustrations, jogged to the dressing room, then leaped straight up into the air.

The Cowboy dressing room was total bedlam. Lyndon Johnson came in and shook Landry's hand. President Nixon called and said the Cowboys had looked great and the offensive line had done a tremendous job. "Thank you, Mr. President," said Landry. Schramm and Clint Murchison were tossed into the shower.

Jimmy Brown had promised Tom Brookshire that Thomas would talk to him on national television, so Duane stepped up onto a makeshift stage in the dressing room as the cameras turned. Brookshire, obviously nervous as he attempted to interview the man who wouldn't talk, said, "Uh, Duane, are you as quick and elusive as you look?"

"Evidently."

"You, uh, your weight seems to fluctuate. You weigh two hundred and five for some games and less for others."

"I weigh what I need to."

"You enjoy football?"

"That's why I'm a pro. It's what I like to do."

Everybody was cheering, howling, and just as Landry had predicted, the emotion came out for the Cowboys after they won the Super Bowl. A great weight had been lifted, a curse, a stigma had been laid to rest. The Dallas Cowboys, for all to see, had won the biggest game.

This day, January 16, 1972, had been a day of total happiness for Tom Landry and the Dallas Cowboys, a landmark time. Tex Schramm talked about a Cowboy "dynasty," and even Duane Thomas was smiling, the anger, over things real and imagined, and the bitterness seemingly gone from his face.

Certainly, the Cowboys were at the top of the world of professional football, and Duane Thomas, in only his second year, was being compared to the great runners of all time. But that afternoon in January 1972 would be his last hurrah.

⌣∴⌣

BY THE SUMMER OF 1972, the Super Bowl championship frenzy had died down to a trophy in a glass case and hard, cold type in the record book. Landry had made it clear to his team that the previous season had passed, that times had changed, and that everybody would be dealt with under the same rules, the same set of standards, including resident dissident Duane Thomas.

Instead of reporting to camp on time, Duane gave his first-class ticket to an old high-school teammate, Roderick Price. Duane had told him to go ahead and try out for the Cowboys. Roderick showed up at practice and started running pass patterns. He was wearing combat boots. "Who the heck is that guy?" asked Landry. Told he was Duane's friend, Landry said, "Get him out of here."

During the off-season, Thomas and his younger brother had been arrested in Greenville, Texas, on charges of possession of marijuana. Duane had been given five years' probation after pleading guilty. Landry had helped by writing a letter, explaining he believed Duane felt remorse over what had happened and was ready to work back into the community. He was wrong.

The end came for Duane Thomas in training camp. He did report, but he had become a vegetarian and often he'd only check in at meals, grab a few pieces of fruit, and go back to his room. He went by the rules but walked a thin line. Duane got through the Cowboys' 20–7 victory over the College All-Stars but didn't play well. He seemed weak, but it was a long preseason and everybody felt he'd come around.

Then one day in camp Thomas missed a meeting and failed to show up for practice. Assistant coach Ray Renfro went to his room. Duane refused to talk to him. Finally, Landry went to Thomas's room.

"Duane, this is Coach Landry. Are you in there?"

"Yeah, can I help you?"

"Well, yes, you weren't at practice."

"Like, uh, I didn't feel like it."

Landry then went into Thomas's room and they talked. When Landry emerged, his face seemed even more stern and determined than usual as he walked from the players' dorm to the one that housed the coaches and officials. Landry found Tex Schramm and said, "That's it. Trade him."

That year the Cowboys had hired Sid Gillman, the longtime San Diego Charger coach who was considered somewhat of an offensive wizard in his own right. At San Diego, Gillman had two young players he felt could be outstanding, running back Mike Montgomery and wide receiver Billy Parks. Schramm made a deal to send Thomas to the Chargers for this pair.

Landry felt he had to explain the Thomas situation to the team and said, "Last night we traded Duane Thomas to San Diego for Billy Parks and Mike Montgomery. I talked to Duane for hours, telling him what he must do to become a part of society, of our team. I took him each step of the way and I felt he was making progress. But then he missed the morning meeting and the afternoon workout. I went to see him in his room to find out the causes. He told me he wasn't paid to attend meetings. He said he was paid to play on Sunday. I told Duane that he had to follow certain rules to be a part of the team, and he refused. I had no choice but to trade him."

Thomas was active for only one game with the Chargers, when they played the Dallas Cowboys. In pregame warmups, he went to the end zone, put his hands on his knees, and stood there for fifteen minutes, looking at the ground. He wandered around, stared at the crowd, sat alone on the bench. He didn't play.

Duane ended up with the Washington Redskins in 1973 and 1974, playing as a backup to Larry Brown. Sometimes he would show spurts of his old self but never consistently, and in the two years with the Redskins he gained about half as much yardage rushing as he had his rookie season with Dallas. In 1975 he went with the World Football League and played for a while in Hawaii, but the league folded. And in the great irony of ironics, he then talked to Landry and asked him for a chance to play in 1976.

"He was very cordial," said Landry. "Duane, I believe, is a good man, and if he can return to the running and pass-catching form he showed when he was with us before, we certainly can use him."

"A man grows," said Duane. "I have grown. I made mistakes. I feel I've learned the things necessary to move ahead now."

Later, Landry said of Thomas: "Duane Thomas was a reflection of the social revolution of the '60s. What happened during that time brought him to where he was, the point to which he had come. I think it was very sad, what happened to him. I felt we were handling the situation until after his rookie year; he spent that summer in California and became involved in the culture out there.

"But those times changed. The players today, the ones coming out of college, are different from those in college in the mid- and late 1960s. They're concerned more about their careers and what their success pattern will be. Yet they still have the carry-overs from the '60s, which are freedom and individualism. That's good. I think those are very good qualities to retain."

Everybody pulled for Duane when he came back, although the

coaches said quietly that he had lost the speed he once had. Landry indicated Duane would have to adjust his running style, that the game had changed now, and a runner, when challenged, had to duck his head and butt for the extra yardage. Duane missed much of training camp with a pulled hamstring. He didn't make it. He was cut at the end of preseason, 1976. As he left the locker room for the last time, he shook hands with Landry and they wished each other well. In 1978 and 1979, Duane requested and was given tryouts with the Green Bay Packers. Each time he was cut in training camp. For all practical purposes, his career ended in 1971 at the age of twenty-four.

CHAPTER 16
Roger Staubach

~:·:~

There's no question that the Cowboys' image around the nation and even the world helped rebuild the image of Dallas after the Kennedy assassination. People were calling Dallas a "City of Hate" and all sorts of things. Tom had a lot to do with changing that image. He was a gentleman with impeccable character, the type person who could have such a broad, strong effect.

—WES WISE
Mayor of Dallas, 1971–1976

THAT AUGUST NIGHT IN 1972 was uncharacteristically warm in Southern California. Yet a shirt-sleeved, capacity crowd of eighty thousand didn't mind because they'd packed the Coliseum to watch the Times-Charity game between the Rams and Dallas Cowboys, who were training in nearby Thousand Oaks. With the preseason game tied 3–3, Dallas faced a third and nine at the Ram twelve when Roger Staubach faded to pass. Then he saw an opening, avoided a rusher, and took off for the goal line. Middle linebacker Marlin McKeever came over to cut him off, but instead of stepping out of bounds or falling after making the first down, Staubach ducked his head like a fullback and tried to ram through McKeever into the end zone. Before he even hit the ground, Roger felt a burning sensation in his right shoulder. As he got up and trotted off the field, he had no control over his right arm, his passing arm. His shoulder was badly separated and would require surgery. Even after he recovered and rejoined the team, he would have trouble with that arm and wonder if it would ever be the same again.

Landry had feared something like this might happen because Staubach's scrambling and running style in those days was closer to that of a running back than a quarterback. A quarterback was supposed to go out of bounds or drop to the ground when danger was near. But when asked about Roger's chances of coming back, Landry said, "The same thing that made him duck his head and try to score will allow him to come back." Fortunately, Landry had an excellent quarterback in the wings, former starter Craig Morton.

Morton stepped in and did a good job, although the drive, the fire that had taken the team to the Super Bowl title, was missing from some elements of the club. Landry had cautioned the team that a natural let-down would come. "It's an unconscious, relaxation-type thing," he said. "You really aren't aware that it's happening, but it kind of creeps in and you let up a little. The teams in the NFL are so close that, when you do that, somebody can move ahead of you."

Duane Thomas was gone, but Calvin Hill was back and running well and Walt Garrison, a real live cowboy who competed in rodeo, was one of the team's toughest, most dependable players. And Landry just thought he'd seen everything until he was faced with the life and times of wide receiver Billy Parks.

Parks, an outstanding receiver, was a sensitive, idealistic guy who was, to say the least, strongly liberal. His feelings on Vietnam used to drive Roger Staubach, a veteran of the war, bananas, and sometimes he just didn't have the competitive instinct. Once he became extremely moody because he was starting in place of his friend Lance Alworth. He didn't want to do that. He was supposed to open against Green Bay, but because he'd learned another friend, Tody Smith, had been deactivated, he said he didn't feel like playing. Before another game when a special pregame program included Secretary of the Navy Melvin Laird induct-ing recruits, Billy had to be restrained in the ramp before the club prepared to go onto the field. Sometimes he wouldn't practice, standing around complaining of a sore leg, a pulled hamstring, whatever. It was clear that Landry would only allow Billy Parks to be part of his team one year, 1972.

Billy decided he wanted to wear white shoes. The team had been wearing black ones. But Landry, trying to be diplomatic, said they would take a vote, the majority ruling. The vote was split, but Landry told Billy his white shoes would be all right.

Parks was a big part of a problem Landry never could solve that year at wide receiver. He used four, including Parks, Bobby Hayes, Lance Alworth, and Ron Sellers, who had come from New England for a draft choice and became Morton's favorite target.

"Everybody makes mistakes, and Tom was wrong in his handling of the receivers," said Hayes. "All of us were messed up because we never knew from week to week whether we were going to play."

Alworth was upset because he was used mostly as a blocker. Actually, he was a good blocker while the other wide receivers mostly made feeble attempts as they waited for the next passing play. Hayes was upset because the receivers never knew when they were going to play. He was also having problems, dropping passes and coming up with nagging injuries. Parks was probably upset because he wasn't upset, so Sellers became the club's top receiver.

Hayes, of course, had been one of the most dangerous threats in the league because, with his speed, he could outrun defenders on deep routes. But a new day was coming to the NFL, and he would not completely adjust to it.

"Wide receivers," said Landry at that time, "must be different than they were three, four years ago when their job was to beat a guy man-to-man and catch the ball. The game has changed. Now they must contribute to the success of the team in any way they can. They have to block. They have to catch the ball in a crowd. There's no place now for an end just running patterns and beating his man. I want people at the position who'll do anything to help us move the ball."

Hill, much more of a power runner than Thomas, became the first player in club history to rush for more than one thousand yards, and Garrison would pass one thousand yards, running and receiving. But the offense wasn't producing as expected. Neither was the defense, due to injuries to Lilly and Renfro and the departure of Herb Adderley, whom Landry replaced with Charlie Waters. Waters, a natural safety, did not have the physical tools to play cornerback, but although he might get beat, he never shied away from contact and actually led the team in interceptions with six.

Landry had upset Danny Reeves when he gave Sid Gillman, originally hired as a special assistant, the additional duties of running the offensive backfield and, in effect, taking that job away from Reeves. Reeves, previously angry because of the way Duane Thomas was allowed to get away with things, did not like Gillman and stewed the entire season because added to his other duties after Staubach was injured was the job of being backup quarterback to Morton.

∽:∾

IN SPITE OF ALL ITS PROBLEMS, Dallas stayed in a close battle with Washington for the NFC Eastern title, splitting the season series with the Redskins. But it also suffered humiliating defeats, such as losing 31–10 to Dick Nolan's 49ers on Thanksgiving Day before a full house in Texas Stadium. This severely hurt the Cowboys' chances to win the division, and Landry had had enough. He told the team:

"It's just pitiful that you'd go out and play a game like that. I tell you, I'm just not built like that. I've got too much pride to sit back and be humiliated like that. When you lose like that, the only thing I know to do is work harder. Heck-fire, we're right in the middle of a championship drive and we're playing like a second-division team. You've got to work and you've got to fight for what you get. We're not doing anything. I guarantee you that's going to change. Anybody in here who is not prepared to fight and work with everything he's got for three more weeks can leave right now. I'll be more than happy to put his name on the reserve list for the remainder of the season. I don't need you. Look, one of the big difficulties in life is to become a man. I've seen thirty-five-year-old men who are still children. Some of us make it, some of us don't. It's going to take men to win the championship."

Landry came up with a new tactic to beat Washington in the second meeting between the two clubs. Alworth, as usual, would start in motion or line up wide. But on a running play to his side, or the side to which he was going, Lance would come back toward the middle and, from the side, block linebacker Jack Pardee, who was so unaccustomed to this happening from a wide receiver that he had problems all afternoon. Dallas won, 34–24, and after the game George Allen and Pardee both claimed Landry had used an illegal crack-back block. But this was the usual smoke screen Allen threw up after a defeat; the block was legal. Actually, Redskins wide receiver Charley Taylor had cracked back on Chuck Howley from behind in a much more questionable block.

Allen's accusations were in the papers all week, and during a Cowboy film session during which the players looked at Alworth blocking Pardee, Mike Ditka yelled out "Pardee, you chicken!" Actually, his language was more colorful, which made even Landry laugh. The NFL later outlawed the tactic.

Washington displaced Dallas as the divisional champion, but the Cowboys made the playoffs as a wild-card, heading to San Francisco to play the 49ers, a team they'd twice defeated in NFL championship games in the first round of playoffs. Howley was out, and Bob Lilly, fighting injuries all year, only made token starts and then retired to the bench. Staubach was still rusty after his return and only had about 90 percent strength in his arm. His shoulder bothered him, but he could play if he had to. He played.

⌁∴⌁

AS HE OFTEN DID, Landry asked Billy Zeoli to give the devotional the morning of the 49er game, which was held in Candlestick Park two days prior to Christmas 1972. Zeoli's topic was "Never give up."

Late in the third period, the inconsistencies that had plagued the Cowboys all season surfaced, and the 49ers led, 28–13. It had not been Craig Morton's fault. Hayes had dropped a touchdown pass and Hill had fumbled at the Dallas one, putting San Francisco in position for an easy touchdown.

"I had stuck with Morton because we were beating ourselves," said Landry. "I had just felt we'd start clicking sooner or later. But when the trend continued near the end of the third period, I felt our only chance was to change the mood of the game. Roger has a way of turning things around, so I sent him in, although I knew our chances were extremely slim."

Staubach entered the game with 1:48 remaining in the third period and also had problems. Certainly the game seemed lost as the Cowboys set up at their own forty-five-yard line with 1:53 left.

"Hey, now you guys know how it feels to lose a game like this!" yelled 49er linebacker Dave Wilcox, a veteran of the frustration Dallas had caused the 49ers in the two NFC championship games.

But Staubach got hot against an all-out rush. He hit three passes in a row, and Dallas had a first down at the 49er twenty-yard line. Staubach had been calling his own plays during the two-minute offense, but time-out was called and on the sidelines Landry told him, "The post to Billy Parks will be open. Let's use that."

Landry knew that cornerback Bruce Taylor sometimes hit to the outside, so Parks made his move downfield, then turned back inside and took a twenty-yard touchdown pass to pull Dallas within five, at 28–23, with just 1:10 left. All the 49ers had to do was get the ball and run out the clock.

"Our hopes were very slim," said Landry. "Everybody in the park knew we'd have to try an onside kick. You just don't expect what took place to happen."

Nolan inserted all his receivers and running backs on the front line for the kickoff. They were more used to handling the ball and, unlike linemen, weren't apt to fumble it. Just before he nudged the ball, Toni Fritsch slung his right foot behind his left to kick the ball in a most surprising and unorthodox manner. Still, it rolled the necessary ten yards to wide receiver Preston Riley, who grabbed it. But as he was falling, Cowboy rookie linebacker Ralph Coleman hit him and the ball squirted loose. Mel Renfro recovered at midfield for the Cowboys.

"When this happened," said Landry, "I felt it must be our day. The 49ers knew we had to pass, but they were revolving their defenses to the weakside, and because of the nature of the defense, we knew our wing [flanker Parks] would be open. And, of course, Roger will surprise you at times."

And so he did. On first down, with just 1:03 left to play, Staubach dropped back to pass but didn't even look for a receiver. He took off running and made a nice thirty-yard gain to the twenty-nine-yard line. Then, as Landry had told him, he found the wing, Parks, open for nineteen yards. Parks took the ball and stepped out of bounds at the 49er ten, stopping the clock.

On the sidelines Landry again talked about going to Parks. But as the huddle broke on the field, Ron Sellers, a wide receiver who came in at tight end on passing situations, told Staubach that he would be open on a hook route, a pattern in which he ran straight upfield then turned and came back for the ball. The 49ers made an all-out blitz, and Staubach had no time to look for Parks. He remembered what Sellers had said and threw the ball toward him. Ron turned, the ball arrived, and he caught it for a touchdown. Unbelievably, Dallas had scored two touchdowns in the final 1:10 and beaten the 49ers, 30–28, to move again into the NFC title game, this time against the Redskins, who had defeated Central Division champion Green Bay.

Landry included that game among the Cowboys' five greatest victories. The others were the Super Bowl victories over Miami, 24–3, and Denver, 27–10, the 1975 playoff upset of Los Angeles, 37–7, and the 1979 final game of the regular season victory over the Redskins, 35–34, in which Staubach brought the team from a thirteen-point deficit to victory in the final minutes.

"When we beat the 49ers, it was one of the greatest moments in our history," he said. "I've never seen our team so excited. Larry Cole was turning cartwheels on the sidelines, and everybody was doing crazy things. There was no way we could win. What happened was that they were asleep, waiting for time to run out so they could play the next game."

⌣∴⌣

GENE STALLINGS, Jerry Tubbs, and Ernie Stautner were over at Tom Landry's house going over the defensive plans the night before Landry had planned to announce whether he would start Roger Staubach or Craig Morton against the Redskins.

Everybody was curious, so as he was leaving, Stallings asked Landry. "Coach, have you decided who's going to start?"

"Yes, I have."

"That was it," recalled Stallings. "He didn't say anything else. I guess he'd been burned so much over the years by things getting out to the press that he wasn't even taking any chances with us."

Landry didn't announce his decision until Thursday. Hindsight is a great advantage, but it would seem his decision was a mistake. Staubach had sat out almost the whole season. He had orchestrated the great comeback against the 49ers but was still very rusty. Morton had played all year and was sharp. Perhaps Landry, like everybody else, was caught up in the spectacle of what Staubach had done. Ah, hindsight.

He called Morton and Staubach over after practice and said, "Craig, you've performed well all year and put us into the playoffs. But I've decided to go with Roger, which is certainly no reflection on you.

"The primary reason is that Roger brought us into this game. I saw us put things together in those last few minutes of the 49er game like we haven't all season. I believe we have momentum going now. If what I saw was right, then Roger will continue this trend against the Redskins."

He was wrong. Allen had the Redskins sky-high, at an emotional peak. Landry had planned to beat them with a running game, but the Redskins shut it off. Staubach was off target, Billy Parks, who had been up and down, was confused over the formations, and as Roger later said in a moment of candor, "Billy sometimes was running pass routes in never-never land." The Redskins destroyed Dallas, 26–3, the worst defeat an Allen team had ever handed the Cowboys.

Dallas had made the NFC title game again in spite of all the injuries, but after winning a Super Bowl, even this was considered a disappointment, a failure. During the off-season, there was discontent among the players as well as the coaching staff.

~:~

DANNY REEVES, then only twenty-eight, had done his job but remained upset much of the season. He did not respect Gillman and also badly wanted a head coaching job. When his name was mentioned in regard to an opening at SMU, Landry told him frankly that he didn't think he was ready or mature enough to accept a head coaching position. (Reeves also heard that Landry had expressed this opinion to SMU officials but later found out it wasn't true.)

Reeves was so upset that he quit after the season and went into the construction and real estate business. He was openly critical of Landry, saying that unlike Don Shula and George Allen, Landry was more of a management's coach than a player's coach. "Coach Landry is a genius in football knowledge but never has had the outward personality that makes a person feel close to him."

But Danny's anger would subside, and Landry would rehire him as an assistant in 1974. Danny would move up the ladder and have great input in the offense and, before leaving, aid Landry in calling plays. Landry recommended Danny for head coaching jobs with Atlanta, Los Angeles, and the New York Giants. Reeves turned down the Falcons and lost the L.A. job when George Allen returned as coach, and the Giants picked Ray Perkins over him. Most people felt Danny would replace Landry, but he took the head coaching job in Denver to begin a very successful head coaching career in the NFL. Until Reeves took over the position in Denver in 1981, the only other Landry assistant to become a head coach was Dick Nolan, who went to the 49ers in 1968. There was some criticism at the time that Landry's assistants just weren't noticed that much because he didn't delegate enough authority to them. Certainly Landry was a very dominant figure, even for a head coach, and made the final decisions on almost all aspects of coaching, but in later years he not only delegated authority more often but also gave more credence to what his assistants said.

Ditka said after he'd become head coach of the Bears, "You look at all Tom's assistants around the league who have head jobs and that shows you who should be coach of the year, every year. Tom encouraged discussions and arguments from us over strategy, but when you stood up to defend your side, whether you were on defense, offense, or the kicking team, you better have had the facts and be ready to back them up."

Landry would have more assistants become head coaches in the league than anyone in the 1980s, with Reeves going to Denver, Ditka to Chicago in 1981, John Mackovich at Kansas City in 1985, and Gene Stallings taking over the Cardinals in 1986. Ray Berry, the New England head coach, was also a Landry assistant in 1968 but left after one year. There was some indication that Berry was too strong-willed to work out over a long term on Landry's staff.

"Sometimes," Landry once pointed out, "I think we tend to overplay our organization and not look specifically at the people who contribute. Our overall success is based on good organization, but those who contributed were often overlooked. Sometimes this has certainly been true of our assistant coaches. Maybe people outside used to look at me too much and not at them, but they deserve the credit. I always hated to lose any of them to head jobs but hoped I did. There was never any doubt they were capable."

"The thing about Tom," said Ed Hughes, who replaced Landry at cornerback for the Giants and later was an assistant for the Cowboys in the 1970s, "is that he does dominate an organization because few people know as much about the game as he does. He just dominates an atmosphere.

"You give him ideas and sometimes he'll accept them and sometimes he won't. Once I was teaching something and Landry said it was in the playbook another way. I was a little embarrassed, but he came up to me and said, 'Ed, I'm sorry. I have a bad habit of doing that.'"

"I can remember that sometimes you'd have liked to have had more authority," said Stallings, "but Tom built the team. When things went wrong he's the one who was criticized. He was the one under pressure."

"I used to argue with him about something and he'd listen to my side," said Reeves. "He was never opposed to making changes, such as when he put in the Spread Formation [1975]."

"It's a good learning experience for a young assistant to work under him," said Nolan. "He just knows more football than anybody."

Landry never tried to force his religious feelings on his assistants. But he never tried to hide them either. Red Hickey, a longtime scout for the Cowboys, recalled that when Landry hired him as an assistant coach in 1964 Tom told him, "Red, I want you to know that the main thing in my life is my religion. Then comes my family and then football. That's the way I live. I'm not expecting my coaches to live that way. I don't tell them how to live their lives. But I want them to know how I feel.

"You have an excellent background in the league [as head coach of the San Francisco 49ers], and if you don't like something you see in our playbook, please mention it to me. Depending on how I feel, we will or will not change it."

"I always was a very emotional type guy," said Hickey. "I remember once in practice Bobby Hayes kept missing something and I yelled at him. Tom quietly came up to me and said, 'He'll get it right, Red. Just be patient. He'll get it.'"

Landry sometimes had problems coming to grips with the more lax (at least on the surface) sexual standards of not only his players but also his assistants. One of his younger assistants took a woman friend, whom he later married, on a road trip, where she stayed with him. Landry just mentioned to him that he didn't think he should be doing that until they were married. He did not tell him he couldn't do it, but the hint was enough.

There was never a big turnover of assistants. Jim Myers was with Landry twenty-four years, Jerry Tubbs and Ernie Stautner twenty-two years, Ermal Allen twenty-one years, Stallings thirteen, Nolan (in two tenures, separated by head coaching jobs in San Francisco and New Orleans) eleven, and Reeves and Ditka each eight. Conditioning coach Bob Ward (who came in 1977), trainer Don Cochren (1965), assistant trainer Ken Locker (1973), and equipment manager Buck Buchanan (1973) were with Landry until he was fired.

❧

IN 1973, there was great unrest in the Dallas Cowboys organization and an air of uncertainty that would grow worse and bottom out in 1974, causing fans and critics to say the glory years of the Dallas Cowboys were over. They said Tom Landry's system was antiquated and once again suggested he should be replaced. Of course, the Cowboys' "bad times" were relative; if the team didn't make the Super Bowl, it was considered an "off" year. When the Cowboys failed to make the playoffs in 1974, ending a record of eight straight appearances, the season was considered a total disaster, even though the club had had a winning season. The Cowboys and their fans didn't really know what a poor season was until the late 1980s.

Two of the team's greatest stars, Bob Lilly and Lee Roy Jordan, and its only decent center, Dave Manders, expressed unhappiness over the way the organization dealt financially with the players. They'd heard about the higher salaries George Allen was paying the Redskins, consistently the Cowboys' greatest nemesis in the NFC East. They wanted to be paid accordingly. So in 1973 Jordan, upset and angry, reported to camp but didn't show up for practice before the regular-season opener against Chicago. The club was without a middle linebacker, but he said he wasn't going to play if he didn't get a better contract. Tex Schramm was forced to appease Jordan, and he never really forgave him.

Jordan reported and had an All-Pro season, his best year, but he never made the coveted Ring of Honor while Schramm ran the team. Schramm controlled the picks, which in 1989 included Lilly, Don Meredith, Don Perkins, Chuck Howley, Mel Renfro, and Roger Staubach. Most everybody believed Jordan should have been there too.

Manders retired. Lilly flew to Los Angeles with plans to go to training camp but, angered by the situation, turned around and went back to Dallas. Schramm jumped on a plane and went after him, talking him into returning. It was the only time he'd ever do such a thing.

Craig Morton also walked out of camp over contract problems and didn't come back until a week before the first preseason game to continue his fight with Roger Staubach for the number one quarterback spot. Chuck Howley, George Andrie, Lance Alworth, and Mike Ditka retired, Danny Reeves went into private business, and Sid Gillman, the reason for Danny's unhappiness, left for Houston to run the Oilers organization.

On the positive side, the club had drafted Robert Newhouse and Jean Fugett in 1972 and Billy Joe Dupree, Golden Richards, and Harvey Martin in 1973. It was also in 1973 that a little-known wide receiver from Tulsa would sign as a free agent. That man, Drew Pearson, would be the third-string wide receiver, moving into the starting lineup after Otto Stowe, who had come to the team in a trade for Ron Sellers, suffered a broken foot and Mike Montgomery was injured as well. Once Drew broke into the lineup, he was not replaced again and became an All-Pro and one of the best, if not the best clutch receivers in the team's history. Dallas also traded Billy Parks and Tody

Smith, the abortive number one draft pick in 1971, to Houston for its 1974 number one pick, which would become Ed "Too Tall" Jones. Craig Morton would also force a trade in 1974, and the number one draft pick the Cowboys would get from the New York Giants would be used in 1975 to get Randy White. So, even though Dallas had begun to blow its number one picks, taking Tody Smith in 1971 and Bill Thomas in 1972, it would more than cover its bases by making deals that would bring in future starters such as White and Jones. They had no such luck with the blown choices in the 1980s.

⌣∴⌢

AS THE 1973 SEASON BEGAN, Landry reflected on what had happened the previous year when Dallas had once again been expected to make the Super Bowl and what can happen if not every player had his mind on the same goal.

"Basically, we had the talent and skill to get into the championship last year," he said. "Once you have this, it is only a matter of dedication and persistence to win the Super Bowl. These things we lacked. That's one of the main things about winning the Super Bowl. It's your goal, you struggle for years to reach it, then react in one of two ways. For us, there were a certain number of players who came back just as hard to try to win it again. Others looked at that ring on their finger and thought it was the ultimate.

"That sort of thing takes the edge from their play. They're no longer dedicated and persistent. They turn their interests in other directions. When that happens, you're no longer a Super Bowl team. And last year [1972], that's what I saw take place. . . . Individuals make the difference. Either you're satisfied or you're not. A man must dedicate himself to a goal. He won't be a success in pro football unless he persists toward that goal. If you don't do it, somebody else will, and you'll watch the Super Bowl on television.

"I see a number of players I can go with to win the Super Bowl. But we can't do it with twenty. It takes forty. We had twenty in last year's NFC championship game against Washington. There are players I know will win again. But there are players who haven't proved to me yet that they can help win a Super Bowl. I want to see some evidence, not conversation. I want to see some work being done, some enthusiasm.

"There is a possibility that some people here have achieved their goals in pro football and started looking elsewhere. Then they lose their capability as a contributing force toward winning a Super Bowl.

"Me? I'm always positive. I know we're going to do it again. I know we'll be back in the Super Bowl. If not this year, then the next or the next. That's my goal and my ambition. All my moves are made according to that."

Landry had again said preseason would determine whether Craig Morton or Roger Staubach would start. Staubach had led the team to the championship in 1971, and Morton had done a good job after Staubach's injury in 1972. This time, Landry reasoned, the question would be settled once and for all. Landry likely preferred Staubach as his quarterback by that time, but he wanted to make sure Morton had an equal chance to win the job.

Staubach finished preseason with an edge in statistics, but Morton came on strong in the final exhibition game against Miami. Some broadcasters had mistakenly said Craig had won the job.

Landry met with Roger and went over the positive and negative points he felt Staubach possessed, and then he asked him how he felt about the situation.

"Coach, I've given this all a lot of thought," said Staubach. "I think you need to make a decision and stick by it. If you aren't going to start me, I want to be traded. If I have any choice in that matter, I'd prefer you trade me to Atlanta."

"You're going to be the starter," said Landry.

Landry asked Morton to come to his house that same evening and, as he had with Staubach, went over what he felt were the positives and negatives. He told Morton he appreciated what he had done but that he was going with Staubach. For the first time, Morton said, "I want to be traded." His wish would be granted by midseason 1974.

For the second time, Staubach would lead the NFL in passing in 1973, and Calvin Hill would rush for 1,142 yards, a 4.2 average, and become the team's leading receiver. D. D. Lewis would do well as Howley's replacement, but a key factor in Dallas's game was Manders's return at center. The snapping duties had become somewhat of a Keystone Kops situation, perhaps being illustrated by a particular snap that went over not only the holder but also the kicker. Staubach even went to Schramm to try to get him to sign Manders. Clint Murchison, never one to pass up a joke, phoned Dave and asked him if he'd hide inside a giant box, all wrapped up, as a birthday present for the owner.

Landry, who when asked about the club's center problems had taken a deep breath and said, "I live in crisis," was at the birthday party and laughed like everybody else when Manders popped out of the box. "I thought you'd retired," he said. Dave returned after the first regular-season game.

As usual during George Allen's tenure in the nation's capital, Dallas and Washington, which had lost 14–7 to Miami in Super Bowl VII, would be in a dogfight for the NFC Eastern title. Allen was everything in his quest to beat the Cowboys; he was the gremlin, the protagonist, the thorn.

CHAPTER 17
The Mid-1970s

∽:∾

I saw him [Landry] as disciplined, self-controlled, and with enormous religious conviction that very few players understood. I suspect that anyone who ever played for Coach Landry will attest that they picked up some of his traits . . . straight-forward, consistent, and disciplined.

—BILLY JOE DUPREE
Cowboy Tight End, 1973–1983

THE WASHINGTON REDSKINS and the Dallas Cowboys were the antithesis of each other. Whereas Dallas built through the draft and signing free agents, Allen traded away all his draft choices for older, proven veterans. "The future is now," he'd say. When he left a team, as he did Los Angeles in 1970 and Washington in 1977, its stock was depleted. Draft choices were gone, and the older guys he'd brought in were over the hill. But he would win while he was there.

Allen left the depleted Redskins and returned to the Rams in 1978. Rams owner Carroll Rosenbloom fired him after two preseason games. When Landry was fired in 1989, Allen sent him a telegram:

"Dear Tom, don't feel bad. It may be the best thing that ever happened to you. I once knew a guy who got bounced after two preseason games and that guy never had a losing season and won over 70 percent of his games. So work out, stay in shape and have a good time. — George."

When Allen's Redskins played the Cowboys, the respected Pulitzer Prize–winning *Washington Post* would have the game as its lead story, with headlines so big they appeared to have been reserved for World War III.

"There was always electricity in the air," said Allen. "Competing against Tom's teams was the reason for our existence. We did everything we could to fuel the rivalry. I encouraged the crowd at RFK Stadium to give us standing ovations for big plays. We tried to challenge Staubach and say things that might throw him off his game. It was the nation's rivalry. Everybody was into it, the fans, the networks, everybody.

"When I first got to Washington and called the squad together, before I ever issued uniforms, I told them, 'We've got to beat Dallas. If we can't beat Dallas, there's no need to issue the equipment.'"

Allen and Landry had once been much closer as friends, but when George was coaching in Los Angeles the first time, the Cowboys found he had people spying on their practices. Club officials traced license plates on rental cars, etc., and had Allen dead to rights. When asked about this, he said he'd also seen Cowboy scout Bucko Kilroy in a tree outside the Rams' practice field. He didn't know Kilroy weighed well over three hundred pounds at that time.

Landry always appeared, at least publicly, not to be overly excited about the game. But his players said he started using the Redskins as a frame of reference as early as training camp. He'd also caution players to watch what they said prior to the Redskins games, knowing the quotes would end up on Allen's bulletin board. Dallas didn't use opponents' quotes on bulletin boards, except before the Redskins games.

After his dismissal, Landry was invited to Washington, D.C., to be inducted into the prestigious Washington Touchdown Club's Hall of Fame, joining members such as U.S. Supreme Court Justice Byron White, Red Grange, and Johnny Unitas.

"I think Tom is one of the greatest coaches of all time," said Allen.

"We had the best rivalry in football," said Landry. "But it lost some of its luster after George left." He paused, smiled, and added, "It was easy to hate George."

The plaque Landry received read: "We cherished the victories, downplayed the defeats, but we always admired the Cowboy coach for his pursuit of excellence and uncommon grace, both on and off the field."

◦⦂◦

DALLAS WAS 7–4 IN 1973, having lost a key 14–7 game to the Redskins in Washington after actually outplaying them and a 14–7 decision to Miami. So Landry called Staubach into his office. He knew Roger was troubled about his mother, who was slowly dying of cancer.

He had allowed Roger to call his own plays but told him that day, "Your play-calling has been good, but we haven't won the close games and seem to be missing some big plays. So I've decided to call the plays again. We'll shuttle our tight ends, Billy Joe DuPree and Jean Fugett."

When the press questioned him about the decisions, Landry said, "In no way do I mean to imply Roger isn't capable of calling the plays. He's as capable of doing it as anybody in the league and has done a good job. I just feel if we pool all our resources we'll be better off. I think my calling the plays is the best way for us to go."

Landry called plays for the remainder of his coaching career. When Landry was with the New York Giants, he had seen Paul Brown use the system in Cleveland. Landry came under criticism from fans and quarterbacks and coaches around the league. Today it would be a rare exception for a quarterback to call his own plays.

"I didn't think it had anything to do with me," said Staubach. "He just liked to do it. Sometimes we would have our differences. One time I told him it was ridiculous when he called a play-action pass [a fake run] on a second and eleven when everybody knew we were going to pass. If I'd called the plays, I would have passed more on first down and probably thrown long more."

An FCA fund-raising dinner once included a mock football game in which Landry coached one side and Staubach the other. As money was pledged for each side, a football would be moved closer to the goal for contributions. Staubach's side was twenty-five thousand dollars short of the goal, and Roger said, "If Coach Landry will let me call the plays, I'll cover the twenty-five thousand dollars we need myself." Landry just smiled, but after the dinner he said, "I've never been so tempted, Roger."

As Dallas prepared to host Washington in the next-to-last regular-season game, one that likely would decide the NFC Eastern title, Landry, who wasn't above a misnomer, was talking about the aggressiveness of Redskins cornerback Pat Fischer. "Now," Landry told the team, "when he starts his carousement . . ." He paused, seemed puzzled, and said, "Where did I get *carousement?*" Somebody said, "You mean *harassment*, Coach." And Landry continued, "When he starts his harassment . . ."

Dallas crushed the Redskins, 27–7. Staubach's mother died prior to the final regular-season game against St. Louis. At Roger's request, Landry did not mention what he was going through. He had an excellent game as Dallas beat the Cardinals, 30–3, to win the East, and

Dallas then took the Rams, 27–17, in the first round of the playoffs, the key being an eighty-three-yard pass from Staubach to Drew Pearson. But Dallas lost Hill to a badly dislocated elbow, and playing without him and with Garrison trying to operate with a broken clavicle, Dallas lost to Minnesota, 27–10, in the NFC title game. Viking coach Bud Grant said he believed the Cowboys were just too battle-weary, having played so many "must" games against Washington for the division title. Once again, Dallas had missed the Super Bowl by a single step.

✥

DURING A VISIT with Tex Schramm the day after the game, Schramm stared out the window as he said, "You know, after we beat Los Angeles in the first round of the playoffs, the Rams left Dallas feeling bad. But they had come a long way to get to the playoffs, and I bet by the time they got to L.A. they'd started talking about what a fine season they'd had. It's not that way for us. We've won the Super Bowl. So when you fail to do so again there's a great disappointment. It lingers."

Down the hall Landry sat behind his desk. He had been very disappointed but smiled cordially and said, "I was just sitting here trying to analyze what happened to us. I'd hoped we'd play better. The biggest disappointment is that we didn't play a better game.

"But I was thinking that this has been an excellent year for us. We had all the problems going into camp, but the players did such a great job and played so well down the stretch. It's just a shame that it had to end for them this way. People tend to remember the way something ended, not what happened before."

Asked if he were about ready to leave the office, Landry said, "No, I'm going to sit here for a while." He seemed so very alone, but watching him, one was reminded that he was the pillar of the Cowboy organization at such times.

✥

THE SEASON OF 1974 was never in focus. Tom Landry was concerned about the age of his team because Bob Lilly was thirty-five, Cornell Green thirty-four, and Lee Roy Jordan thirty-three, and before the season ended, Mel Renfro would be thirty-four and Dave Edwards thirty-five. But Landry believed they could all play well for at least another year and Dallas might, just might, make it to the Super Bowl again. However, his best-laid plans went up in smoke due to circumstances beyond his control. First, the World Football League swept through the NFL, raiding teams and signing players. Then the differences between the NFL Management Council and the NFL Players Association became so heated that the entire preseason was threatened, and threatened to get worse.

At first, nobody took the WFL seriously, but with money and sleight of hand the fledgling league signed Larry Csonka, Jim Kiick, and Paul Warfield of the World Champion Miami Dolphins and, to future contracts, Calvin Hill, Craig Morton, Otto Stowe, Pat Toomay, Mike Montgomery, Jethro Pugh, Rayfield Wright, D. D. Lewis, and Danny White. It became obvious the WFL was concentrating on the NFL's strongest teams. Some players, such as Hill, had one year remaining on their contracts and others two. Thus was created the "Lame Duck" player, a term that Landry didn't like but had to admit was appropriate.

The way it turned out, only Hill and White would have their contracts honored by the WFL, but the disruption and distraction of the signings were evident. When Hill phoned Landry to tell him that he was considering joining the WFL, they discussed the situation, and initial indications were that Calvin would consider both sides. However, it was later learned that before Hill phoned Landry *Sports Illustrated* had already shot a possible cover featuring Calvin posed in a WFL uniform.

Those who signed with the WFL claimed that, as professionals, they would play just as hard during their "Lame Duck" seasons as they normally would have, and most of their teammates seemed to think they did. Landry did not.

"When they signed with the WFL, it created an almost impossible situation from my standpoint," he said. "As a team sport, we must have a joint effort in a championship drive. There can be no doubts about any player putting out everything he has. Every player must be rewarded if we win, or suffer if we lose. I just don't believe the players who signed future contracts will suffer if we lose. They'll be rewarded regardless."

Landry, of course, came up in a generation of football players who had great loyalty to their teams, and for a time it was difficult for him to relate to a player who would go elsewhere for more money. But in later years he began to better understand that security for one's self and family can supersede loyalty to a team.

Although he diplomatically remained neutral over the NFLPA-NFLMC problems, he grew impatient with the players who agreed to strike. He was too fair a man to hold it against them, but again, it was something those in his generation would not have thought about doing. The NFLPA was good to the extent that it certainly gained the players better benefits, but difficult in that it unleashed some militant elements who sought to become the all-powerful dragon they were trying to strike down.

In 1974 players boycotted training camps and wore T-shirts that said, "No Freedom, No Football," and showed the figure of a clenched fist, the sign of revolution. Indeed, for a while, there was no football. The College All-Star game was canceled. Veteran players finally reported to camp and the strike ended August 14, but the veterans had reported late and rookies had to play the early preseason games.

Landry's patience was running thin by the time the veterans got to camp. So he not only extended the length of camp but for a while also instituted, in effect, three-a-day workouts. He had players up before breakfast, running the trail leading up the mountain behind the practice field. The veterans were calling it the "Ho Chi Minh Trail." Then there would be midmorning and midafternoon practices. The players continually complained of fatigue as Landry kept training camp open for eight weeks, trying to get the veterans through two full-scale weeks of workouts despite the strike and the fact that they were already playing preseason games.

The strange case of Otto Stowe emerged. He had been great until he broke his leg at midseason in 1973. But he didn't seem to care much in camp. He had signed with the WFL and was not really trying to get into condition, claiming his foot was still sore. Doctors told Landry that Stowe could and should work. He became moody and participated little in practice, but the days of a Duane Thomas were over.

"He doesn't seem happy any place," said Landry. "He won't be happy in the WFL. When we traded Miami for him he wasn't happy in Miami. He said that was because he wasn't starting for the Dolphins. He was starting for us, and now he isn't happy because he's not making enough money here." Stowe was dropped from the roster and never played in the WFL, or anywhere else.

Staubach had worried about his arm and shoulder going into the 1973 season, but the soreness had finally subsided and he was able to throw normally again. But he had undergone foot surgery during the off-season and suffered cracked ribs in early preseason. He never really felt right during the year, and Dallas kept losing close games much as they would in Landry's final season of 1988, games that could have gone either way. For instance, leading the Vikings 21–20 with time running out, Harvey Martin tackled Fran Tarkenton, who fumbled to Dallas. An official ruled Tarkenton was down and there was no fumble. Films showed otherwise. Minnesota kept the ball and Fred Cox kicked a twenty-one-yard field goal to win the game, 24–21. The field goal appeared to go wide right, and even Landry questioned it. But he said, "If we had been playing as we should have, we wouldn't be in a position where a call by an official settles the outcome of a game."

Landry, like the entire team, became terribly frustrated with the continual plague of narrow losses. Once on the sidelines when a call went against Dallas, Landry yelled at an official, "Damnit, watch the play! DAMNIT!" Then he paused, thought about the situation for a minute, and turned to Danny Reeves. "Did I say what I thought I said?" he asked. Told that, indeed, he had, Landry sighed and started watching the game again.

"That," said Lee Roy Jordan, "is about the extent of Tom's profanity. But, listen, he gets as upset and excited as the rest of us. He's just not as verbal. You can look at him and see agony or joy on his face, if you know how to read him. If we thought he was throwing tantrums and screaming, we might lose control ourselves. He projects confidence, poise, and composure to us. It doesn't bother us that he's not always yelling or patting somebody on the back."

Just before the halfway mark in the season, Morton demanded to be traded, and a young, free-spirited rookie from Abilene Christian College named Clint Longley became Staubach's backup. When Dallas hosted the Redskins on Thanksgiving Day, it had a 6–5 record, and Allen and his key spokesman, Diron Talbert, were taunting Staubach, telling the press that Roger might get hurt if he ran out of the pocket and that Dallas didn't have any help behind him. Sure enough, Staubach was hit and suffered a concussion and had to leave the game with the Cowboys trailing, 16–3. Longley had not played a down in regular season, but he had to go in. There was nobody else.

"The plays we set up against Washington were good, sound plays," said Landry. "But there was a great deal of tension among our regulars, and Roger was not sharp. He wasn't seeing the plays. When Clint went in, he wasn't even concerned about keying the defense. All he was doing was fading and hitting a receiver he saw open. It just so happened that Washington was in a prevent defense a lot of the time and keying wasn't that important. If the Redskins had played all types of defenses, Clint would have had to key, and this would have been difficult for him."

Longley's performance was called by Blaine Nye "a victory for the uncluttered mind." He was magnificent, passing the Redskins silly. But his performance seemed to have fallen short as Dallas set up at midfield, trailing 23–17 and facing second and ten with thirty-five seconds left in the game and no time-outs. George Allen had employed his Nickel Defense in which an extra back, Ken Stone, replaced a linebacker, Harold McLinton. Teams had completed only about 20 percent of their passes against this particular defense, which had five defensive backs. Nobody in memory had gotten beyond it.

Unknown to Landry, Pearson was working a little strategy of his own with Longley. "I'm going to fake inside and then go deep," Pearson told Longley. Landry recalled, "Drew obviously had felt he could start in and the inside guy would be waiting. Then he felt he might turn back and go deep when the back switched back on him. What happened was just amazing."

Pearson faked inside and cut back deep. Ken Stone took the fake and let Drew get behind him, and the Cowboy receiver then got into a footrace with Stone and Mike Bass for the goal line. Longley hung the ball out there, and, in a final burst of speed, Drew caught the ball behind the two defenders for a touchdown. Dallas had won, 24–23.

"There was no way we could complete that pass, but we did," said Landry. "Nobody on our team could believe what happened, and the shock of winning was tremendous. It was definitely the highlight of our season."

Longley, a free spirit who liked fast cars and boats and had a hobby of wearing twin six-shooters and hunting rattlesnakes, was the backup again in 1975, although in order for him to have that job Landry cut Jim Zorn, who would go on to Seattle and become a star. Most people felt Landry kept Longley because of what he'd seen him do in that single game against the Redskins. Landry had considered keeping Zorn and Longley but let Zorn go so he could add Preston Pearson to the roster.

Danny White joined the club in 1976 after the WFL folded. White caught onto the system quickly and was battling for the number two quarterback spot when Longley's attitude seemed to change. Longley withdrew from his teammates and would sometimes mutter insults about other players, especially Staubach, behind their backs. Roger talked to him but got nowhere. During a passing drill in training camp, Drew Pearson failed to make a catch on a Longley pass and Clint called him a name. Staubach challenged him, they exchanged words, and they agreed to meet and settle the issue after practice. Longley threw a glancing punch and Staubach was all over him and had him on the ground, with the option of pounding away, when Danny Reeves broke up the fight. Landry told them in no uncertain terms that any recurrence would cost them more money than anybody had ever been fined before.

Longley was simmering over newspaper accounts that Staubach had bested him. The next day he waited in the locker room as Staubach came in and started to dress for practice. Just as Staubach had his arms up to put on his shoulder pads, Longley smashed him in the head, sending him falling against a weight scale and causing him to cut his face. Staubach was trying to come out of the daze and to get his pads off, but Longley was coming after him. Randy White, then a rookie, grabbed Longley and held him.

Staubach later said that he was ashamed but that after he was treated in the hospital, he came back to the dorm looking for Longley. But Clint had talked Allen Stone, a Dallas radio man, into taking him to the airport. He was gone. Landry traded him to San Diego, where he played for a while but did little, and soon he was out of the league.

So 1974 was a dismal season, one in which Dallas finished 8–6 and failed to make the playoffs for the first time since 1965. And it was a season in which Clint Longley would have his one great shining moment in pro football.

~:~

PEOPLE WERE TALKING ABOUT THE DEMISE of the Dallas Cowboys, something that had happened to other great teams, such as the New York Giants, the Green Bay Packers, and the Baltimore Colts. Landry was faced with crucial retirements and the defection of Calvin Hill to the WFL, and yet he seemed more relaxed and was talking more than ever and even joking around. He was excited because of the great challenge of reshaping the Cowboys in 1975, and Landry was usually at his best when faced with a big challenge because he became more innovative and, perhaps, tapped the workings of his mind more than he would otherwise.

"When he's faced with a big challenge, then you really see his great competitive spirit come out," observed former defensive lineman Larry Cole. "It's interesting to see the fighter in him emerge. He's smiling more, mainly having more fun in a competitive way. He loves it."

Before the 1975 season began, John Niland, an All-Pro guard during the Super Bowl years who had not played as well in 1974, asked Tom and Alicia over for dinner.

"When he accepted I was shocked," said Niland. "But then I got to thinking that Tom probably was receptive to such things, but none of the players ever thought to ask him. My wife liked to be innovative for such occasions, so she decided to have Chinese food, decorations, and even use chopsticks to eat.

"I can still see Tom sitting at the end of the table trying to eat with chopsticks."

Landry would try to hold the food with the chopsticks, and then it would drop back onto his plate before he could get it to his mouth. But he kept trying to get the knack of it. Here was an extremely intelligent man, an intellect, but he couldn't solve the mystery of the chopsticks and finally asked for a fork.

Before the 1975 season began, Landry asked Niland to come to his office. "John," said Landry, "these things are extremely difficult to do, but . . . we've traded you to Philadelphia."

"Coach, listen, I fully understand," said Niland. They talked for a while, and as John started to leave he said, "You really didn't like that meal, did you?" Landry seemed puzzled at first, and then they both laughed. "I really respect and love that guy," said Niland.

During training camp Landry also traded Bobby Hayes to San Francisco. Hayes was in the twilight of his career and had lost his starting job in 1974 to Golden Richards. However, during the off-season Landry had said he felt Bobby could have one more surge. Bobby left the Cowboys feeling he'd been treated unfairly by Landry. He played for Dick Nolan in San Francisco for a while but early in the season was placed on waivers and not claimed. In 1979 when Hayes went to trial and pleaded guilty to selling drugs, Landry came to court as a character witness. He said Bobby was a fine man but was easily misled and he hoped the court would be lenient on him.

"When Bob Hayes came into the league, he changed defenses," recalled Landry. "His speed and ability to get deep against the man-to-man coverages they played in those days caused the defenses to start using zones. I think if any one man did that, it was the Bullet. He was fantastic."

Walt Garrison tore up a knee bulldogging during the off-season and decided to retire. Cornell Green went through part of camp and then ended his career and joined the club's scouting department. Charlie Waters became the starting strong safety, a much more natural position for him, and was an immediate success, becoming one of the very best at the position in the NFL.

But the most significant retirement was that of Bob Lilly, the brightest of the Dallas Cowboys stars. Landry called Lilly a player who comes along once in a coach's career and the best defensive tackle he'd ever seen play the game.

Lee Roy Jordan recalled how Landry always seemed to have praise for Lilly during the Monday film sessions, which most of the players feared. Landry had been known to embarrass players during such sessions.

"It was always like Tom really got psyched up for the film sessions," said Jordan. "But, man, you'd sit there and it would be Lilly-this and Lilly-that, what a great play Bob had made here and another one there. Bob, of course, was a great player, but sometimes you wanted to say, 'Hey, we were out there too.'"

"That Lilly," recalled Dave Manders, "he always sat right next to the projector, which was buzzing right along. After we'd played an awful game, Tom would be pretty critical of us and Lilly would just talk right back to him. I thought, this really is Lilly's team. Then one time it occurred to all of us that, because Lilly was sitting next to the projector, Tom couldn't hear a word he said."

"There have been some really great people on this team," Landry once reflected. "For instance, Bob Lilly. What a great guy. I think I'd really have liked to have gotten closer to Lilly, become friends, but sometimes you just can't do that when you're a coach."

"Tom Landry," said Lilly at that time, "is a fine man, a very high-caliber person, and he did an awful lot for me. But I don't think anyone really knows him personally, except his family. We respect him an awful lot but don't really know him. Tom is a very complex person. He doesn't mince a lot of words.

"I just know he's a fine person. We've talked a few times, but basically it's been about business. There hasn't been a lot of association outside of football. He has been concerned when things have happened to me down the line. So I know he's very concerned about individuals on the team and their children."

For the first time in ten years, nobody really expected the Dallas Cowboys to be a championship contender in 1975. As Landry said, "The pressure's off. Nobody will be picking us to do anything. They'll be talking about how we're on the way down. A lot of negative things will be said. They'll say we're leveling off, that other top teams before us went down and now so will we. We'll just have to fight to prove we're not going down, and I'm personally very excited about the reshaping of this football team."

Landry had a new toy. He had given a great deal of thought to ways to combat the popular new trend in pass defenses, used by Dallas and others, in which one or two extra backs enter the game, replacing linebackers or linemen on obvious passing situations. The extra backs made defenses more difficult to read. Landry was also concerned with the fact that Roger Staubach had been trapped ninety times in the past two seasons. Landry did not come up with something new . . . he came up with something old, the Spread formation, called by many the Shotgun.

Landry reasoned that when you face a second and long, a third and long, your opponents know you are going to pass, so why not just go ahead and line up in a passing formation, such as the Spread? By lining up five yards back of the center, Staubach would have more time to see what was happening, to read the pass coverages. The formation also spread out the defenses because of the positions of the receivers.

Landry had used the formation briefly in the early years, but Meredith wasn't comfortable with it. Red Hickey had employed both the Spread, more of a passing formation, and the Shotgun, more of a running formation, when he was head coach of the San Francisco 49ers in 1960.

There were a number of chuckles around the league when Dallas unveiled the formation as part of its offensive arsenal in preseason, but the formation was to leave the people who were laughing behind.

Dallas needed more than a new formation. With retirements and defections, the Cowboys were a team with tired blood. The draft looked good, but even Landry had no idea then just how good it would be or the effect the newcomers would have on the team. Dallas had fine drafts before, but the 1975 group was the best in the club's history and one of the best ever in the league. Landry was never happier than with the group that came to training camp that year. They were Landry's kind of football players. Often during camp he would remark that they were the hardest-hitting bunch he'd had.

An unbelievable number of rookies, twelve, made the team and would be called the "Dirty Dozen." It wasn't just their physical presence that helped the club, but also the new spirit they brought. They were Randy White, Thomas Henderson, Burton Lawless, Bob Breunig, Pat Donovan, Randy Hughes, Kyle Davis, Rolly Woolsey, Mike Hegman, Mitch Hoopes, Herb Scott, and Scott Laidlaw. Hoopes became the club's punter. Lawless was the only other rookie who became an immediate starter, moving in to replace John Niland. But some of them were used on obvious passing situations, and they added a new dimension to specialty-team play.

Experts say it takes four or five years to really make a judgment on a draft, but in 1975 the dividends were immediate. Using the accepted yardstick, the rookies measured up: White, Henderson, Lawless, Breunig, Donovan, and Scott would become starters; Laidlaw, Hegman, and Hughes would also start at times.

As said earlier, Randy White, who would one day be in the NFL Hall of Fame, was frightened of Landry in his early years with the team. White recalled, "I was scared to death of Coach Landry. Hey, I studied that middle linebacker spot like crazy before he moved me to defensive tackle. I memorized everything and knew it all perfectly. Then I'd go into a meeting and he'd ask me a question. I knew the darn answer and would try to tell him, but I was so nervous it just wouldn't come out. I'd grab the sides of my chair, grind my teeth, and nothing would come out.

"I'd get so mad at myself and could just imagine him saying, 'Here's our number one draft choice and the guy is so dumb he can't even talk.'"

"The draft we had in 1975 helped point our team in the right direction again," said Landry. "I'm not sure what would have happened without it, but we'd have had a lot of problems."

But Landry knew he needed another running back. Of course none was available, but then strange circumstances took place. As preseason ended, Pittsburgh cut nine-year veteran Preston Pearson. Nobody claimed Pearson when he was cut except Dallas. Nobody wanted him except Dallas. So the Cowboys picked him up, and he became the final missing link for the surprise team, the Cinderella team of 1975.

Landry used Preston beautifully. He wasn't a big running back, a guy you could give the ball to twenty times. But he was a good route runner, an excellent receiver, and superb on screens when he was out of the congestion of tacklers and had room to weave and maneuver. What Landry would do was run him nine or ten times a game, insert Doug Dennison for short-yardage plays, and utilize fullback Robert Newhouse as the key down-to-down runner.

"The man [Landry] used me perfectly, let me do the things I do best," said Preston. "I'm best in one-on-one situations, where I can beat one man at a time, and that's the situation he tried to get me in. Nobody has ever utilized the things I do best as Coach Landry did."

"Tom did his best job of coaching that year," said Lee Roy Jordan. "We had a great, exciting feeling on the team and a lot of enthusiasm."

People downgraded the formation, but by the end of the season the third-down success rate of the Spread was 44.5 percent compared to the usual success rate on third downs of 33 percent.

Landry knew if Dallas could split its first two games he'd be happy. So after it beat L.A., he just didn't believe the team could handle the Cardinals. For the Cowboys to have a chance, they'd have to outscore St. Louis, because nobody could stop Jim Hart, Mel Gray, Terry Metcalf, and Co. from putting up points. With Staubach passing for 307 yards and three touchdowns, Dallas did outscore the Cardinals, posting a 37–31 overtime victory.

"When we upset Los Angeles and St. Louis," said Landry, "we gained the momentum necessary to catapult us the rest of the season. None of us dared think about making the Super Bowl at that time, but we were just concentrating on having a better season than we'd had in 1974."

But with Staubach at his best and Landry finding success on everything from fullback passes, featuring Robert Newhouse, to reverses on kickoffs, starring Thomas Henderson, the Cowboys posted a 10–4 record to finish a single game behind the Cardinals in the NFC East and gain the wild-card spot in the playoffs.

AS THE WILD-CARD TEAM, Dallas couldn't be at home during the play-offs, so in the first round it traveled to Bloomington to play the defending NFC champions, the Minnesota Vikings.

Landry had confidence the team could play with anybody. "It kept surprising me, and then, finally, the things that happened were no surprise," he said. Dallas actually outplayed the Vikings but trailed 14–10 as Minnesota got one gimme touchdown when a Viking punt touched a Cowboy blocker and was recovered at the Dallas four.

The crowd, like that in the 1972 San Francisco playoff game, began to go to the exits, holding up their hands and signifying the Vikings were number one. The Cowboys set up deep in their own territory in the final minute but seemed stopped when they faced a fourth and sixteen from their own twenty-five with forty-four seconds left. Staubach threw for the sidelines, and Drew Pearson, the club's great clutch receiver, made a fine catch, stepping out of bounds at the fifty. Two plays later the Cowboys were still at the fifty with twenty-four seconds left, perhaps time for one more play, maybe two.

From the Spread, Staubach faded, waited as long as he could, and then arched a long pass toward Pearson, speeding down the sidelines step-to-step with cornerback Nate Wright. As the ball came down, Pearson and Wright both slowed down to wait, but somehow, miraculously, Pearson maneuvered and caught the ball just off his hip around the five-yard line as Wright fell. Drew then lunged into the end zone. The Cowboys, who had been beaten, won 17–14. After the game, Staubach was asked what happened and he said, "I threw it as far as I could and said a Hail Mary." That pass became known as a "Hail Mary," a term still used today on last-second desperation passes.

"It was amazing, unbelievable," said Landry. "I can't believe the ball stuck on Drew's hip like that. It was a thousand-to-one shot, but I tell you, I'll take it. The game was out of my hands. Roger called the play, and he and Drew executed it."

Los Angeles and Minnesota had the best regular-season records in the NFC, 12–2, and most had conceded they would meet for the conference title in Bloomington. The Rams crushed St. Louis 35–23 in the divisional playoff and had expected to watch the Vikings beat Dallas on television the next day.

"Psychologically, our victory over Minnesota worked against the Rams," explained Landry. "They had expected to have to go north to Minnesota for the championship game. They were more concerned over playing Minnesota than they were over having to play us. The Ram players had written off our regular-season victory over them as a fluke. I'm sure Chuck Knox tried to tell them we had a pretty good football team, but the Rams already were talking about playing in the Super Bowl."

That season, Los Angeles had allowed just 135 points, the second lowest in a fourteen-game schedule in NFL history. Quarterback Jimmy Harris had been injured, but Ron Jaworski had moved in and led the team to a victory over the Pittsburgh Steelers. Some of the Ram players talked about how they'd beaten Pittsburgh once and they could do it again, if the Steelers went on to win the AFC. They had not calculated the team Dallas had become, or the effectiveness of what L.A. linebacker Isaiah Robertson had called Landry's "rinky-dink" Spread formation.

~:~

ON A FINE SUNNY DAY in the Los Angeles Coliseum, a standing-room-only crowd of 84,483 watched the Cowboys totally fool and dismantle the Rams. Landry had geared his Flex Defense to stop Lawrence McCutcheon, and it was never more effective, holding the fine Ram running back to 10 yards on eleven carries and the entire Ram offensive to a net 118 yards.

Meanwhile, Roger Staubach and Preston Pearson, the halfback nobody wanted, were going wild. Before the afternoon ended, Staubach would complete sixteen of twenty-six passes for 220 yards and four touchdowns, three of which would be caught by Pearson. Dallas took a 21–0 halftime lead with Pearson making a tremendous, diving stab on his fingertips from eighteen yards out for the first score.

As the second half began, the Rams felt they still had a chance. Dallas moved to a third and nine at the L.A. nineteen in the third period, and Landry called for the old shuttle pass out of the Spread. Only this time, he decided to run it to the weakside, taking advantage of end Fred Dryer's aggressive pass rush and linebacker Isaiah Robertson's great pride in pass coverage. The play moved from the drawing board to the field without a hitch. Staubach took the snap and started to his left. Dryer shot in after him, and Robertson chased a back coming out of the backfield on a deep route. Suddenly, Preston, lined up far to the right, came galloping across field behind the line of scrimmage. Staubach just tossed him a basketball-like pass, and Preston went right up the alley, vacated by Dryer and Robertson, and scored. If the game had not been over already, it was then, as Dallas won 37–7 to move into Super Bowl X in Miami. The clock had never struck midnight for what they were calling Landry's Cinderella team. It had become the first wild-card club ever to win a conference championship and advance to the Super Bowl.

"I had thought," admitted Landry, "the final score might be in the 13–7 area, but everything we tried worked."

⌣∴⌣

THE PITTSBURGH STEELERS had won Super Bowl IX over Minnesota, 16–6, to give Art Rooney, one of the great old men of the NFL, his first championship ever. In Super Bowl X on January 18, 1976, against Dallas, the Steelers were favored to join Green Bay and Miami as two-time Super Bowl champs. The strengths of the team were a tremendous defense featuring a front four of Joe Greene, Ernie Holmes, Dwight White, and L. C. Greenwood, a hard-hitting secondary led by Mel Blount, and an offense featuring Terry Bradshaw, Franco Harris, and Lynn Swann.

Landry knew he could not match the Steelers, so he again planned to open things up and try to catch them by surprise. The thing he did not expect was that the Steelers would be able to rough up his receivers without receiving a single penalty. There is no doubt Pittsburgh was better than Dallas, but it was unbelievable that the Steelers, the most penalized team in the NFL, could go through the entire Super Bowl game without being penalized a single time.

On the opening kickoff, Dallas tried a reverse to Thomas Henderson, who almost broke all the way and, even though he was stopped, set up a twenty-nine-yard scoring pass from Staubach to Drew Pearson. Dallas held the lead until the final period, but the Cowboy receivers, Golden Richards and Drew Pearson, both on the small side, were being bounced around by the Steelers. Richards was finally knocked out of the game with broken ribs after taking an elbow. Lynn Swann was killing Dallas by making fine catches with Mark

Washington draped all over him. One catch set up a Steeler touch-down, but Dallas still led 10–7 in the final period when Mitch Hoopes went into his own end zone to punt. Veteran Dave Edwards failed to pick up Reggie Harrison, who blocked the punt out of the end zone for a safety. Pittsburgh, with good field position, scored a field goal after Hoopes's free kick from the twenty, giving the Steelers a 12–10 lead. Roy Gerela hit another field goal, making it 15–10, and then Bradshaw and Swann combined on a tremendous play to put the game away despite a furious finish by the Cowboys, who never quit.

With third down from its own thirty-six, Dallas had a blitz on. As Bradshaw faded, linebacker D. D. Lewis went in too high and missed him, allowing him to arch a long pass down the middle of the field. Swann went up, took the ball from Washington at the five, and scored with 2:54 remaining. Staubach took Dallas eighty yards to bring the count to 21–17, but his final desperation pass for Drew Pearson in the end zone was intercepted as time ran out. The Cowboy magic had ended.

"We didn't play a bad football game," Landry said after watching game films. "The fact that Pittsburgh didn't get any penalties was very unusual. It also looked like some of our receivers were being held and couldn't get downfield. But we played well. We were a team.

"Had we known the way the game would be called [the tactics allowed by defensive backs], we might have been more ready for it. But still, we had our chances and we lost to a great team."

Staubach didn't lead the NFL in passing, finishing second in the NFC to Fran Tarkenton, but Landry said, "Nobody in the league did more for his team than Roger."

"At that time, that season was the most satisfying I'd had as a coach," Landry added. "It was exciting in 1966 when we became a top team for the first time. But in 1975 we had one of the best groups I've ever coached as far as character, morale, spirit, and teamwork. They were the type people who give you your greatest reward in coaching, who really made it enjoyable."

He said the only team he might have enjoyed coaching even more was the 1985 club. "It did more with less as far as achieving the Eastern Division title," he said. "It probably did more than the 1975 team, really, because that club had some quality. We had a lot of rookies, but we also had Roger Staubach. . . . They're still trying to figure out how we beat out Washington and New York for the championship. I think that's the best achievement we ever had with a team."

But what happened with the 1975 group ranked close. With the new formation and the new players, it was the most exciting year for the team, and it proved that the much talked-about demise of the Cowboys was just a mirage. The Cowboys were back.

CHAPTER 18
America's Team

᳁

Coach Landry was a man of vision. He could see things players couldn't see because their minds were locked on a position or just what they wanted to do. Coach Landry looked beyond the surface.

—RAYFIELD WRIGHT
Offensive Tackle, 1967–1979

TOM LANDRY never particularly cared for the title "America's Team." He believed that it just gave opponents another reason to become more emotional when they played the Dallas Cowboys. It was not until he got out of football that he began to like it more and more, accepting it as a special compliment for the years he coached the team.

The term did not actually originate with the Cowboy organization, although Tex Schramm and his marketing and publicity people loved it. The people who do such a fine job at NFL Films had observed as they traveled around the country taking footage for their shows that they'd continually see Dallas Cowboy banners, pennants, and hats in the crowds. It didn't matter whether the Cowboys were playing in the New Orleans SuperDome or Giants Stadium in East Rutherford; wherever they played, there always seemed to be an abundance of Cowboy fans. NFL Films does a yearly highlight film for each NFL team, and remembering the national popularity of the Cowboys, they titled the 1978 Dallas film "America's Team." The term caught on.

Explaining the phenomenon, Schramm said, "The first reason we became so popular around the country is that we were winning. It all starts there, and without it, nothing else would have been possible. Then you have to remember we've had a number of very colorful players, the kind who have captured the public's imagination."

He mentioned the laid-back Don Meredith, Bobby Hayes, the Olympic hero who became the "World's Fastest Man," a rodeo cowboy like Walt Garrison, the country boy from Throckmorton, Bob Lilly, Randy White, Tony Dorsett, and Staubach, whom Schramm called "the greatest sports hero of his time." And there were the storybook success stories of free agents such as Cliff Harris and Drew Pearson, who personified the Great American Dream.

"Then, of course, there was Tom Landry," continued Schramm. "He's steady, cool, calculating, a man who never seems to get rattled. He exudes confidence and coolness under fire, the way we'd like our leaders to do. He's God-fearing, moral, and all those things that made up the heroes of our youth. Yet he had a flair, coming up with the multiple wide-open formations in the 1960s and putting the Spread formation back into pro football in 1975. He was using an exciting brand of football all those years. Tom Landry was the constant in so many people's lives."

By 1980, Dallas had been involved in three of the four top-rated sports events on national television and held the highest ranking for Sunday, Thursday, and Saturday and for divisional, wild-card, and conference playoff games. The Cowboys also played the game that was the highest-ranked Monday-night football game until 1986. Through the mid-1980s, Cowboy-related products sold by NFL Properties accounted for 20 to 30 percent of all sales involving all teams.

If there indeed was an "America's Team," it was the Dallas Cowboys.

ACTUALLY, when Tom Landry was honored in 1989 with his special day, it was not the first time that the city of Dallas had recognized him. He was given an appreciation dinner in March 1976 after Dallas sent Roger Staubach, some excellent veterans, and the "Dirty Dozen" to the Super Bowl against Pittsburgh with a chance of beating the Steelers. A capacity crowd of fourteen hundred paid one hundred dollars a plate, the proceeds benefiting Trinity Christian Academy, to see Landry lauded by people such as Frank Gifford, Sam Huff, Dick Nolan, Mrs. Marie Lombardi, widow of the late coach, and Bob Lilly, who had retired in 1974.

"Tom is the best coach in the NFL," said Gifford.

"It's about time somebody around here realized what Tom's done and honored him," said Huff. "I think people just take him for granted. They don't appreciate him like they should."

"I taught him everything he knows," said Nolan, grinning.

Lilly talked about Landry and then became very serious. "I regret that my true feelings about Tom Landry have never become a matter of public record," he said. "He's the finest man I've ever come in contact with, and I can honestly say he's had more of a positive influence on my life than anybody."

For only the second, and final, time in his career, Landry had been named "Coach of the Year" in 1975, and he was cited for the first time in 1976 as one of the "Best Dressed Men" in the country. Most believed the credit for this should have gone to Alicia, who said, "Tom just doesn't have time to shop. But he'd look good in anything."

◡:∾

LANDRY WAS FEELING GOOD and ready for another challenge when he went to training camp in 1976. He was still doing a lot of jogging in those days, although favoring his bad knee. He would even run, as the players were required to do, up the steep hill overlooking the practice field. Thomas Henderson recalled he was about halfway up when he heard this odd-sounding gallop of a person coming up behind him. It was Landry, slightly limping as he ran up the hill. "He caught up with me, and then, as he passed me, he said, 'Come on, Thomas, let's go.'"

Henderson showed tremendous potential at linebacker, a promise that would never be fulfilled. In 1976, Landry would continue to make a middle linebacker out of Randy White, but he would also begin to use him as a down lineman on passing situations. White proved excellent at rushing the passer, and when in 1977 it became apparent that it would take him at least another year to become a linebacker, Landry switched him to defensive tackle. There he would make All-Pro eight straight times, go to the Pro Bowl nine times, and no doubt be headed for the NFL Hall of Fame. Randy, who played fourteen years, had planned on being a player-coach for Landry in 1989, but new coach Jimmy Johnson suggested retirement might be better.

During the height of White's career, Landry would call him "the premier defensive tackle in the business. He's got such intensity and competitiveness. I've never seen another player, other than Ernie Stautner, who could match Randy's constant intensity for the game."

346

With injuries to Preston Pearson and Robert Newhouse, Dallas continually had problems at running back in 1976, but Staubach took up the slack, hitting 70 percent of his passes in the first seven games and threatening to set new standards for NFL quarterbacks. Jack Pardee, then head coach with the Bears, said, "Staubach isn't all-NFL anymore, he's all-world. He's doing the best job anybody has ever done."

Dallas was 5–1, but for all practical purposes Landry's hopes for another Super Bowl ended once again with an injury to Staubach. In the second period of the game against the Bears, Staubach's right hand was stepped on and he suffered a deep bruise and a chipped bone. He tried to play the following week against Washington but reinjured the hand. The greatest season he might ever have had ended. The Cowboy defense, with the addition of linebacker Bob Breunig and the outstanding play of Charlie Waters, then established at strong safety, came alive, and Dallas finished with an 11–3 record and the NFC Eastern title and hosted Western Division winner Los Angeles in Texas Stadium.

As usual, there were some controversial calls, the final one being when Dallas faced a fourth and ten at the Los Angeles seventeen with 1:37 left. Staubach, who completed only fifteen of twenty-seven passes and suffered three interceptions, found Billy Joe Dupree for an apparent first down at the seven-yard line, but an official marked the ball at the ten, a yard short of the first down. Los Angeles won, 14–12.

Landry admitted Dallas got the short end of a couple of calls but added that, over the long haul, those things tended to even out. He also had to face a very despondent Roger Staubach after the game.

"Trade me," said Staubach. "I've let the team down, and I don't think I have them with me anymore."

"That's crazy," said Landry. "We had problems with the running game all year and you were injured. You played well under the circumstances. We just didn't have the support in other areas."

Landry later commented, "Roger is as good as anybody playing the game today. He literally took us to the Super Bowl in 1975 and might have done it again had he not been injured."

Staubach calmed down and prepared to make 1977 a banner year. But the Cowboys still needed a lift at running back, a threat to go all the way and one who would take some of the defensive pressure off Staubach.

⌣∴⌣

WITH ITS RECORD, there was no way Dallas would get a top running back by the time it drafted in the first round, but with the blessing of Schramm, Gil Brandt pulled off his best deal ever. He conjured, hustled, and talked Seattle into making a trade in which Dallas would swap first-round draft positions with the Seahawks, twenty-fifth for second, and also give Seattle three second-round choices the club had accumulated.

Prior to the draft, Rosy Waters mentioned to Charlie that when they were jogging, Mrs. Landry had remarked, "I told Tommie to draft that Tony Dorsett because he's so cute." Straight-faced, Charlie inquired, "You mean that's how we make our draft choices?"

After Tampa Bay made USC's Ricky Bell the first player chosen in the draft, the Cowboys did indeed pick Tony Dorsett, the Heisman Trophy winner from Pittsburgh and the all-time leading NCAA rusher until Ricky Williams of the University of Texas broke his record in 1998. Some had felt Tony was not big enough, at 5'-10", 190 pounds, to withstand the punishment and preferred Bell. Bell would never really distinguish himself, but when he retired, Dorsett was the second-leading rusher in NFL history. He would easily be the greatest breakaway threat Landry ever coached. He would rush for 1,007 yards his rookie season, including runs of eighty-four and seventy-seven yards even though Landry didn't make him a starter over Preston Pearson until the tenth game of the year.

Tony was hampered by minor injuries during training camp and wasn't overly attentive during meetings. When the season started, Landry did play his rookie a lot, but he didn't start him. He wanted to make sure Tony would clearly see what was supposed to happen on plays, where the blocks and the tacklers were coming from, rather than just turn him loose and, perhaps, risk an unnecessary injury. There was also some diplomacy involved because some of the veterans resented Tony's somewhat lackadaisical attitude during meetings and practices and, no doubt, the contract and attention he had gotten.

Landry worked in the young players, dealt with injuries, and coached the team's first successful season without Lee Roy Jordan, who had retired. Lee Roy, who had played collegiate football under Paul "Bear" Bryant at Alabama, compared that legendary coach to Landry:

"They were alike only in that they both were winners. Bryant was the greatest motivator I've ever been around. He wasn't a genius like Landry as far as the technical aspects of the game. But he could get you very excited about playing. You'd get to such a high emotional pitch that you'd sometimes play over your head. You thought you were going to win because Bryant made you believe you were.

"Tom is a brilliant man, no doubt about that. He wasn't a guy who motivated you. He left that to the players themselves. He just stated the facts. He was so intelligent that he could coach offense and defense at the same time. I don't think there was anybody else who could do that.

"Playing under both men, I learned there are two different ways, two approaches to winning. Both were their own men, did things their own way, and were very successful."

"Lee Roy was an extremely tough competitor," said Landry. "He was a leader. Not everybody liked him, but that happens when you're a leader. It's not a popularity contest. But they all respected him. Being a leader is trying to get people to do what it takes to win games. Lee Roy could do that type of thing."

Landry moved Bob Breunig from strongside linebacker into Jordan's spot in the middle and inserted Thomas Henderson as a starter on the outside. With Aaron Kyle becoming a starter and Randy White moving to weakside tackle to stay, there were four new starters playing new positions on defense. However, with Harvey Martin posting twenty-three quarterback sacks, becoming the NFL's defensive player of the year and having, along with Waters, Harris, and White, a Pro Bowl year, the defense was tremendous.

Dallas won its first eight games, and Cardinal coach Don Coryell said, "The Cowboys are the best team I've seen since I've been in the league."

Dallas, when it was 8–2, hosted the Redskins, the only other team with a chance to catch it in the NFC East. Dallas had beaten the Redskins 34–16 in the first meeting and won again, 14–7, marking the only time Landry's Cowboys would sweep the season series against George Allen's Redskins. When asked to compare Allen's feelings that "losing is like dying" to his own, Landry said, "The world doesn't stop when you lose. You must think about the good things that happened to you. You must look ahead. The only way a person can really become strong is to have setbacks.

"No, I certainly don't believe in winning at all cost, if that means cheating or spying on the other team or doing things that are wrong. But if you think winning is not too important, then you are not willing to pay the price to win. Take away winning and you've taken away everything that is strong about America. If you don't believe in free enterprise, capitalism, our way of life, you lose something. Our way of life means trying to succeed, and you must win to do that.

"Today [the late 1970s] in America it is, 'Let's be free. Let's be ourselves.' But that eliminates responsibility. If you have freedom, you must have responsibility. If you're going to have free enterprise, have a country like ours, you've got to try to win, to pay the price, to do the things that make our country progressive. Once you start moving away from that, and that's what I mean about what's happening in America today, sooner or later you're going to fail. You won't remain strong.

"This country is organized no differently from a football team. It's built on discipline, competition, and paying the price. Take away those things and you have chaos, weakness, and immorality, and all the things that are taking place today. So winning is important. It has to be."

Oddly enough, Landry had worked without a contract for two and a half years after signing one for three years in 1974. He signed a new one in 1977, which called for some one hundred fifty thousand to one hundred seventy thousand dollars annually to 1981, but Murchison let it be known that Landry could coach the team as long as he wanted.

∾⋮∾

AFTER DALLAS BEAT WASHINGTON in that 1977 season, the final time Landry would face Allen (Dallas won 8, lost 7 during Allen's tenure), the club went on to take its final three games, beating Super Bowl–bound Denver, which was resting starting quarterback Craig Morton, in the regular season's last game, 14–7.

Dallas defeated the Chicago Bears, featuring Walter Payton, 37–7, in the first round of the playoffs, after which Waters, who intercepted three passes, said, "Coach Landry is a genius. All you have to do is convince yourself to do as he says, and you'll win."

"He never forgets anything," said Harris. "About six years ago when we were playing Chicago I tried to run with a punt I'd caught inside our ten. It was late in the game, and I knew I should have fair caught it, but I just thought I'd run upfield as far as I could, then step out of bounds and stop the clock. I got hit near the sidelines, fumbled, and Chicago recovered. I looked up, and there was Coach Landry standing over me and looking right into my eyes.

350

"So, six years later I got back for a punt return against Chicago and he said, 'Cliff, fair catch the ball. You remember what happened last time.'"

In conference title games, Denver, which had defeated Pittsburgh, 34–21, in the first playoff round, beat Oakland, 20–17, for the AFC title. Dallas had no problems in winning over Minnesota, 23–6, and moved into New Orleans for the Super Bowl, which it had won there six years earlier.

~.:.~

TOM LANDRY brought an almost entirely different team to New Orleans from the one that had won the Super Bowl in January 1972. He had done an amazing rebuilding job, with only the slight setback in 1974, and became the first coach to bring practically different teams to the Super Bowl.

There were only two holdover starters from that championship club—Roger Staubach and Cliff Harris. Mel Renfro, one of the club's great stars, was coming to the end of his career and only seeing part-time duty. "Mel was as talented an athlete as we ever had," Landry said. "He could have played on offense or defense. When he made up his mind, he could cover anybody and played cornerback as well as anybody I've ever seen."

Coach Red Miller said, bluntly, the Broncos were going to win. Landry recalled, "I knew we were going to win with the 1971 team, but I wasn't really certain what we were going to do against Denver. I believed we had an excellent chance because of the defense we had been playing. But I believed we had to play great defense and come up with turnovers to win."

Landry was truly proud of Morton, who had come over from New York to give the Broncos enough offensive leadership to go with Miller's outstanding defense. "We think the world of Craig Morton," said Landry. "He was a winner when we had him, and he's come onto a fine team and done an outstanding job, much as Y. A. Tittle did when he went to the New York Giants years ago and Billy Kilmer when he came to the Redskins. Craig is talented, smart, and can beat you. You have to put a lot of pressure on him or he'll pick you apart."

On January 15, 1978, Super Bowl XII was played in the gigantic SuperDome before 76,400 fans and was billed as the contest between the "cool" of the Cowboys and the "emotion" of the Broncos. Landry would later recall that it was the highest a team of his had been for a game.

As Landry said was necessary, the defense, led by White and Martin, simply swamped Morton, who had played so well in victories over Pittsburgh and Oakland and had led the AFC in passing. Against a torrid rush, he managed to complete just four of fifteen passes, was trapped twice, and was hurried six other times. He also had four passes intercepted. "He didn't," said Landry, "have a chance to show what he could do."

Dallas, leading 13–0, had dominated the first half, and during intermission, Landry reminded his players that Denver had had the characteristic all season of making a big play and surging back into a game. This is exactly what happened as Rick Upchurch returned a kickoff for a Super Bowl record of sixty-seven yards to set up a touchdown. Dallas was ahead 20–10 in the final period, but Martin slammed into Norris Weese, who had replaced the ineffective Morton, causing him to cough up the ball at the Bronco twenty-nine.

All week the Cowboys had worked on a fullback pass by Robert Newhouse. Landry had waited for the right moment to use the play, and it came with the fumble. On first down from the twenty-nine, Staubach lateraled to Newhouse, going to his left. Golden Richards, the split end, started toward cornerback Steve Foley as if to try to block him. Foley, as had been his tendency, already had come up too fast on the play to challenge what appeared to be a fullback sweep. He couldn't recover, and safety Bernard Jackson could not get over quickly enough as Newhouse pulled up, then lofted a fine pass to Richards, who caught the ball and scored with 7:11 remaining. Dallas had put the game away, 27–10. Defensive linemen Harvey Martin and Randy White were named Super Bowl co-MVPs.

Dallas joined Green Bay, Miami, and Pittsburgh in having won two Super Bowls. "I think," said Landry, "that the ones of us who were at both games probably felt more satisfaction with the one in 1972 because everybody was saying we couldn't win the Big One. That team had gone through a lot of heartbreak, so it was a great feeling to do it, finally.

"The team that beat Denver probably didn't have the experience but did have more top athletes. It did what it had to do, put together a string of three outstanding games, two to get to the Super Bowl, and one to win it. It was one of the best defensive performances we've ever had."

Landry had been asked by a television crew, prior to the game, if he thought he could smile for their audience. "Not until the game is over," he said. "A man can't smile and think at the same time." He smiled a lot after the game.

~:~

THE PLAYERS HAD SAID FOR SOME TIME that they had begun to feel closer to Landry, that he had loosened up. At a team party in early June 1978, the players, coaches, and club officials were standing around the swimming pool at a Dallas country club when somebody got the idea to start tossing people into the pool. After the first Super Bowl victory, the players had thrown Schramm and Clint Murchison into the showers, but nobody had had the nerve to do it to Landry.

This time they did. A group of players grabbed him and threw him into the pool. He took three of them with him. They crawled out, wet and smiling. It was a great time for Landry. He had rebuilt his team and gotten back to the top of the NFL. Dallas certainly had an excellent chance of becoming the top team of the 1970s. Pittsburgh had had an off year, and nobody had any idea just how strongly the Steelers would come back.

~:~

RAY LANDRY, Tom's father, had had a wonderful time at the Super Bowl, attending the game and both the pregame and postgame festivities. It was something he needed, because he'd gone through a difficult time. His wife, Ruth Della, Tom's mother, had died on May 12, 1975, at the age of seventy-six. They had dated since high school and had been married for fifty-five years. Her death had left a terribly empty place in his heart and life. He missed her presence, her quiet dignity, and sometimes he would forget she was gone and expect to see her.

Ray had done little for almost six months after she died. But then he had begun to hunt and fish and do the things he once had loved. Then one day while he was deer hunting, he seemed to lose control and fell. He'd suffered a stroke, and it was awfully difficult for him for a while. But he was determined to come back, to be able to take care of himself again, and he had.

"My goodness." said Viola Bourgeois, Ray's sister. "When he got back from New Orleans, he was so happy. Just bubbling over with pride over what Tommy's team had done and what he had accomplished."

On October 10, 1978, two days after the Dallas Cowboys had beaten the New York Giants and brought their record to 4–2, Ray and his brother Arthur, visiting from Oklahoma, were waiting to watch the World Series when Ray became restless. He told Arthur he was going out to mow the yard, and after a few minutes, his brother went out to join him. Suddenly, Ray stopped mowing, sighed, then fell over backward. He was dead, just over a month before his eightieth birthday. Tom went to Mission to make funeral arrangements. The entire town seemed to attend, and a procession went through the city, passing the park that had been named for Ray Landry. Relatives kept coming up to Tom after the funeral to tell him how proud Ray was of him, how proud they were of him. After the funeral, Tom left Mission and wouldn't return to the town where he was born and raised until the 1980s when it named the high-school stadium after him.

～•∴～

SO OFTEN THE TRAVEL POSTERS you see from places like the southern part of Florida show the ocean too blue and the beach too clean and the people too healthy, vibrant, and young as they bask in the sun, ride the Big Wave, or embrace under swaying palms with the moon, which of course is big and round and yellow and glowing, unhindered by clouds. People depicted in the posters are living the Good Life, having the Great Time as we imagine it to be.

Once you get to these places, you find that the posters are not exactly in focus. The young are usually not at the big hotels. Rather, you find the older people there, the people who have the money to spend for long Miami vacations or have come to the area to retire. They seek the sun as though it were the Fountain of Youth.

This does tend to change during special events, and there are few things more special than the Super Bowl. People from all walks of life beg, borrow, steal, or mortgage to come from all over the country to be a part of the atmosphere surrounding the biggest sporting event of any year. But so often the game, the actual game itself, is as misleading as the travel posters. It simply does not match the pregame hype, the publicity (with two notable exceptions being the Dallas Cowboys–Pittsburgh Steelers Super Bowl games in the 1970s).

But there is nothing quite like the fine madness surrounding the

354

Super Bowl, and unless you have been there, you can't fully appreciate it. Certainly the Super Bowl is a game, a sport, and yet because of that unbelievable hype and the public relations of the NFL, it becomes in our minds much more. The Super Bowl is almost worshiped as we go to its altar to make sacrifices in papier-maché. So, indeed, we make it bigger than life, not only because of the effect of the hype but also, perhaps, because we need to do so, need to have the greatest of distractions from everyday life and what comes with it.

Outside of the political conventions, there is more media attention given to the Super Bowl than to any other single event. It is on television and radio. It is screaming headlines and pictures, and the NFL encourages us to hold it in reverence by using Roman numerals to designate its particular year. Tom Landry and the Dallas Cowboys were a part of Super Bowl madness for the fifth time in 1978, and nobody could have imagined it would be the last time he would take a team to the Super Bowl.

⌣∶∿

JUST ABOUT EVERYBODY favored the Steelers to win. They had the best record, 14–2 to 12–4 for Dallas, and had come through a tougher schedule because, at that time, the AFC Central Division was the strongest in the NFL. Oddly enough, in the 1980s the NFC East would have that distinction. The Pittsburgh defense had been superb, allowing a league low of just 195 points. Terry Bradshaw was having a magnificent season, and there were no better receivers than the very acrobatic Lynn Swann and James Stallworth. And Pittsburgh had destroyed good teams in the playoffs—Denver, 33–10, and Houston, 34–5.

For Dallas, the NFC championship season of 1978 had taken the shape of so many other successful ones. It had been a year in which the Cowboys had been hot and cold before settling down to streak for the NFC Eastern Division title and the playoffs. This seemed to be Landry's formula, planned or unplanned. With the retirement of Ralph Neely and the slow rehabilitation of Rayfield Wright's knee after surgery, the line had problems for much of the year. Further, Harvey Martin had been idled or played with injuries and Tony Dorsett was guilty of a rash of fumbles.

Landry had credited some of the early problems to an easy 38–0 opening victory over Baltimore in a game many believed to be a preview of the Super Bowl to come. But the Colts had played without quarterback Bert Jones, had other malfunctions, and never were the team they were supposed to be. Landry believed the victory caused the Cowboys to think they were better than they were, giving them a sense of false security that bottomed out in a 6–4 record with six games to play in what was then the new sixteen-game format for a regular season. As was traditional, fans were asking the ageless question, "What's wrong with the Cowboys?" But Cliff Harris, who had played on teams that were 5–4 and 4–3 and still streaked to the Super Bowl, said the team had the NFC right where it wanted it. And, indeed, Dallas won its final six games and took the division over the Eagles by three full games.

There had been no great problems during the season, although Landry had to become accustomed to the shenanigans of Thomas Henderson and the lapses in devotion by Tony Dorsett, something Landry would not tolerate on game day.

Tony missed a light practice before a home game against the Eagles, claiming he'd failed to hear the alarm clock and had overslept. He had not bothered to call and explain why he wasn't there.

"Tony," Landry told him, "you're not going to start, and you might not even play."

Dorsett's family had made the trip from Pennsylvania to watch him play, and so, as they looked at each other, tears came into Tony's eyes.

"I was furious," he said, "I did play quite a bit, though, but he didn't start me and I was embarrassed in front of my family and all those fans."

Later, in the light of the perspective of years, Tony said, "Maybe you didn't always like his decisions, but he was fair. He would listen to all sides of an issue and then decide what was best for the team."

Dorsett had a fine year in 1978, rushing for 1,325 yards; Staubach led the NFL in passing for the third time; and Randy White, Charlie Waters, and Cliff Harris all made All-Pro and kept the defense in championship form.

Dallas beat wild-card representative Atlanta, 27–20, in the first round of the playoffs, relying on backup Danny White after Staubach was knocked out in the first half. As usual, insiders believed the Rams, 34–10 playoff winners over Minnesota and a club that had beaten Pittsburgh, 10–7, during the regular season, would defeat Dallas.

Asked prior to the game if calling the plays against such a fine defense presented a special challenge to him, Landry said, "It's always a challenge." The way it turned out, he called a conservative game because his defense outplayed the Ram offense.

Los Angeles, under Chuck Knox and his successor, Ray Malavsai, had a very simple offense. Pittsburgh All-Pro linebacker Jack Ham noted, "Landry's offense is so complicated it takes a book to explain it. You could put the Ram offense on a postcard."

Dallas beat the Rams, 28–0, as Charlie Waters recovered a fumble to set up one touchdown and intercepted passes to put his team in position for two others. Linebacker Thomas Henderson applied the coup de grace by picking off a pass and returning it sixty-eight yards for the final touchdown. Prior to the game, he had said, "The Rams don't have enough class to make the Super Bowl." Landry had cringed when he heard this but said nothing to Henderson.

◡⋮∾

DURING THE WEEK PRIOR to Super Bowl XIII, the players, from top to bottom of the roster, became celebrities, folk heroes, philosophers. The media hung on their every word, the irony being that in ordinary times some members of the press might not have walked around the corner to talk to them. But there were daily press conferences with the competing teams and coaches, and all that was written was a form of overkill.

The image of a stoic Tom Landry was so implanted in the mind of the general public and press that it wouldn't have changed had he put a feather in his hat and, carrying a cane, done a soft-shoe on the sidelines. But he gave a good, honest interview, could be witty at times, and just had great powers of concentration when he was working with his team or in a game.

Landry seemed more relaxed and philosophical than usual when he met with the press before the 1978 Super Bowl, whereas Steeler coach Chuck Noll, for the most part, was serious and blunt. He would say things like, "I'm not a wordsmith," or "I'm a historian," or "We're ready to play." He did, however, get in a zinger at Thomas "Hollywood" Henderson. Thomas was reminded that Steeler defensive end L. C. Greenwood was also called "Hollywood." Thomas responded, "Come on. How does that sound? L. C. "Hollywood" Greenwood. Or Greenwood "Hollywood" L. C. Or "Hollywood" Three Rivers [for the Steeler stadium] L. C. Greenwood. That's the most ridiculous thing I've ever heard. If he's the original Hollywood,

I'm going to give it up. There's only one Hollywood. If L. C. can be Hollywood, I'm gonna be Cinderella."

"I understand," said Noll, dryly, "empty barrels make the most noise."

When Landry showed up for a midweek press conference, the room was overflowing with media. "I'm not sure," he deadpanned, "if this room is big enough to handle the Thomas Henderson interview, but we'll try."

But he discussed the subject more seriously. "I sort of mind the things he says because it's not my style. But we're in a different time now. A player should have freedom of expression. My criteria is not to let it bother me too much until it starts bothering the team and its effectiveness. Then I'll do something about it. It hasn't so far. But it's the way Henderson psyches himself up for a game. So he has to back it up, and so far, he has. It will be interesting to see what happens if he doesn't. The only time I'll say anything to him is if he doesn't do well, and then I might suggest he change his tactics a little.

"For me to sound off is out of character. But, once again, we find in the NFL today and in other professions a lot of expression by individuals, no matter whether they spike the ball or what. It's part of the times, and we deal with it as best we can. I don't resent it. I don't resent people very easily. I tolerate people pretty well. I feel no resentment at all toward Henderson. He underlines positive things too."

But in less than a year, Landry would not only be surprised at what was behind some of Henderson's actions, but also have to do something about him.

⌣∴⌣

COMEDIAN DON RICKLES noted the somber reputations of the two coaches and remarked, "Chuck Noll and Tom Landry got into a grinning contest, and neither won. So they brought in another playoff team, Mount Rushmore, and it beat both of them."

Regarding the buildup for a Super Bowl game, Landry said, "The game has become so big that what surrounds it takes away from the contest itself. But I understand this because everybody has a job to do and this is what people want to read about. It can be distracting if you let it. But I just accept it, set aside time for different things we have to do, try to enjoy the situation we're in. I imagine a lot of coaches would like to go through the so-called distractions. We're happy to be here.

"The biggest problem for the players is that they have to get up so early and burn up a lot of energy before the game. There's a lot of tension before the game, and so much of the energy is used while waiting for the kickoff. Personally, I'm sure my [cool] appearance is misleading because, sure, I'm nervous. But in this situation we know what to expect because we've been here before and have had the Super Bowl experience. I'm not sure, however, that the playoffs are a true indication of the best team. You win a playoff game and it means you're the best team on that given day."

At least Landry appeared very loose and relaxed. But then, how could you really tell? When he bumped into Doug Todd, then the Cowboy publicity director, at 10:00 A.M., he asked, "What are you doing up so early?" "Oh," said Todd, "I've been up for hours." Landry became very serious and said, as he walked away, "Hmm. Nobody could have been up that long and look as sleepy as you do."

Cowboy president Tex Schramm had brought his boat up from Key West and had docked near Fort Lauderdale, where the Cowboys were staying. Landry was looking for Schramm and was told he was off on his boat. Shaking his head slowly, Landry said, "Boy, I'm going to come back in my other life as the president of a team instead of a coach."

A fan stopped Landry. He looked to be in his sixties. "Tom, I saw you play when you were with the Giants. You seem so calm now. But you used to get pretty mad in those days. You had a temper, all right. You were awfully fiery."

"I guess we all grow a little, mature a little," said Landry.

"Yessir, he sure had a bad temper back in those days," the man said after Landry had left. "But you wouldn't know it now, huh?"

⚬∴∾

THERE HAD BEEN QUITE A DEBATE after Pittsburgh beat Dallas the first time they met in the January 1976 Super Bowl. Fans and members of the Cowboy organization believed the officials had allowed the Steelers to get away with virtual muggings on pass coverage. Even under the rules of that year, a defender could only bump a receiver two or three times. But, as said earlier, the Steelers appeared to be hitting and holding receivers all the way downfield. The Steelers had been tough and intimidating. Coming into the game they had been the most penalized team in the NFL. Yet not one flag had been thrown on them in the Super Bowl.

359

"It was miraculous how clean they got two weeks before the game," said Billy Joe Dupree. Frankly, Landry appeared to be trying to alert the officials to the Steelers' tactics in Super Bowl X by mentioning them prior to Super XIII.

Chuck Noll let it be known that he resented the implications that his team had been successful because it bent the rules. Landry said that if he were Chuck he'd have said the same thing. And Commissioner Pete Rozelle, asked to comment about the Steeler tactics, said, "Tom's half right . . . well, maybe three-fourths right. But this is more of a problem than just one for the officials. It has to start with the coaches in the league controlling the players."

Rules would soon be changed to protect not only the receivers but also the quarterbacks.

Landry expected the Steelers to use the same tactics, to try to intimidate the Cowboys and draw them away from their game plan. Most of the Cowboy players wanted to retaliate.

"Pittsburgh is a basic team and will continue to do the same things," Landry told the team. "I want you to remember this: Don't fight with them. Stick to what you know you must do to win. If you fight with them, you'll lose your poise and concentration. We know what to expect. We know how to counter what they do. Don't descend to their level."

Preston Pearson later remarked, "The same thing happened. The Steelers mugged Drew again because Golden Richards [the other wide receiver] was out."

Preston had the rare distinction of playing for Don Shula in Baltimore, Noll in Pittsburgh, and of course, Landry. "The dealings I had weren't that much different. All three can stand on their records." He would later add, "Both Landry and Noll were religious. Noll had to get his word in and made it known that he knew about everything—wine, food, politics, whatever. With Shula you always knew where you stood. That wasn't true with Noll or Landry. Landry understood football better than Noll, so Noll went for the physical players."

∾:∾

DALLAS SURPRISED EVERYBODY by moving the ball on the ground at the outset of the game. With Dorsett running wide, Dallas moved to a first and ten at the Steeler thirty-four the first time it had the ball.

Landry had planned to shoot the works, so instead of staying on the ground until the Steelers stopped his team, he sent in a trick play, for which he'd later draw a great deal of criticism. Staubach was supposed to hand the ball to Dorsett, who, in turn, would give it to Drew Pearson, who would appear to be running a reverse from his flanker position. Drew would then pull up and pass to tight end Dupree. Dupree was wide open for a touchdown, but Dorsett and Pearson fumbled on the exchange and Pittsburgh recovered. Landry, looking ahead, felt the Steelers would stop his running game and hoped to strike while they were on their heels. His attempt to gain an early advantage almost looked silly. Had the pass worked, and it should have, he would have been a genius again.

Bradshaw was excellent as usual against Dallas, and Cowboy defenders were having trouble tackling his receivers once they caught the ball. He threw three touchdowns in the first half, and Staubach threw one. Also in the first half, linebacker Mike Hegman stole the ball from Bradshaw on a blitz and ran thirty-seven yards for a touchdown.

Staubach and Landry had words on a play Tom called during the two-minute period before the half. Dallas had a first down at the Steeler thirty-two and Landry called for play-action, which Roger thought was the wrong play because the Steelers were looking for a pass all the way. But Staubach was supposed to fake a run with Dorsett, stop, and throw to Dupree. The ball was intercepted, and Pittsburgh quickly marched downfield to score. It was a seven-point swing.

"Why didn't you throw the ball to Billy Joe?" snapped Landry.

"Why did you call such a ridiculous play?" said Staubach, adding that Dupree wasn't open anyway.

Pittsburgh led 21–14 at intermission, but as the second half got under way, the Cowboy defense held Pittsburgh to twelve yards on three straight possessions, and Staubach took the offense to a third and three at the Pittsburgh ten. On a play that will forever be embedded in the minds of the Cowboys and their followers, Staubach faked a play-action and then threw the ball to Jackie Smith, all alone in the end zone. Smith had the soft pass and then, as he fell to his knees, let it get away. Smith had had a great career with the Cardinals but waited for all his playing days for such a chance in a big game, the biggest of games. It was as if time stopped for those seconds and real life became pictures . . . the picture of Smith showing such awful agony on the ground in the end zone, of Staubach jerking his head around in anger, more at himself for throwing the ball too soft than for Jackie dropping it, and Landry grimacing on the sidelines.

But the Cowboys seemed to have momentum when Bradshaw brought the Steelers out on a second and five at the Pittsburgh forty-four in the final period. He dropped back to pass as Swann ran downfield toward cornerback Benny Barnes, who back-pedaled. Barnes then got tangled up with Swann as the Steeler receiver turned back toward the middle of the field to try to catch Bradshaw's pass. Both fell. Field judge Fred Swearingen called interference on Barnes, a thirty-three-yard penalty. Landry was yelling at the officials from the sidelines, feeling Swann had caused the contact. But it did no good. He would later say he was more upset with official Pat Knight, who had a much clearer view of the play than Swearingen and should have told him what had happened.

Pittsburgh went on to score and then, after recovering Randy White's fumble on the ensuing kickoff at the Dallas eighteen, scored again, taking a 35–17 lead with 6:51 left to play. Staubach, who had not played particularly well, got hot and led Dallas eighty-nine yards for a touchdown with 2:27 left. When the Cowboys recovered an onside kick, reminding fans of the 1972 playoff comeback against San Francisco, Staubach again took his team for a touchdown. Dallas trailed 35–31 with just twenty-two seconds left, and this time the onside kick failed. Time had run out on Landry and the Cowboys and their chance to make history, to be the team of the '70s.

Landry said Dallas might not have won but it was a shame a call like that involving Swann and Barnes would take away part of the focus on a fine game. "I'm upset, not so much for myself but for the players who worked so hard. But, sure, it bothers me because this game was the culmination of a decade in which we went to five Super Bowls. We could have been the first team to win three Super Bowls, and that would have been a great climax to an era. But . . . we didn't do it."

Tom and Alicia appeared at the team party about an hour after it started. They moved around a number of tables, greeting people, and then ate and left early. The previous year they had stayed for all of the party, an annual event for both winners and losers of the Super Bowl, but Dallas had beaten Denver that year. That was the difference for Landry between victory and defeat. He did not talk loud enough or laugh hard enough, and the music was not strong enough to change what happened, even for a while.

Speculation was that he had gone to look at the game films, but when asked this the next morning, he said, "No. They weren't ready yet."

That morning after, his eyes were clear, his face was only slightly drawn, and he showed only vague signs of lack of sleep, but he seemed more upset than he had been in the past and actually displayed normal, human bitterness over the interference call.

Billy Carter, the brother of then president Jimmy Carter, had been in the room that morning just before Landry got there. He had poured himself a rather large drink and walked out with it. "I'm glad," said Landry, "he isn't running the country this morning."

~:~

TOM LANDRY KNEW exactly the type of player he wanted when he first took control of the Dallas Cowboys. He talked to Gil Brandt and others who might be involved and told them he would like to have, as much as possible, players with intelligence and character. He believed that type of player would be trying just as hard at the end of a game as he was when it started, no matter what the score might be.

Perhaps more than any other player, Roger Staubach personified this trait. During his career with the Cowboys, Staubach helped bring the team from behind to win twenty-one games in the final period, fourteen of those in the last two minutes or in overtime.

"If Tom Landry was going to create a perfect quarterback for his system, it would be Roger," said Don Meredith. "He has great character, which Tom loves, and the intensity and dedication to give that one hundred ten percent, go that extra hundred yards. Roger adapted well to the Landry system, and consequently, Dallas won a lot more games."

There was probably never a season that emphasized this more than Staubach's final one, 1979. Dallas beat St. Louis, 22–21, with 1:16 left on Rafael Septien's field goal. Staubach's pass to Tony Hill beat Chicago, 24–20, with 1:57 left. Staubach led Dallas to ten points in the final two minutes for a 16–14 win over the Giants, and then there was the Redskin game that year, considered by Landry to be one of the two greatest comebacks by Dallas (the other being the playoff victory over Atlanta in January 1981).

Dallas and Washington played in mid-December in Texas Stadium for the NFC Eastern title, and with all their close games and other problems, it had not been easy for the Cowboys to get in that position.

Dallas had gone into a three-game tailspin in November, including a 34–20 loss to the Redskins in RFK, and this would be the last game Thomas Henderson would play. Henderson had shown such great promise, but he had both angered and saddened Landry, who finally gave up on him as a football player, if not as a person.

Henderson had seemed to be the same old jovial cut-up when he reported to training camp, albeit in a rather auspicious way. Thomas had hired a long black limousine for the trip from L.A. International to the practice field in Thousand Oaks. When he arrived at camp, he sat in the limo and watched the workout for a while, then got out and staggered past Landry across the field to greet some of the other players. He seemed a little drunk but had actually been sitting in the limo snorting cocaine. Landry had no idea what his problem was, but Thomas frequently missed workouts completely or was not able to go full speed. He'd contracted hepatitis during the off-season, which affected Landry in more ways than one.

Members of the team had to be given painful hepatitis shots, and Landry called Henderson into his office. He looked at Thomas and said, unsmilingly, "Thomas, I had to get one of those shots."

Henderson missed time in camp due to weakness, ankle problems, etc. When this pattern continued into the season, Landry told him they'd make a deal: If he practiced all week and worked, he'd start. If he didn't, he wouldn't.

As Henderson would later admit, due to drugs he was not in control of himself. Henderson was walking a fine line and had been warned by Landry to straighten up, but he seemed to have lost complete reality somewhere over the rainbow.

Then there was the first meeting with the Redskins. Dallas was getting clobbered as the national television cameras zoomed in on the bench and Thomas Henderson. He immediately started waving a towel and mugging for the camera. Jerry Tubbs had seen this on a monitor in the press box, and when the game was over he bawled out Henderson. They almost fought. On the charter back to Dallas, Henderson threatened assistant coach Jim Myers and kept telling everybody, including Landry, to trade him. He later said he was high on coke.

The following morning, Marge Kelly phoned Thomas and told him Coach Landry wanted to see him. Landry reminded him that they had a deal and that he hadn't kept his part of it. "You've been disruptive for the team, shown disrespect for the staff, and your behavior in Washington is unforgivable."

He explained to Henderson that he understood he'd had problems and had grown up without a father but that he still had to be disciplined. "You're up one day and down the next," said Landry. "Your attitude has gone from bad to worse. I've never had a player approach me like you did on the flight coming back to Dallas.

"I could put you on the bench, but it's not in our best interests right now. I'm not going to try to trade you either." Henderson recalled that at that time Landry seemed to be about to break down but had continued and told him he was going to put him on waivers because "I can't handle you anymore."

When Henderson was trying to get in shape to catch on with another team, Landry allowed him to use the Cowboy facilities. Henderson finally admitted his problems with drugs and then served a term in federal prison for a charge by two women, one in a wheelchair, that he'd assaulted them. Landry wrote letters, asking for leniency.

"Hey," Randy White said, "I was there when he had a lot of those misfits, and Coach Landry would bend over backward giving them a second and even a third chance. That's two or three more than they'd have gotten from anybody else or from anybody in any other kind of business. He did it because he has faith in people. Then most of them come out and start saying bad things about him."

Henderson did, Duane Thomas did. But as years passed and their perspectives changed, they said only nice things about Tom Landry.

～∴～

IN THE 1979 GAME for the NFC East Division championship against the Washington Redskins in Texas Stadium, the momentum went back and forth. The Cowboys finally seemed to go down for the count when John Riggins broke for a sixty-six-yard touchdown run, putting the Redskins ahead, 34–21. It was then that Staubach rallied the Cowboys to victory in the final four minutes. He threw a touchdown pass of twenty-six yards to Ron Springs and then took his team on a drive to try to beat the clock. A field goal obviously wouldn't help, and with time running out the Cowboys were at the Redskins' seven.

Landry called a play in which Staubach was supposed to throw to tight end Billy Joe Dupree, but as the huddle broke, Staubach looked at the Redskins defense, the way it was apparently going to line up, and felt a blitz was coming. He grabbed Tony Hill, the split end, and told him to go straight into the end zone and he would float a pass on a play called "13 Route," which had worked so well so often for them. It worked once again, and Dallas won, 35–34.

"That was the most remarkable game we ever played," said Landry.

"We had to make a lot of big plays to win, and it had seemed certain we were defeated."

Staubach had been at his best, so it would seem a little odd in his final game as a Cowboy when the last pass he'd ever throw was caught by guard Herb Scott, an ineligible receiver. On the other hand, everything the forgettable Vince Ferragamo threw for the Rams that day in the first round of the playoffs seemed to be caught. He threw touchdowns of thirty-two, forty-three, and fifty yards, the last one going to Billy Waddy in a roundabout way to defeat Dallas and rob it of another chance to play Pittsburgh in the Super Bowl. In spite of everything, it appeared the Cowboys would win, but Mike Hegman tipped an off-target throw from Ferragamo and it fell right into the arms of Waddy to give L.A. a 21–19 victory.

Meanwhile, there had been some confusion on the Cowboys' last possession on a screen pass, and Staubach threw to guard Herb Scott instead of the intended receiver. He joked that that would be what he'd always be remembered for.

⌣∵∽

ROGER STAUBACH had mentioned to both Tom Landry and Tex Schramm that he was considering retirement prior to the January Pro Bowl game, which Landry coached. But Roger was thirty-seven, on top of his game, and Landry never dreamed he'd really retire. Landry told him he should continue to play, and Schramm, much more aggressively, tried to talk him out of any thoughts of retirement. Landry said, calmly, that Roger's play had been analyzed and he had not reached a point where he should retire. "You should continue playing, and we want you to play. But if it's something that you feel strongly about, then you have to make that decision."

Landry objectively evaluated players reaching the end of their careers and told them as honestly as he could what they should do, but he never tried to talk them out of a decision. He had told Rayfield

Wright, a former All-Pro tackle and one of the best offensive linemen in the club's history, that he should retire after the 1979 season. But Wright had wanted to play, and when Landry put him on waivers the Eagles picked him up. He left the club without any fanfare, something that would bother Landry.

Staubach had suffered twenty concussions during his playing career, five with the Cowboys. Although doctors didn't tell him to quit, they indicated there might be some neurological changes on the left side of his brain that could be related to his head injuries. It was possible further damage could occur. But Staubach had also reasoned that he wasn't looking forward to training camp again and that his family life had been too much in a fishbowl. So in March 1980, two hundred members of the media showed up at a press conference in Texas Stadium to hear Roger officially announce his retirement.

"We'll miss him tremendously, but I'm not sure the National Football League won't miss him as much or even more," said Landry. "He has the type image you want in the game because young people look up to him. You can't afford to lose a person like Roger."

"Tom Landry is a towering figure," said Roger. "To me he was, is, and always will be special—a man apart from other men. What made him so beyond others was his brilliant technical grasp of football and two bedrock Landry characteristics: enormous self-discipline and consistency. Tom Landry is the rock against which we all lean, often without realizing it, at some point in our careers.

"Of course, the nuts and bolts of the Cowboys is . . ." Roger's voice broke. He choked up, then regained control and continued, ". . . the man who wears the funny hat on the sidelines, Tom Landry."

As Roger walked to the door, he grinned and said, "If I do come back next year, will you let me call the plays?"

"Oh, sure," said Landry. "You can call them from the press box."

Then Landry smiled too and said, "Well, we have a system here that we have to keep going."

Both Landry and Staubach had tremendous respect for Danny White, and although the team would certainly miss Roger, Landry believed the Cowboys would . . . keep going.

CHAPTER 19
The Landry Years in Decline

⌢∵⌢

I saw Dallas play Miami [1987] and noticed Shula and Landry. Those two old dogs were fighting each other to death. There was fire in their eyes. It was the same thing in the Cowboys' game against Minnesota. Landry almost brought them back to win both times. You can't tell me the guy can't coach anymore, that he's lost it. That's nonsense.

—GEORGE YOUNG
Former New York Giants General Manager

A CAPACITY CROWD and a national television audience were watching Dallas play the Los Angeles Rams in Anaheim on a Sunday night in early December 1986. Tom Landry was deeply concentrating on the game as usual when Larry Wansley, the former FBI agent who had become director of counseling services and security for the team, hurried down from the press box onto the field to see him.

"Coach Landry," said Wansley, "there's been a threat on your life. There's probably nothing to it, but there might be a sniper up there somewhere. You're going to have to come with me now to the dressing room."

Landry thought for a few seconds then handed Danny White the game plan and walked away with Wansley, who kept his eyes on the stands as they made their way to the ramp leading to the dressing room. Ordinarily, Landry would tell White the play he wanted to run and Danny, who was out for the year recovering from a broken wrist, would signal the information to Steve Pelluer on the field during games. But Danny was totally puzzled when Landry just handed him the game plan and walked away.

In the dressing room, Wansley urged Landry to remain off the field. He said that there was probably nothing to the threat but somebody had telephoned to make it and there were a lot of kooks out there.

Landry was concerned about the game and convinced Wansley that he would be safe back on the field if he wore a bulletproof vest. When Landry got back to the bench, White handed him the game plan and asked what was going on.

"Oh, nothing much," said Landry. "There's supposed to be a sniper in the stands. They wanted me to stay in the locker room, but I put on a bulletproof vest and persuaded them I'd be all right."

Landry then turned back toward the field and began concentrating again. Meanwhile, White edged away from him, and so did the other players, because frightening news travels fast.

As Landry turned to give Danny the play, he looked momentarily puzzled. Danny was five yards away from him. "Coach," said Danny, "you're going to have to speak up!"

Landry grinned. "Coach," said Danny, "you don't even have to tell me not to stand close to you! The way this season has gone for me, that sucker might be drunk, think he's aiming at you, and shoot me!" Landry laughed.

White later said of the incident, "If it had been my life that was threatened and I was standing out there in front of seventy-six thousand fruitcakes, knowing one of them might have the crosshairs on me, I don't know what I would have done. But it really didn't seem to faze him. He went right on calling the plays and running the game like nothing was wrong."

⌣∶∾

IN THE HOSPITALITY ROOM set up by the Dallas Cowboys in the Stouffer Hotel in Tower City, downtown Cleveland, various groups of visitors were holding conversations the night before Dallas played the Browns. The 1988 season had already gone down the drain, record-wise, and minority owner Ed Smith was offering his unsolicited opinions to assistant coaches Jerry Tubbs and Alan Lowry. He often sought listeners to whom to offer his opinions, but although he sat near Tom Landry and Tex Schramm on the team's charter flights, he never took the opportunity to express his opinions to them.

Tubbs and Lowry were very patient and polite to Smith, as both tended to be. I was an innocent bystander, along for the ride while working on a book. Smith said a key reason the club had not been successful was that its cornerbacks were too short to play in the NFL.

"Look at the good cornerbacks," he opined. "They're 6'-1", 6'-2"."

"But Robert Williams is, what, 5'-10", and he's been outstanding," I offered.

"Too short," said Smith. "None of them are any good."

"Well," said Lowry, "Cleveland has a pretty good pair. They're not tall."

Smith shook his head, somewhat impatiently. Cleveland Browns cornerbacks Frank Minifield and Hanford Dixon were considered among the best, if not the best pair in the league at that time. Dixon is 5'-11" and Minifield 5'-9".

The following afternoon, the Cowboys, with a 2–11 record, took Cleveland, a contender for the AFC title, down to the wire before losing, 24–21. Roger Ruzek had kicked a field goal early in the game after a turnover, but an official had ruled that Randy White, who blocked on field goal attempts, had tripped a rusher. The field goal was disallowed. With 1:43 remaining in the game, Ruzek kicked a forty-yard field goal that appeared to have tied the game, 24–24. An official again ruled that White had tripped a rusher. White and the coaches said he had used the very same blocking technique all season.

On the return charter, play-by-plays were passed out, and Landry, as always, went over each possession and marked penalties and various things. Smith, sitting across the aisle, got a play-by-play and started marking it up. Smith later conferred with Paul Hackett, who by then had been relegated to little more than a quarterback coach.

Those scenes, the sniping and second-guessing, and the way in which the game was lost, seemed as much as anything to exemplify the craziness of Tom Landry's final season with the Dallas Cowboys and, to a degree, the years the team went into decline.

~:~

ROGER STAUBACH AND DANNY WHITE had been competitors, certainly, but they were also friends. Danny was an excellent backup for Roger but also an outstanding punter. He certainly caused defenders worries when he lined up to punt because he might have taken off running. He had done it successfully a number of times, but it was something Landry didn't like. It was too much of a gamble.

The Cowboys were fighting Pittsburgh to become what people were calling the "Team of the Decade" in the 1970s. And in October of 1979, the teams were playing in Pittsburgh with the Steelers leading, 7–0. The Steel Curtain had shut down Staubach and the offense, and as White trotted onto the field to punt, he decided, without Landry's knowledge, to fake a kick and take off running. If he made the first down, it could cause the momentum to change. So White called the fake punt in the huddle, got the snap, and took off. But he was stopped just short of a first down.

"Coach Landry was the last person in the world I wanted to see when I came off the field," recalled Danny. "That was probably the worst I've felt about anything I'd ever done on the football field. I wanted to avoid him, but sure enough, he came over to me when I got back to the bench."

"Danny," said Landry, calmly, "you just can't do that. You just can't do that."

Pittsburgh went on to win, 14–3. "I was worried the next week and got a little paranoid when I felt he wasn't talking to me," continued Danny. "But that was all just in my mind. Coach Landry doesn't hold grudges against anybody, not even some of the people who over the years have really betrayed or disappointed him." Danny didn't say Amen, but he must have felt like it.

❧

DANNY WHITE wasn't exactly in an ideal situation replacing Roger Staubach, who had retired after the 1979 season. Roger was America's Quarterback of America's Team. He'd established himself as one of the best to play the game. And when you put together his talent and drive and incredible knack for comebacks, you have a legend. It was difficult enough to follow a Roger Staubach; it was even more difficult to follow a legend.

Danny was the man Landry had prepared to take Roger Staubach's place. His arm wasn't as strong as Roger's, but he was accurate and very smart and everybody had a lot of confidence in him. He played amazingly well until injuries, misfortune, and diminishing talent around him made him a part of the decline of the Landry years.

The end of the championship era for the Dallas Cowboys of Tom Landry did not come with Staubach's retirement. The team still had talent and was capable of winning another Super Bowl. But if you wanted to be specific and cite the final seconds when it slipped away, then you would probably point to the 1981 NFC conference championship when Dallas played the 49ers in San Francisco. Cincinnati would win the AFC title, and experts believed neither the Cowboys nor the 49ers would have much trouble beating Cincinnati in the Super Bowl. That honor would belong to the 49ers after one of the more heartbreaking defeats in Cowboys history.

Many things happened in the game before Dallas seemed to be on its way to winning. The Cowboys were leading 27–21 and moving into field goal range as time was running out. But White missed a wide-open Doug Donley on third and eight, and the Cowboys had to punt. Had he hit the pass, Dallas might have been able to run down the clock and kick a field goal.

The 49ers drove the length of the field and faced a third down from the Dallas six. Joe Montana, trying to throw the ball out of the end to stop the clock, watched in amazement as Dwight Clark leaped high in the back of the end zone to catch the pass for a touchdown, giving San Francisco a 28–27 lead with less than a minute remaining.

With time running out, White brought the Cowboys downfield and Drew Pearson almost broke loose when a 49er was just able to grab his jersey and bring him down. Dallas was at the 49er's forty and with one more first down would have been in field goal range. The crowd was too loud for Danny to use the Shotgun, so he had to run the play from under center. Tony Hill was wide open for the first down and field goal chance, but White tripped as he faded back. He dropped the ball, and the 49ers recovered. That, perhaps, was the minute in time when Super Bowl hopes ended. And it seemed to illustrate White's plight. But for the noise, he'd have already been back in the Shotgun and might not have tripped. Had he completed the pass and Dallas won, Landry might have been right that the Cowboys could have remained a Super Bowl contender for a few more years. But sports have always been full of "might haves" and certainly the Cowboys have had their share.

White took a great deal of blame for the loss, remindful of Craig Morton when he was in Dallas. He was very good, but unfortunate things just seemed to happen to him. It was just the opposite for Staubach; had Morton or White thrown the Hail Mary pass, which actually wasn't a very good throw, you wonder if Drew Pearson would have caught it.

"Danny White," said Landry, "was probably as fine a winner as we ever had. He didn't have the natural gifts of some of the other quarter-backs, but he knew how to win. I don't think anybody could have followed Roger and done as well as Danny. If we had beaten San Francisco that year and gone to the Super Bowl with Danny, I think we might have gone a couple of more times with him. He was an excellent quarterback, but a lot of people were critical of him and just didn't recognize that."

~:~

THERE WAS A NEW POWER in the NFC East in 1980. Dick Vermeil had taken over as coach of the Philadelphia Eagles and seemed to bring a new enthusiasm to the team. Vermeil had been a successful college coach and was very emotional and enthusiastic. He'd often grab players and hug them on the sidelines. And his Eagles beat Dallas (12–4 during the regular season) 20–7 for the NFC title.

Landry said he really didn't mind his image of being cool and collected, rather than fiery. "My image is based on how people see me reacting on the sidelines," he said. "It's just that I've trained myself to concentrate. I blank out everything else. If you do that, you don't show emotion. I trained myself by watching Ben Hogan, who had tremendous concentration. He never let anything break his concentration. The image never bothered me too much. My friends know me.

"I think . . . at least you hope . . . that people who know me are aware I'm not a stoic or unemotional person. I can't help my image because that's the way it'll be as long as I coach. I won't change that."

When asked about the enthusiasm Vermeil showed, he said, "There's nothing wrong with that. There's a number of ways to do things, to be, and still be successful. I just won't have that relationship with players. I did when I was an assistant coach with the Giants, but it's a lot different when you're a head coach. If I was that way with the players now, it would affect my coaching.

"The players are in my hands, and that's an awesome responsibility. Therefore, my feeling is that you must have some distance from the players in order to make the correct judgments and do the things that you have to do. When you get close, you can lose your objectivity and it also sometimes gives a player an out because he feels he doesn't have to do what you want him to do. Sure, I've seen a lot of players I'd like to be close to, but it might affect my job.

"I think emotion is misunderstood. You create emotion by the way you react. Emotion comes from preparation and confidence. There are very few athletes who don't play emotionally when they're prepared and have confidence. I don't believe you can go out and give them that fiery pep talk before a game and that they'll charge through the door. I believe we can play as emotionally as anybody, but that it comes from being ready and prepared for a game."

Vermeil, who retired from coaching after seven seasons in Philadelphia because he suffered burnout, said, "Everything we did with the Eagles was based on beating Tom Landry. It was the respect we had for him that motivated us. The Cowboys were always the best-disciplined team we faced on game day, especially on defense."

Vermeil shocked the football world when he ended his long hiatus from football and left the broadcast booth to return to coaching with the St. Louis Rams. In the musical chairs of modern-day professional sports, the team had once been the Los Angeles Rams. He took the Rams to the Super Bowl championship in January 2000 then retired again.

DALLAS GOT OFF TO AN EXCELLENT START under Danny White in 1980 by beating the Redskins at RFK and also defeating them later in the year in Dallas. Dallas split games with the Eagles, a team they were to lose the divisional title to on a tiebreaker when both clubs finished 12–4, and then beat Los Angeles, 34–13, in the first round of the play-offs.

Dallas seemed in a hopeless situation against Atlanta the following week. With 8:23 left, Dallas trailed, 27–17, and Danny White became a big hero as he passed to Drew Pearson for two touchdowns, the last one coming with forty-two seconds left, as Dallas won, 30–27. On the final touchdown, Danny laid the ball into Pearson's arms a split second before two defenders converged on the Cowboy receiver. Landry considered that game and the one Staubach engineered in the 1979 Redskins game to be his team's greatest comebacks.

The Eagles flattened Dallas, 20–7, for the NFC title in cold Philadelphia as White didn't have a good day and Tony Hill, who had become the team's leading receiver, didn't appear to want to play all that much in the cold. Hill would continually draw criticism, and his attitude certainly suffered by comparison to that of Pearson, who was fearless. But he also made some big plays.

Landry had believed White would do well, and Danny went beyond all his expectations. White still had a solid team around him in those days with Tony Dorsett, one of the league's best runners, and good offensive linemen such as Pat Donovan and Herb Scott. The defense had gotten an amazing forty-seven turnovers in 1980, and the defensive line with Randy White, Ed "Too Tall" Jones, and Harvey Martin was excellent. The secondary got a boost in 1981 with rookies Everson Walls and Michael Downs, but D. D. Lewis was playing his final year at linebacker and that particular position would never again be what it had been with Lewis, Dave Edwards, Chuck Howley, and Lee Roy Jordan. The defense, Landry's pride, would hold seven opponents to thirteen points or less in 1981.

The team had surprised Landry in 1980, but in 1981 he believed it could indeed return to the Super Bowl. For the second straight year, Dallas finished 12–4 to win the NFC East and ran over Tampa Bay, 38–0, in the playoffs to get to the finals against the 49ers, losing a Super Bowl bid in the final seconds.

Dallas had been so close, and Landry was excited about the 1982 season. Those feelings would fade with the NFLPA strike, which forced the cancellation of eight games, half the season, and caused the league to come up with a playoff tournament to see which clubs made the Super Bowl.

"We had the talent to win that year," said Landry, "but the dedication was lacking from some of the players. With the strike, I didn't like that season [1982] much at all."

Once, when asked about the plight of coaches, Landry talked about the strike. "It had nothing to do with the coaches," he said. "It was the owners and players. The coaches had to try to bring everything back together. It seemed like the people who suffered most were the coaches. They were the ones getting fired or burned out."

After the Eagle and San Francisco games, White, who made the Pro Bowl that year, was taking a lot of flak about not being able to win the big games. Meanwhile, Dallas beat Tampa Bay, 30–17, and Green Bay, 37–26, to make the NFC title game against Washington. Danny got knocked out of the Redskin game in the first half with Dallas trailing, 14–3, and Gary Hogeboom came in. Although he gave the club some excitement, Dallas lost, 30–17. White, still groggy, cried on the sideline. As had San Francisco the year before, Washington went on to win the Super Bowl. Reflecting on the strike and the season, when Landry was asked what kind of animal he would want to be if he could be reincarnated, he responded candidly, without pausing, "A bird. Then I could fly above all this."

⌣∴∿

THE TALENT ON THE CLUB seemed to be diminishing as high draft choices failed, but commenting about this, Landry said, "I've never seen a team that couldn't improve. But I have seen in recent years a Washington team that was not blessed with great talent win the Super Bowl and a 49er team not blessed with a lot of experience do the same thing. Five, six, seven years ago you couldn't do that. You had to have experience and good, quality players."

There were rumblings that Hogeboom should be starting in 1983, but White was on top of his game. With an offense that also featured Dorsett, Danny would lead the team to its highest point totals in history at that time, 479, and throw a club record of twenty-nine touchdown passes. These stats are for a sixteen-game season, the format having been changed from fourteen games in 1978, but are still very impressive. The press had begun to say that Landry favored White over Hogeboom simply because he liked him. Players, such as Everson Walls, were talking about this too; players had changed a lot over the years.

"Coach Landry," said White, "would change his focus at times over the years. It would depend on what he believed the particular team needed at the time. He had a great knack for looking ahead and projecting what the team would need in a particular situation, and he would focus on that.

"He would change in the way he dealt with players somewhat too. He would try to focus in on what a team needed and be real firm, take a strong stand, or relax a little and back off. I think he was able to change his approach and the way he treated different teams in regard to the players he was working with.

"Of course, the players changed. They became harder to deal with. As salaries went up, they worked hard and expected a lot but didn't like to be told what to do and be pushed around. Nowadays, players just seem less coachable. It wasn't that way when I started. But, to his great credit, Coach Landry was able to adapt to that."

As with Staubach, Landry would telephone White the night before a game and go over the game plan with him, checking last-minute details and making sure everybody was on the same page. When his quarterback would answer the phone, it was never, "Hello, how are you," but Landry would just begin talking about the game plan right away.

"He was never very receptive to ideas during the week, but if you saw something and pointed it out to him during a game, he would listen," said White. "But on the field if you did something without consulting with him, he'd get a little upset. I ought to know."

During a game against the Redskins, shown on national television, each team was trying to get an advantage when White, also the punter, decided to go up to the line of scrimmage and, with a slow count, try to draw the Redskins offsides on a fourth down. If this didn't work, he believed, Ron Springs could make the short yardage off-tackle. As the Cowboys came out of the huddle, the television cameras focused in on Landry on the sidelines. He was yelling, "No, Danny! No, Danny!" The play lost yardage and the Redskins won, 28–10.

Announcers told this joke on national television: "A man died and went to heaven. He shook hands with Saint Peter and noticed that everybody in heaven had gathered to watch a football game. The man looked closer and saw a fellow with a funny hat standing on the sidelines. 'Hey,' he said. 'Is that Tom Landry?' Saint Peter said, 'No. That's God. He just thinks he's Tom Landry.'" Landry didn't particularly care for that joke.

Dallas couldn't run the ball in the first round of the playoffs against the Rams, so White threw a record fifty-three passes, hitting thirty-two. Still, the Cowboys lost, 24–17. It was during the off-season that Drew Pearson was in an automobile accident that prematurely ended his career and took the club's best clutch receiver away. Landry called Pearson "one of the great clutch receivers of all time with the Cowboys. He probably made more big plays than anyone. It was the confidence he had and the rapport with the quarterbacks. Most guys wouldn't throw it to a lot of receivers in such tough places, but they did to Drew because they believed in him so much."

Although they would win the East one more time in 1985, the Dallas

Cowboys were never as good again under Tom Landry. For all practical purposes, the 1983 club was the last one Landry would ever have that had a chance to make the Super Bowl.

By the late 1980s, Tom Landry knew it would take a massive rebuilding job for the Cowboys to be Super Bowl contenders again, but he had no idea that by February 1989 he would not be there to try to do the job.

⌣∶⌢

THE COWBOYS' DECLINE actually began in 1984 when the team lost key players such as Drew Pearson, Pat Donovan, Billy Joe Dupree, and Harvey Martin, whose ability had diminished in his final year. Bob Breunig was also having problems playing up to earlier standards and would retire the following year. The draft hurt the team because good replacements were not coming in. And Landry also faced yet another serious quarterback controversy. Danny White had replaced Staubach, and the team had gone to three straight NFC title games only to lose them. People were saying White couldn't win the Big One. Gary Hogeboom had become a favorite of most of the media and fans. But, as it turned out, he couldn't always win the Little One.

During the strike year of 1982, a problem had developed between White and some of his more outspoken teammates. He had taken somewhat of a promanagement stance, which had angered some of the players. Many had already begun to believe that Hogeboom, who had a much stronger arm and was better liked by his teammates, should replace White. In a poll taken by the *Dallas Morning News* of thirty-four Cowboy players, a landslide majority favored Hogeboom.

After seeing the poll, Staubach became angry. Reflecting on that situation and what happened to the team thereafter, Staubach said the team had become "whiners" and a lot of players performed to their weaknesses instead of forgetting about them and playing to their strengths. He said that had been apparent in the poll.

"If I had been Danny," he said, "I'd have gone into the locker room after that and confronted each and every one of them."

Landry threw the job open in training camp, and White and Hogeboom seemed to finish about even. The draft was promising, with the addition of Billy Cannon, Victor Scott, and Eugene Lockhart. The giant holdover lineman, tackle Phil Pozderac (6'-9", 282 pounds), appeared ready to assert himself. But Landry had to make a decision about his quarterback and called a press conference to announce his choice.

There was a great deal of tension as he said, ". . . so I've decided my starting quarterback in our first game against the Rams will be . . . Phil Pozderac."

After momentary shock, there were chuckles in the crowd, and Landry, who at times had trouble with names, corrected himself and said Gary Hogeboom would start. (He'd also referred to him as "Hogenbloom.")

There was also a new receiver in camp, Mike Renfro. Butch Johnson didn't like Tony Hill, or his work habits. Hill had become overweight and asked to be traded. He was swapped for Renfro, an instant crowd favorite, and what seemed an unimportant fifth-round draft choice. That choice turned out to be Herschel Walker.

Hogeboom started well and drew a great deal of praise from sports-writers, who were saying I told you so. There were also a few chuckles going around when something called "Dull Folks Unlimited" of Rochester, New York, named Erma Bombeck, Ed McMahon, and Tom Landry among its Top Ten Dull Folks. Landry paid no attention. Alicia didn't think it was at all funny.

Sometimes Landry would insert White, but usually he would go back to Hogeboom until that awful afternoon in Buffalo. The Bills had the worst defense in the league, and one of the poorest teams overall. Yet they beat Dallas 14–3. Landry stuck with Hogeboom all the way, hoping to watch him pull it out but also proving, in a way, that he had to go back to White if the team was to have a chance to make the play-offs. Dallas won two in a row and, with a victory in either of the final two games against Washington and Miami, would make the playoffs.

~:~

THE REDSKINS EDGED DALLAS, 30–28, and the following week Miami beat the Cowboys, 28–21. Dallas tied the Redskins and Giants with a 9–7 record for the final playoff spot but lost the tiebreaker because it had been beaten twice by each team.

This broke a record-setting nine straight playoff appearances for the Cowboys. It was only the second time in nineteen years the club hadn't made the championship round.

But Danny White was back, and some said and wrote that if Landry had started him earlier Dallas might have made it. "The strike was a bad year for the Cowboys," Landry was to explain. "It was a year of dissension. It took a long time to get over that. Even though it had happened two years before, my feeling was that Danny would have problems leading the team because of what was said during the strike and the way the players felt. I decided to make a change and use Gary Hogeboom and give Danny a chance to recover, and he did. He worked himself back up and got the confidence of the team again."

⌣∶∾

LANDRY HAD A MOST UNUSUAL SEASON in 1985 as his team actually seemed mediocre but still reclaimed the NFC East title. It beat the Redskins twice and also the Giants, but it lost to a poor Detroit team and was demolished by Chicago 44–0, Cincinnati 50–24, and San Francisco 31–16. If the Cowboys had won, they would have had home field advantage in the playoffs.

Unusual things happened that angered Schramm more than Landry. There was a distraction when the *Miami News* ran a story with the headline: "NFL, FBI Probing Allegations Cowboys Fixed Games for Coke." It turned out the story was based on statements by a former FBI agent who had pleaded guilty to charges of bribery, conspiracy, and possession of cocaine. He said a convicted smuggler had told him about the players. The story was never investigated. Some of the Cowboys did get a laugh when Danny White's name appeared in the story. He didn't drink or smoke, much less take drugs. Also, prior to the loss to Detroit, Landry had given the players the option of missing a meeting to go to court to support Ron Springs, who had been charged with being drunk, disorderly, resisting arrest, and assaulting a Dallas woman police officer at a striptease club.

Schramm was very angry when members of the team said it didn't really matter that they had lost to San Francisco because they had the playoffs clinched. "If you don't want to go out there and win, then why play the [blankety-blank] game?" reasoned Schramm.

Landry knew the team had overachieved, considering that the offensive line, the linebackers, parts of the secondary, and the wide receiving corps sometimes seemed to be held together by glue and gum.

Dallas was pathetic in the first round of the playoffs, losing to Los

380

Angeles 20–0. Eric Dickerson rushed for a playoff record of 248 yards as Dieter Brock was able to complete only six of twenty-two passes for fifty yards.

"I'm proud of the team," said Landry. "We had a long way to come. We just didn't have the togetherness a team should have had, and that could be traced all the way back to the strike. We proved all that year that we had to play as well as we possibly could to win. When we didn't, we lost."

Years later, Landry would call the 1985 team that won the NFC East the one he enjoyed most. "It was so outmanned. There's no reason why New York or Washington shouldn't have won the division that year. We won it because of guys like Mike Renfro. And Steve Pelluer coming in and throwing the ball to an unknown Karl Powe. I remember we beat Washington on a take-off-and-go on third and ten. That was a thrilling team. I enjoyed coaching them and seeing them perform."

Landry actually did go to the Super Bowl game that year, but without his team. Roone Arledge of ABC selected him as an expert commentator opposite O. J. Simpson. "You know, if I had to pick one guy I'd like to have next to me in my living room to talk to during the Super Bowl, it would be Tom Landry," said O. J., one of pro football's greatest running backs who would gain even more fame after being accused of killing his wife and her friend. "This is not my element, really," said Landry. "But I'm going to try my best. I think O. J. has the toughest assignment, trying to get me to smile."

As he studied the 1985 season, Landry knew the team would need help, agreeing with Schramm that changes had to be made. That was when he agreed to hire Paul Hackett and listened to him more than anybody thought he would. And an unexpected surprise developed when the USFL folded and Herschel Walker, chosen by Schramm as a flyer on the fifth round of the 1984 draft, reported to training camp.

❧

THERE WAS A GREAT DEAL OF OPTIMISM when Herschel Walker came to training camp in July 1986, although Tom Landry had to change his plans abruptly. Disgruntled Gary Hogeboom had been traded to the Colts after telling the Cowboys to play him or trade him. But Steve Pelluer was making great strides, and Danny White was established again at quarterback. The new offense, a combination of the philosophies of

Landry and new assistant Paul Hackett, had been predicated on White's know-how, and once again, the attack was to feature Tony Dorsett at tailback running the ball and Timmy Newsome at fullback, doing the lead blocking.

Walker presented a problem, but a good one. He turned out to be not only a top runner but also an outstanding receiver, a talent the Cowboys did not know he had. He was used at tailback, fullback, and flanker—and as the man in motion—and continually came up with big plays. But he was spending too much time on the bench. Dorsett was still the starting tailback. Cowboy coaches just never could work out a method of keeping them both on the field at the same time. Dorsett was not a good blocker, and nobody wanted to use Walker as one, although he blocked well.

Dorsett was never happy to have his role diminished. When Schramm signed Walker to a $5 million contract over five years, Dorsett almost bolted training camp.

"I'm not playing second fiddle to anybody," he said. He also noted that Walker's rushing yards had come in the USFL and added that if he continued to be unhappy he could be "a very disruptive force on this team."

Dorsett later apologized, but although it had happened in the past, club officials were a little surprised over his outburst considering what had been done for him the previous year. Tony was in a hopeless situation with the IRS in 1985 because of amazingly bad investments by both him and his agents. The IRS had liens on both his houses and his car and was picking up his check each month for back payments. He had also borrowed five hundred thousand dollars from the Cowboys. He had three years left on his contract, which was to run through 1987 and which specified that he would not try to renegotiate. So he was late for camp and wanted to renegotiate.

Schramm called in experts and had Tony's contract restructured so he could settle with the IRS, draw a substantial yearly salary, and have his future secure. Among other things, the Cowboys funded an annuity that was supposed to pay him fifty thousand dollars over the ensuing five years. The club had saved him. He was happy. But he became upset when Walker got $5 million.

"The Cowboys were really a big part of helping Tony Dorsett," said Landry. "The club came in and helped him [financially] when he needed it most, and he could never return that favor. . . . The ego that made him react [after Walker signed] is the same one that makes him a great football player on the field."

Over the years, Dorsett, small for a running back at 5'-10", 180 pounds, proved to be extremely durable. But he continually criticized Landry for not letting him run the ball more. Landry remained stubborn, feeling Tony would last much longer if he didn't. And, indeed, in 1989, Dorsett would be going into his fourteenth season in the NFL, where running backs usually last about five or six years, passing Jimmy Brown as the second all-time leading rusher in the league and ranking only behind Walter Payton, who played twelve years. Of the top ten all-time rushers at the time of Dorsett's retirement, only king-sized backs Franco Harris and John Riggins had lasted fourteen years.

"People criticized Tony at times, but he handled himself extremely well for a player who had had more publicity than anyone we ever had coming out of college," said Landry, reflecting on Tony's career. "A lot of guys wouldn't have been able to handle it. I remember the first training camp [1977] reporters were everywhere. They were even putting cameras in his face during calisthenics.

"Tony was a great runner. He didn't work a lot on other things, such as receiving and blocking. He just didn't develop his overall skills or he would have made much more yardage, such as a guy like Roger Craig. But he felt running was his calling, and he was like Jimmy Brown, who also didn't work much on those other things.

"Oh, Tony fussed about me a lot because I wouldn't let him run more. Yet he gained over twelve thousand yards when he was with us. So I guess it wasn't all that bad."

~:~

HERSCHEL WALKER never dreamed he'd play for Landry, and Landry, in turn, never would have imagined he'd coach a player like Herschel Walker, especially in a winning season.

As he had with Staubach and would later with Chad Hennings, who still had to serve time in the air force, Schramm took a flyer on Walker in the fifth round of the 1985 draft. Herschel was still playing in the USFL, but Tex gambled on the league folding and his chances of signing him. Landry usually lost interest in the later rounds of the draft and had already left the draft room when the pick was made. Tex's gamble paid off. The USFL folded, and Schramm signed Walker during negotiations in training camp in 1986.

Landry called it a "once-in-a-lifetime stroke of good fortune." And after he had coached Walker and gotten to know him, Landry would say, "Herschel is a unique person. They don't come around too often like Herschel, a superstar with humility. Not too many great athletes have that, and the reason is that their egos get so big. Herschel is a rare individual . . . the way he handles players, whether they're rookies or whatever, the way he sits on the front row of every meeting to make sure he doesn't miss anything."

There were problems finding a place to play Herschel, but Landry moved him around from fullback, to halfback, and to wide receiver. Herschel made some big plays that first year and brought a new enthusiasm to the team.

Rookie Mike Sherrard became the long threat the team had been trying to find, and Danny White got off to a tremendous start, leading the NFC in passing. Dallas went into New York with a 6–2 record, one of the losses being 37–35 to Atlanta when a desperation pass was taken away from two Cowboy defenders by a Falcon receiver and the other being to Denver when Danny White was injured and couldn't play. But the great promise that the team had come back would fade in New York on that first Sunday in October in the Meadowlands in a game that would propel the Giants on their way to the Super Bowl championship.

In the second period, linebacker Carl Banks blitzed and crashed untouched into Danny White, who extended his right arm, hit a helmet or shoulder pad, and suffered a fractured wrist. His season ended.

Steve Pelluer wasn't as brittle as White. He had a stronger arm and could run away from the rush. He replaced White, and in spite of Rafael Septien missing two field goals, one a chip shot, Dallas trailed just 17–14 in the final three minutes.

Pelluer dropped off a screen pass to Dorsett, who ran thirty yards for a first down at the Giants' six. The play was called back for holding by tackle Phil Pozderac. All seemed lost, but Pelluer found Newsome for another thirty-yard gain inside the New York ten. Again, the celebration was short-lived. End George Martin said he knew, because of the tremendous crowd noise, which the officials could not quiet, that Pozderac would not hear the snap count. So he raised his hand, giving the impression the ball had been snapped, and Pozderac jumped offsides. New York was no better than Dallas that day, but as the season continued, the Giants got much better.

The coup de grace of the year came, perhaps, the following week. Dallas had never dominated a team more than it did the Los Angeles Raiders in the first half of the game. Yet, Dallas led only 13–3. Pelluer had run twenty-five yards for a touchdown, but it had been called back for Glen Titensor's holding, and Everson Walls had run an interception forty-seven yards for a touchdown, only to see it nullified by Ed Jones's clip.

The Raiders won the game 17–13 when Jim Plunkett lofted a forty-yard pass that Dokie Williams out-leaped three defenders to catch in the end zone. During that game, it became apparent that the ankle Walker had injured against the Giants would bother him the remainder of the season and that Dorsett's knees, both of which were operated on after the season, were problematic.

Pelluer, who had begun with promise and excitement, was hit so much and became so confused when he stayed in the pocket that he looked like a punch-drunk boxer by the end of the year. Dallas finished 1–7 the final half of the season, and the string of twenty straight winning seasons was broken.

~:~

TOM LANDRY SAW PLAYOFF POTENTIAL for his team in 1987, but the writing seemed to be on the wall before the first exhibition game was ever played. First a story broke during the off-season that Rafael Septien, the best place-kicker the team had ever had, was involved with a minor. Septien later pleaded guilty to charges of sexual abuse of a ten-year-old.

Tex Schramm immediately wanted to trade him, but Landry, as was always his custom, sought to give Septien a second chance. Knowing the severity of the public reaction to such an offense, Schramm and other club officials talked the coach out of his earlier position and Septien was waived.

During training camp, Mike Sherrard suffered a severely broken fibula, or shin bone, while running a simple pass pattern and was lost for the season. Furthermore, a fear arose that Danny White's wrist would become a problem (and that fear would later be realized often) because at times he'd lose all control of his passes. Then the NFLPA struck again, and after the third game of the season was canceled, the owners went ahead with a plan to have replacement games using substitute players.

Veteran players such as Randy White, Danny White, Ed Jones, Tony Dorsett, Doug Cosbie, and Everson Walls had contracts with annuities that specified that they would never miss a practice, a meeting, or a game unless they were physically unable to be there. Schramm sent out letters reminding them of this, so Randy White and Ed Jones crossed the picket line and all but Cosbie and Walls followed later. Landry wanted to keep them sharp for the time the strike would end and worked them in with the replacement players, causing some dissension on the team.

Gil Brandt and staff had done their homework, and Dallas had an excellent replacement team that beat the Jets, 38–24, and the Eagles, 41–22, and captured the imagination of the fans. The new heroes were guys such as quarterback Kevin Sweeney and receiver Kevin Edwards.

When Dorsett reported, he said he didn't want to play in the games, that he'd get down on his knees at the fifty-yard line and beg Landry not to play him because he didn't want any yardage tainted in his pursuit of Jimmy Brown on the all-time rushing list.

In the final replacement game against Washington, Landry made a decision that would greatly anger fans as well as people within the organization. He decided to start not only Dorsett at running back but also Danny White at quarterback in place of the very popular Sweeney, who had led the NFL in passing during the replacement games. This seemed to take the edge off the team. Dorsett lost two key fumbles and White did little as Dallas lost 13–7. Landry had just wanted to get the veterans back into the groove, but his decision may have cost the team a game.

White was brilliant against Minnesota but when the game went into overtime and Dallas was in position for a winning field goal, the ball got away from White on a pass. The Vikings intercepted and went on to win, 44–38. Dallas had also lost to poor Detroit and Atlanta teams.

Landry was getting criticized from all directions, just as he would in 1988, and admitted some of what was being said bothered him. "Sure, it bothers me. I'm human. But they have a right to say whatever they want. When a team beats you up-front, it doesn't matter which play you call because it's not going to work. We have a quarterback with a bad wrist, an offensive line that keeps getting banged up, and we lost our best receiver before the season ever started.

"I could step down today, but I've made a commitment to bring this team back. But who knows? I don't have time to think about it right now. The only important thing is what happens right now. People are paying their money to go out there and see us win.

"Oh, nobody is ever really fair when it comes to coaches, but that's just the nature of the business."

Gene Stallings called Landry after all the criticism surfaced and said he just wanted to see how he was doing. "Coach Landry gave me a job when I didn't have one, and I appreciate that," said Stallings, recalling how Landry hired him as an assistant after he had been fired at Texas A&M. "He's tough-minded, but to think the criticism doesn't bother him is wrong. It does."

Danny Reeves said, "Losing hurts anybody. It hurts a lot more when you've been winning and you're trying to turn things back around and you're not getting the loyalty or support around you. You need to have everybody sticking together."

George Young, a former history professor and general manager of the New York Giants at the time, was asked about the situation and was quoted as saying:

"I saw Dallas play Miami [1987] and noticed Shula and Landry. Those two old dogs were fighting each other to death. There was fire in their eyes. It was the same thing in the Cowboys' game against Minnesota. Landry almost brought them back to win both times. You can't tell me the guy can't coach anymore, that he's lost it. That's nonsense.

"They said the same thing about the Duke of Wellington; they voted Winston Churchill out of office before the war was over. The Duke of Marlborough got fired in the eighteenth century. They demeaned Napoleon because he lost that last battle. I can't, however, say I'm surprised. Coaching is the only profession that, as you get older, most people think you get dumber."

Certainly, Landry had worked hard and concentrated to a great extent on the team. Once when he was told that David Letterman wanted him to appear on his show, Landry said, "Who's David Letterman?" He was being honest; he didn't know.

With a strong showing in the final two games, Dallas finished with a 7–8 record. It had hope for the future, for the next season. That hope, of course, turned out to be hollow.

IT HAD BEEN IN 1987 that Tom Landry had changed his mind about retiring, asked for and got a three-year contract, and begun his plans to rebuild the team, something he believed could be accomplished to a great degree by 1989. He later would say he might coach into the 1990s. But, as astonishing as it might sound, Landry believed the 1988 team that finished 3–13 was actually better than clubs in previous years that had better, if still losing, records. In 1987 Dallas had finished 7–8, one game being canceled by the NFLPA strike and three being played mostly by replacement players.

In the final two games of the year, Landry seemed to have established a trend that would be successful. He installed Steve Pelluer at quarterback and launched an attack featuring Herschel Walker behind a much-improved offensive line. Pelluer would be conservative, his passing only serving to vary from Walker's running, and it worked as Dallas beat Los Angeles, 29–21, and St. Louis, 21–16. L.A. and the Cardinals had everything to gain because each had a shot at the playoffs. Yet Dallas had beaten them. There was hope again.

But one of the best examples of Murphy's Law was Landry's final year. Dallas lost the opener in Pittsburgh, 24–21. The Cowboys had seized momentum and faced a third and two at the Stealers' four late in the game. Pelluer was supposed to fake, roll out, and try to hit right end Doug Cosbie if he was open. If not, he was supposed to dump the ball. Ruzek then could kick an easy field goal. Steve got mixed up and ran the wrong play. He then threw the ball at three Steeler defenders, one of whom did the only thing he could: He intercepted. Dallas lost to the Giants, 12–10, when an official awarded New York a safety, later admitting he'd made a mistake and should not have done so.

Pelluer was great against New Orleans, passing for 271 yards and scrambling for 54 more, but Thornton Chandler dropped an apparent touchdown pass on the goal line, and Ruzek missed an easy field goal before he kicked one to tie the score with twenty-four seconds left. The Saints then won the game, 20–17, as Morton Anderson kicked a forty-nine-yard field goal as time ran out. Dallas had Philadelphia 20–0 at halftime and could have had twenty-three, except Pelluer again became confused and failed to get a time-out so Ruzek could try a short field goal. The Eagles won 24–23 when they scored after a long pass-interference penalty was called with two seconds left. Dallas led Phoenix 10–0, then lost 16–10. Midway through the third period, Dallas was ahead of Houston 17–10, but lost 25–17. The key play occurred when Cornell Burbage fumbled a kickoff return with 4:32 left. Then there was the loss to Cleveland.

Dallas did get it together to beat the Redskins, 24–17. Tom Rafferty gave Landry the game ball because Tom had stood by the team through an awful season. It was an act of respect. "We thought we had won the Super Bowl," said Landry. "In the locker room it was like everybody was looking for the champagne."

It was such an odd season. Dallas certainly had been lucky in beating Atlanta, 26–20, when a Falcon receiver dropped the ball in the end zone, but Lady Luck was only teasing. Dallas lost five of seven games in the final minute during one stretch. One play could have turned losses into wins against New Orleans, Philadelphia, and New York. Interceptions at the goal line or in the end zone cost Dallas three games.

"This is a better team than we were last year," said Landry. "There is better quality. There is better camaraderie. There is better morale. I didn't see anybody quitting. They practiced well. The only problem was the shock of going out every week and losing. We kept getting shocked, and it kept us from getting over the top.

"With an easier schedule, we could very easily have been .500. When you start from scratch, it takes you four or five years before you see daylight. But I see daylight here already. Back in the early days, I didn't see daylight until 1964.

"We lost because we couldn't get the ball across the goal at the end or because we couldn't stop the other team when we needed to. That's the sign of inexperience."

During the season, the criticism that had followed Landry in every losing situation since he came to the Cowboys resurfaced. He just wasn't a motivator . . . a motivator of grown men, many of whom were in their late twenties and thirties and knew full well that they had a job to do and were getting paid very well to do it.

"So he didn't go around yelling and screaming," said Randy White. "He told you what to do, and if you did it you were successful. It was that simple. And, hey, he motivated me because we had those film sessions. If you did good, he'd tell you. But if you did bad, he'd also let you know right in front of everybody, and it didn't matter if you were a star or not.

"I tell you about these so-called rah-rah type guys. They might get you going for a while, but tricks like that wear thin after a while. The pro players are older, and it's not like in college. The seasons are a lot longer, and that rah-rah stuff won't keep working over the long haul. What works is if you have a coach who knows what he's doing and tells you what it takes to be successful. Then you have that confidence in him and you go out and do your best."

White laughed and added, "When we won the Super Bowl that last time [over Denver], Harvey Martin and I were co-MVPs in the game. The next year we got to training camp and Coach Landry was telling everybody that nobody's job was secure. I honestly believed him, and I got out there and worked my tail off."

Safety Bill Bates was always a guy who became extremely emotional, very fired up when he played. "I'm the type guy who turns it up a notch when the coach gets on me," he said. "It gets me more motivated.

"One day we were having a light practice, working out with helmets, shoulder pads, and shorts the day before a game. I ran a defensive play wrong, and Coach Landry just steps up and starts telling me how to do it. He wasn't loud or excited or anything, but just stating the facts. Timmy Newsome was my assignment. I turned it up a notch, and the next time we ran that play I knocked Timmy down. Hey, we were only going half speed and I'd blasted him."

"Bill," Landry told him, "you've got to be more under control."

"Coach Landry didn't really compliment players a lot, but the little things he did meant just as much," said Ray Alexander, the team's leading receiver in 1988. "He had ways of letting you know he was pleased. You make a good catch in practice and go back to the huddle and he wouldn't smile but just kind of tilt his head real quick or maybe give you a wink."

Alexander had signed with Dallas from the Canadian League, spent the 1987 season on the injured reserve with a broken left wrist, and worried prior to 1988 whether he would make the team. Landry said little to players until they did or did not make it. Alexander got tired of waiting and went to see him.

"Coach, I just wanted to know how I'm doing. That's all."

"You're doing just fine," said Landry. "Just keep up what you're doing and give it your best shot and everything will work out for you."

Alexander was a sleeper but kept working hard, and not only did he make the team but he became a bright spot in a dim season.

"Coach Landry liked that team [1988]," said guard Nate Thurman, who would become a holdover star for Jimmy Johnson. "I hated to see him not coming back. Coach Landry and I were just getting to where we were going to start cracking jokes at each other."

"Considering what all happened, that last season was amazing," said Ed Jones. "Our morale was always high, which is really something when you consider we kept losing those close games over and over. But something positive developed out of all of that. You just don't see that happening in situations like this."

Landry was asked if he wasn't relieved the season had ended, and he said, "Relief comes when you have to do the things you don't enjoy doing. I don't feel any relief. I don't need to have the pressure lifted off my shoulders because it's what I enjoy."

He did, however, admit it had been tough. "It was the most difficult season I've ever coached. But you have to go through it as a team. And if you do, you'll look back and say, 'Hey, I don't have to do that again.'

"The key was the team always played for me. As I keep saying, I'd have quit a long time ago if it hadn't. But it always picked itself up and went back out and played hard.

"Next year we're going to be a much better team coming out of training camp because we now have a higher experience level. Then we can start thinking about going back to the playoffs."

Danny White reflected again on Landry and the final season. "I think there's one thing I'll remember about him more than anything. He's a throwback to the work-ethic days when people were willing to pay a price and be patient and work and have faith that sooner or later success would come. Not overnight, but it would come. You always got that feeling about him.

"Even in the face of all that adversity and failure, he was just sure it wasn't a matter of whether we'd be successful, but when. That was true even when we were struggling at the very end."

At thirty-seven years of age, Danny White believed he could pick up the pieces of his career and perhaps find an important place for himself under new coach Jimmy Johnson. The wrist that had been broken and threatened to end his career in 1986 had healed, and the knee he'd injured in 1988 was much better.

White went through the off-season voluntary-mandatory mini-camps. He was getting very little work, with Troy Aikman and Steve

Walsh the center of attention. He talked to Johnson, who apparently encouraged him to retire. In July 1989, he did. He had been with the Cowboys thirteen years.

Herschel Walker would join White as an ex-Cowboy. In his three years under Landry, Walker was one of the best all-around players in the league. One year he rushed for 1,514 yards, and always a threat catching the ball, another season he caught seventy-six passes for 837 yards. But he never fit into Jimmy Johnson's offense and was traded to the Vikings for players and draft choices that would help the team become contenders in the Jerry Jones era. Walker's career fizzled after that, and he never again approached the results he had under Landry.

⌣∴⌢

"COACHES COACH, but when a football player gets on the field, he's got to play," said Herschel Walker. "Coach Landry took a lot of flack over things we should have been criticized for. If we're in a game and we're winning, then suddenly we lose, it's not all the coach's fault. We're professionals, and I feel like when we step on the field we have to take responsibility for our actions sooner or later."

"When I played for him, he was tough because he wanted things to be done the correct way. I think that's good. He didn't want anyone cheating themselves or the team, which is the way it should be.

"The X's and O's represented just one side of him. What made him the legend he is today is the excellent role model he was for the people. Coach Landry was a consistent, concerned citizen who realized the value of displaying a clean image. He was a great contribution to society."

Even if Jones hadn't fired him, Landry would never have been able to work for an owner who inserted himself into the middle of everything that was going on with the team, on and off the field. Landry was better off being away from the new Cowboys, and the people and organizations he had more time to help were better off as well.

⌣∴⌢

CHAPTER 20
Alicia

∿∴∿

Tom and Alicia were a unique couple. I feel so honored to have known them. Subconsciously, they had an influence on our community regarding what family values were all about.

—WES WISE
Mayor of Dallas, 1971–1976

THE FRENCH COLONIAL–style home the Landrys bought in the mid-1970s is located on an incline overlooking a creek with visiting ducks in a cul-de-sac on an acre-and-a-third plot near a busy North Dallas intersection. It is secluded behind trees and a wall that help buffer the sounds of traffic and give you a feeling of being in the country. Some fine, affluent homes seem cold no matter how they are decorated or how expensively they are furnished. You cannot manufacture the warmth of love, kindness, and affection. But there is the feeling of that warmth in the Landry home.

It has been a house of laughter, happiness, disappointments, and tragedy that we all experience, but it has always been a place of love . . . the love affair of Tom and Alicia, which endured for more than half a century.

I remember a momentary, seemingly meaningless episode during training camp at California Lutheran in Thousand Oaks, California, that showed so much about their love. Tom Landry spent most of his time tending to football matters. He would jog and work out after practice, but during the time he put aside for relaxation he was in his room, reading his ever-present Western paperback novels (his favorite author was Louis L'Amour) or the Bible. The routine only changed when Alicia made her annual visit. She'd stay a week or so near the end of

393

camp at a nearby motel, and they would go out to dinner and church and spend time together.

That particular time, Alicia, who hadn't seen Tom in four weeks, had just arrived and had been driven to the practice field just as the players and coaches were arriving for the afternoon session. She knew Tom would be conducting practice, but she wanted to at least get a glimpse of him. Tom jogged onto the field, saw her, and veered toward her car. He slowed down briefly, and as he passed by, he said, "Haven't I seen you somewhere before?" Their eyes met, their faces brightened, and big smiles crossed their faces. Then he jogged on to practice. I thought that said more about love than words ever could.

Over the years, sometimes you would also see them laughing as they shared something humorous. Tom, as often stated, had a strong power of concentration, blocking out whatever was going on around him. Once he took Alicia to a downtown luncheon where he was speaking. He finished the speech, his mind returned to football, and he headed back to his office. About halfway there, he remembered he'd left Alicia at the luncheon. He hurried back, and when he picked her up she told him, "I won't give you a touchdown but I suppose I'll give you a field goal for remembering to come back and get me."

∿∶∿

LANDRY WORKED ENDLESS HOURS during football season but always set aside time to spend with his family. When Tom Jr. was young, he'd spend time at training camp, and all the kids went to home games. Landry would take Alicia out to dinner on road trips. When the team was in New York, they'd usually dine with their old friends the Wellington Maras. During the week, he'd go home after practice, have dinner with his family, and then work in his office at home. Often he'd call whomever was his number one quarterback at the time. He would also do this on the road, asking the quarterback to come to his room to go over the game plan. Roger Staubach remembers that when it was getting late Alicia would often interrupt Tom and say, "Tommy, let him get some sleep."

During the week, Tom would set aside Friday night to go out to dinner with Alicia and use his great concentration to forget football. His football schedule allowing, he celebrated the holidays with family and friends just as most people do.

Gil Brandt remembered once having Thanksgiving dinner with the Landrys when the doorbell rang. Tom excused himself, got up from the table, and went to the door. "It was a woman who had gotten lost looking for a friend's house in the neighborhood," said Gil. "Tom invited her in and then made some calls and found out where the friend lived. Then he gave the woman directions how to get there. That was Tom Landry for you. There was nothing aloof about him, nothing at all."

Another example of Landry's kindness comes to mind. During training camp one year an older woman marched right onto the field during practice before anyone could stop her. She was Opal Mills, who was there with her son-in-law Bill Lemmons, a Rockwall, Texas, resident living in Thousand Oaks at the time.

"She wanted to get his autograph. So while we were watching practice, I looked around and she was gone, marching toward Coach Landry on the field. But you know, Coach Landry saw her and was very nice. He signed his autograph and politely told her that she could get hurt out there with all the players running around. And then he escorted her back to the sidelines."

～∴～

OF COURSE, after the season he would spend more time with his family. Fortunately, Alicia was an avid football fan. "By the end of the season, I was usually exhausted, but after a week or so, I was ready for the season to get started again. When the season was over he was usually home, except for the weekends when he'd travel for his work with the FCA and things such as that."

Alicia never felt as though she were taking a backseat to Tom because of his celebrity status. "He never made me feel like I was. He always made me feel so important. . . . There was never anything difficult about being Mrs. Tom Landry." She called him the "greatest thing going," and besides their deep love for one another they were also best friends.

A child psychology major before leaving UT her sophomore year to marry Tom, Alicia had taken courses in design and interior decorating. She decorated the Landrys' house herself, with Tom in mind. She decorated it with love.

～∴～

THE HOUSE was where Tom played with his grandchildren, just as he had once played with his own children in their childhood home. If there was any stoicism in his nature, it melted away in his home.

During a discussion some years ago, Alicia said, "When he got home from work, I would just turn the grandkids, and our children before them, over to Tommy. He would get up in the middle of the night if they needed him. And he fed them, dressed them, and bathed them. I told him I just needed more sleep than he did."

Vacations were always family affairs for the Landrys, as they'd go to the coast or to Yellowstone Park, or go fishing, play golf, or go boating or skiing together. Later the Landrys would include their grandchildren in their vacation plans.

"The children always loved him so much," continued Alicia. "He was better with them when they were growing up than I was. He just kept calm and had a great understanding."

⌣∴∾

OFTEN CHILDREN of successful, well-known parents will be diminished by them before they ever get started with their own lives. The shadows are just too big. Landry was certainly confident and obviously successful, but he never made a big deal out of his accomplishments to his children, nor for that matter to anybody else. And he never tried to live their lives for them.

Tom Landry Jr. recalled that his father never pushed him in the direction of football. "I don't recall ever feeling any pressure to play football at all," he said. "We always were an active family, participating in sports and games, and I just liked football. Dad would encourage me if I wanted his help, and when I was growing up, he'd play catch with me if I asked him.

"When I did play, I never thought about being the son of Tom Landry and living up to anything. I'm sure that had a lot to do with his attitude. I liked the game, but for me it was more a form of recreation, something I enjoyed, rather than something I wanted to be involved in the rest of my life."

Tom Jr. played at St. Mark's Academy in Dallas and went on a football scholarship to Duke, where he was a defensive back. After his sophomore year, he underwent surgery on the same knee for the third time and was advised by doctors to give up the sport. "I never talked to Dad about my decision to quit," he said. "I didn't have to."

When he was growing up his father was gone a lot, but he remembered, "We had a pretty normal life when he was at home. He set the highest standards for us but wasn't any big, strict disciplinarian. He never was a back-slapper either, or a person who carried emotions on his sleeve. He wasn't particularly warm outwardly, but the warmth was there and you knew it. I couldn't have had a better father."

Tom Jr. got a law degree from the University of Texas, was in the oil business, then joined his father in the investment business.

"When he corrected us, he was usually right, and we knew it," recalled the Landry's older daughter Kitty. "There wasn't any of that big boss type stuff."

"You try to influence your children to think the way you do in regard to things such as Christian ideals," said Landry. "Some will lean more than others toward a Christian life. You just hope to lay a foundation where someday, if they've taken another direction, they'll return to the Christian way."

∾⁖∾

DURING ALL HIS YEARS COACHING, Landry never changed his basic ideals, but he did become more comfortable and tolerant of others. In the later stages with the Cowboys, he talked about the reasons for this:

"Maybe in my early years I didn't always appreciate some of the problems people had or accept them in a realistic way. But as I grew older, things didn't seem to bother me as much. I don't know if it was age or my faith just grew stronger. But I stopped getting so hung up on perfection, of people doing things perfectly. You look for perfection and you'll be disappointed."

He added that he began to accept the limitations of people because of his faith, which he continued to study and learn more about. "Everything is so much more enjoyable as your faith strengthens," he said.

The players and people with whom he worked in the organization certainly felt the change. They played a number of tricks on him, something they might not have done in the 1960s. Once on Landry's birthday, Bob Lilly stood up at the team meeting and said there was a special guest coming to join them in a brief celebration. A disfigured, deformed, gruesome man hobbled in and started picking his nose and grabbing for the birthday cake. Then he walked toward Landry, who backed away and almost knocked over the podium. Everybody laughed. The man was Walt Garrison, wearing a mask and acting the part.

Longtime Cowboy photographer Bob Friedman was filming practice in Thousand Oaks when he happened to glance down and see a well-endowed woman, who wasn't overly dressed, walking past. Unable to resist, he turned the camera on her. He was showing the film to the assistant coaches, planning to take it off the reel before Landry saw it. But in walked Landry, and Friedman almost had a heart attack.

"Hmm," said Landry. "Bring that part to the meeting when we look at films tonight. Maybe it'll liven things up."

"He hasn't changed a lot over the years," said Alicia. "But he became more outward than he was when he first took over the Cowboys. He was the youngest head coach who had ever been in the NFL and was taking over a new, expansion team. It was the most difficult job anybody had ever had and took his full concentration. He did the job too.

"But he was never that cold, stoic person people liked to paint him as being. He's a very warm person with a great sense of humor. I think most very intelligent people are witty."

❧❀❧

AFTER TOM WAS FIRED, he took Alicia on a three-week vacation that he said was one of the best vacations he'd ever had. He didn't have to call back to check on what was happening with the football team or be concerned about anything, really, except their time together. They went to New York and saw the old places where they'd lived when they were very young and he played for the Giants. They visited Central Park, where they'd taken their children to play. They went to some Broadway shows, just as they once had done. Then they returned to Dallas, where there was such a great outpouring of love and appreciation for him on that special day, bringing back memories of the best years with the Cowboys.

"It's been a wonderful life, and I look back and wouldn't have traded it for anything. And I'm looking forward to it being a wonderful life from now on," said Alicia, not knowing it would end too soon.

❧❀❧

TWO MONTHS AFTER TOM LANDRY'S DEATH, I went to see Alicia in the North Dallas house they'd shared. She'd just returned from spending a couple of weeks in Austin with eight-year-old Christina. After their daughter Lisa died in 1995, Tom and Alicia tried to be with Christina as much as possible.

Alicia was doing extremely well under the circumstances and was friendly and cordial as always, but tears, as they would be for sometime, were only a memory away. When we were talking about our mutual love for Austin, she remembered her recent visit to Christina. She had been driving near downtown when she saw the Texas Tower. That brought back memories of the "sweet times" she had had with Tom when they were students at Texas, and tears came to her eyes.

She was so thankful for the cards and letters of condolences she and the family had received from people all over the country. As we were looking through the letters, Tom Jr. came by with some papers for her to sign. Outside, workmen were replacing the windshield of her car, which had a crack in it. Life had to go on.

She loved Tom so dearly. She'd shared her life with him for fifty-one years of marriage and raised children and enjoyed grandchildren together. When he died, he took such a big part of her with him. When someone you love so deeply dies, you sometimes half expect them to walk through the door, to still be there in so many ways in so many places. Then you realize that they never will be there again but that you have to go on. The awful pain subsides, ever so slowly, but you have to live every second of it until it does.

"We just had a wonderful life. I just didn't think about it ending like this," she said.

We talked about so many nice things Tom had quietly done for so many people. Alicia is proud of the man Tom was. He so loved flying, and she said it made her very sad when he got sick and could no longer take off in his beloved Cessna.

Asked what the best of times were for them, she said so many of their years together were wonderful. Then she added, "Tommy had happy years after he retired, but the best ones were the ones with the Cowboys and the friends we made and relationships we had." She smiled when we talked about what a great run it was . . . those years with the Cowboys. And she was so proud about the good deeds he'd done, the people he'd helped after those years with the Cowboys, and how they were looking forward to many more in their golden years.

She enjoyed talking about her grandkids. Kitty's son, Ryan, nineteen, was at Auburn, and her daughter, Jennifer, sixteen, was at Highland Park High School, where Alicia had gone, and "was such a sweet girl." And there was Lisa's daughter, Christina, and Tom Jr.'s kids, Taylor, Logan, and Tommy III. Her children and grandchildren needed her.

As I left, I remembered something Lamar Hunt had said about how Tom Landry had such an incredible legacy because of football, his faith, his religious work, his class and dignity, and his being such a loving family man. "His legacy will last for generations and generations and perhaps forever because he influenced so many lives in such a positive way," said Lamar.

When Tom Landry died, we were saddened, yet we appreciated even more what he was about. Perhaps we realized that a Tom Landry isn't likely to pass our way again.